THE WRITER
AND SOCIETY

Heinrich Mann and Literary Politics
in Germany, 1890–1940

David Gross

HUMANITIES PRESS
Atlantic Highlands, N. J.

To LaVerne and Lois Gross

Library of Congress Cataloging in Publication Data

Gross, David, 1940–
  The writer and society.

  Bibliography: p.
  1. Mann, Heinrich, 1871–1950—Political and social
views. 2. Authors, German—19th century.
3. Authors, German—20th century. 4. Literature
and society. I. Title.
PT2625.A43Z645   838'.9'1209 [B] 79–11707
ISBN 0–391–00972-9

Manufactured in the United States of America

CONTENTS

PART I.
THE WRITER AS AESTHETE

PART II.
THE WRITER AS EDUCATOR

PART III.
WRITING AND POLITICAL POWER

Preface

This study is an attempt at what might broadly be called the sociology of literature. In the pages which follow I have tried to describe, first, how much a modern writer's political, intellectual, and literary development is affected by an ongoing reciprocity with the age in which he lives, and second, the extent to which the substance of an author's thought is a *response* to his social environment.

The context of the discussion is Germany between the 1890s and the 1940s, and the main focus is on the writer Heinrich Mann. Mann has generally been neglected in this country and as a result is often remembered simply as the older brother of Thomas. When he has been dealt with, it has usually been from a strictly literary rather than historical point of view. Here, I have attempted to open up other avenues of investigation by exploring new approaches to the understanding of both Heinrich Mann as an individual writer, and the whole field of literary biography as an area of research. The degree to which I have succeeded, even on a modest level, must be left for the reader to judge.

For help in gathering material for this work I want to express thanks to Ulrich Dietzel and Rosemarie Eggert of the Heinrich-Mann-Archiv, East Berlin; Serge Fischer of the Bibliothèque Nationale et Universitaire, Strasbourg; and the staff of the Schiller-National-museum, Marbach-am-Neckar, for their aid and advice.

Generous financial support to carry out this project was provided by the University of Colorado's Council on Research and Creative Work, the Committee on University Scholarly Publications, and the American Philosophical Society. Without this help the study could not have been completed.

I am also grateful to Professor Robert A. Pois of the University of Colorado for many useful suggestions, and to Professors Reinhold Grimm and George L. Mosse of the University of Wisconsin for reading an early draft of this book. To the latter, under whose direction this work was originally conceived, I owe an additional intellectual debt which it would be impossible to repay.

Finally, my deepest and warmest thanks go to Ruthanne, Stefan and David, whose love and willingness to sacrifice lightened the burden of writing and made me realize that life begins not with, but on the other side of, scholarship.

Introduction

Who is the poet? He whose life is symbolic. I have always believed
that I need only speak of myself in order to tell the story of my age.

Thomas Mann

The Vortex of Events

Heinrich Mann was born in 1871, two months after the founding
of the Second Reich; he died in 1950, five years after the collapse of
the Third. During this span of eighty years Germany experienced
what were perhaps the most tumultuous decades in modern history.
Beginning with the deceptive calmness of the *Gründerzeit*, and
accelerating at a more frenetic pace after the 1890s, the German
tempo of events soon took on the appearance of a *danse macabre*.
Besides witnessing two world wars and the Hitler era, Germany was,
during these years, a crucial battleground for a number of ideological
and literary movements which disturbed the peace of the European
continent. Not only were some of the first and last battles of Marxism
and fascism fought out on German soil, but so were a series of
important intellectual engagements, including those of Naturalism,
Neo-Romanticism, and Expressionism. The decades between the
1870s and the 1940s were anything but peaceful, and to those
sensitive to the clash of ideas and world-views, the times must have
seemed especially tense and strained. There was hardly a single year
that could be called serene or uneventful.

Mann not only lived through, but was passionately involved in,
most of these struggles. Moreover, as an author he wrote insightfully
enough about his age to create several novels which rank among the
best social documents of the period. Of course, he did not intend for
his works to be treated retrospectively as social or literary "documents."
He wrote about his era simply out of the sense of obligation he felt
as a writer to record and criticize his times. Some authors who lived
through the same decades did not feel this need and consequently
defined their literary tasks in a different way than did Mann. Rudolf
Pannwitz, Alfred Mombert, or Theodor Däubler, for example (all

born within a few years of Mann), were only minimally bound up with their age and did not see what being a writer had to do with commitment to the world around them. For this reason their work is more introspective and mystical than Mann's; the resonances of Germany's social and political realities are only faintly echoed in their poems or novels. By contrast, a glance at Mann's literary production makes it immediately clear that he was in the center of events—and not by accident, but by choice. It is this quality of being-in-the-middle-of-things (and, more particularly, the ability to translate the concentrated experience of this involvement into print) that gives Mann's work such a vital, transcriptive appearance. Few could equal him in this respect, which is one reason why his intellectual biography reads much like the biography of the era itself.

Because the interrelations between Mann and his age were so close, there are various ways in which his work could be approached. One would be to study his novels and essays as historical sources—that is, to discount their value as literary texts and treat them only as indicators of social reality. Here his *oeuvres* would be dealt with solely for their reflective qualities—for the special kinds of historical knowledge they provide about post-Bismarckian Germany. Another approach would be to engage in a stylistic analysis of Mann's writings in order to understand how his language, method of presentation, and even syntax were integrally connected with the period in which he lived. If this were done well (e.g., in the manner of Leo Spitzer) one could learn a great deal not only about the historicity of style, but also about the specific forms, literary strategies, and modes of expression a writer had access to in late nineteenth and early twentieth-century Germany.

Both of these approaches, among others, would result in valid projects and would no doubt produce interesting results. Neither is, however, the primary focus of this study. Instead, I have tried to do three things which need to be made clear from the start.

The Writer and His Role

First of all, in the first two sections of the book I have attempted to trace Heinrich Mann's evolution as a writer from roughly his twentieth to his fiftieth year. At the beginning of this time-span (around 1890), Mann hesitantly began to consider himself an "author." This designation meant something special to him, for in *fin-de-siècle* Germany authorship carried with it marks of social and cultural esteem which Mann wanted to acquire for himself. By the end of this period (around 1920) Mann had achieved his full stature as an author, but in the process had become a different kind of writer. In his youth, he viewed writing as an aesthetic divertissement; by the time he reached maturity he regarded it as a moral obligation. In the first instance the written word was an escape from an oppressive society, in the second a necessary means for confronting and changing it. After 1920 (the period treated in the third section of this study), Mann maintained this latter position with even greater conviction than before and began to view writing as not only a moral, but also a political, obligation.

These changes in outlook were considerable but represented no sudden *volte face*. The transition from one position to the other was slow and laborious, and was achieved only at the cost of great inner turmoil. In no sense can it be said that Mann was compelled to become an engaged literary intellectual. There was no immanent logic to his development and there were no mysterious forces pushing him in that direction. On the contrary, Mann had to fight every step of the way to become the writer he was in the 1920s or 1930s. This struggle can be seen, for example, in the developing conflict he felt between different interpretations of his role as an author. At first the idea of a "role" presented no problems. Being a writer was simply equated with artistic sensitivity, and since Mann was sure he possessed this quality, he knew he was cut out for authorship. At this stage, in the early 1890s, his self-image (as a "man of feeling") was perfectly compatible with the persona he presented to the outside world (the cultured, literary aesthete). But as time passed, both Mann's self-concept and his view of the writer's place in society began to change. In large measure this happened because of the shifting social and political configurations of Wilhelmian, and later Weimar, Germany. The more unacceptable the Empire and then the Republic began to seem, the more Mann felt drawn into a posture of concern and involvement. Eventually his aesthetic interpretation of authorship appeared completely inappropriate when viewed against the background of an egregious social reality. Hence, he revolted not only against his earlier conception of the author's role (which seemed incongruous with his new social orientation), but also against that part of himself still attached to the old role. In short, Mann's evolution as a writer occurred as the result of a two-fold struggle: the first, between his changing literary image and the dynamics of the age in which he lived; and the second, between different aspects of the "self" he was or wanted to become.

The secret of Mann's development was his creative interaction with the world. Had he not accepted the challenge of engagement he would have become a different kind of author. Or, had he lived in more placid times, he might not have felt even the need to become involved. But because Mann's era was so problematic, and because his relation to it was so intense, external problems were inextricably linked to inner ones, and both, taken together, strongly affected his self-definition as a writer. One of the consequences of this was a gradual shift in his role as author, beginning with his initial pose as a poetic *Lyriker* and ending with one as a politically conscious *Literat*.

Literary Politics

In addition to dealing with Mann's literary evolution, I have also tried to deal with his politics. More specifically, I have attempted to relate the changing nature of Mann's intellectual politics to his changing conception of himself as an author, on the grounds that these two matters are integrally connected with one another.

Nearly every kind of writing is political, even the kind that tries to stand above the fray. If a writer metamorphoses himself from one type of author into an entirely different type, it is hard to imagine that his politics has not been transformed in the meantime. This relationship between writing and politics is true of Mann's development between the early 1890s and the late 1930s.

At the beginning, when he fashioned himself as an artist of subtle moods and evocations, his politics was right-wing; at the end, when he had become a master of the social novel, his politics shifted to the Left. Still, a word of caution ought to be inserted here. Even though a writer's style, literary intention, and thematic content change with his changing perceptions of political reality, this correspondence rarely develops as a one-to-one relationship. There are times, especially in periods of rapid social change, when one's political views evolve very quickly while one's style lags behind. When this happens, an author might continue to express himself in an earlier aesthetic mode despite the fact that he has begun to write about political matters for which such a style is no longer appropriate. There are other times when the opposite might be true. A writer could make a number of technical or literary innovations and not immediately realize that these signal deeper, more permanent, changes in his total *Weltanschauung*. In Mann's case, there were moments when his style changed more rapidly than his politics, and other moments when his politics shot beyond his style. After 1915, however, a synthesis was finally achieved whereby his literary form and political content came into conjunction, at least to Mann's satisfaction. It was at this point that he reached his pinnacle as a writer, since he not only knew what he wanted to say but also had gained control of the technical means for saying it.

In addition to the issue of Mann's literary disequilibrium, another aspect of his politics on which this book focuses is the increasingly conscious politicization of his work after 1900.

Though, as I have suggested, most literature is unavoidably political, there are many different ways in which a writer's politics might be expressed in his literature. Some writers make their politics covert, others overt; some try to hide their views behind subtleties, while others write in a clearly polemical vein. The curious thing about Mann is that during the years discussed here he evolved from the first to the second of these types. Initially, he was a conservative aesthete who disguised his politics as much as possible (sometimes under the pretense of being apolitical). Three decades later, he had become one of Germany's leading "left intellectuals" and as such never hesitated to spell out the political message of his work. This transition from an implicit to an explicit mode of political expression is an interesting story in itself, but like everything else in Mann's development it cannot be treated in isolation. The heightened political tone of his later novels and essays was closely bound up with a whole kaleidoscope of ideological changes, not the least of which was a more radical conception of the writer's task in society. Eventually Mann began to suggest that literature should not merely incorporate a politics, it should *be* politics. The writer, he thought, had to take responsibility for his world; he had to turn his work into social and political criticism, even into a critique of life itself. Perhaps, if a writer did his job well, his words could actually affect political decision-making and, in the end, move Germany along in a more humane and democratic direction. This notion—that literature might have something to do with changing the world—began to predom-

inate in Mann's work after the turn of the century. At first he dealt
with the idea from a conservative perspective, later from a liberal one
and, finally, from a radical one. Despite these differences in perspective, the certainty that writing was a political act and that the committed writer was an activist *par excellence* came increasingly to the
forefront of Mann's thought.

Throughout the following pages, the term "literary politics" refers
to this attempt to effect social or political consequences by exclusively literary means. The deliberate effort to both politicize writing
and intellectualize politics preoccupied Mann to an extraordinary
degree, especially during the latter half of his career. It might justi-
fiably be said that he cannot be understood as a writer without
taking into account this central concern which permeates so much of
his work.

The Trans-Individual Subject

The third and final goal of this study is to look at Mann in relation
to others of his generation, and to deal with him, in so far as it is
possible, as a socio-literary type. In the following pages I have
attempted to show that Mann's development was far from unique.
Instead, it was in several respects paradigmatic of a whole stratum of
literary intellectuals who went through much the same transition,
though of course with individual variations.

"A man lives not only his personal life as an individual, but also,
consciously or unconsciously, the life of his epoch and his contemporaries."[1] So wrote Thomas Mann in *The Magic Mountain* and the
same can be applied, with caution, to Heinrich Mann. As he exter-
nalized himself in his work and objectified in literature his encounter
with his times, he seemed to capture a mood which others of similar
age and background also felt. Though he did not notice it at first,
Heinrich Mann had much in common with a large number of his
contemporaries. Not only did he involve himself in the same issues as
others, but he also gave his works a comparable structure and
internal coherence, often without knowing of the writings of like-
minded authors, or without being influenced by them in any significant way. When this sort of concurrence happens in literary history it
is either because the writers involved came out of, or were decisively
affected by, a common lived experience, or because they were unified

by a problematic which they all perceived and agreed had to be faced and overcome.[2]

What is striking about Mann's literary work is how much it resembles that of other German writers of the period. Among those contemporaries to whom Mann was spiritually and intellectually very close one could mention Lion Feuchtwanger, René Schickele, Bernhard Kellermann, Paul Zech, Alfred Döblin, Rudolf Leonhard, Wilhelm Herzog, Georg Hermann, Kurt Findeisen, Otto Flake, Friedrich Huch, Adam Kuckhoff, Georg Kaiser, Carl Sternheim, Bruno Frank, Herbert Eulenberg, and Georg Hirschfeld. The bond that tied Mann to this group was not simply the fact that he shared with it certain literary themes and social values; it was also that each member came from the same kind of background and went through parallel developments at similar points in their lives. The bare outline of this "collective" evolution would be as follows: Almost all were born between the early 1870s and mid–1880s. All but one or two grew up in conventional middle class homes. In their twenties, each tended to reject the status quo or at least to see his relationship to it as highly ambiguous. Then, having turned away from the existing social order, they all sought private avenues of escape, usually in art or literature but sometimes in extensive travel (to Italy, generally, but also to Latin America and the Orient). In time each came to view these solutions as inadequate, mainly because they lacked any real element of social commitment which, in the face of a deteriorating situation in Germany after 1900, each eventually began to accept as necessary. Hence, in order to acquire a sense of involvement, these writers gradually abandoned their expedients of personal or aesthetic withdrawal for a moral critique of society. In different ways, each of them slowly moved toward the ideology of liberal humanism, and then eventually toward that of democratic socialism. Finally, after World War I, all were united in realizing that the classical bourgeois age was over and that a new form of society had to be constructed. The quest for the "new form," the "new ethic," or the "new man" (all approached within a left-wing, usually socialist, framework) occupied much of their later lives.[3]

As it stands, this is only a literary profile. It indicates that several German writers acquired an identity because of the way they *corresponded* to the same "lived situation." But might there not be more involved here than a correspondence? The French literary sociologist Lucien Goldmann has argued that behind the *oeuvres* of any group there exists a larger entity which always expresses itself in the structure of literary texts. This larger presence is the social class or stratum to which one belongs, something Goldmann has referred to as the "trans-individual subject." Each social class (so he alleges) has a particular outlook of its own—its own collective consciousness—and every individual, to the extent that he is a member of a class, participates in its world-view as a small part suffused with the spirit of the whole. If a person (a writer, for example) should attempt to articulate his own feelings and attitudes, he would inadvertently express and externalize the attitudes of the social grouping which invariably speaks through him. Embedded within works of literature, then, are certain presuppositions, values, and modes of structuring experience which reflect not only an author's philosophy of life but, more importantly, the core assumptions of the class to which he belongs. If, in a series of literary texts written by different authors living at the same time, a similar world-view is continually reproduced, it then appears likely that the same trans-individual subject is being made manifest. According to Goldmann, individual authors should not be discussed as a group or "school" simply because they influenced one another in matters of style or content. The notion of influence, after all, is only the most elementary way of accounting for identities; its explanatory value often leaves much to be desired, especially when similarities can be detected in contemporaneous writers who did not read each other's works. Much more helpful, in his view, is the concept of a mutual (though not necessarily conscious) participation in the same social whole, since this leads to a shared mental predisposition and outlook on life. Had Goldmann made a study of the writers mentioned here, it is likely he would have concluded that they all collaborated, however unknowingly, in a common frame of reference and "world vision." Hence, he would no doubt have argued that Mann was linked to the others by an affinity of mental structures, class experience, and membership in the same social totality.[4]

Can this approach be accepted and used here with respect to Mann and his contemporaries? It seems that Goldmann is right in much of what he says (his entire theory of literature is far more complex than I have indicated here), but his insights apply more to tight-knit groups, like the Surrealists or the Storm-and-Stress writers, than to the comparatively loose collection of German authors whose profile has been given above. In light of this, it is important to explain the position of this study relative to Goldmann's methodology, and in the process to clarify the connections I have made—and think permissible to make—between Mann and the literary group described earlier.

First, I have not tried to argue that Mann participated in a German collective consciousness or that he directly transferred this consciousness to his novels. Possibly there was something like an *a priori* mind at work behind the authors treated in this book, but if so I am not interested in uncovering it since to follow in this direction would move the discussion well beyond Mann and his literary politics, which is the major focus of this study. Second, I have not attempted to establish absolute links between Mann and the other writers dealt with here, nor have I tried to prove that they shared an integral world vision. Instead, my intention has been to suggest that they were held together mainly by the similarity and simultaneity of their reactions. What made them so similar to one another intellectually was the fact that they came from the same general background, saw the same problematic, and embraced the same political solutions. At issue here is more a set of "elective affinities" than any immanent unifying principle. Finally, I have tried to infer that Mann was in many ways typical of his generation, but not representative (if by the latter term is meant that he spoke *for* the group and articulated the group's every concern). The most that can be said is that Mann was moving in a direction parallel with the others and that, under similar circumstances, his responses tended to be the same as theirs. He was not, however, part of an intimate literary "cohort" and his works are not emblematic in any mystical sense.

In sum, one of the goals of this study has been to draw out Mann's common ties with the others without at the same time allowing him to be swallowed up by too many comparisons. Mann the writer was a particular person who related to his world in a particular way. But in so doing he produced a multiplicity of attitudes which happened to be characteristic of others as well. The idea of a trans-individual subject has not been introduced in order to obfuscate what is still essentially a literary biography. Mann's artistic and political development against the backdrop of German society remains the central, pivotal theme of the following pages. His relationship to like-minded writers is dealt with here as an important and clarifying, but nonetheless subsidiary, motif.

Footnotes
Introduction

1. Thomas Mann, *The Magic Mountain*, trans. H. T. Lowe-Porter (New York, 1961), p. 32.

2. See, for example, Julius Petersen, *Die literarischen Generationen* (Berlin, 1930), pp. 35-40.

3. This sketch depicts nothing more than an "ideal type." Still, allowing for individual differences, it holds true to a suprising degree for all of the writers mentioned here. To be sure, a novelist like Friedrich Huch (1873-1913), whose development was remarkably close to Mann's up to the eve of World War I, died prematurely, and another like Otto Flake (1880-1963) flirted with conservative and elitist ideas in the 1930s. Then, too, there is some question about the middle-class origins of a writer like Alfred Döblin (1878-1957) whose family fortunes changed for the worse when he was ten (though he still retained the deeply rooted goals and aspirations of a *bürgerlich* upbringing). With these few exceptions, all the authors listed above were politically and intellectually very close to each other. They all shared what has frequently been called a "middle-class humanist outlook" or a "socialist-humanist *Weltanschauung*." (See the *Deutsches Schriftstellerlexikon*, ed. Günter Albrecht, et. al., Weimar, 1963.)

Thomas Mann (1875-1955), though he went through many of these stages, cannot be included as part of this literary group because his growth as an author and political writer was too idiosyncratic. Though in broad terms he did follow a pattern similar to the one described here, his pace of development was considerably slower and more elliptical than that of the others. For example as a young man, he, like the writers mentioned above, viewed the world as ambiguous, but for artistic rather than political reasons. Likewise, he eventually embraced a social-democratic world-view, but only in the 1920s, not around 1910 when most of the others did.

4. For a further elaboration of Goldmann's views see *The Hidden God*, trans. Philip Thody (New York, 1964); *Pour une sociologie du roman* (Paris, 1964); *Structures mentales et création culturelle* (Paris, 1970); and "The Sociology of Literature," in *The Sociology of Art and Literature*, ed. Milton C. Albrecht, James H. Barnett, and Mason Griff (New York, 1970), pp. 582-609.

Part 1

THE WRITER AS AESTHETE

Chapter 1

The Making of a Novelist

Doubtless, one could find at the origin of every artistic calling a certain undifferentiated choice which circumstances, education, and contact with the world particularize only later.

Jean-Paul Sartre

The Decision to Write

Heinrich Mann appears to have been predisposed toward a writing career from an extremely early age, possibly as early as his tenth or eleventh year. The question that needs to be asked at the beginning of this study is: what specific factors shaped or caused this inclination toward a literary vocation? It is not enough to attribute authorship to some sort of unavoidable destiny, nor is it sufficient to deal with it as something purely accidental or arbitrary. The act of writing is always a choice, and generally a rare one at that. Perhaps no more than one in a thousand chooses a literary profession, and thus it seems reasonable to think that there might be unusual factors affecting such a decision. For our purposes, the question of talent as a cause for an individual's desire to become an author must be suspended temporarily. Real talent probably does not exist at the onset except in the vaguest form, i.e., as active imagination or a highly developed fantasy life. But even when individuals possess these prerequisite qualities there is no guarantee that they will turn toward a literary calling rather than some other creative endeavor. To speak of Heinrich Mann, for example, as having a "natural gift for writing," or being "destined for a literary career," is to avoid the root of the matter. Mann himself candidly admitted that he was in no sense a born literary artist.[1] Instead, he spoke of a "decision to write" (*Beschluss zu schreiben*),[2] indicating that he became an author through discipline, hard work, and a firm commitment to the art of writing well.

What needs to be investigated initially, then, is the etiology of authorship. The central point of concern is why Mann chose to

3

become a writer even before his work had been tested by a reading audience or his abililties validated by public opinion. In examining this problem, one would expect psychoanalytic theories to be helpful, but in many ways they do not go far enough in providing answers to essential questions. Freud, for instance, correctly pointed out that writers are people who turn their fantasies into art (who "dream in broad daylight," as he put it) but he was unable to identify the source of this phenomenon. Instead, he shifted his discussion to the technical aspects of art, which he then admitted psychoanalysis was incapable of handling.[3] Jung picked up the issue of artistic creativity but, although he wrote extensively on the subject, he never explicitly dealt with the origin of the need to write. Similarly, Otto Rank, who wrote what is perhaps the best book on the genesis of the will to create, also eluded the question. "The artist," he wrote, "creates essentially by an inward urge which we may describe as an individual's will-to-form, and whether he objectifies this in a picture, a statue, [a book], or a symphony is rather a technical and formal matter than an individual problem."[4] What I wish to suggest here is that the direction one's "will-to-form" takes is not, as Rank put it, merely a "technical and formal matter." Rather, it is induced to a considerable degree by a facilitating environment which encourages one type of creative expression over another, even one entire mode of cultural objectification over another.

In order to remedy the shortcomings of the psychoanalytic approach, a broader perspective is needed. The origins of authorship should be seen as intimately bound up with a writer's entire *Lebenswelt*, including the social dimensions of childhood development. Neither the growth of a child's mind nor the awareness of himself as a person takes place in a vacuum; both are inseparable from a social context which manifests itself in and through one's psychic development. Unless the ambience in which a child matures is taken into consideration, neither his later value orientation nor the career projects he eventually sets for himself can be adequately comprehended.[5]

With regard to a writer like Heinrich Mann, at least three things have to be understood: first, how his personal development was influenced by his family relations; second, how he was affected, consciously or unconsciously, by the class to which he belonged; and third, how he was implicated in, and learned to perceive, the complete social structure within which his family and class were located. Each of these layers represents a filter or "mediation" through which the whole of social reality was seen and interpreted by Mann; and each, in its own way, supplied a grid for conceptualizing not only the world at large, but his relation to it.

In discussing Mann or any other literary figure, then, each of these three dimensions of reality needs to be kept in mind. At the broadest level there is society itself, with its elaborate set of presuppositions which everyone acquires to a greater or lesser extent. (Among the societal presuppositions in nineteenth-century Germany one would include certain commonly-acknowledged values such as the formal acceptance of a Christian ethic or the strong emphasis on rationality and order.) At the next level below this are the more clearly defined enclaves, or strata, within the whole. (In nineteenth-century Germany, once again, these would include specific class groupings, each carrying with it historically-developed attitudes based upon collective experience and location within the general social framework.) Every class possesses, to some degree, not only its own level of culture and power, but also its own social perspective. Furthermore, each class assumes a certain position toward the whole of society, thereby deciding which aspects of social reality will be reinforced or encouraged, and which rejected or played down. To be born within a class is to receive the world already screened, already charged with meaning. But one can go further. Inside each class there is still another layer of mediation, the individual family unit. Each family has its own unique composition, its own reciprocal relationships, its own conception of itself; each provides a singularly original milieu for a child to grow up in. Because every family regulates the kind and amount of social reality it transmits to the children, it automatically deciphers the class and societal values which are impressed upon it. Just as each family is shaped by the social life around it, so too each shapes the mental space of its own members. For this reason, the family is perhaps the most important mediator between the outer world (society, class relations) and the inner world (individual consciousness). This is especially true with respect to young children for whom the family group is virtually the only social context within which to experience the first few years of life.

Heinrich Mann was born into his family "not as an independent person but as a *member*."[6] The importance of this point cannot be overestimated. It means that Mann experienced his world as filtered three times over, with his family being perhaps the most decisive influence. As Erich Fromm, among others, has emphasized, "[t]he family is the medium through which the society [or] class imprints its specific structure on the child and therefore on the adult. *The family is the psychological agency of society.*"[7] True though this may be, it should also be stressed that the family is an active as well as a passive agent. It not only receives impressions from without but also helps generate attitudes from within, by either encouraging its members to confront the world or escape it, by urging them either to affirm or question dominant values.[8] Since the family plays such a crucial role in psychologically situating its members and giving them their basic orientation towards life, it is reasonable to suppose that it may also be a central factor in predisposing some individuals towards authorship.

The following is an attempt to show that not only the kind of writer one becomes, but whether or not one becomes a writer at all, is greatly affected by one's social and familial relations. To be sure, a child has no choice about the world he inherits or about how it is interpreted by the family. But he is free to constitute his world as much as he is constituted by it. Each individual can decide how he is going to address himself to the ensemble of relations in which he is enmeshed. This margin of freedom is the extent of a writer's early creative space. It is the area in which he can maneuver according to his own will, the area wherein he decides who he is and how he will react to the larger forces which shape him. No writer's attitudes are really "determined" by external realities even if they do stake out the parameters of his initial reflections about the world. Between the circumstances of an author's early life and the writer he eventually becomes there is a *décalage*—a wedge of irreducible freedom where one chooses to make what he wants out of himself and his situation.

The Mann Family and the "Crisis" of the Middle Class

An understanding of Heinrich Mann's "decision to write" begins with a look at the Mann family itself. As the first of five children, Heinrich was born into one of the more prominent middle-class families in Lübeck. It is important to note immediately that the Mann family was without any noticeable literary traditions. Hence, the urge to write (which gripped both Heinrich and Thomas when they were still young) can in no way be attributed to familial pressures to emulate or "live up to" the accomplishments of predecessors.[9]

On the contrary, Thomas Johann Heinrich Mann, the boys' father, felt wholly uneasy in a literary environment. What little reading he did was secretive (as once, on the seashore at Travemünde, when he tried to read a Zola novel surreptitiously, beyond the pale of friends and family).[10] If the father communicated anything to his sons, it was not an encouragement to write but rather the notion that writing is a superfluous and wasteful activity—a vocation chosen by essentially "indolent" and dreamy people.[11]

The father's hope for Heinrich was that he would follow in his own footsteps and take up a career in business. Since the late eighteenth century, the Manns had operated a thriving grain import and export trade in Lübeck. The father was the fourth successor to the Mann firm and there was every reason to expect that Heinrich would be the fifth. To this end, the father made all the appropriate gestures to initiate his son into the business; he took him on commercial jaunts, he let him christen cargo ships, and he introduced him to numerous customers, all to no avail. The boy did not seem interested, and worse yet, his mind was so unsystematic that he could not even remember the street numbers of the houses which they passed.[12] Clearly Heinrich Mann was not attracted to business life. Instead, he appeared drawn to reading and writing in a way that seemed unhealthy and disturbing to his father. Later, the feelings of disappointment harbored by the father broke out in recriminations; Thomas Johann Mann accused his son of being lazy, apathetic, and spiteful because he rejected hard work in favor of an artist's personality.[13]

Heinrich Mann's decision to controvert his father's will and become a writer was not the result of impulse or caprice. It was arrived at because he concluded that, for him personally, not business but writing was the only authentic mode of being-in-the-world. To understand why he came to such a conclusion, it is important to look briefly at a complex of events in German social life which peaked during the years of Heinrich's childhood. These occurrences had repercussions on the Mann family and particularly on the way in which Heinrich internalized the values of family life. I refer to the totality of these events as the "crisis of the middle class."

The social stratum to which the Manns belonged was the so-called *Bürgertum,* or "old middle class." With its roots in pre-industrial Germany, especially in old trading towns like Lübeck, this sector of the population came to develop an identifiable style and outlook on life. In summary fashion one could say that the German *Bürger* was recognized by his traditionalist mentality, his high esteem for work and discipline, his strong sense of moderation and propriety, his great emphasis on respectability and personal character, and his convictions about authority, status, and "sense of place." Culturally, the *bürgerlich* type tended to be conservative, and therefore generally suspicious of change or experimentation; personally, he usually inclined towards an old-fashioned, perhaps somewhat formal bearing; politically, he was a firm believer in civic-mindedness, local self-determination and responsible involvement in politics.[14] There were, of course, exceptions to this typology, but as a rule the German *Bürger* stayed close to this pattern (and to the extent that he diverged from it, he no doubt felt out-of-step with his class).

It was, however, not only this common style and world-view which unified the members of the old middle class. They were also held together occupationally, both by their predominance in traditional businesses such as small-scale trading and manufacturing, and geographically, by their deep roots in the urban areas of Germany. These factors, taken together, gave the *Bürgertum* a sense of identity, a sense of being part of the same social class. It should be emphasized that wealth as such was not a measure of inclusion in, or exclusion from, the traditional middle class since the amount of money one possessed did not determine class alignment. A person could, in fact, be fairly well-off and yet feel a kind of bondedness and loyalty to the social stratum into which he was born. This was so because the true burgher rejected vertical mobility as betrayal—as the abandonment not only of one's class, but also of the whole way of life bound up with that class.[15] The Mann family was a case in point. In spite of the fact that the Manns were financially secure ("We are not rich," Heinrich's mother told him as a child, "but we are well-to-do"[16]), the family was still tied up morally, culturally, and socially with what Werner Sombart called the *Bourgeoisie alten Stils* (the old-style middle class).[17]

The important thing to note, however, is that this class, the traditional German *Bürgertum,* was in decline in late nineteenth-century Germany. Above it was rising another class: the bourgeoisie, or what Sombart termed *der moderne Wirtschaftsmensch* (the modern business man). The characteristics of this emergent economic type were markedly different from those of the old middle class. The "new people," as Heinrich Mann later called them, were not interested in permanence or stability but in rapid change and a high turnover of profit. As a recognizable class which both introduced and profited from novelty, the bourgeoisie affirmed all the allegedly "progressive" tendencies of the century: industrialism, finance capitalism, the cartelization of shipping and commerce, *la transformation economique du monde*. Where the traditional merchant emphasized austerity and hard work, the *nouveaux riches* stressed conspicuous consumption and display. Where the burgher was proud of his civic virtue and sense of community, the bourgeoisie seemed indifferent to local politics or unconcerned that their economic acquisitiveness was up-rooting the social order. Where the old-fashioned middle class considered itself cultured, composed, and responsible, the "new wealth" appeared by contrast to be superficial, pretentious and un-conscionably greedy.

The conflict between these two types—the one slipping on the social scale, the other ascending—was real and deeply felt. In part, the antagonism was between, on the one hand, an essentially pre-industrial middle class firmly anchored to an urban or *ständisch* framework, and, on the other, an entrepreneurial bourgeoisie inter-ested in high finance or industrial *Konkurrenz* and operating best in an international framework. Putting aside for the moment the economic causes of these differences, there can be no doubt that the social and psychological effects of this cleavage were everywhere in evidence in nineteenth-century Germany.[18] Certainly they left their mark on the Mann family, and even appeared in the early works of Heinrich and Thomas. As writers, both sons gave considerable attention to the burgher versus bourgeoisie theme, Heinrich especially in *Im Schlaraffenland* (1900) and Thomas in *Buddenbrooks* (1901).

The Father: A Problem of Identity

Within the Mann family unit, the one person who felt the crisis of the middle class most strongly was the father, Thomas Johann Mann (1840–1891). Born when the family fortunes were still high, he took over its grain business in 1863 at the age of twenty-three. At first things went well, and Thomas Johann felt prosperous enough to marry in 1869 and start a family. He even built a new house in the fashionable Makart style, and later (1877) became one of the senators of the city. By all indications he seemed successful, but in truth he was presiding over a business whose foundations were slowly eroding. In the 1860s and the 1870s, new economic and political forces were changing the face of North Germany and introducing a different sort of reality which Mann was quite helpless to check. It was the reality of industrialization, cartelization, and consolidation—of the new Reich and the "new spirit." It was, in short, the reality of modernization which threatened to undermine not only Mann's traditional business, but his traditional way of life as well.

As early as 1864, with the war in nearby Schleswig-Holstein, the shadow of Prussian influence over the free city of Lübeck was strongly felt. Two years later many of Lübeck's company and trade privileges (which had helped sustain the Mann firm) were removed. After 1871, when the city became part of the Second Reich, its economic situation further deteriorated. With Berlin as the new capital, it was natural, for geographic reasons, that Stettin and Hamburg would be Berlin's ports to the sea, not Lübeck which was relegated to secondary importance. By the 1880s, the building of the North Sea canal at Kiel placed Lübeck still further into the backwater; and, to make matters worse, the port cities of Hamburg, Kiel, and Stettin consolidated many of their operations, leaving Lübeck out once again. The profitable thing now, for an increasingly industrialized German economy, was the traffic in industrial raw materials, not grain. For Mann, these reverses meant a rather severe decline in his grain trade—a decline accentuated by yet another lifting of company privileges (1886), and by Bismarck's imposition of protective tariffs (thus freezing the cheap importation of wheat from Russia on which the Mann business depended).[19]

The conflict being acted out here was one between merchant and industrial capitalism. On the one side were the old commercial and trading interests, on the other the new entrepreneurial bourgeoisie, with its risk capital and *laissez-faire* ethic. The former wanted things to remain basically fixed and stable; the latter wanted a shift in the distribution of wealth and power, a liberalization of finance and trade legislation, and a breaking up of old town privileges. The outcome of this conflict was never in doubt. The victor was "big business allied with capital and science"; the loser was "the independent tradesman" who now fell upon "a time of insecurity, hardship, and fear."[20] For Thomas Johann Mann, whose business interests and life-style were tied up with the declining *Bürgertum,* these conflicts led to a steadily worsening economic situation. In the 1870s there was a

point where he was in danger of losing everything, but in the succeeding years he recovered many of his losses.[21] By the time of his
premature death at age fifty-one (1891), Mann was able to leave a
substantial sum of money to his wife and children. Nevertheless, the
firm was liquidated, and the family house put up for sale, thus ending, as his youngest son Viktor Mann put it, "the proud middle-class
period of our family history."[22]

Given the fact that "new forces" permeated German economic life
in the latter half of the nineteenth century, Thomas Johann Mann
had at least two options. For one, he could have gone over to the
bourgeois spirit, tried to adapt himself to the so-called "new era,"
and learned to play by the rules of a different game. This he refused
to do. The bourgeoisie represented a world he could not embrace.
"[My father]," Heinrich later recalled, "had an uncontrollable hatred
of newness which threatened him socially, in the form of the *nouveaux
riches*, and spiritually, through [his fear of] insecurity."[23] Hence,
instead of adjusting to the new forces enveloping him, he opted for
an alternative course—namely, ensconcing himself in a traditional,
middle-class mode of life at precisely the time when this was becoming
an obsolete and no longer adequate way of coping with the world.
As both Heinrich and Thomas later attested, their father seemed to
cultivate, almost to an exaggerated degree, the classical traits of the
bürgerlich character. In the midst of a world in transition, he held
firmly to his "formal bearing," his dedication to work, his obsessive
sense of "middle-class solidity."[24] To Thomas, his father appeared "a
model in matters of discipline," the very personification of "the
serious conduct of life."[25] To Heinrich he seemed extraordinarily
steadfast, conscientious, exact, and rigorous.[26] In a word, the father
embodied what Thomas referred to as *"Lebensbürgerlichkeit"*—the
old middle-class style of life, with its traditional straight-forwardness
and overwhelming sense of duty.[27]

For whatever reasons, Thomas Johann Mann chose a stance of
retrenchment *vis-à-vis* an increasingly hostile modern world. This
decision had a number of interesting repercussions on his children,
especially on his two eldest sons. In the long run, it seems to have
strongly affected their decisions to choose writing as a career.

To begin with, the father's retreat into formality prevented him
from "acting out" his proper social role with regard to his children.
According to Talcott Parsons, the function of the father is to embody

an adequate conception of social reality and objectify or represent it
to the children within the context of the family group.[28] Thomas
Johann Mann could not do this because he had turned his back on
the ascendent social reality (or rather social reality had turned its
back on him). Between the cultural-ethical world the father clung to,
and the objective world coming into being, there was a gap too great
to be bridged. As a result, he lost his ascriptive function in relation
to the children, since he would not socialize them into conditions
which he opposed with his whole being. In a curious way, the integrative tasks of the traditional family unit began to break down in
the case of the Manns. If, as it seems, the purpose of the family is to
produce "socially necessary mental structures"; if its basic goal is to
instill "role dispositions" and "role expectations"; and if its existence
is geared to shaping "the kind of personality that guarantees the
frictionless operation of bourgeois society," then the Manns failed
abysmally in fulfilling their parental duties.[29] Both Heinrich and
Thomas grew up without a firm attachment to the given and with no
strong sense of responsibility toward it.

It seems clear that the father did not encourage his sons to develop
a psychological disposition compatible with an emerging bourgeois
society. What is less clear, however, is the sort of attitudes he *did*
try to encourage in them. Apparently, he presented himself to his
children as a prototype of "middle-class solidity"; he even tried to
implant in them the same kind of practical, responsible qualities he
himself possessed.[30] But he did not succeed in this because, in the
last analysis, he appears not to have been all that sure of precisely
what function he was supposed to perform with regard to them. If
reality had not become problematic, and if he had been able to go on
socializing his children into a world he felt secure about, there would
likely have been no dilemma. But Thomas Johann Mann was fighting a rear-guard action against modernity for a way of life that was
disappearing. Because his own social and economic position was in
jeopardy, he could not act out with confidence or conviction the role
of the patriarchal father resolutely leading his children into the future.
That role made sense, after all, only when there was a future, but
about this he was not at all certain. All too frequently the father
talked about his discomfiture in the modern world, his "fear" with
regard to contemporary tendencies and the "still more ominous"
future on the horizon.[31] Under the circumstances, he could hardly
(as Parsons suggests) have embodied social reality and represented it

to his children. On the contrary, he was too deeply troubled and filled with self-doubts, not only about his business affairs but about his very *raison d'etre*. It appears that at this time Thomas Johann Mann—in his own way, and over a more protracted period—went through the same sort of identity crisis described in the novel *Buddenbrooks*. In fact, the title character Thomas Buddenbrook (whose crisis is indirectly brought on, as Thomas Johann Mann's was, by a general unsettlement in his family, class, and personal life) was partly based on the real-life character of the father.

In sum, the father failed to become an object of emulation to his children. Both Heinrich and Thomas indicate that as children they were aware not only of their father's deteriorating position, but of his basic insecurity on a personal level. As a result, a strong identification between father and sons never materialized in the Mann family. This was especially true with Heinrich, who even at the beginning showed little inclination to internalize his father as an exemplar.[32] Instead, he seems to have considered him more a "limit situation" than a valid ego ideal.

Heinrich Mann's decision to write was made against his father's wishes, and, as such, was an implicit act of rebellion. Still, it would be wrong to think that he became a writer simply on the rebound. He was also drawn to writing for a positive reason, because he came to believe that expressing oneself artistically was the most creative way in which to establish one's presence in the world. He got this notion from his mother, and it is therefore important to turn for a moment to her influence on his early development.

The Mother: An Artistic Alternative

Julia da Silva-Bruhns Mann (1851–1923) was the daughter of a German father and a mother of Portuguese-creole descent. Born in Brazil near Rio de Janeiro, she was brought to Lübeck at the age of seven. At seventeen she married Thomas Johann, who was eleven years her senior. Although detailed information about her is lacking, these things at least are known: that she was "extraordinarily beautiful," charming, and sensitive; that she was musically talented, especially at the piano; that she felt out of place in Lübeck, a "foreign element" in a city of Protestant burghers; and most importantly, that she was by all indications the affective center of the family circle, and in

this role exerted an emotional influence on the children which was
far greater than that exercised by the father.[33] It could in fact be
argued that Julia Mann was decisive in shaping the temperament,
values, and inclination towards phantasy which were evident in both
Heinrich and Thomas. Not only did she initiate them into her own
unique outlook on life—that of an outsider and an *artiste*—but she
also encouraged them to be different, to see art and everyday life as
irreconcilably opposed, and, as a way out of this dichotomy, to
choose art as the only meaningful path toward personal redemption.

By all appearances, Julia Mann was a striking contrast to her
husband in temperament, in interest, and in what she represented to
her children. As both sons later recalled, it was their mother who
had the most significant influence on their early development. This,
they indicated, was not only because she was "warm and empathetic"
while the father was distant and aloof, but also because she introduced
them to music and poetry, cultivated their sense of word and tone,
and stimulated in them a sensitivity toward the lyrical and the
romantic. To Thomas, for instance, Julia Mann seemed to be a
"distinctly Romanic" personality: sensuous, artistic, literary, and
gifted with what Goethe called "the delight in story-telling" (*Lust zu
fabulieren*).[34] Heinrich confirmed this impression, and emphasized
especially the importance of her Brazilian personality and artistic
disposition which, as a child, seemed to him strange and extraordinary.
To Heinrich, Julia Mann—who had come from over the sea, from
dark and obscure origins—personified everything *künstlerisch*, non-
Lübeckian, enchanting, and mysterious.[35]

Thus, both Heinrich and Thomas Mann perceived the parents as
not only different but as representatives of opposing world-views: one
bürgerlich, the other artistic; one punctual and exact, the other
sensitive and musical; one ethical and duty-bound, the other emotional and spiritual. Of these two styles, the father's naturally seemed
less inviting, while the mother's was far more attractive and the one
which, it appears, the sons tended to imitate. Heinrich, in particular,
assimilated the artistic-literary mode of life which she personified. In
fact, in Freudian terms it could be argued that he internalized the
mother as a primary ego ideal. This concept refers to the set of self-
definitions and introjected cultural values which are integrated into a
child's personality at the deepest level. The primary ego ideal unavoidably affects, sometimes decisively, the nature of a child's earliest
commitments and aspirations. If it happens to be the mother who

provides the substance of this ideal, then a child will tend to incorporate her *imago* and emulate what she, not the father, represents. As two recent writers have summarized it: "The way in which ego and primary ego ideal are structured will determine the way in which an individual will use personal energy for social ends. The goals that one strives for, the ends that one aspires to, are defined as the result of primary identifications . . . [Thus, because of] a sense that is acquired initially from objects cathected at the primary level . . . [a] child will act unconsciously in the direction of fulfilling certain commitments consistent with the demands of the primary object."[36]

The point to be made here is that Julia Mann supplied the content and general structure of her sons' ideals. As the dominant figure in their early lives, she not only helped shape their artistic orientation, but she encouraged them to believe that there was something mysterious and special about writing (perhaps even that imaginative expression was a higher and more worthwhile calling than the business life). Emotionally as well as financially she did everything she could to support her children's literary interests; in Heinrich's case, she eventually went so far as to pay the entire publication costs of his first book.[37] Had the father been the object of identification, Heinrich and Thomas Mann might have been drawn to mercantile rather then literary careers. But as it happened the mother was the pivotal influence, and to the extent that she represented the way of the *artiste* and outsider, she became the major source of creative inspiration to her sons. In short, Julia Mann provided a third option between an obsolete *bürgerlich* world on the one hand, and a newly emerging, but vulgar, bourgeois world on the other. As they reacted against the father and his values, Heinrich and Thomas simultaneously embraced the mother and her values, thereby moving towards literary expression as a mode of relating to the world.[38]

Heinrich Mann and His Generation

No single factor mentioned above (family, class, social structure), nor all of them together, *caused* Heinrich Mann to become a writer. At most, they set the conditions which made it possible or even likely that he would orient himself toward a writing career. This is not the same as saying that his career was determined by his circumstances. His family situation, on the first level, did no more than provide a certain milieu favorable to the choice of literature as a way of life. But the decision to actually take up this option rested exclusively with Heinrich Mann. He had the freedom to affirm or reject the artistic tendencies he found inherent in his family setting, and as it turned out he affirmed them. This put him squarely on the path toward a creative career as an author. Why he chose this form of artistic expression and not another cannot be definitively answered since an attempt to do so would take one to an ontic level of the personality which cannot be explored *post mortem*.

It is important to note, however, that although Mann's development was unique it was by no means atypical. The specific details of his turn toward literature are singular and distinctive, but the general configurations of his evolution reflect a pattern that was not at all uncommon. As has been touched on above and will be seen later, a number of writers in Mann's generation shared roughly the same background, and were drawn to writing for the same kinds of reasons. In fact, it seems permissible to talk about a literary type which began to surface in Germany in the 1890s, just at the time Mann began self-consciously referring to himself as an "author." The pattern shared by the majority of writers who belonged to this type was roughly the following: most were descended from *bürgerlich* origins and hence found themselves caught in the general "crisis" of their class; moreover, each rejected a business career for essentially the same reason as Mann; and lastly, each found someone in his personal life who, by embodying the artistic ideal, served as a model for a literary vocation. For all of these reasons, writing became a way out of a bad situation. Not only was reality conceptualized as problematic in nearly the same terms by each of these individuals, but the solutions arrived at were virtually identical. As the example of Mann makes clear, the goal was to be an aesthete, a *Wortkünstler,* a connoisseur of art and literature. In nearly every case, writing was viewed as a medium through which one entered an alternate reality far removed from the banality of everyday existence.

More will be said about this "type" in succeeding chapters. In the meantime, it is enlightening to look at Mann's first attempts at literary expression in terms of how they contributed to his later writing style, and what they reveal about the way in which he viewed himself in relation to society.

Footnotes
Chapter 1

1. See Heinrich Mann, "Kurze Selbstbiographie," March 27, 1947 (manuscript in Schiller-Nationalmuseum, Marbach-am-Neckar).

2. Heinrich Mann, cited in Klaus Schröter, *Heinrich Mann* (Hamburg, 1967), p. 33.

3. Sigmund Freud, "The Poet and Day Dreaming," *On Creativity and the Unconscious,* ed. Benjamin Nelson (New York, 1958), pp. 44–54.

4. Otto Rank, *Art and Artists,* trans. Charles Francis Atkinson (New York, 1968), p.78.

5. On the necessity for both social and psychological analysis see Theodor W. Adorno, "Zum Verhältnis von Soziologie und Psychologie," in *Sociologica: Aufsätze für Max Horkheimer: Frankfurter Beiträge zur Soziologie* (Frankfurt, 1955), pp. 11–45. The best example of social psychology as applied to a writer is Jean-Paul Sartre's, *L'idiot de la famille; Gustave Flaubert de 1821–1857,* 3 vols. (Paris, 1971–1973).

6. The phrase is Hegel's. See G. W. F. Hegel, *Philosophy of Right,* trans. T. M. Knox (London, 1952), p. 110, italics added.

7. Erich Fromm, "Über Methode und Aufgabe einer analytischen Sozialpsychologie," *Zeitschrift für Sozialforschung* (1932), I:35, Fromm's italics.

8. On this, see René König, *Materialien zur Soziologie der Familie* (Bern, 1946).

9. There is an entirely different psychology which goes with being born into a family in which the father, for example, has already achieved literary fame. Though a child with ambitions to write might have more opportunities for development (the culture of the home, literary connections, etc.), it may actually be much harder psychologically to overcome the father and achieve an identity of one's own. The psychology of Thomas Mann's son Klaus, for instance, was altogether different and more complex than that of either Heinrich or Thomas, who did not have to compete with a successful literary father. This may have had something to do with Klaus's suicide in 1949.

10. See Thomas Mann, "Ansprache in Lübeck," *Autobiographisches,* ed. Erika Mann (Oldenburg, 1968), p. 287.

11. See his letter to Heinrich, May 26, 1890, in *Heinrich Mann 1871–1950: Werk und Leben in Dokumenten und Bildern,* ed. Sigrid Anger (Berlin, 1971), p. 44.

12. Heinrich Mann, *Ein Zeitalter wird besichtigt* (Stockholm, 1945), p. 234.

13. See Thomas Johann Mann's letter of May 26, 1890, and his references to Heinrich in his last testament, October 13, 1891, in *Heinrich Mann 1871–1950: Werk und Leben,* pp. 44, 50.

14. These qualities are the ones generally found in an urban middle class up until the beginning of the twentieth century. One can already find traces of these in the Hanseatic cities of the Middle Ages, and in the Italian city-states of the early fourteenth century. See Max Hoffmann, *Geschichte der freien und hansestadt Lübeck* (Lübeck, 1889); and Hans Baron, *The Crisis of the Early Italian Renaissance,* 2 vols. (Princeton, 1955).

15. Some of the most unwholesome characters in Mann's novels were those who, though born into the *Bürgertum,* later shunned it and tried to "move up" (e.g., Diederich Hessling in *Der Untertan*). These people lost their moorings, became twisted, cruel, grotesque. The very fact that they left, or wanted to leave, their class already indicated that they were bad seeds.

16. Heinrich Mann, "Das Kind," *Novellen* (Hamburg, 1963), p. 453. The Mann estate at the time of the father's death (1891) amounted to 30,000 marks, a large sum but by no means a fortune.

17. See Werner Sombart, *Der Bourgeois: zur Geistesgeschichte des modernen Wirtschaftsmenschen* (Munich and Leipzig, 1923), pp. 194–243.

18. This point is discussed in detail in Theodore Hamerow, *The Social Foundations of German Unification,* 2 vols. (Princeton, 1969–1972).

19. In general, see Heinrich Bechtel, *Wirtschaftsgeschichte Deutschlands,* 3 vols. (Munich, 1951–1956); Helmut Böhme, *Deutschlands Weg zur Grossmacht* (Cologne, 1966); Ivo Nikolai Lambi, *Free Trade and Protection in Germany, 1868–1879* (Wiesbaden, 1963); Friedrich Lütge, *Deutsche Sozial-und Wirtschafts-geschichte* (Berlin, 1966); Ludwig Pohle and Max Muss, *Das deutsche Wirtschafts-leben seit Beginn des neunzehnten Jahrhunderts* (Leipzig and Berlin, 1930); Percy Schramm, *Hamburg, Deutschland und die Welt* (Munich, 1943); and Werner Sombart, *Die deutsche Volkswirtschaft in neunzehnten Jahrhundert* (Berlin, 1903). For Mann and the situation in Lübeck see Roman Karst, *Thomas Mann oder Der deutsche Zwiespalt* (Vienna, 1970), p. 19; Ferdinand Lion, *Thomas Mann in seiner Zeit* (Zurich, 1935), pp. 5–7; and Klaus Schröter, *Thomas Mann* (Hamburg, 1964), pp. 24–25.

20. Theodore Hamerow, *Social Foundations,* II: 82, 96.

21. Later in life Heinrich Mann remembered how, as a child, he had seen his father despondent over money losses while his mother tried to comfort him. "It was," he recalled, "my first impression of the change in fortune." (See his "Das Kind," *Novellen,* p. 454.)

22. Viktor Mann, *Wir waren fünf: Bildnis der Familie Mann* (Constance, 1949), p. 13.

23. Heinrich Mann, *Ein Zeitalter wird besichtigt,* p. 235.

24. Thomas Mann, "Hundert Jahre Reklam," *Schriften und Reden zur Literatur, Kunst und Philosophie* (Frankfurt, 1960), p. 334.

25. Thomas Mann, "Lebensabriss," *Autobiographisches,* p. 15. See also his "Lübeck als geistige Lebensform," *ibid.,* p. 81; and Erika Mann, *Das letze Jahr: Bericht über meinen Vater* (Oldenburg, 1968), p. 320.

26. Heinrich Mann, *Ein Zeitalter wird besichtigt,* pp. 234–35.

27. Thomas Mann, "Lübeck als geistige Lebensform," *Autobiographisches,* p. 81.

28. Talcott Parsons, cited in David Cooper, *Psychiatry and Anti-Psychiatry* (New York, 1971), p. 42. See also Talcott Parsons and Robert Bales, *Family, Socialization, and the Interaction Process* (New York, 1966); and R. D. Laing, *Politics of the Family and Other Essays* (New York, 1972).

29. The citations have been extracted from the following works: Erich Fromm, "Sozialpsychologischer Teil," *Studien über Autorität und Familie,* ed. Max Horkheimer (Paris, 1936), pp. 77–135; S. N. Eisenstadt, *From Generation to Generation* (Glencoe, 1956), p. 288; and Mihàly Vajda and Agnes Heller, "Family Structure," *Telos* (1971), VII:99–111. On the social function of the family in general see also: Wilhelm Reich, *The Mass Psychology of Fascism,* trans. Vincent Carfagno (New York, 1970); Max Horkheimer, *Kritische Theorie,* ed. Alfred Schmidt, 2 vols. (Frankfurt, 1968); Alice Solomon, ed., *Forschungen über Bestand und Erschütterung der Familie* (Berlin, 1930); and Ruth Anshen, ed., *The Family: Its Function and Destiny* (New York, 1955).

30. When, for example, both sons turned away from the firm, he nonetheless tried to guide each of them toward a "practical occupation" (*praktischer Beruf*) or at least give each a "practical education" (*praktische Erziehung*). See Ulrich Dietzel, ed., *Aus den Familienpapieren der Manns* (Berlin, 1965), p. 47.

31. See Thomas Johann Mann's letter to Heinrich, February 22, 1890, in *Heinrich Mann 1871–1950: Werk und Leben,* p. 43; and Heinrich Mann, *Ein Zeitalter wird besichtigt,* p. 235.

32. Heinrich Mann, in rejecting his father, also rejected the *bürgerlich* world his

father represented. Thomas Mann remained more ambivalent. He did not turn away from his father as sharply as did Heinrich, and hence he felt more keenly the struggle between the burgher and the artist (a theme which dominated his early work).

33. See Viktor Mann, *Wir waren fünf,* pp. 17–29; Thomas Mann, "Das Bild meiner Mutter," *Autobiographisches,* pp. 64–66; and "Lübeck als geistige Lebensform," *ibid.,* pp. 80–81.

34. Thomas Mann, "Lebensabriss," *ibid.,* p. 15; and Richard and Clara Winston, "Introduction," *Letters of Thomas Mann 1889–1955* (New York, 1971), p. xv.

35. See Heinrich Mann, "Lebenslauf," *Heinrich Mann 1871–1950: Werk and Leben,* pp. 493–94.

36. Fred Weinstein and Gerald Platt, *The Wish to be Free: Society, Psyche and Value Change* (Berkeley, 1969), pp. 183–84; also, pp. 145–52, 168–96. Weinstein and Platt discuss with great insight both the primary ego ideal and the general crisis of the family.

37. See Heinrich Mann's letter to Karl Lemke, January 29, 1947, in *Briefe an Karl Lemke, 1917–1949* (Berlin, 1963), p. 71.

38. There is a great deal of recent psychological literature which tends to support the conclusions arrived at here about the Mann household (particularly about the boys' identification with their mother). It is too extensive to mention in detail, but a few of the more important works should be cited since they provided helpful theoretical guidelines for this chapter.

On the problem of "identification" see Roy Shafer, *Aspects of Internalization* (New York, 1968); Robert Winch, *Identification and Its Familial Determinants* (Indianapolis, 1962); and Heinz Hartmann and Rudolph Löwenstein, "Notes on the Super-ego." *The Psychoanalytic Study of the Child* (New York, 1962), XVII:42–81.

On mother-son relationships see Henry Guntrip. *Personality Structure and Human Interaction* (London, 1961); Helen Faigin Antonovsky, "A Contribution to Research in the Area of the Mother-Child Relationship," *Child Development* (1959), XXX:37–51; Walter Emmerich, "Parental Identification in Young Children," *Genetic Psychological Monographs,* (1959), LX:32–51; and Joseph Sandler and Bernard Rosenblatt, "The Concept of the Representational World," *The Psychoanalytic Study of the Child* (New York, 1962), XVII: 128–45.

On inadequate father-son relationships see Alexander Mitscherlich, *Society Without the Father,* trans. Eric Mosbacher (New York, 1969), pp. 137–64, 268–304; Urie Bronfenbrenner, "The Study of Identification through Interpersonal Perception," *Person Perception and Interpersonal Behavior,* ed. Renato Tagiuri and Luigi Petrullo (Palo Alto, 1958), pp. 110–30; Walter Emmerich, "Young Children's Discrimination of Parent and Child Roles," *Child Development* (1959), XXX:402–19; Paul Mussen and Louis Distler, "Masculinity, Identification, and Father–Son Relationships," *Journal of Abnormal and Social Psychology* (1959), LIX: 350–56; and Tess Forrest, "Paternal Roots of Male Character Development," *The Psychoanalytic Review* (1967), LIV: 51–68.

Chapter 2

Fin-de-Siècle

The aesthete . . . is one of the last forms of expression of the middle class.

Gustave Flaubert

Early Work

Mann's decision to become a writer was inseparably related to the kind of writer he became. In the early 1890s, at the start of his literary career, Mann held certain clear-cut notions as to what authorship meant. For one thing, it meant being aloof and above the tumult of ordinary existence. As Mann viewed it, the professional writer was, by virtue of his higher calling, both more refined and more "inward" than others. For this reason, he was seen as deserving a special status which would place him far above the demands of everyday life. Of course, it followed that the writer would necessarily be more alone than the rest of mankind since his unique nature would prevent him from fitting into the work-a-day world around him. But to the young Heinrich Mann this was not considered a serious problem, at least not at first. On the contrary, he affirmed the alienation of the man-of-letters as a mark of distinction: a sign that one was different from, and somehow superior to, others.

In a similar vein, Mann believed that writing carried with it the task of portraying middle-class existence as sordid and contemptible. This stance implied an initial rejection of the *Bürgertum* as well as of the bourgeoisie since both were viewed as "unaesthetic." (Later Mann would reverse this position and draw sharp distinctions between the two, making the bourgeoisie his special adversary.) What he seemed to do at the beginning was to assume that creative expression and the appreciation of beauty were the highest goals in life. From this premise he concluded that whatever hindered these ends had to be shunned. But the whole of conventional society in the

21

1880s and 1890s hindered these ends, so middle-class life itself had to be repudiated. Escape from the quotidian and non-involvement with the world as given were objectives Mann considered integral to the choice of being a writer.

These conceptions of what a writer is and what he does are implicit in several of Mann's earliest pieces, especially those written in late adolescence and not intended for publication.[1] In the short story "Apart" (1885), for example, the world is described through the hero's eyes as "insipid and loathsome." Still, it is inferred, one can maintain a measure of integrity by holding aloof and standing apart, even if this attitude leads in the end to "a very lonely death."[2] In other novellas such as "Haltlos" ("Rootless," 1889), "Mondschein-phantasien" ("Moonlight Phantasies," 1889), or "Tilli" (1891), Mann gave the impression that artistic individuals are by nature delicate, ethereal, and uncontaminated by the everyday world. Clear lines are drawn between art and ideals, on the one hand, and a commonplace reality on the other, with little doubt left in the reader's mind as to which side Mann was on.

Perhaps the most interesting of these early documents is a fragment from the year 1889 entitled "Fantasien über meine Vaterstadt L." ("Fantasies on my Hometown L.").[3] It bears looking into for what it reveals both about Mann's view of the middle class, and his notion that artists are exceptional individuals who have no place in German society.

The "Fantasien" takes the form of a letter addressed to a young lady, whom the author warns not to come to "L." (Lübeck) because it "smells miserable." Why does it smell, he asks rhetorically; because that is a sign of progress. In the modern world the town that is filled with the most pungent odors of leather and petroleum is obviously the most successful. And Lübeck is proud of its stink since this indicates that it is high on the list of important cities. There are, however, a few streets which do not reek, and one of these is the street where the opera house is located. But no one appreciates the opera. It is simply a memorial to Lübeck's putative greatness—a kind of victory monument which the middle class has erected to itself. Likewise, there are five large churches in Lübeck, which everyone takes as a sign of the city's religiosity. But to draw such an inference would be misleading, for the churches are filled only with the "Sunday public" which never includes the rich and prosperous, but only their "poor relatives," who must pray for the wealth they were not fortunate enough to obtain by other means.

The town of Lübeck, Mann continues, is also graced with a cultural elite which is active in its support of the arts. And yet it would be a mistake to conclude from this fact that such people are actually cultured. The financial support they provide is the result of political considerations, since the arts give an aura of refinement and security to the town which, then, becomes an insurance against revolution. Mann suggests that the support of culture and the defense of the status quo are one and the same thing; what takes place under the guise of cultural beneficence is in effect another means of political control.[4] But here Mann pushes his point still further. In a satirical way he hints that the locus of power lies in neither the cultural nor the political spheres, but in an institution that stands behind both: the stock exchange. Symbolically, the stock exchange represents the spirit of enterprise itself, the very motive force of middle-class life. In this context, Mann infers that the freer the market is to define existence in economic terms, and hence to relegate other matters to secondary importance, the more it becomes the major cause of the unaesthetic atmosphere of Lübeck. The conclusion is extreme but unavoidable: whenever business interests prevail, an impoverished cultural life invariably follows, since money-making and genuine culture are hostile to one another. Even when Lübeck appears to be making an honest cultural gesture (like dedicating a statue to the poet Geibel), it does so either for political reasons, or to avoid being out-classed by other cities which honor their men-of-letters.

How does the "poetic" individual fare in the midst of all this? The answer, Mann believed, is very badly. Because poetic natures deal only with "unpractical things" there is no place for them in Lübeck, or perhaps in the modern world in general. The truly creative individual does not belong, does not "fit in"; instead, he is left to puzzle out a role for himself in a society whose very ethos militates against the creative impulse. Toward the end of the "Fantasien" Mann posed this question: "How can there be, in our thoroughly practical age, any people who occupy themselves with unpractical things? Who today still believes in the world of fables about which the 'poet' makes such a fuss? The other fairy tales, namely those of religion, have long ago been done away with, and no reasonable person considers them true anymore—not even the 'poor relatives' who fill the churches of L. Who, then, is left to get enthusiastic about 'poetic' nonsense?"[5]

In the "Fantasien" Mann offered no clear answer to this question, nor did he suggest that there would be a solution in the future. The fragment ends on a weak and indecisive note, leaving the reader only with the inference that art and middle-class life are unbridgeable opposites. Mann seemed to imply that by choosing to pursue art, he had cut himself off from the ordinary, everyday world. But this theme remained muted and undeveloped, since he did not go on to discuss what the artist's role would then be in or against society.

Three Modes of Writing

By 1891, the year of his father's death, Mann had decisively committed himself to a literary career. Two years earlier he had left Lübeck to work first in Dresden (as a bookdealer's assistant) and later in Berlin (for the newly-founded S. Fischer Verlag). In the meantime, he continued to improve his style and literary method by writing several short stories and then discarding or re-working them. At this point, the act of writing was still for the most part a private affair.[6] However, at the moment when he felt ready to present himself to the public (that is, to write in order to be read) he had to take into account a number of things which had not seemed important before.

The transition from writing as personal therapy to writing *for others* is always difficult because the latter involves so much more than self-expression. In order to be published a young writer cannot simply say what he feels; he must express himself within the framework of an acceptable genre, and according to at least basic agreed-upon rules of syntax and style. The very language he is forced to use confines him to certain restricted forms and contents, especially if the literary market is controlled by people who know exactly what they want to read and are able to set the standards of taste accordingly.

So far, Mann has been viewed from the inside, i.e., from the perspective of his need to write. Now it is important to see him in the reverse, from the point of view of the German literary world of the 1890s. Once he had decided to become an author he had to choose what sort of socially-acceptable mode of writing he would commit himself to.

In making this decision Mann was forced to come to terms with the cultural world in which he found himself. Every author, whether he likes it or not, is situated in a certain milieu and surrounded by a definite climate of opinion. Unless he is extraordinarily original, he tends to accept the boundaries of his *Ideenwelt* and identify with one tendency against others; he begins to take sides, choose models, and enter the literary battles raging at the time. Thus, the type of writing Mann was attracted to, and eventually appropriated as his own, was predictably the kind for which his background had prepared him all along. It may already be obvious from what has been said that Mann would be interested in an aesthetic, refined, and cultivated sort of literature, one which viewed itself as spiritually elevated above the everyday. In *fin-de-siècle* Germany, only Impressionism could have satisfied Mann on these points, and hence it was towards this movement that he naturally gravitated in the early 1890s.[7]

Impressionism was one of three literary camps prevalent in Germany during the last decade of the nineteenth century; the other two were Naturalism and *Heimatkunst*.

Naturalism was the first and most aggressive of these movements.[8] Its origins can be traced partly to the cultural influences from France and Scandinavia, and partly to an indigenous literary reaction against the obscurantism of *Gründerzeit* literature and the social injustices of the new industrial order. Essentially, Naturalism stood for objectivism and "consistent realism." Its credo revolved around the dictum that art had to strive for absolute trueness to reality; good art was that which represented nature exactly, while bad art was that which was furthest removed from reality. The task of literature, as the Naturalists conceived of it, was to replace the false charm and finished grace of a writer like Paul Heyse with down-to-earth realism. What they termed "proletarian art" and "urban art" were therefore intended as counterpoises to the alleged prudishness, dilettantism, and pseudo-eloquence of German literature in the 1870s and 1880s. *Wirklichkeit ist Wahrheit* (reality is truth), they insisted; consequently, their mission was to submerge themselves completely in what one Naturalist writer called "the joys and miseries of the surrounding world."[9] In substance this meant resurrecting the "fourth estate," including the criminal, the prostitute, the bohemian, the outcast, the proletarian and all the dispossessed of society, because these uprooted people embodied the actual conditions and quintessential truth of contemporary Germany. Previously, they argued, acceptable literature focused on only middle-class figures (the doctor, the merchant, the officer), but for the Naturalists this focus was no longer tenable because it did

not mirror the misery and despair of real life. For them, literature
in the modern era would have to be as tough and brutal as the
industrial age which it was called upon to reflect.

The second movement, *Heimatkunst* (Homeland Art), stood in many
ways at the opposite pole from Naturalism.[10] It emerged in the 1890s,
when the ideas of Romanticism and the peasant novel were fused
with certain aspects of late nineteenth-century reactionary thought.
The fundamentals of its program revolved around the concern for a
new "Germanic" form of literature dedicated to peasant, or at least
rural, themes. In order for art to be creative, argued the *Heimat-
künstler*, it had to become self-consciously *deutschnational.* This meant
that a German style based on racial and cultural uniqueness had to
be developed. And since the essence of the *Volk* lay with those
closest to the soil, it was necessary for literature to return to the land
and extoll the values of the simple life rooted to the earth. Here the
idea of the "landscape" became important. It was felt that a symbiotic relationship existed between the German landscape and the
Germanic soul, but that this was being eroded in the metropolis,
where men were separated from their surroundings and deprived of
their souls. As a response, the cry "Away from Berlin!" was sounded,
meaning away from industrialism and materialism and back to
nature, simplicity, and community. Given this ideological framework,
the *Heimatkunst* view of literature was quite different from that of
Naturalism. A good literary work was not one which exposed working-
class conditions, but one which expressed reverence for the German
family, praised the virtues of rootedness, lauded the qualities of the
German *Volksgeist,* and advocated closeness to nature and a new
feeling for the peasant.[11] Thus, *Heimatkunst* was essentially rural
and romantic, while Naturalism was urban and realistic.

The third movement of the *fin-de-siècle*—the one which Mann most
readily identified with—was Impressionism. Its origins in Germany
dated back to at least the 1880s, though it did not reach full bloom
until around 1900. Like Naturalism, Impressionism received much of
its thematic and stylistic inspiration from a European-wide group of
authors who formed the avant-garde of the movement. These included, among others, Oscar Wilde, Walter Pater, August Strindberg,
Maurice Maeterlinck, Gabriele D'Annunzio, J. K. Huysmans, and
Paul Bourget. But if its inspiration was European in scope, its
impetus was closely bound up with the turn-of-the-century mood in
Germany. Like the adherents of the other two movements, the Im-

pressionists began with a psychological revulsion against all the vulgar and dehumanizing features of the German Empire. Again like the others, they were upset by the commercialism and cultural philistinism which seemed to be gaining ground everywhere. But rather than immerse themselves in the foulest aspects of modernity or flee to the countryside, they chose the stance of aesthetic withdrawal. Thus, each of the three movements started with an abhorrence of the quotidian and went on to criticize the brutalizing features of modern industrial society, but after this their ways diverged sharply. A comparison between the two most important literary movements, Naturalism and Impressionism, may help to clarify this point.

The Naturalists chose to criticize society by showing what it was, the Impressionists by showing what it had failed to become. Both alternatives were based on valid conceptions, but where the one attempted to reveal the ugliness of daily life, the other tried to negate it with aesthetics and point the way toward personal modes of escape. In some cases, Impressionism led to a denial that the existing world was in any sense real. Nietzsche, an unwitting precursor of Impressionism, sounded almost Hegelian when he asserted that the real was the apparent, and the apparent the real: "things, matter, bodies," he wrote, "are mere phantasmagoria."[12] Hermann Bahr followed in the same vein by declaring that "the rule of mere factuality is over"; what existed was only what "seemed" to exist, only sensations, impressions, nerve reactions. Likewise, the poet Alfred Mombert denied the coarse reality of urban life by affirming that only the transcendental, the symbolic, and the cosmic were real. The conditions of actual existence were deemed interesting only to the extent that they could be transformed by the mind and the imagination. This response to German society was quite different from that of Naturalism, but it was nonetheless a reaction to the same things. Thus, what distinguished these two movements was not their attitude toward society, but the way they reacted to its problems and the different prescriptions they offered to cure the ailments of the modern age.

For Impressionism, the most salutary remedy was art, but art defined as fabrication rather than representation. "The truth of nature must be obscured," wrote Oskar Bie in his *Ästhetik der Lüge*, "so that the lies of art can shine forth. . . . Naturalism is base because it is too much concerned with [representing] nature. The further art is removed from reality—that is, the more unreal, centaur-like, exotic, and musical it becomes—the higher it stands."[13] Here, in the world of phantasy and imagination, lay the freedom to break through the dark realm of necessity; here, beauty was possible as an antidote to the crassness of contemporary life.

Again in contrast to Naturalism, the Impressionists rejected the notion that man was the product of his environment. Instead, they asserted that man shapes his destiny by grasping his innermost being and fashioning it according to his desires. The hero of an impressionist piece was generally self-determining (and also wealthy and free enough to have the luxury of self-determination). If he suffered character defects it was because of flaws in his own ego, not because of the milieu. For this reason, entire plays and novels were given over to the analysis of *Seelenzustände* rather than to social criticism or the minute description of the environment, as in the works of Naturalism.

By withdrawing into the labyrinth of the self, the Impressionists tended to lose touch with the reality of the external world. Since they were not convinced that what merely existed was for that reason real, they came to think of the world simply as a mode of fiction. To the most conscientious it became increasingly difficult to determine whether there was any truth behind the fiction or any substance behind the whirl of sensations. "Try as we may," wrote Oscar Wilde, summarizing the Impressionist's dilemma, "we cannot get behind the appearance of things to reality. And the terrible reality may be, that there is no reality in things apart from their experiences."[14] And yet, the more the world eluded their grasp, the more they emphasized a "quickened, multiplied consciousness" in order to gain a sense of the real, the living, the palpable. This led them even further into a kind of solipsistic self-scrutiny which virtually made a cult of private experience. Here again, Impressionism stood poles apart from Naturalism.

Other differences also existed. For objectivity, the Impressionists substituted subjectivity. Instead of the emphasis on the typical, they stressed the unique. In the place of a hard-hitting crudeness of language and expression, they reintroduced an exquisite and precious manner of writing. And finally, rather than "equality" as a watchword, they substituted its opposite: *Vornehmheit*, or aristocratic individualism. It was clear to most commentators of the period that the two movements stood diametrically opposed to one another in almost every way.

Although the characteristics of Impressionism can be defined, it is still difficult to trace its advance in Germany. The movement was too diffuse and its origins too diverse to stimulate within its ranks any firm sense of unity. What is more, there were no stirring manifestos to lay out directions for the future or to rally poets and writers to a common cause. Nonetheless, this new artistic trend steadily gained ground so that by the turn of the century several of the most important works of Impressionism had already been published and were well-received by the German *Bildungspublikum*.

Heinrich Mann and Impressionism

When Mann set out to pursue his career in the nineties, it seemed natural for him to gravitate toward Impressionism. Of the three predominant trends of the period, only Impressionism was compatible with the style he had developed in his youth, because it alone agreed with his temperament and aesthetic disposition. In a notebook entry entitled "My Plan" and dated November 11, 1893, Mann expressed himself in a very revealing way:

> If I am generally drawn to analysis, I believe it is only that of the *haute vie* or rather the elegant life which has been appointed as my subject matter. The moral disposition that I wish to address myself to one finds only there. A cosmopolitan, cultured and ceremonious existence (which is the last cultural legacy of the old world) I must at all events acquire so that I can have the occasion and the space to express the form and utterances of that which I now 'feel' more than I 'know'. . . . At present I lead the cosmopolitan life as well as I can within my limited means. I cultivate the various manners of speech, live the lives of different peoples, and generally take pleasure in unusual [*eigentümlich*] art.[15]

These were the sentiments of one who shared the impressionist view of the world. Indeed, the passage could have been written by the character Des Esseintes in Huysmans' novel *À Rebours*, who was looked upon as the prototype of the *Empfindungsdilettant*. Like Des Esseintes, Mann was not interested in extolling the proletariat or the German *Volk*. At this point, he was solely interested in cultivating his art and in perfecting his subjective, psychological, and highly nuanced mode of writing. Hence, in his first literary efforts, Mann tended to associate himself with the movement of Impressionism, and to write about the world from an impressionist perspective. One need only look at his early work to verify this. Nearly everything he wrote between 1892 and 1896 (the period of his initial entry into the literary world) is in accordance with the style, form, and psychological emphasis of German Impressionism.[16]

In style, Mann painted his words carefully. His mode of expression was excessively refined, and thus his prose often gives the appearance of being mannered and overworked.[17] In some of his early novellas, Mann seemed to strive for a kind of musical effect through language, as though the sonority of words or word-combinations were the chief purpose in writing. In other novellas, he used a style designed to mystify his readers or induce in them a longing for the infinite. This, too, was typical of Impressionism. The evocation of mood—frequently one of melancholy, world-weariness, or the yearning for the inexpressible—was often the primary objective of a work. In contrast, the story itself became simply a medium through which the mood was expressed. Furthermore, Mann's portrayal of atmosphere was precisely the opposite of the exactness of detail which characterized the naturalist writers. What interested him was tone-coloring, the play of illusion, and even the "truth" of hallucinations. Hence the focus of his art was not everyday existence, but that mysterious realm between dream and reality which could only be captured by a subtle, evocative style.

Also typically impressionist was the form of Mann's early pieces.[18] Nearly all of them were written in the first person in order to maximize the subjectivism of the work. The narrator of the story rarely related events as they actually happened, but only as he perceived them in his imagination. It is not surprising, then, that novellas like "Ist sie's?" ("Is it she?," 1894) or "Ein Verbrechen" ("A Crime," 1897) take place entirely within the story-teller's memory, so that the reader is unable to distinguish what is true from what is merely imagined. Others, like "Contessina" (1894), deal with the world of dreams; one cannot tell the difference between real life and phantasy since the borderline between the two is hazy and undefined. Still others are set in far-away places, or in the chiaroscuro atmosphere of twilight, to heighten the sense of mystery and anticipation. Often, even the action of a novella is foreshortened so that the story rushes quickly to an unexpected conclusion, from which one realizes that nothing is as it appears.

The impressionist emphasis on the psychological was likewise a feature of Mann's early efforts. Consequently, there is a noticeable lack of action in all of his novellas dating from this period; none of his figures set out on heroic adventures, and there are no epic-dramatic scenes of the kind found in the works of contemporary writers like Tolstoy or Spielhagen. On the contrary, everything takes place within a confined space, such as the upper middle-class setting of *In einer Familie* (*In a Family*, 1894), and the actions of individuals are limited to their strained and problematic relations with one another. Mann chose to let his stories unfold almost exclusively on a psychological level. Very seldom did he attempt to deal with more than two or three figures at a time, but around these few he constructed a miniature *roman de caractère* which penetrated deeply into mental processes and emotional states. In all of this, Mann betrayed his debt to the French novelist Paul Bourget. Bourget's theory of literature made a great impact on him, and he self-consciously adopted not only Bourget's style and literary technique, but also some of his reactionary political and social views.[19]

What put Mann clearly in the impressionist camp, however, was not only his style, form, and psychological emphasis, but also the thematic content of his work. If it is true, as historians of German Impressionism have maintained, that the impressionist movement was dominated by certain recognizable motifs (among them, the split between art and life, decadence, dilettantism, the difference between appearance and reality, eroticism, the daemonic woman, the bourgeois citizen versus the *Lebenskünstler,* Nietzscheanism and Renaissancism), then it can be said that Mann's early prose sketches were unmistakably impressionist in orientation.[20] In "Contessina," for instance, Mann depicted the cleavage between art and life. A young girl, who lives alone with her mother, longs for fulfillment. An artist from Florence (symbolic of the rejuvenating power of art) visits their estate and offers hope of this fulfillment. The girl discovers that the way to inner satisfaction is through art, but the Florentine leaves for good and she drowns herself, convinced that life would be meaningless without him.[21] Another novella, "Eine Erinnerung" ("A Memory," 1894), accentuates the conflict between bourgeois duty and artistic ideals.[22] The protagonist, von Dillstedt, is torn between his sense of responsibility and his urge to give himself up to life. This conflict between a practical *Bürgerlichkeit* on the one hand, and an impractical longing to experience everything on the other, was a common subject for the impressionist writer. Still other novellas are concerned with disillusionment and isolation, the strong woman, and even such exotic phenomena as the transmigration of souls and autosuggestion. The best story Mann wrote during this period, "Das Wunderbare" ("The Marvellous," 1894), is also typically impressionist, bringing together a number of the themes mentioned above. It is also significant in that it expresses the same attitudes found in his earlier "Fantasien," only with a great deal more subtlety and sophistication. These attitudes indicate a pronounced anti-bourgeois bias, a fascination with aestheticism, and a concern with the artist's need to separate himself from the banality of ordinary existence. It is no coincidence that these themes were some of the most overworked in the Impressionist's repertoire. Mann had no trouble at all in adapting his personal world-view to that of Impressionism.

In summary, when Mann reached literary maturity in the early 1890s he found that his personal disposition, artistic taste, and socially-acquired attitudes all inclined him towards Impressionism.[23] Of the other two movements he had mixed opinions. Generally, he was hostile to Naturalism because it seemed to delight in presenting social facts which were, as he said in his notebook, *"foncièrement antipathique à mon goût."*[24] He was somewhat more favorably impressed with *Heimatkunst*, though chiefly for the value it placed on feeling, not for its right-wing ideology. But it was only with Impressionism that Mann felt completely at home. Throughout the 1890s he remained closely bound up with its spirit and atmosphere. And even after he moved outside its commanding influence, he was still mistakenly regarded by many as an impressionist author.

Footnotes

Chapter 2

1. The Heinrich-Mann-Archiv in East Berlin (a branch of the Deutsche Akademie der Künste) contains a large number of poems and nearly a dozen short stories dating from the late 1880s and early 1890s. All are hand-written, and many exist without date or place. A few of these pieces, including some of the poems, have been collected in the (already cited) 100th anniversary edition of Mann documents: *Heinrich Mann 1871–1950: Werk und Leben in Dokumenten und Bildern,* ed. Sigrid Anger (Berlin, 1971).

2. Heinrich Mann, "Apart," Heinrich-Mann-Archiv, no. 433; also in *Heinrich Mann 1871–1950: Werk und Leben,* pp. 27–32.

3. In *Heinrich Mann 1871–1950: Werk und Leben,* pp. 12–17.

4. Heinrich Mann, "Fantasien über meine Vaterstadt L.," *ibid.,* pp. 15–16.

5. *Ibid.,* p. 16.

6. With the exception of four poems and four newspaper pieces, Mann did not publish anything before 1892. For a sample of his very earliest work, see the poem "Geh schlafen," in *Die Gesellschaft* (1890), VI:1663, and the short stories "Beppo als Trauzeuge" and "Der Geburtstag der Frau Baronin" in *Lübecker Zeitung,* May 23, 1889, and July 14, 1889, respectively.

7. The term "Impressionism" is used here instead of "Neo-Romanticism" since the latter term is too imprecise and misleading if thought of as merely derivative of the early romantic movement. Admittedly, the word "Impressionism" also has its problems. When used with reference to Germany in the 1890s, it must be distinguished from the artistic movement of French Impressionism, even though the aesthetic tastes of both were sometimes quite close. See the excellent discussion of German Impressionism in Richard Hamann and Jost Hermand, *Impressionismus* (Berlin, 1966).

8. For a more comprehensive treatment of Naturalism than can be given here see Erich Ruprecht, ed., *Literarische Manifeste des Naturalismus 1880–1892* (Stuttgart, 1962); and Richard Hamann and Jost Hermand, *Naturalismus* (Berlin, 1959).

9. Karl Bleibtreu, *Revolution der Literatur* (Leipzig, 1886), p. 13; see also Konrad Alberti, "Die Bourgeoisie und die Kunst," *Die Gesellschaft* (1888), IV:841.

10. See Jethro Bithell, *Modern German Literature 1880–1938* (London, 1939),

p. 382. There has not been a great deal of work done on *Heimatkunst.* The most helpful sources on the movement are Richard Hamann and Jost Hermand, *Stilkunst um 1900* (Berlin, 1967), pp. 364–94; Albert Soergel, *Dichtung und Dichter der Zeit,* 1st ed. (Leipzig, 1911), pp. 737–70; and two uncritical but useful books by Adolf Bartels: *Die deutsche Dichtung der Gegenwart* (Leipzig, 1907), pp. 311–25, and his shorter *Heimatkunst* (Munich, 1904).

11. Fritz Lienhard, "Literaturjugend von heute: eine Fastenpredigt," *Neue Ideale* (Leipzig, 1901).

12. Friedrich Nietzsche, cited in Richard Hamann and Jost Hermand, *Gründerzeit* (Berlin, 1965), p. 136.

13. Oskar Bie, cited in Richard Hamann and Jost Hermand, *Impressionismus,* p. 149.

14. Oscar Wilde quoted in Thomas Mann, *Last Essays,* trans. Richard and Clara Winston (London, 1959), p. 157.

15. Heinrich Mann, "Mein Plan," November 11, 1893; in *Heinrich Mann 1871–1950; Werk und Leben,* p. 55.

16. Mann's earliest short stories—including "Das Wunderbare" (1894), "Der Hund" (1894), "Die Gemme" (1896), "Contessina" (1894), "Enttäuschung" (1896), and "Geschichten aus Rocca de'Fichi (1896)—were published in *Das Wunderbare* (Munich, 1897). Another volume, which included, among others, "Der Löwe" (1894), "Irrtum" (1894), and "Ist sie's?" (1894), appeared the following year under the title *Ein Verbrechen und andere Geschichten* (Leipzig, 1898).

17. Herbert Ihering, *Heinrich Mann* (Berlin, 1951), p. 43; and Ulrich Weisstein, *Heinrich Mann. Eine historisch-kritische Einführung in sein dichterisches Werk* (Tübingen, 1963), pp. 205–06.

18. The fact that most of his early works took the form of novellas or sketches rather than long-winded novels is in itself characteristic of Impressionism. The novel never became as important to the Impressionists as it did to the Naturalists.

19. The influence of Bourget is discussed most thoroughly in Klaus Schröter, *Anfänge Heinrich Manns. Zu den Grundlagen seines Gesamtwerks* (Stuttgart, 1965), pp. 18–42.

20. Richard Hamann and Jost Hermand, *Impressionismus, passim;* Walter Rehm, "Der Renaissancekult um 1900 und seine Überwindung," *Zeitschrift für deutsche Philologie* (1929), LIV:296–328.

21. Heinrich Mann, "Contessina," *Novellen* I, in *Ausgewählte Werke in Einzelausgaben,* 12 vols., ed. Alfred Kantorowicz (Berlin, 1951–1962), VIII:63–78.

22. Heinrich Mann, "Eine Erinnerung," hand-written manuscript in Heinrich-Mann-Archiv.

23. Mann's initial commitment to Impressionism is evident not only in his early novellas but in his literary criticism as well. See his "Neue Romantik," *Die Gegenwart* (1892), XLII:40–42; "Bourget als Kosmopolit," *Die Gegenwart* (1894), CLV:53–58; and "Barbey d'Aurevilly," *Die Gegenwart* (1895), XLVIII, no. 47–48: 325–28, 342–46.

24. Heinrich Mann in his hand-written *Tagebuch, 1892–1894,* Heinrich-Mann-Archiv, no. 466. Mann's attack on Naturalism is best represented in his essays in *Das Zwanzigste Jahrhundert,* most notably: "Moderne Literatur," (1895), V, Halbband 2, pp. 402–04; and "Niederlage des Naturalismus," (1896), VI, Halbband I, pp. 467–68.

Chapter 3

Literature and Politics

No one . . . can write without passionately taking sides (whatever the apparent detachment of his message) as to all that happens or does not happen in the world.

Roland Barthes

The Politics of Literary Expression

As has been shown, Mann's earliest proclivities were towards an impressionist mode of literature. To the extent that he conformed to this model, he tended to incorporate into his own literary work certain political and ideological assumptions which were woven into the fabric of the impressionist *Weltanschauung.* Here the political implications of Mann's writings need to be examined and understood in relationship to the political spectrum of the 1890s.

In *fin-de-siècle* Germany, the "politicization of everything" (which Thomas Mann later called the foremost characteristic of the twentieth century) had already become a reality. The distinction between social and political questions, even between literary and political ones, was blurred or no longer clearly perceived by either writers or readers.[1] The three movements mentioned in the last chapter were not exceptions to this rule. Each became associated with a political world-view which was consonant with its literary principles.

Naturalism, for example, tended to become tied up with the social and political outlook of socialism (if this word is understood in its broadest context, without connection to political parties). Both Naturalism and socialism opposed capitalist exploitation, existing social institutions and bourgeois moral hypocrisy, and both made use of a scientific methodology which defined the problems of industrial society in similar ways. Moreover, both adopted a revolutionary rhetoric, agitated for social justice, and demanded the alleviation of working-class misery. It was hardly accidental, then, that several leading Naturalists aligned themselves with socialist ideals and programs. The significant mutuality of interest between the two movements caused them to be identified with one another. In fact, in the popular press Naturalism was often referred to, rather simplistically, as the "artistic equivalent" of socialism.[2]

Heimatkunst was likewise alive with political connotations. At its core was the longing for a renewed relationship to the *Stamm,* the landscape, and the *Volk*—a longing which was easily translatable into political categories. Furthermore, the emphasis on heroic vitalism and rootedness, and on will and instinct, often merged with the slogans of the extreme Right and later of National Socialism. Even the language of *Heimatkunst* reflected a reactionary ethos that was part of the revolt against modernity. When the author Adolf Bartels wrote in 1904 that "The German *Volk* must have an art that strengthens and fertilizes the roots of its existence, an art which makes life rich, beautiful and great, and which exalts in its power of resistance and expansion," he was already expressing the same sentiments and imagery he would use when he later joined the Nazi movement.[3] This is not to say that there was a one-to-one relationship between *Heimatkunst* and National Socialism, since they did in fact differ on a number of points.[4] Nevertheless, it is hard to deny that *Heimatkunst* was, politically speaking, a literature of the far Right. As such, it stood at the opposite pole from Naturalism and therefore became the "aesthetic equivalent" of cultural and political reaction.

Impressionism, no less than the other two movements, was suffused with political implications. What these were, however, is more difficult to ascertain since many impressionist writers and poets claimed to be apolitical. Most of them certainly were (if "apolitical" is taken to mean a turning away from ordinary political issues), but in spite of this, tendencies existed within their work which easily lent themselves to political interpretation. Initially the Impressionists were interested almost exclusively in matters of beauty, form, and style. In time, however, they began to expand these categories and apply them to cultural and political life as well. Why, they asked, should not a culture have "style" just like a work of art? Why should not the state have "form"? Why could poetic values not be applied to contemporary life? These questions belonged more appropriately to the realm of aesthetics than politics, but they were politicized when it became clear that aesthetics could not be compartmentalized, since it too had a social aspect which compelled one to take a stand. This notion of "taking a stand" on cultural issues—and still more, of advocating solutions—necessitated a kind of political posture, even if it was not directly intended.[5] The Impressionists, then, became political almost against their will. Nevertheless, they made it known that theirs was not the usual practical politics, which they condemned as vulgar. Rather, it was *Kunstpolitik,* a term which evoked for them the notion of transforming life through art instead of through endless parliamentary resolutions.

In contrast to the reactionary nature of *Heimatkunst* and the social humanitarian overtones of Naturalism, the literature of Impressionism can most accurately be called "neo-conservative." Here this term must be understood quite apart from its ordinary political connotations. For the Impressionists, it was above all a cultural concept which meant resisting the tendencies of modernity, usually through the renewal of existing institutions. It would be inviting disaster, they thought, to believe that the "masses" could reinvigorate social life. This could never be accomplished by the vast majority but only by that small segment of the population which had already achieved moral or spiritual perfection. Thus the poet Hugo von Hofmannsthal talked about the "two or three thousand people" who could still save Europe from abasement, and Stefan George created his "community of monks" as a basis for transfiguring a decadent society. On the whole, the Impressionists were unashamedly elitist in that they believed decaying social forms could only be reawakened by the sensitive few who could impart the needed values to society. They despised industrialism, bourgeois philistinism, and the oppressiveness of urban life as much as did the other two literary movements, but they were convinced that salvation would come not through the *Volk* or the working class, but only through an intellectual and aesthetic aristocracy of superior individuals.

If they could have had their way, perhaps the Impressionists would have chosen to live entirely apart from what they considered to be a decadent society. But in the 1890s many came to see that the bifurcation between the private and public realm could no longer be maintained. There could be no pure aesthetics in an age dominated by the mass press, the standardization of taste, and the democratization of art. In order to defend the citadel of art against the onslaught of cultural levelling, several Impressionists felt compelled to offer alternatives to "massification." From their standpoint, the two best alternatives were either social rejuvenation based upon the leadership of a cultural elite, or transformation of oneself (and through oneself, all of society) by means of "love" or "art." Some, like Stefan George, emphasized the first, while others, like Mann, tended to put more stress on the second approach. In either case, the goal was to make social existence beautiful again.

This orientation led to the common conviction that life needed to become more spiritual. In a significant number of impressionist works, from Rainer Maria Rilke to Max Dauthendey, there was an effort to reinvest matter with spirit so that the world would once again be infused with meaning. Since things appeared to be falling apart, and every particle of life seemed to be floating without relation to any other, the impressionist writers attempted to remedy this by "evoking the whole" in the reader's consciousness and thereby ending the disjointedness of modern life. Impressionism opposed the forces of atomization and fragmentation in art as well as in social life, and stood against the reduction of everything to facts measurable in purely quantitative terms. It attempted to counter these tendencies by a renewed emphasis on the spiritual side of life.[6] In this respect, Impressionism was much closer to *Heimatkunst* than to Naturalism, but nonetheless, the two rightist movements were not comfortable bed-fellows by any means. There were, among the Impressionists, no overt traces of chauvinism or racial thought, and no wish to have their work identified as *deutschnational*. On the contrary, many specifically proclaimed themselves above national boundaries, "free from every bond of house and home" as Hofmannsthal put it.[7] Furthermore, they had no desire for a *Volksstaat* based upon mass participation, but generally preferred an "aesthetic state," i.e., a state as a "work of art" in the fashion of Jacob Burckhardt. On some points, the neo-conservatism of the Impressionists blended with a reactionary outlook and at times seemed almost indistinguishable from it. Nevertheless there were usually noticeable differences in tone and emphasis between the two. It goes without saying that none of the leading Impressionists had any sympathy for National Socialism, though many took a prominent part in the "Conservative Revolution" of the 1920s.[8]

On the whole, Impressionism was not so much reactionary as it was neo-conservative in character. What kept it from becoming representative of the radical Right was its suspicion of mass movements as well as its traditional elitism and emphasis on inner renewal over outward change. The call for the "idealization" of life through *Kunst-*

politik was never a threat to the status quo as were some of the ideas of *Heimatkunst.* In fact, it tended to legitimize the existing structure of society by accepting it as given. According to most Impressionists, the way to change the tenor of modern life was not through mechanistic, exterior alterations but through inward, spiritual rebirth. Consequently, they did not waste their energies on polemical or agitational activity, since this was beside the point, but concentrated on the "beautification of existence." Ironically, the class most interested in this concept was the upper bourgeoisie. It was seeking a way to spiritualize its own naked power relationships in society, and Impressionism offered the most satisfying way of doing this. The impressionist writers often came to depend upon this class for their livelihood, even though they realized that it was perhaps the main cause of the vulgarity of modern life which they condemned.

Despite their criticisms of the existing order, few Impressionists suggested any viable social alternative. Each in his own way argued for the maximum development of individuality within the present system and saw no need to attack capitalistic exploitation as such, but only those aspects of it which limited individuality.[9] This narrowness of vision was the result of what Georg Lukács, echoing Thomas Mann, has called "power-protected inwardness."[10] The Impressionists failed to see that their very inwardness justified the existing political and economic structures which made such a state of mind possible. While they proceeded to rhapsodize about the transfiguration of society through art, the militaristic, imperialistic, and nationalistic elements of Wilhelmian Germany continued to grow at an alarming pace. By seeking to spiritualize a mode of life which was inherently unspiritual, the Impressionists in effect sanctioned the very aspects of society which disturbed them aesthetically.

Passive Neo-Conservatism

Just as Heinrich Mann found it natural in the early 1890s to regard himself aesthetically as an impressionist writer, so too he found it natural to assume the conservative political perspective which tended to accompany such a choice.

However, some distinctions between these two alignments need to be made, since a particular politics did not automatically spring into Mann's head as soon as he wrote his first impressionist piece. It took

time for Mann's attitudes to surface. At first (1889–1892), his
manner of writing was impressionist but his work lacked an overt
political tone or content. Even such potentially political attitudes as
his hatred for "the rule of money" or his aesthetic anti-capitalism
never ripened into a mature world-view at this first stage in his writing
career, though such attitudes may have been implicit. On the whole,
Mann started out by either limiting his observations to a single locale
like Lübeck (thereby preventing a larger political message from
coming to the fore), or by smothering any latent political content
with heavy doses of irony and satire. In either case, the potentially
critical side of his early work was obscured by a general *mal du
monde* which, by its very nature, hindered the emergence of an overt
political perspective.[11]

In the following years (1892–1895), however, this was no longer
the case. As Mann continued to develop as a writer, an immanent
impressionist politics began to catch up and merge with his impressionist style and literary approach. At this point in his life, when he
achieved some identity between his literary form and content, Mann
became a quintessential impressionist author. He himself recognized
that he had entered a more sophisticated phase of his career when, in
the spring of 1892, he wrote a friend that he had begun "a new spiritual
epoch."[12]

One finds in Mann's work at this stage a more focused political
and social message. Several different themes which were not evident
before now began to come into prominence. Collectively, they constituted what Mann himself referred to as a "neo-conservative"
political content.

Basically, there were four new elements in Mann's work. First,
existing society was seen as a totality and, moreover, as totally problematic. The narrow and fragmentary perspective of the "Fantasien"
was transcended as Mann began to view the world from a different
vantage point than that of a Lübeckean adolescent. He still kept the
dichotomy between the artistic "I" and "everyday life" (*gemeine
Alltäglichkeit*), but now social existence was seen as something that
could be overcome, not something that was unalterably "out there"
and incapable of being acted upon. After 1892, in other words,
Mann gradually began to treat society as something malleable and
open to solutions rather than as a fixed and immutable entity from
which one's only recourse was escape. Second, there was a new
concern about renewing society and somehow restoring it to "health."

The inference was, therefore, that social improvement could be accomplished only by returning to some earlier social norm, i.e., by "regeneration" rather than revolution. The images that began to appear at this point were those representing sickness versus health. Contemporary life was pictured as "diseased," and the age was said to be "sterile and disabled," but it was inferred that the patient could still be saved through proper care and the right kind of convalescence.[13] Third, dilettantism was by now rejected as an acceptable solution to the crisis of the age. Mann began to hint that dilettantism (now referred to as a "sickness of the will") contributed to the general decadence of the epoch. The aesthete was pictured as, in a way, no better than the capitalist, since he also left reality essentially as it is— although by withdrawing into art, rather than by pursuing profit. And finally, Mann began to offer a rudimentary analysis of what he called the "sickness of the century" and, in the process of diagnosing the illness, suggested a few tentative remedies. Among these were the notion of individual self-renewal as the source of social health, love as the key to a revitalized society, and a strong family unit as the chief fulcrum for social regeneration.[14]

All of these ideas started to appear in Mann's writings between the years 1892 and 1895. Taken together, they manifest a neo-conservative posture *vis-à-vis* existing society. Still, it should be pointed out that at this stage Mann was only a *passive* neo-conservative. By this is meant that his overriding interest in the early nineties was literature and belles lettres, and consequently his political biases were present only implicitly. He never thought through or gave concentrated attention to politics as such during these years. In fact, Mann continually avoided specific political issues and chose instead to confront the problems of his age only obliquely, through his literary works. Later (1895–96), Mann moved to a position of *active* neo-conservatism, becoming an engaged right-wing intellectual. He threw himself more decisively into the political arena, took aggressive stands on a whole spectrum of contemporary issues, and worked out to his own satisfaction an explicitly neo-conservative ideology. But prior to 1895, he was viewed, and rightly so, as primarily an aesthetic author.

In Mann's literary production between 1892 and 1895, two works in particular stand out and deserve special comment. The first of these is his most artistically successful novella of the 1890s, "Das Wunderbare" (written 1894, published 1897), and the second is the only novel he completed during the same decade, *In einer Familie* (written 1893, published 1894). Both reveal traces of what is here described as Mann's passive neo-conservatism.

"Das Wunderbare" is the story of a man who returns to see his school friend after many years, and finds that his friend's eagerness for ideals has been replaced by a corpulent body and a love of comfort. Once, as schoolboys, the two shared common experiences: both had "lyrical-artistic" natures and both vowed their undying commitment to art and ideals. Now this had changed. Siegmund Rohde, the friend and former idealist, had become burgher Rohde, a small-town lawyer. His home, his possessions, his occupation, the public affairs he was involved in (such as the building of a small canal for the city), were now his primary concerns. Though he was still conversant in aesthetic matters, he had come to experience art as something "unreal" and essentially irrelevant to his daily life.[15]

This attitude toward art and life was precisely what Mann wished to criticize. His point was that art could not be trivialized or confined to after-dinner conversations, since it contained within it the demand that life live up to an aesthetic ideal; to compartmentalize art was to destroy the sense of obligation which lay at its very core. Rohde, as a typical bourgeois, saw no necessary connection between ideals and action, between art and ethics. He regarded ideals and art as beautiful things because they added to the enchantment of life, but did not consider them to be imperative goals. To Rohde, they appeared to be only abstractions and ornaments which helped enhance his rather humdrum existence as a provincial lawyer.

Rohde's problem lay in the fact that he did not grasp the role that art should play in social life. As a youth, he was misguided because he thought of art as escape. As a middle-aged bourgeois he again missed the point by thinking of it as mere decoration. In both instances, the transforming power of art was never recognized, and consequently the quality of existence was not changed in the slightest. The proper course, Mann seemed to suggest, would have been to bring art back into an immediate relationship with life, but as a transforming and spiritualizing agent rather than a distraction or amusement. This could have been done by understanding that art can be used as a social force to reintegrate a bifurcated reality. Mann did not take issue with Rohde's statement that "one must not make the marvellous banal," for he agreed that when art is brought down to the commonplace in a compromised way it becomes as trivial as everyday life.[16] But Mann could never have accepted, as his character

Rohde did, that art and life should be kept apart, or that the one bore no necessary relationship to the other.

"Ideals come and go," says Rohde at the end of the story, "and we grasp their fragments in our hands without realizing them or entirely forgetting them."[17] In Mann's view, this was a fundamentally erroneous conception of ideals and how integral they are to life. An individual like Rohde regards ideals as disembodied concepts which carry no responsibilities. He feels no compelling impulse to reconcile them with activities, that is, to unify his thoughts and his acts. Instead, he compartmentalizes: he keeps his artistic interests private, and carries on with business as usual. This, Mann believed, is exactly what should not be done. Art must suffuse all of life, personal and social, and help spiritualize it. Again, Mann offered no precise solutions as to how this could be accomplished, perhaps because he found it impossible to be programatic in a novella. Nonetheless, he did introduce in "Das Wunderbare" a problem which continued to occupy him during his early years as a writer. The issue that had to be confronted was the split between pure spirituality on the one hand and a banal, undemanding middle-class existence on the other. Mann still held out the hope that the hiatus could be bridged through the regenerative power of art (if only the aesthete would leave his ivory tower and re-enter the everyday world without, at the same time, forsaking his ideals). To alter a pharase of Max Weber's, the goal seemed to be one of "this-worldly aestheticism," where the spiritual individual would transform ordinary existence through the energizing principle of art.

In *In einer Familie* the emphasis was somewhat different. Here, Mann suggested that a revitalized family unit might do more to end the alienation of modern life than aesthetic idealism. But even though the solution was different, the general conceptualization of the problem did not vary much from that which one finds in "Das Wunderbare."

The plot of the novel is simple. Erich Wellkamp, the thirty-two-year old protagonist, returns to Germany after a ten-year trip during which he lived a life of carefree dilettantism. He now intends to build his life upon a new foundation, since aestheticism seems to him a dead-end. He meets a nineteen-year-old girl, Anna von Grubeck, and marries her. The novel concludes with the two expecting a child and looking forward to a happy family life.

As in much of Mann's work during this period, the notion of spiritual renewal is integral to the novel. Wellkamp, who in some measure is Heinrich Mann himself, at first finds repose in art and inwardness only because he can find no place in the world. His personal stance in *modus contradictorius* to his age is directly related to his aesthetic revulsion against the predominant trends of his time.[18] But Wellkamp does not find his individualistic rejection of the world very satisfying. Though longing for ever-stronger aesthetic "impressions," he begins to feel himself enervated by art, and weakened by its subtle ability to paralyze the will. Hence, he resolves to pull himself out of his lassitude before it is too late, and to establish a more meaningful relationship with the world. This he eventaully does in two ways: first, by re-thinking, and rejecting, his earlier aestheticism; and second, by marrying and laying down "roots" (which are now seen as the precondition for health).

In a long passage, Mann describes Wellkamp's new world-view. He is, Mann says, a "reactionary," but a reactionary of a new sort. Like other "natural born conservative[s]" he longs for an "earlier, more spiritual epoch," but at the same time he is aesthetically more sensitive than the unthinking right-winger and "feels" the problems of the age more keenly.[19] For this reason, Mann continues, he can only be described as a "new kind" of conservative, one who has little in common with traditional forms of reaction. Not only is Wellkamp's opposition to the present more spiritual and cultural than that of the ordinary political conservative; but he is also, as a matter of principle, opposed to business interests and "the mob-rule of money" (*Pöbel-herrschaft des Geldes*). At bottom, Wellkamp's opposition is not intellectual, for he is not really informed or concerned enough to work out a conservative opinion on concrete political issues. Rather, he is opposed to the whole tenor of his era on a more fundamental, inner level, and out of this opposition stems a deep need for moral and spiritual regeneration.

There is, then, a change in Wellkamp as he reflects on his earlier life. Initially he thought of renewal in personal terms, as the retreat into art. In time, however, this choice seemed like escapism. He gradually became convinced that aestheticism was part and parcel of the general sickness of the age, incapable of contributing to social recovery, since the dilettante's over-refinement only added to the un-healthy emotional atmosphere. At the same time, Wellkamp did not believe that renewal could come through politics either, since the purely political individual was too abstract and unfeeling. He might achieve a theoretical identity between himself and mankind, but only by circumventing the more pressing need to interrelate with others and bind himself to them through "love."[20]

Realizing this, Wellkamp seeks redemption through Anna, the symbol of health. As a nineteen-year-old, she is as yet uncorrupted by either society or aestheticism. Wellkamp chooses Anna instead of her rival Dora because Dora has too "nervous" a temperament and is open to the same "mystical susceptibility" and self-destructive impulses that Wellkamp once possessed.[21] If he should attach himself to Dora he would be opting for death, but to marry Anna is to find the way to life. Mann hints that dilettantism is a *cul-de-sac;* there can be no social renewal within a strictly personal framework. Wellkamp is saved because he realizes that the family is the proper medium for social reconstruction. In the end, Wellkamp and Anna settle down to a "meaningful family life, enriched by a genuine, simple, constant, and harmonious tranquility."[22] By means of the homely family unit, Mann achieved a fusion between rootless aestheticism and middle-class existence. The spiritualized family constellation was now seen as a *point d'appui* for new social possibilities in the future.

Here the influence of Paul Bourget is clearly evident. In the early 1890s Mann was strongly impressed by Bourget, and traces of this attachment are not hard to find in *In einer Familie*. Not only was the novel dedicated to his French mentor, but the style and treatment of characters—even the form of the work and its analysis of the *vie interieure et morale*—bear the marks of the political ideas which Mann borrowed from Bourget.[23] As an implacable critic of the French Third Republic and one of the founders of the *Action Française,* Bourget was one of the leading aesthetic ideologues of French conservatism. His name is now associated with, among other things, monarchism, anti-liberalism, organicism, and the attack upon decadence. Mann was influenced in varying degrees by each of these movements, but what may have struck him most was Bourget's theory of the family. According to this theory the family, not the individual, is the fundamental unit of society. Any attempt to transform social life on the basis of personal solutions would be ineffective, in so far as they take place outside the only viable framework for social change. However, if an attempt at spiritual renewal were to occur through the mediation of the family, it could register an effect on society as a whole, since the family is not only the foundation of social life but also the source of its moral strength.[24] Mann, following

Bourget, set his two main characters on the road to health and renewal by uniting them in marriage and blessing them with a child.
Here the primacy of personal relations replaced the primacy of the
individual ego, which was the familiar theme of Mann's earlier work.
The notion that the familial *Intimgruppe* could lead to a revival of
moral and spiritual values did not, strictly speaking, represent a
complete socio-political world-view, but it was as close as Mann had
come to one by the year 1894.[25]

A Generation and Its Discontents

It seems clear, then, that by the mid-1890s Heinrich Mann had
begun to view himself artistically as an Impressionist and politically
as a neo-conservative.

Several other German writers, born about the same time and under
similar circumstances, and all of whom later moved to the Left to
one degree or another, also tended to assume an identity close to
Mann's in the 1890s or early 1900s. Georg Hermann (b. 1871), the
product of a traditional Berlin middle-class family, began composing
highly-stylized impressionist pieces when he was in his early twenties;
later he, like Mann, went on to write socially-critical novels depicting
Wilhelmian society under the sway of a parvenu bourgeoisie. Georg
Kaiser (b. 1878), son of a Magdeburg businessman, grew up in an
old-fashioned *bürgerlich* home with its usual emphasis on frugality
and duty. After rejecting a business career (which he tried temporarily),
Kaiser turned to writing. Though he was greatly influenced by
Gerhart Hauptmann, several of Kaiser's early works were informed
by impressionist motifs such as the flight from reality, the notion of
beauty as an antidote to banality, and disgust with the materialism of
modern life. Alfred Döblin (b. 1878), born into a trade and business
family in Stettin, developed for familial reasons the attitude of an
outsider; the predominant themes of his early work, written around
1900, were the incompleteness of middle-class existence, the search
for "love," and the longing for an imaginary life. Carl Sternheim
(b. 1878), the product of a conservative upper-middle class home in
Leipzig, began in the 1890s to rebel against "things as they are,"
and in the process developed a political philosophy based on aesthetic
"pseudo-traditionalism." Like Mann in the 1890s, he hoped for
some (unspecified) kind of social rejuventation; at the same time, he

cultivated an artistic style which alternated between preciosity and lyrical aestheticism. Bernhard Kellermann (b. 1879) came from the solid *Bürgertum,* his father being a city official. After an early decision to write novels and travel literature, Kellermann went on to cultivate a subjective and highly impressionist mode of writing. At this point he was an aesthetic elitist but later, like Mann, he turned away from this toward a moral critique of German society. René Schickele (b. 1883), the son of a middle class Alsatian wine-grower, became during World War I a radical pacifist and socialist. In his earliest poetic and literary efforts, however, he adopted a conservative outlook and expressed himself in a romantic prose style. Finally, Lion Feuchtwanger (b. 1884) grew up in a tradition-minded burgher home, his father being a Jewish manufacturer in Munich. Like Mann, he gradually moved to the far Left, wrote politically-committed literature, and viewed himself as a moral intellectual in deadly combat with immoral power. Nevertheless, in his youth Feuchtwanger wrote in a mannered, artificial style which he himself later described as "over-refined" and "excessively aesthetic." Again like Mann in the nineties, the young Feuchtwanger perceived the world in artistic categories and showed few traces of the radical social critic he would later become.[26]

These are only a few of Mann's contemporaries who appeared to follow a common line of development. The pattern seems more than coincidental, which suggests that, taken collectively, these writers formed something like a literary generation. They were unified by the fact that they were impinged upon by the same events, and tried to cope with these events by recourse to the same set of mental reactions. This phenomenon has been aptly labeled by Karl Mannheim as an "identity of responses."[27] It occured for some of the reasons alluded to earlier: namely, that all the writers shared a common historical and class location; all were drawn into the same intellectual-cultural world during early adolescence; all acquired similar values, mental attitudes, and psychological dispositions; all reacted to the same things in nineteenth-century German society (e.g., the mechanization of the world, the alienation of modern life, the absence of *Gemeinschaft,* and the isolation of the artist); and finally, all opted initially for similar aesthetic solutions. These similarities made them something more than a mere aggregate of individuals, and gave them a certain amount of inner cohesion which allows one to speak of them as a "generational unit."[28]

Footnotes
Chapter 3

1. See Fritz Stern, *The Politics of Cultural Despair* (New York, 1965), pp. 5, 327.

2. See Albert Soergel, *Dichtung und Dichter,* p. 215. This alliance, it should be noted, was less with Marxian socialism than with a humanistic, non-programmatic socialism.

3. Adolf Bartels, *Heimatkunst,* p. 18.

4. There was in *Heimatkunst* a strong sense of tradition which was hard to reconcile with revolutionary nihilism. Moreover, there was as yet no call for a *Führer* nor any rabid anti-Semitism, though something of the sort was implied. For the National Socialist view of *Heimatkunst* see Walter Linden, *Geschichte der deutschen Literatur* (Leipzig, 1944), pp. 431–37; and Helmuth Langenbucher, *Volkhafte Dichtung der Zeit* (Berlin, 1941), pp. 390–409.

5. See Claude David, "Stefan George: Aesthetes or Terrorists?," *The Third Reich,* ed. Maurice Baumont, et al., (New York, 1955), pp. 287–315.

6. Wolfdietrich Rasch, *Zur deutschen Literatur seit der Jahrhundertwende* (Stuttgart, 1967), pp. 7–19.

7. See Theodor W. Adorno, "The George-Hofmannsthal Correspondence, 1891–1906," *Prisms,* trans. Samuel and Shierry Weber (London, 1967), pp. 198, 202.

8. See Armin Mohler, *Die konservative Revolution in Deutschland 1918–1932* (Stuttgart, 1950); and Klemens von Klemperer, *Germany's New Conservatism* (Princeton, 1957).

9. Richard Hamann and Jost Hermand, *Impressionismus,* pp. 14–32.

10. Georg Lukács, *Essays on Thomas Mann,* trans. Stanley Mitchell (New York, 1965), pp. 27–31, 61–62.

11. Typical of Mann's writing at this point was his unpublished novella "Haltlos" (Heinrich-Mann-Archiv, no. 165). Written during September and October, 1890, the story reflects the introspective and generally apolitical tone which pervaded much of his work during this early period. The intense subjectivism of the piece, the overdone sense of *Weltschmerz,* and the mood of what Mann called an "innere Verbitterung, Welt-und-Ich-Verachtung," all blocked the emergence of a more obvious political message.

51

12. Heinrich Mann, letter of May 29, 1892, to Frau Dr. Lehmann, in Heinrich-Mann-Archiv, no. 52/56.

13. Heinrich Mann, *In einer Familie* (Munich, 1894), p. 131.

14. For an overview of Mann's work at this time see Manfred Hahn, "Zum frühen Schaffen Heinrich Manns," *Weimarer Beiträge* (1966), XII, no. 3: 363-73.

15. Heinrich Mann, "Das Wunderbare," *Novellen,* I, *Ausgewählte Werke,* VII:9-10.

16. *Ibid.*, p. 11.

17. *Ibid.*, p. 37.

18. Heinrich Mann, *In einer Familie,* p. 161. "The feeling of dissatisfaction leads in the end just as easily to artistic sensitivity . . . as it does to political partisanship on the other side of the interpretation of life."

19. *Ibid.*, pp. 61-62.

20. This interpretation follows that of Manfred Hahn, whose work on this period of Mann's life has surpassed all previous studies. See Manfred Hahn, "Das Werk Heinrich Manns von den Anfängen bis zum 'Untertan'," Ph.D. dissertation, Leipzig, 1965, pp. 62-88.

21. Heinrich Mann, *In einer Familie,* pp. 159, 184. Dora is Anna's young step-mother, to whom Wellkamp feels drawn after meeting Anna. Interestingly enough Dora is half-Jewish and therefore perhaps more dangerously seductive than Anna, whose roots are purely German. In his essay "Bourget als Kosmopolit" (in *Die Gegenwart,* 1894), Mann seemed to accept the principle, formulated by Bourget and Taine, that race and milieu play a crucial part in determining character. It is possible that this idea found its way into *In einer Familie,* since the novel appeared in the same year as the essay on Bourget. If so, it is probably not accidental that Dora was made out to be Jewish. In the 1890s Mann betrayed a rather strong streak of anti-Semitism, which came out most clearly in his articles in *Das Zwanzigste Jahrhundert* (1895-1896).

22. Heinrich Mann, *In einer Familie,* p. 268.

23. According to Klaus Schröter, Bourget had a more profound impact on Mann than any other writer up until 1894 (see his *Anfänge Heinrich Manns,* pp. 18ff.). Manfred Hahn reached a similar conclusion in his own work (see "Das Werk Heinrich Manns," p. 88).

24. Heinrich Mann, *In einer Familie,* p. 12.

25. It should be noted that the structural limitations of Mann's novel hindered the possibilities of a more extended political discussion. The confined space, the small number of characters, and the rarity of social interaction kept the novel on a private rather than a social level. Then, too, since most of the conflicts were individualized and psychologized, the "critical possibilities contain[ed] within [the novel] remained unutilized." See Manfred Hahn, "Zum frühen Schaffen Heinrich Manns," *Weimarer Beiträge*, XII, no. 3: 372.

26. Most of the above information can be found in biographies of the respective authors. On Hermann and Kellermann see the *Deutsches Schriftstellerlexikon*, ed. Günter Albrecht, et al., (Weimar, 1963), pp. 275–76, 348. On Kaiser see Ernst Schürer, *Georg Kaiser* (New York, 1971), pp. 22–31, 44–58. On Döblin: Ernst Ribbat, *Die Wahrheit des Lebens im frühen Werk Alfred Döblins* (Münster, 1970), pp. 8–27; and Klaus Müller-Salget, *Alfred Döblin: Werk und Entwicklung* (Bonn, 1972), pp. 12–43. On Sternheim: Winifred Georg Sebald, *Carl Sternheim: Kritiker und Opfer der Wilhelminischen Ära* (Stuttgart, 1969), pp. 21–38, 50–55. On Schickele: Francine Bradley, *René Schickele: der Kampf um einen persönlichen Stil* (New York, 1942); and Hermann Kesten, "René Schickele," introduction to *Werke in drei Bänden* (Cologne and Berlin, 1959), pp. 7–18. On Feuchtwanger: Y. E. Yuill, "Lion Feuchtwanger," *German Men of Letters*, 4 vols., ed. Alex Natan (London, 1964), III:179–205; and John M. Spalek, ed., *Lion Feuchtwanger: The Man, His Ideas, His Work* (Los Angeles, 1972).

27. Karl Mannheim, "The Problem of Generations," *Essays on the Sociology of Knowledge*, ed. Paul Kecskemeti (London, 1959), p. 306.

28. See *Ibid.*, pp. 276–320; and Henri Peyre, *Les générations littéraires* (Paris, 1948), pp. 173–206.

29. Goldmann has argued that when these qualities are found in literary works it is an indication of shared mental structures. See Lucien Goldmann, *Pour une sociologie du roman*, pp. 15–37, 213–29.

Chapter 4

Dialectics of Engagement

The more bitterly and acutely we form a thesis, the more irresistibly it clamors for an antithesis.

Hermann Hesse

From Passive to Active Neo-Conservatism

Mann's earliest work should be viewed in terms of three stages. The first covers the period of his unpublished writings up to 1892, while the second extends from 1892 to 1894 and includes his initial reception as a published author. The third, which concerns his move toward conservative political journalism, is the subject of this chapter.

In the first stage, Mann's fragmentary work contained a latent, not a manifest, political character. In all of his pieces written before 1892, with the possible exception of the short story "Fantasien über meine Vaterstadt L.," the concern with form and style tended to obscure any explicit political content. Although Mann was sure the world-as-given was not for him, he offered no social solutions to the problems he saw around him. Usually the suggested remedy was retreat into art and phantasy, or withdrawal into the chrysalis of the self. When Mann did talk about the will to change he meant the will to change oneself. Thus in the novella "Tilli" (December, 1891), Mann inferred that bourgeois existence could be transcended by an act of will, and that health could be achieved through the personal exercise of one's "inner resources."[1]

In the second stage, Mann moved beyond this point to a position I have described as passive neo-conservatism. By this is meant not only that he began to search for supra-individual rather than personal solutions to social issues, but that he began to approach these issues through an implicitly conservative political framework. Hence in *In einer Familie*, Mann indicated that the major task ahead was social regeneration and that there were two ways to achieve it: through love

55

and the revitalized family unit. By the notion of social regeneration through love, Mann vaguely envisioned the emergence of a new élan in society without the need for concrete social mediations. With the concept of the spiritualized family he became more specific about desired solutions without, however, becoming any less conservative. By regarding the family as the agency for a healthier social life Mann placed himself not only on the side of a rightest like Bourget, but also on the side of a whole line of nineteenth-century German traditionalists who argued precisely the same point.[2]

The fact that Mann borrowed most of these ideas from others and then failed to develop them in any systematic way is significant. At this stage, Mann was not concerned with politics as such. He was still interested almost exclusively in "being a writer," and to the extent that politics entered his work it did so passively and indirectly. Like so many other young middle-class writers, Mann seems to have come to politics *through* literature. At first he withdrew into aestheticism in order to leave politics behind, but he began to see that even aestheticism had a political side to it which was inescapable. It was not long before his supposedly pure aestheticism became a political aestheticism. The more Mann and his literary generation faced social reality, the more critical they became of it. Nevertheless, theirs was a uniquely aesthetic mode of criticism in which the central categories were often artistic rather than social or political. At work here was a process of withdrawal from the world (into a cult of beauty) and then a return to it, but the return was always dialectically enriched by the artistic experience. By becoming more critical of their culture, Mann and the others dispensed with the formalities of aestheticism but not with its informing spirit. In this way the aesthetic vision was both preserved and transcended, not discarded. What makes the conservative social criticism of the nineties interesting as well as potentially explosive is that it contained simultaneously an attack on things as they were, and the radical hope that life could be made beautiful again. This kind of sentiment would most naturally tend to align itself with rightist views, but there were also leftist aspects to it that cannot be overlooked (since even Marx spoke of altering reality "in accordance with the laws of beauty").[3] Mann himself, who even later in life never completely abandoned the artistic approach to social problems, moved in both directions, but at different times. At first, in the mid-1890s, he fused his aestheticism with right-wing politics, and then much later took his aesthetic concepts to the far left of the political spectrum.

In the third stage of his artistic development, which was reached around the year 1895, Mann moved from a passive to an active neo-conservatism. This meant two things: that he began to meet contemporary issues head-on, without using fiction as a medium, and that he began to articulate a more reactionary position which placed him closer to the far Right than at any time in his life. These two developments went hand in hand and appeared to affect one another mutually. In 1895, Mann began for the first time to deal with social and political problems as autonomous issues entirely distinct from aesthetic ones—something that would have been inconceivable five years earlier. At the same time, he attempted to carve out for himself a role as a social critic without totally abandoning his previous image as an aesthetic writer. Between 1895 and 1896 Mann produced virtually nothing in the way of fiction, but he did write over three dozen essays dealing with specific cultural-political problems of the 1890s.[4] It is important to note that in the process of trying to separate political issues from aesthetic ones, Mann shot beyond his restrained impressionist *Kunstpolitik* and began expressing opinions which seemed dangerously reactionary. This is not suprising. Given the fact that Impressionism had no clearly developed body of political thought, it was easy to fall back on the rhetoric and ideology of the extreme Right when one attempted to say something concrete. And yet there is an irony here, for in the very act of becoming engaged rightists Mann and some of the other Impressionists of his generation sumultaneously laid the groundwork for later becoming engaged leftists. How this occurred, through a dialectical involvement with society, is discussed below; but first, a few comments about Mann's active neo-conservatism.

Das Zwanzigste Jahrhundert

Mann's most extreme social and political views can be found in the journal *Das Zwanzigste Jahrhundert* (The Twentieth Century) which he edited in 1895–1896. The nature of his work for this journal has been discussed elsewhere.[5] Here it is necessary to describe only the general tone of his politics during his period as editor.

Das Zwanzigste Jahrhundert: Blätter für deutsche Art und Wohlfahrt was a monthly journal founded in Berlin by Erwin Bauer in November, 1890. Bauer was managing editor until 1893, when the poet Friedrich Lienhard took over. In April, 1895, Heinrich Mann assumed

the editorship and maintained that position—at first alone, later in
collaboration with others—until December, 1896, when the journal
closed down.[6]

Essentially, *Das Zwanzigste Jahrhundert* was a journal of critical
thought with a right-wing, at times almost *völkisch,* point of view.
Its programme, in so far as it had one, was to achieve a "healthy
modern realism in art and literature" and a revived German national
consciousness.[7] It was hostile to socialism, liberalism, science, tech-
nology, industrialism, the metropolis—in short, to everything which
ran counter to the tried and true virtues of German *Volkstum.* In
foreign policy, it advocated rapprochement with France, but was
suspicious of Russia and England. In literature, it carried on a
prolonged vendetta against the proponents of Naturalism (especially
Hauptmann), and supported instead the best of the neo-romantic
writers as well as regional *Bauerndichter* such as Friedrich Lienhard.
On the whole, those who wrote for the journal were undistinguished,
with the names of most of them hardly remembered now even by
historians of the period. Of the entire group, only Lienhard and
Mann went on to establish literary reputations of their own.

Mann's first article in the journal, entitled simply "Reaction," set
the tone for those which followed. In it he summarized the main
ideas which he hoped to encourage as an editor.

Why, he began by asking, had the word "reaction" come to have
such bad connotations while the word "progress" was received so
enthusiastically? His answer was simple: since the liberal bourgeoisie
had played a decisive part in defining these two concepts, it naturally
exaggerated the benefits of the one while denigrating the qualities of
the other. He concluded that this perspective needed to be reversed
so that the positive meaning of reaction could be brought to light. To
accomplish this, Mann launched an attack on materialism and
science, the two mainstays of the bourgeois view of progress. Materialism was unsatisfactory because it denied mystery, the unconscious,
and the darker well-springs of human action and belief. Similarly,
the idea that progress was synonymous with the expansion of science
or industry was erroneous because it was too narrow and one-sided;
it failed to see that science and industrialism only increased the
general spiritual impoverishment of the age. Materialism, science,
and the liberalism of the *nouveaux riches* had conspired together to
define the meaning of progress, and in so doing each strengthened
and reinforced the other. The task of the age was to expose the

shallowness of this point of view. The "errors of materialism" and the "bankruptcy of science" had to be revealed for what they were, so that the "wonderful abysses of the human soul" could be affirmed once again.[8]

Mann admitted that this revelation would not be easy since so-called progressive ideas had already taken hold of the masses, and materialistic attitudes were widespread at all levels of society. But the situation was not yet hopeless. If one could reactivate in the German mind such conservative values as community, religious belief, and high spiritual ideals, the nation might still be saved. Should these qualities be revived, the term "reaction" would no longer be a derogatory one. On the contrary, to be labelled reactionary would be a compliment since it would indicate a healthier view of what progress really means, namely moral and spiritual growth rather than material accumulation. The word "reaction" is not popular, Mann noted in conclusion, "but he who constantly finds himself in the minority will in the end be right."[9]

In German society at that time, it was the Social Democrats who most clearly shared the scientific and materialistic attitudes which Mann opposed, and it was against them that he vented much of his anger. As a matter of course, he accused them of embodying all the fraudulent ideas on progress already mentioned. At the same time, he expanded his critique to include the internationalist tendencies which he associated with the socialist movement. Socialist internationalism was, in Mann's view, a force which was essentially evil since it cut ruthlessly into the national consciousness and replaced it with a standardized and rootless frame of mind.[10] To destroy the *National-prinzip*, as the socialists threatened to do, would be to destroy the very source of Western culture. Furthermore, Mann was convinced that the principle of monarchy and the feeling for hierarchy were firmly implanted in the German soul. To suppress these attitudes by emphasizing proletarian internationalism would be to strike at the root of German consciousness and dissolve a system of order into chaos.[11] The Social Democrats had to be opposed not only because they stood for a radical subversion of the existing order, but also because they wanted to replace nationalism with a levelling internationalism which, in his opinion, was incompatible with the very principles of civilization. (In this, Mann seemed to express the typical middle class view of socialism as a threat to *Ordnung* and, just as important, to *Kultur* and the individuality of the artist or writer.)

Next to socialism, Mann felt that modern liberalism, based on classical economics and interest-group politics, was the most harmful ideology of the time. His case against it was built up rather unsystematically, but essentially he maintained that liberalism was polluting Germany with four harmful elements: democratic ideas, moral decay, parliamentarianism, and the rule of money (*Geldherrschaft*).

Mann had nothing against democratic ideas in themselves so long as they remained indigenous to the people who bred them. In France, for instance, democratic and republican sentiments were legitimate because they were a product of national consciousness. The German people, however, were supposedly attached to an organic rather than a democratic conception of society, so it would be wrong to impose upon them a foreign import. All that a nation really needed would develop spontaneously within its own borders. Thus, it was fatuous to speak of supra-national abstractions such as freedom and humanity. These generalities (necessarily lacking in substance since they were not grounded in particular cultures) were the essence of the liberal creed, and yet they also explained why this creed was at once both vacuous and dangerous: vacuous because it was without concreteness, and dangerous because it destroyed the organic political forms that were best suited to the German people. To Mann, one of the tragicomic aspects of the Revolution of 1848 was that the German liberals strove to imitate political models which lay completely outside the German mode of experience. "For our nature as Germans," he wrote in one article, "[democracy] is an entirely irrelevant ideology."[12]

Nevertheless, even after 1848 liberal ideas continued to encroach upon Germany, so that by the 1890s their presence was once again decisively felt. This led Mann to discover a second consequence of liberalism: the widespread "moral decay" he witnessed in his own time. There seemed to be a direct correlation between the anarchy of ideas in liberalism and the anarchy of morals in society; it followed that as liberalism gained a foothold, traditional religious and ethical codes of behavior began to decline.[13] This is what Mann referred to as "degeneration," or the corruption of popular morality, for which liberal influences were chiefly to blame.

A third indictment of liberalism rested upon the political divisiveness it allegedly brought to the German people. This was especially evident in the parties and parliamentarianism which the liberals had introduced into political life. The result was not a harmony of interests as they promised, but a situation where whole segments of the population were set against one another, breeding hostility and resentment instead of mutual understanding.[14]

Finally, Mann attacked liberalism because of certain economic developments which he imputed to it, most notably the rise of a modern plutocracy. Just how liberalism caused or was linked with *Geldherrschaft* is not clear, except that the *nouveaux riches* who brought liberal ideas to Germany later became, in many cases, the magnates of industry who profited from the liberal conception of the free play of forces. Mann saw a close connection between a loosening up of the political sphere and a breakdown in Germany's economic equilibrium; out of the chaos of liberalization a new moneyed class had emerged, the wealthy bourgeoisie, who promoted liberal ideas because it was in their financial interest to do so. Similarly, these newly-arrived plutocrats encouraged the liberal attack on religion and the "natural order" since both were viewed as checks on the accumulation of more economic power for themselves. The consequences, again, were economic anarchy and ruthless individualism.

It is evident from a number of passages that Mann was strongly anti-capitalistic, but his was a reactionary anti-capitalism rather than a socialist one. Furthermore, it was primarily large-scale capital (*Grosskapital*) that he opposed, not capitalism in general, and most certainly not the "responsible" capitalism of the old *Bürgertum*. His objection to the rise of money values brought by liberalism was that they destroyed higher values, especially the concept of community. As with Max Stirner, whom Mann placed in the forefront of the liberal movement, the concept of "we" was reduced to a single concept "I".[15] Although this had some merit on a human level, in the realm of economics it was disastrous because it created "modern money morality," which dissolved all ties and loyalties incompatible with the profit motive. The result was the same kind of moral indifference on a social plane which Stirner manifested on an individual one. Here Mann agreed with Karl Marx who, in *The German Ideology*, singled out Stirner on the same grounds. Also like Marx, Mann abhorred all the embodied symbols of capitalism, such as the stock exchange, the monopolies, the trusts and cartels.[16] But unlike the German revolutionary, he did not want to see liberalism replaced by communism, nor the rule of plutocrats by the dictatorship of the proletariat. Mann wanted a new simplicity and a new community, by which he really meant the return of old social relationships and concerns which he saw bourgeois liberalism destroying.[17] When he described the kind of society he wanted, he used the more traditional term *Gemeinschaft* (community) in contrast to Marx's more radical *Gemeinwesen* (communality). In every respect, Mann's critique of large-scale capitalism was thoroughly conservative.

As he continued to write articles opposing all these tendencies— socialism, imported liberalism, modern capitalism—it apparently struck him that large numbers of German Jews were at the head of each of these three movements. Presumably this was one factor which led Mann to take a belligerent attitude towards the Jews, since they were helping to destroy the values he thought should be upheld. Hence, by the mid-1890s, Mann was drawn into an explicit, though qualified, anti-Semitism. His attitude towards the Jews was presented in extremely banal and platitudinous terms in an essay entitled "Jüdischen Glaubens" ("Of Jewish Faith"). Here he argued that there was no such thing as a Jewish middle class in the proper sense of the word; there were only Jewish businessmen who existed outside the structure of the traditional German *Mittelstand*. They rose and fell quickly because they were essentially a "transitory" people, "not lasting or firmly established like a cooperatively ordered *Stand* from which one never grows away."[18] Thus, to Mann, the Jewish mind remained something separate and different from the German mind, just as Jewish business practices differed from middle-class ethics as a whole. Because of this, and because they were not a true *Volk* and therefore not rooted in a particular land or language, the Jews were a foreign and undesirable element. "Against all the tendencies and fundamental laws of modern European state-systems, they remain a living contradiction. Simply by their presence they daily do harm to the community of states in Europe."[19] What, then, should be done about them? Mann's answer was straightforward: their harmful influence should be opposed by a healthy, "spiritual" kind of anti-Semitism:

> The Jews . . . are not persecuted as a 'people' because they have not earned that name yet. The only reason they are set upon is that they are the embodied negation of both nationality and faith. And so they are tormented not so much for themselves, but as symbols of everything which is destructive and degenerate. . . . It is for us, therefore, to reaffirm the condition of our healthy nature, in order to make the ominous signs of decline disappear. Everyone who would then be a protector of [our] natural social conscience would by nature be an anti-Semite. But for this kind of anti-Semitism the suppression of Judaism would not be the purpose or goal, but only its most immediate manifestation.[20]

Dangerous as these ideas appear, Mann nonetheless tried to dissociate himself from anti-Semitism as an organized movement, for which he seems to have had only contempt. His brand of anti-Semitism was treated as something spiritual and elevated, but the "popular ground-swell which one calls anti-Semitism" seemed to him vulgar and plebian, built on hatred rather than on high cultural ideals.

The final concern with which Mann dealt in the journal was the broader issue of war and peace. War, he argued, was beneficial because it helped to perpetuate the fit rather than the unfit. Moreover, it gave an order to society out of which sprang the roots of a sound culture. Peace, on the other hand, led to the "anarchical free play of ideas" which was destructive of order and culture. Thus Mann opposed what he called the "middle-class peace movement," which was gaining some adherents at the time, because it hindered the salutary effects of struggle and consequently set the conditions for general decline.

In an article entitled "Kriegs-und Friedensmoral" ("The Morality of War and Peace"), Mann admitted the horrors of war. But, he argued, when "unreconciled enemies" loom up on all sides, the German people have to accept a perpetual state of battle-readiness. In light of this, he could not understand the talk about disarmament or the new enthusiasm for "peace leagues." A peace league, he pointed out, was ineffectual because there would never be eternal peace; it was also dangerous because it whittled away at national pride and denigrated the greatness of those personalities whose fame rested on their exploits in war.[21]

Although Mann considered liberal peace efforts to be misdirected, he did believe it was important to work for a unified Europe. The basis of unity, however, should not be general disarmament but a general re-armament *vis-à-vis* the "crude and unscrupulous East." Without using the term "yellow peril," Mann conjured up all the associations the phrase implies. He warned that it was wrong to think the age of barbarian hordes was past. It was still possible that a leader could arouse the whole Eastern world against the West. And if, in the meantime, Europe should have disarmed itself, what would become of Western civilization? His conclusion was that the European states should band together and prepare for war against a future and unavoidable enemy. "This enemy may seem far afield today, but we know that one must fear him from a distance in order to encounter him fearlessly up close."[22]

The sentiments expressed at this point were so different from what they would be twenty years later that it is enlightening to quote a typical passage at length:

> For us today, war is a model of the true social order. . . . Without war there would be no concept of heroism; with it comes all moral and aesthetic value. Even painting and art would not be worthwhile if it were not for war. Homer, the Nibelungenlied, the Pantheon frieze, the dying gladiator . . . would all be gone. . . . For it is precisely in war that everyone's consciousness becomes simple and complete. A warlike epoch lifts it children to heights that are usually thought unreachable in ordinary times. The view from above is comprehensive and simplified. Commonplace, petty attitudes disappear; envy and greed are silenced, and honesty replaces the usual hypocrisy of daily life. Those who are enemies try to come to terms with their hostility, and in this way they become real and respectful friends who feel themselves lifted up, through their participation in great designs, into a single unified purpose. The life-interests of the individual are set aside because the life of the individual in itself is no longer considered of great importance. . . . Such a condition among men is not brought about by works of culture (if it is necessary to contrast war and culture) but is produced only by war. Certainly this is brutal, but then so is truth.[23]

"Volk" or "Mittelstand"?

There can be no doubt that the opinions Mann expressed in these and other articles in *Das Zwanzigste Jahrhundert* drew him deeply into cultural and political reaction. For nearly twenty months between April, 1895, and December, 1896, Mann put forth a number of ideas which seemed not far removed from the *völkisch* Right. His previous impressionist concern with personal renewal appeared to be subsumed into a larger emphasis on social harmony and national regeneration. At this stage in his career, Mann seemed to have moved significantly to the right of the moderate neo-conservatism of his earlier literary period.

Two points need to be emphasized here, both of which have a bearing on Mann's later development. First, the ideas he articulated in the pages of *Das Zwanzigste Jahrhundert* were, objectively speaking, neo-conservative, even if the rhetoric suggested something more dangerous; and secondly, embedded within Mann's politics were the seeds of a liberal *Weltanschauung*. These seeds, though not evident on the surface, were nonetheless there, and when Mann eventually broke with his neo-conservative outlook, these half-hidden liberal possibilities were at hand waiting to be utilized.

Both points are important. If Mann had thrown himself into a genuinely *völkisch* ideology of the kind represented by, say, Julius Langbehn in *Rembrandt als Erzieher,* it would have been difficult for him ever to embrace a liberal world-view since the about face required would have been too psychologically wrenching. Furthermore, if there had not been at least the potential of a liberal outlook ensconced within his conservative frame of mind, Mann might not have had anything to draw on in building a new perspective. When he was eventually faced with the bankruptcy of neo-conservatism, he was able to construct a new social and political philosophy, but it seems unlikely that he could have done this if certain core ideas had not been present *in nuce* in his earlier thought. Particularly in the years after he left the journal, Mann, like a hesitant but skillful *bricoleur,* re-examined his previous opinions, rejecting some and re-working others, often by placing them in a completely new context. The initial result was a cautious but rudimentary form of liberal humanism.

Before dealing with the political complexion of Mann's work for *Das Zwanzigste Jahrhundert* it must be repeated that the ideology he elaborated was neo-conservative and not *völkisch*. Despite the virulence of language and crudeness of opinion, there were several moderating influences in Mann's thought which restrained him from the worst excesses of the Right.

One of these restraining influences was his attitude towards religion. By almost any definition it was conservative rather than *völkisch,* since Mann carefully avoided encouraging any notion of a nationalized religion or a "Germanic Christianity." Unlike Paul de Lagarde or, later on, Alfred Rosenberg, Mann had no desire to mix race and religion, or to create a new kind of *Volk*-centered Christianity. His emphasis was always on a traditional, hierarchical form of religious organization, whereas the far Right wished to fuse religion with a social movement in order to shatter moribund religious structures or, if possible, to "Germanize" them. Mann felt that any tampering with established religion would always do more harm than good.[24]

His attitude towards existing society was also basically conservative since, at bottom, he did not want to see it radically changed. Despite an occasional lapse into romantic nostalgia, Mann had no wish to turn Germany into a land of peasants and poets (though it is true that he wanted the bourgeoisie removed from their position at the top of the social structure). The important thing was to consolidate the best of what already existed, including the monarchy, but not to risk the loss of everything by carrying out the utopian schemes of either the Right or the Left. "We still believe," he wrote, "in the vitality of the German people and the present system. . . . Reformation is what we strive for, not revolution."[25] And in another place: "A nameless resentment is rising in the lower orders. It is strong and threatening and is directed precisely against the liberal power structure that is now falling into the hands of the few."[26] Rather than join the assault forces against the present system, as the radical Right was inclined to do, Mann advised moderation. As bad as things were, it was still better to modify the status quo and, where possible, to spiritualize it, than to open the floodgates to mass energies which might rush out beyond control. "Our duty," he concluded, "is to see that this resentment does not grow out of hand [and] . . . that the injustices of capitalism are meliorated as much as possible."[27]

For Mann, the salient concept at this point was stability. To be sure, an organic past based on traditional *Stände* did at times appear attractive, but mainly because it seemed to promise a kind of security missing in the 1890s.[28] By contrast, the ideologues of the radical Right were never so intent on defending the established order or the residues of traditionalism contained within it. Likewise, Mann did not have the respect for the German peasantry that was characteristic of the extreme Right, nor did he advocate a *Volksstaat* as the base for a new social order. In truth, Mann suspected and feared the common people more than he loved them. When he spoke of a "nameless resentment" from below, he talked in terms of containing it rather than unleashing its fury.[29] In this respect he was a conservative rather than a proto-fascist, having much less in common with Langbehn than with Gustave Le Bon, whose defense of reactionary politics (*Psychologie des foules*, 1895) came out the same year Mann became editor of *Das Zwanzigste Jahrhundert*.

In other fundamental ways as well, Mann did not share the world-view of the *völkisch* Right. There was no dynamic to his thought, no emphasis on youth or movement, no hint of a *Führerprinzip*, no "blood and soil" ideology and no deliberate evocation of racial myths or symbols. In place of these, Mann continued to stress the need for re-activating "monarchical feelings" and the old corporate consciousness as the means to social regeneration. Only his anti-Semitism poses a question which cannot easily be answered. It was, more than

anything else in the journal, tendentious and did come close to a
völkisch attitude towards the Jews. Nevertheless, there are important
distinctions to be made here as well. Mann's attack on the Jews was
not intended to be racial; it was their social function which he
despised, especially the way they allegedly imposed capitalism and an
irresponsible brand of liberalism upon Germany. The Jews did not
fit into the German framework because they belonged to no legitimate *Stamm*. Being outsiders, they had accumulated for themselves
tremendous power which they used to undermine the foundations of
society.[30] This view is hardly excusable on any terms. Nonetheless, it
should be distinguished from the usual *völkisch* fare which turned
anti-Semitism into a theory of history and made of the Jew a bio-
logical enemy.

Perhaps the conservative element in Mann's thought which most
decisively distinguished it from the ideology of the radical Right was
his strong defense of the German *Mittelstand*. The word *Mittelstand*,
at least as Mann used it, referred to Germany's middle strata, i.e., to
the practical, old-fashioned, pre-industrial *Bürgertum*.[31] Mann frequently relied on this concept (sometimes using the term inaccurately)
in order to contrast the virtues of the old middle class with the
qualities of the emergent bourgeoisie, and to argue that a return to
power by these middle strata would lead to a social and spiritual
reawakening in Germany.

His critique of the bourgeoisie, which pervades all of his writings in
the journal, derived from his belief that this class was destroying the
"feeling of community" and the old corporate relationships, unleashing a *laissez-aller* liberalism, and introducing the evils of industrial
and finance capitalism. Not only did Mann deplore their *arrivisme*
and crude parvenu tastes; he also accused the bourgeoisie of turning
all questions of value into questions of money, and in this way
dominating German social and intellectual life. The whole tenor of
the period was affected by the *nouveaux riches;* indeed, the 1890s
had become the bourgeois age *par excellence.* Even the changeover
from Bismarck to Wilhelm II was symbolic in this respect. Where the
Bismarckian era had been one of order and stability, the Wilhelmian
epoch—with its "new course" abroad and its vulgar ostentation at
home—was typically and thoroughly bourgeois in character. Formerly
the *Mittelstand* had been the very foundation of society, but since the
rise of the bourgeoisie, this traditional middle class had lost its social
importance. The floodgates had been thrown open and Germany was

falling into dissolution. Still, this course could be reversed if old middle-class virtues regained their hold on society. Germany would then be restored to its earlier healthy condition and proper moral feelings would be reasserted. Religion and the monarchy would also be reaffirmed, and the desire for stability would replace the quest for novelty. Above all, "social conscience" would take root again, and a sense of community would supersede an aggressive individualism based upon the profit motive.[32]

Once it is understood that Mann's bête noire was the bourgeoisie and not the middle classes in general, the real thrust of his articles in *Das Zwanzigste Jahrhundert* comes more clearly into focus. His anti-Semitism, for example, can be explained at least in part by the fact that for Mann, the Jews epitomized the worst qualities of the ascendant bourgeoisie. As a "terrible simplifier," he was inclined to picture the Jews as the physical embodiment of greed, unscrupulousness, and all the other qualities which he regarded as foreign to the German *Bürgertum*. Similarly, his critique of the money economy was not a critique of capitalism as such, but only of its latest large-scale excesses, which again were attributed to the bourgeoisie. What he singled out for attack were the stock exchange and the monopolies, but he had only good words for the small proprietor (*kleine Kapitalisten*).[33]

It is true that Mann often used the rhetoric of the extreme Right, but fundamentally his ideas were grounded in neo-conservatism. His emphasis on the *Mittelstand* over the *Volk* placed him outside the mainstream of pre-fascist thought. During the conservative revival of the 1920s, the man who came closest to his position was not Adolf Hitler, but the romantic conservative Eugen Diederichs. In his journal *Die Tat,* Diederichs proclaimed that what was needed was "not the destruction of the *Bürgertum* . . . but the formulation of a social theory which could justify the position of the *Bürgertum* as a ruling class".[34] This is an echo of Mann's view in 1895–96. Social renewal, if it was to come, would take place under the leadership of the old middle class. In spite of his flirtation with the radical Right, Mann put his trust in the German *citoyen* and not in the idealized peasant.

Negative Dialectics: From a Neo-Conservative to a Liberal Weltanschauung

Ironically, Mann's very involvement in right-wing social commentary was one factor which later drew him towards a liberal political perspective. Had he held onto the "aesthetic politics" of his impressionist period (1892–1894), Mann's development would not have taken the shape it did. And without committing himself to solving concrete social problems, as he did in *Das Zwanzigste Jahrhundert,* it is possible that Mann's vague, untested, and essentially uninformed political opinions would have been absolutized into what Fritz Stern has called *Vulgäridealismus.*[35] If this had happened, he would have continued his idealistic criticism of modernity, materialism, and mass society, but he would not have felt obliged to confront these issues directly. Mann might have remained a "vulgar idealist," choosing to hide behind abstractions rather than to try seriously to change things, had he not become editor of *Das Zwanzigste Jahrhundert.* His position on the journal compelled him to become an engaged publicist, and as a result he was drawn into the maelstrom of the social and political currents of his age. Previously, he had viewed most contemporary problems from a distance and replied to them with the stock answers of an impressionist writer; now, as a critic responsible for commenting intelligently on the social scene, he could no longer afford the luxury of being *au dessus de la mêlée.* By placing himself in the journalistic arena Mann forced himself to work out a consistent position on topics he had not thought much about before. As a result of doing this, he presented the image of a stereotypical rightist thinker. But underneath his formal neo-conservatism there were significant traces, even though undeveloped, of a basically liberal philosophy. During the years after he left the journal, Mann would gradually come to recognize these liberal tendencies within his own thought and do what he could to bring them out into the open.

What were these traces of liberalism embedded within Mann's right-wing politics? Several could be mentioned but the most important are the following.

First, as has already been pointed out, Mann placed a strong emphasis on the old-fashioned burgher as the basis of a healthy society. Coincidentally, this was the same emphasis one could find in some aspects of classical German liberalism. Where the Junkers stressed the importance of a paternalistic nobility, and the extreme Right stressed the mystical qualities of the *Volk,* the traditional German liberal tended to view the old *Bürgertum* as the core of a sound social system.

Second, Mann seemed to argue that the values of the traditional middle class were superior to those of other classes and for this

reason ought to become the values guiding the whole of society.
What Mann had in mind were the increasingly antiquated qualities of
piety, civic responsibility, local autonomy, personal moderation,
social conscience, and a respect for traditional rights and privileges—
precisely those qualities which his father embodied. Some years
earlier, in his "Fantasien," Mann had made no distinction between a
bürgerlich and a bourgeois society, since both were to be equally
shunned. By 1896, however, Mann portrayed the difference between
the two as absolute. Bourgeois society (along with its hybrid liberalism
which espoused the "free play of forces") was unqualifiably bad,
while traditional middle-class society (with its "responsible" liberalism
and its rejection of cutthroat *laissez-faire* economics) was unqualifiably
good.[36] So by a curious turn of events, Mann came to embrace the
world his father had represented, a world which he had previously
rejected. It should be recalled that Mann became a writer in the first
place because he tended to identify with his mother's artistic sensibilities over his father's *Ethik*. But now that he was called upon to
make social and political judgments, the *artiste* in him had nothing
to contribute. In response, Mann fell back upon the ethos of his father
and began to defend exactly those qualities which, in his aesthetic
period, he had severely criticized: namely, rectitude, discipline, civic-
mindedness. By now Mann no longer looked upon these qualities as
stuffy virtues to be rebelled against. Instead, he considered them the
indispensable ingredients of a healthy social system. The tradition-
minded German liberal would have agreed; inadvertently, Mann was
expounding an essentially liberal idea in conservative guise.

Third, in his journal articles Mann placed great weight on morality
as a key concept in political judgment. This, too, represented a liberal
tendency, even if Mann was not fully aware of it. Classical German
liberalism always had a heavy streak of moralism in it, and this
became especially pronounced around 1900 under the influence of
the neo-Kantian revival. Mann's work in *Das Zwanzigste Jahrhundert*
continually stressed the need for "moral progress" as opposed to the
emphasis on material progress in *Vulgärliberalismus*. Moreover, he
relentlessly argued that society had to be confronted not simply as an
empirical reality but as a moral order.[37] While this kind of argument
could exist outside a liberal framework, it had nevertheless come to
be identified with a typically liberal mode of reasoning. Nowhere
was this reliance on moral categories more evident than in Mann's
own thinking after he had begun moving towards a basically ethical-
liberal point of view.

Finally, Mann's notion of the role that "critical intelligence" can play in society also carried essentially liberal connotations. In the pages of *Das Zwanzigste Jahrhundert,* Mann began to suggest that the concerned writer should abandon the thoroughly impressionist view that art ought to be purposeless. Instead, the literary intellectual should strive to develop a "social conscience" and place himself "in the service of ideas."[38] Mann now inferred that critical engagement, not artistic withdrawal, was the most authentic mode of relating to the world. If an entire epoch is sick, then everyone who mindlessly participates in it is also sick. But the possibility exists that the intellectual can extract himself from the age and critically react back upon it; in the words of Nietzsche (who, as will be seen shortly, had a great impact on Mann in the 1890s), he can cut "vivesectionally into the very virtues of the time" and reveal the "hypocrisy, comfortableness, . . . [and] lies" which pass for virtues in a bourgeois epoch.[39] If it turns out that a writer does successfully lift himself above a bad reality, the way opens up for him to see the world as it is and begin to change it.

Though Mann did not yet make use of the antinomies *Geist* (spirit) versus *Macht* (power), he did set up an intrinsic dualism between the spiritual intellect and the forces which keep the world sick and enchained.[40] Later, in his phase as a liberal democrat, Mann would make this dualism the main rationale of his opposition to Wilhelmian Germany. Power, as he would eventually come to view it, made the world base, but spirit was the means by which everything could be set right again.

It must be re-emphasized that Mann was in no sense a "liberal" in 1895–1896, even though there were liberal elements in his thought. After he left the journal, however, he began to have serious doubts about the validity of his conservative world-view. In the process of rethinking and re-evaluating his opinions, his conservative principles began to dissolve or lose their coherence. When this occurred, many of the liberal tendencies which had once been muted or suppressed began to come more freely to the surface. The result was that a "progressive" content gradually broke through a reactionary form, and in time Mann came to view himself as a liberal democratic writer instead of a neo-conservative one. Of course this did not happen overnight. It took several years for Mann to move from one perspective to another, and this very complex interlude, which is the subject of the next chapter, might best be described as his transitional period.

Footnotes
Chapter 4

1. Heinrich Mann, "Tilli," novella written December 17–21, 1891, Berlin; in Heinrich-Mann-Archiv, no. 183/184. Mann's phrase is "Gesundwerden aus eigener Kraft."

2. When Mann wrote in *In einer Familie* (p. 12) that "patrician families [are] like princely houses, so exalted [are] they above the day-to-day social changes and so firmly entrenched in the noble traditions of their houses," he was arguing (as W. H. Riehl and others had done before him) for the family as a bulwark of value and social continuity in the midst of unwelcomed social change. On this see Herbert Marcuse, "Autorität und Familie in der deutschen Soziologie bis 1933," in *Studien über Autorität und Familie,* ed. Max Horkheimer (Paris, 1936), pp. 437–52; and René König, "Family and Authority," *The Sociological Review* (1957), V:107–27.

3. Fritz Stern has documented the right-wing tendencies within aesthetic criticism, but others like Ernst Bloch and Georg Lukács have pointed out the revolutionary potential implicit in an aesthetic critique of the world.

4. Between "Das Wunderbare" (written in November, 1894) and "Das gestohlene Dokument" (written in September, 1896) there is no record that Mann wrote any novellas. Nor did he begin writing another novel until 1898. During the years 1895–1896, Mann could more accurately be described as a *Publizist* than a *Schriftsteller.*

5. See David Gross, "Heinrich Mann and the Politics of Reaction," *Journal of Contemporary History* (1973), VIII, no. 1: 125–45. The remainder of this section is an abbreviated version of this article.

6. His role as editor extended from April, 1895, to March, 1896, but he continued working with the journal until December, 1896. It is not known why Mann accepted the editorship. Possibly he became acquainted with Erwin Bauer when he lived in Dresden in the early 1890s, and it is conceivable that Bauer may have subsequently asked Mann to take over as editor. See André Banuls, *Heinrich Mann* (Stuttgart, 1970), p. 38.

7. See Fritz Schlawe, *Literarische Zeitschriften 1885–1910* (Stuttgart, 1961), p. 63.

8. Heinrich Mann, "Reaction," *Das Zwanzigste Jahrhundert,* V, Halbband 2, p. 4. (hereafter *DZJ*).

9. *Ibid.*, p. 8.

10. "To be international," as Mann put it, "is the same thing as being a traitor." Heinrich Mann, "Jüdischen Glaubens," *DZJ*, V, Halbband 2, p. 461.

11. Heinrich Mann, "Das Reichstags-Wahlrecht," *DZJ*, V, Halbband 2, p. 472.

12. *Ibid.*, p. 474.

13. Heinrich Mann, "Degeneration," *DZJ*, V, Halbband 2, pp. 185–88; "Bei den Deutschen," *DZJ*, V, Halbband 2, pp. 575–83; and "Kriegs-und Friedensmoral II," *DZJ*, VI, Halbband 1, p. 19.

14. Heinrich Mann, "Das Reichstags-Wahlrecht," *DZJ*, V, Halbband 2, pp. 469–73.

15. Heinrich Mann, "Zum Verständnisse Nietzsches," *DZJ*, VI, Halbband 2, p. 245.

16. Heinrich Mann, "Weltstadt und Grossstädte," *DZJ*, VI, Halbband 1, pp. 204ff.

17. Mann saw only the negative, destructive aspects of modern capitalism, and failed (as Marx did not) to grasp its inherently "progressive" qualities. See Manfred Hahn, "Heinrich Manns Beiträge in der Zeitschrift 'Das Zwanzigste Jahrhundert'," *Weimarer Beiträge*, (1967), XIII, no. 6:1015.

18. Heinrich Mann, "Jüdischen Glaubens," *DZJ*, V, Halbband 2, pp. 456–63.

19. *Ibid.*, p. 461.

20. *Ibid.*, pp. 462–63.

21. Heinrich Mann, "Kriegs-und Friedensmoral I," *DZJ*, V, Halbband 2, p. 595.

22. *Ibid.*, pp. 593–95. This argument is expanded in a sequel, where Mann suggests that Europe may have to prepare for a new "Battle of Lepanto" against the East. See "Kriegs-und Friedensmoral II," *DZJ*, VI, Halbband 1, pp. 17–26.

23. Heinrich Mann, "Kriegs-und Friedensmoral II," *op. cit.*, pp. 21–25.

24. Cf. Mann's new emphasis on "religious sanctification" (in "Reaction," *DZJ*, V, Halbband 2, p. 7) with his earlier (1889) critique of the "Sunday public" (in "Fantasien über meine Vaterstadt L.," *Heinrich Mann 1871–1950: Werk und Leben*, pp. 13–14).

25. Heinrich Mann, "Hauptmanns Weber," *DZJ*, V, Halbband 2, p. 92.

26. Heinrich Mann, "Reaction," *DZJ*, V, Halbband 2, p. 7.

27. *Ibid.,* p. 7.

28. For a while Mann was interested in a *ständisch,* or corporate, view of society where the four great segments of the population (agriculture, industry, trade and commerce, and the intelligentsia) would mutually interrelate with one another. Manfred Hahn has suggested in his "Das Werk Heinrich Manns" (p. 136) that Mann borrowed this notion from Otto Henne am Rhyn, whose *Aria, Das Reich des ewigen Friedens im zwanzigsten Jahrhundert* (1895) was published at the time. Rhyn's book presented a scheme for a society based on ranks and corporations.

29. Mann did not begin to show any confidence in the "masses" (that is, ordinary people) until his novel *Die kleine Stadt* (1909).

30. See Heinrich Mann, "Jüdischen Glaubens," *DZJ,* V, Halbband 2, pp. 455–62.

31. Technically, there is a difference between the *Bürgertum* and the *Mittelstand* which Mann often overlooked. See Emil Grünberg, *Der Mittelstand in der kapitalistischen Gesellschaft: Eine ökonomische und soziologische Untersuchung* (Leipzig, 1932); Herman Lebovics, *Social Conservatism and the Middle Class in Germany, 1914–1933* (Princeton, 1969); and Heinrich Winkler, "Der rückversicherte Mittelstand," *Zur Soziologischen Theorie und Analyse des 19. Jahrhunderts,* ed. W. Rüegg and O. Neuloh (Göttingen, 1971), pp. 163–79.

32. For an excellent discussion of Mann's view of the *Mittelstand* see Manfred Hahn, "Heinrich Manns Beiträge in der Zeitschrift 'Das Zwanzigste Jahrhundert'," *Weimarer Beiträge,* XIII, no. 6:998–1000.

33. Heinrich Mann, "Weltstadt und Grossstädte," *DZJ,* VI, Halbband 1, p. 204.

34. Eugen Diederichs, cited in Klemens von Klemperer, *Germany's New Conservatism,* p. 100.

35. Fritz Stern, *The Failure of Illiberalism* (New York, 1972), pp. 17–19.

36. See Heinrich Mann, "Kriegs-und Friedensmoral II," *DZJ,* VI, Halbband 1, p. 21; and "Jüdischen Glaubens," *DZJ,* V, Halbband 2, p. 460.

37. Heinrich Mann, "Kriegs-und Friedensmoral I," *DZJ,* V, Halbband 2, pp. 590ff.; and Manfred Hahn, "Heinrich Manns Beiträge," *Weimarer Beiträge,* XIII, no. 6: 1007–08.

38. Heinrich Mann, cited in Manfred Hahn, "Heinrich Manns Beiträge," *op. cit.,* pp. 1002, 1012.

39. Friedrich Nietzsche, *Beyond Good and Evil,* trans. Walter Kaufmann (New York, 1966), p. 137.

40. See Manfred Hahn, "Heinrich Manns Beiträge," *Weimarer Beiträge,* XIII, no. 6:1010–11.

Part II

THE WRITER AS EDUCATOR

Chapter 5

Transition

The honest man must be a perpetual renegade; the life of the honest man must be a perpetual infidelity.

Charles Péguy

Rebelling Backwards—and Forwards

The reactionary cultural politics which Mann articulated in *Das Zwanzigste Jahrhundert* reflected the feelings of a certain type of middle-class intellectual: one who felt ensnared in a network of new forces which he could neither comprehend nor control. Some of these intellectuals resolved the dilemma by opting out (into aestheticism or "vulgar idealism"); others, often after an initial period of retreat, chose to face it. Mann's choice during the mid-1890s was the latter. In his articles for the journal he tried to turn his impressionist politics into something more tough-minded, and the result was right-wing reaction. This tendency for artistic elitism to slide into some form of conservatism was fairly common among those who found themselves in Mann's position. So long as they could remain aloof, their aestheticism made no great political demands upon them; but as soon as they were compelled to deal with specific social problems, their inclination was to fall back upon a politics of reaction. In Mann's case, his position as the son of an old *bürgerlich* family made it difficult for him to look ahead with any enthusiasm. The present, too, seemed an *Irrweg*, a disastrous wrong turn in history. The only hope was to try to conserve the past and retain the best of what had already been achieved. In this way Mann became a neo-conservative author.

The predicament which he faced in the nineties has perhaps been captured best by the psychotherapist Wilhelm Reich. In discussing those who, like Mann and his contemporaries, had "rebellious feelings" toward existing reality, Reich asserted that no individual is

77

a "clear-cut revolutionary" or a "clear-cut conservative." On the contrary, each "bears a contradiction within himself" between what his social situation would lead him to believe, and the convictions he acquires from the ideological superstructure. Every individual's psychic make-up derives from a combination of these two ingredients. Even if one is dominant, the other is still present.[1]

When this conception is applied to Mann, it becomes evident that his particular social condition induced him to rebel backwards. But at the same time, and paradoxically, he could not help affirming certain liberal values which did not fit the mold of pure reaction. He seemed to have acquired these from a re-examination of what his father represented and from an idealized picture of the German *Mittelstand*. Hence, in the 1890s, his world-view was a mixture of conservative and forward-looking tendencies which he tried, unsuccessfully, to integrate. When the tension became too great, this superficial harmony broke down and Mann was forced to re-think everything. In doing so he began to rebel forwards rather than backwards, and in the process laid the groundwork for a liberal-democratic *Weltanschauung*.

"Fruitful Incongruities"

This period of re-evaluation (which I am calling Mann's transitional period) lasted for nearly a decade. It began in late 1896 or early 1897, when Mann severed his ties with *Das Zwanzigste Jahrhundert* and became an independent writer once again. It ended around 1906–1907, with Mann's decisive (and by then irrevocable) commitment to liberal democracy. The intervening years were ones of confusion, inconsistency, false starts and stops. It is virtually impossible to trace Mann's evolution as a writer during this span of time, since his thought did not evolve in a steady manner but zig-zagged in an elusive way. On the one hand he could write a novella like "Das gestohlene Dokument" ("The Stolen Document," September, 1896) which seemed to be critical of existing society, and particularly of the *Untertan*-types which the society engendered; on the other, he could write a story like "Doktor Biebers Versuchung" ("Doctor Bieber's Temptation," February, 1898) which appeared to be imbued with all the aesthetic attitudes Mann was supposedly rejecting.[2] Similarly, in a letter to *Die Zukunft* in 1904, he could present himself as a concerned, democratic-minded intellectual who was able to make comparative judgments on French and German socialism; yet in the same year, in the *Albert Langens Verlagskatalog,* Mann conveyed the opposite impression by depicting himself as a neur-asthenic artist who, because of his unusual geneology (a "product of two races"), was forced to remain detached, isolated, and committed to nothing but his art.[3]

In these and other cases, it is extremely hard to pin Mann down. Nonetheless, it cannot be said that this was a form of game-playing, but rather a sincere struggle to determine exactly what his convictions were and what he, as a writer, had to do in order to live up to them. It would have been much easier not only on Mann but also on his readers (many of whom were no doubt confused by his apparently chameleon-like changes) if he had known precisely what it was he stood for, and then had brought his art into correlation with his ideas. Had this been the only issue, it would have been simply a matter of living up to one's principles—of achieving a certain con-sistency between form and content. But Mann's basic problem was that he had not yet decided what his principles were. Until he was clear about them he could not be clear about anything, including his style and method or even his role as a writer. By 1907 Mann had finally determined what he stood for and what he wanted to accom- plish. From that point on the reading public knew what Mann repre-sented, and could accept or reject his *oeuvres* on that basis. But until then there seemed to be nothing but incongruities in Mann's work: fruitful ones as it turned out, but incongruities nonetheless.

Mann's development as a writer is typical, most literary biographies notwithstanding. A serious author almost never evolves from one point to another in a logical, apodictic way. Neither does his con-ception of himself or his relation to the surrounding *Ideenwelt* grow in a natural, undisturbed fashion; rather, real development is a dialectical, not a linear, process. The creative individual always undergoes a period in which he takes in and tries to cope with more material than he can handle. His mind becomes a battleground of conflicting, and even antithetical, ideas which struggle to achieve a larger unity. Contrasts and unreconciled elements exist side by side in what Nietzsche called "an enormous multiplicity which is never-theless the opposite of chaos."[4] To an onlooker this might seem to be a period of setback, but it is in fact a period of creative fermen-tation. On the surface, the individual in such a condition may appear to be overwhelmed and confused, but he is really in a state of preparatory uneasiness which makes possible a great leap forward. With Mann, the years 1897–1906 were such a period of dialectical tension, of "carry[ing] everything heavy," to quote Nietzsche once again. However, as a result Mann was eventually able to re-think and re-integrate these conflicting elements into a larger, more coherent, and more critical synthesis. Had this intervening stage of doubt and re-evaluation not occurred it is questionable whether he could ever have arrived at a liberal-democratic viewpoint. To connect neo-conservatism and radical republicanism there had to be a transformative interlude—an interlude of intense soul-searching and *approfondissement* out of which a new cast of mind could eventually emerge.

Despite the general ambivalence of this period in Mann's life, several developments took place which were important for his later career as an engaged *littérateur*. A few of the more significant ones need to be mentioned here.

First, Mann rejected the neo-conservative ideas of *Das Zwanzigste Jahrhundert* without knowing, at least at first, exactly what it was he was moving towards. Even the subcutaneous liberal ideas concealed beneath his neo-conservatism were not decisively affirmed until around 1906–1907. During and after the years 1906–1907 Mann never mentioned, either publicly or in his personal letters, the work he did for *Das Zwanzigste Jahrhundert.* Moreover, he refused to allow any of it to be reprinted in his collected works. Many of his friends and acquaintances in later years were not aware that Mann, the exemplary liberal, had edited a reactionary journal defending anti-Semitism and justifying war.[5] Like Thomas Mann's *Betrachtungen eines Unpolitischen* (1918), Heinrich's own work for the journal increasingly seemed to him like the "last great rear-guard action of the romantic middle class mentality in the face of advancing 'modernity'."[6] This stance towards the contemporary world no longer seemed satisfactory to him. In fact, the first novella Mann wrote after leaving the journal appears to be an attack on many of the things he passionately defended a few months earlier.[7]

Also significant was the fact that Mann held onto his anti-bourgeois attitudes throughout this transitional period, and continued to oppose the new forces of capitalism which were achieving hegemony around 1900. In some socially-critical novels, like *Im Schlaraffenland (In the Land of Cockaigne,* 1900), it is clear who the bourgeoisie were. They were the "fine people" represented by the financier James L. Türkheimer and his friends, i.e., the new wealth, the parvenu middle class.[8] In other works, however, Mann was not so precise. Occasionally he took liberties with the word "bourgeois" and even went so far as to use it in a non-class sense. In one place, for example, Mann cited favorably Flaubert's statement, "I call bourgeois those who think basely," and in another he wrote: "Bourgeois, this is how I refer to those whose feelings are loathsome and who express these loathsome feelings deceitfully."[9] Here the word became more an aesthetic than a class term. Though Mann remained consistently anti-bourgeois during this time, his anger was sometimes directed against a psychological state of mind instead of a specific social group. This was nevertheless only a temporary blurring of distinctions. After 1906 Mann once again treated the bourgeoisie as a definite socio-economic class and not just as a people whose feelings were "loathsome."

A third significant observation is that Mann persisted in his opposition to the status quo during the transitional years, but now on partly different grounds than in *Das Zwanzigste Jahrhundert*. After leaving the journal, the rationale for his critique began to center on the fact that existing society either prevented genuine individuality from developing, or perpetuated a system of unjust social relations. The first of these arguments seems to have stemmed from his impressionist period, while the second can be more accurately tied to the old middle-class viewpoint which Mann portrayed so favorably in *Das Zwanzigste Jahrhundert*.

Around 1900, Mann held up the "full personality"—the complete, harmonious individual—as a supreme ideal.[10] But at the same time he was convinced that German society as it then existed was not fostering this ideal; in fact, it seemed to be hindering the "full personality" in every way possible. As a result, wholeness appeared to be a quality which was difficult, if not impossible, to achieve in contemporary Germany. Instead, the tight, pinched personality—the so-called "good subject" whom Mann had already pictured in "Das gestohlene Dokument" (1896) and "Ein Verbrechen" (1897)—was seen as the rule rather than the exception.[11] Society, through its emphasis on obedience and submission, created the prototype of the fearful, other-directed individual instead of the autonomous personality. Since every society ought to be held responsible for the human wreckage it produces, Mann inferred that Wilhelmian Germany

should also be called to account for the way it prevented the emergence of full, self-contained individuals. In nearly all his work during
this time, Mann demonstrated that those who tried to be total human
beings were dashed on the rocks of the social system. (The character
who came closest to being an autonomous personality was not a man
but a woman: the Duchess of Assy in *Die Göttinnen* [*The Godesses*,
1903]. Even in this case, the setting was not contemporary Germany
but an imaginary kingdon in Dalmatia.)

The other rationale for Mann's critique, and admittedly one not as
yet very well-developed, was that modern German society was
basically unjust. The inference here was that wherever injustice exists
to any significant degree, both it and the social order which harbors
it have to be opposed. One can get indications of this in *Die Göttinnen*,
especially in the figure of San Bacco but also, at times, in the Duchess
of Assy herself.[12] An essay on Flaubert in 1905 echoes this theme,
and further hints appear the following year in a piece entitled "Der
Fall Murri" ("The Murri Case").[13] Later, this idea of opposing
obstacles to justice would become even more important as an instrument of social criticism.

These two major reasons which Mann offered for opposing the
established order—because it prevented the fullness of individuality
and because it appeared to be essentially unjust—were of course only
negative, but they were the best Mann could come up with during
the years 1897-1906. Even his best works like *Im Schlaraffenland* or
Professor Unrat (1905) registered only a negative protest against
existing conditions, not a positive affirmation of anything.[14] After
1907, and more particularly after 1910 (by which time Mann knew
what kind of society he did want), he began to oppose the social order
for positive reasons.

The fourth and last of Mann's tendencies during this period was to
turn gradually toward moral rather than aesthetic categories of
criticism. This is not to say that he by any means abandoned the use
of aesthetics, either during this pivotal decade or later. Throughout
his work words like "unfein," "grotesk," "unsauber," or phrases
like "ohne Reiz" or "unfeine Beschäftigungen" were utilized as
hostile terms, intended to reflect a society which standardized (or
institutionalized) ugliness.[15] Nevertheless, as time went on such words
were used with diminishing effectiveness until Mann eventually came
to depend on ethical categories for his most convincing arguments.
Aesthetic judgments were often retained, but his language and force

of argumentation became increasingly moralistic. Thus, the ground was unwittingly laid for Mann's conversion to liberal democracy. In light of this progression, Harry Pross's remark that "aesthetic, not political, insights turned [Heinrich Mann] into a Jacobin" is not entirely correct.[16] Pross failed to recognize Mann's intermediary moralism and his re-affirmation of the same *bürgerlich* ethical ideals which he had earlier dismissed when he considered himself a pure *artiste*. Such a transformation probably needed to take place before Mann could turn into the kind of liberal he became by 1910. Thus it seems more correct to say that the aesthete became a moralist, and the moralist eventually a Jacobin.

These, then, are some of the more important generalizations one can make about the transitional stage of Mann's development. In spite of a great deal of intellectual fluctuation, it appears that Mann began this period by doubting the tenets of his previous neo-conservatism, and concluded it by having established a basic predisposition toward liberal democracy. By late 1907 Mann could be unambiguous about his political convictions. "I am no aesthete," he wrote his friend Maximilian Brantl. "What makes me an exception in present-day Germany is my radicalism; I am radical in thoughts, feelings, and formulas."[17]

To be more specific about how this transformation occurred, it is useful to focus on two concrete examples. One is the way Mann purged himself of the aesthetic mode of relating to the world, and the other is the way he decisively overcame the influence of Nietzsche. In both cases, Mann's path towards democracy was essentially a negative one; he weeded out and rejected ideas which no longer seemed desirable, but he was slow to fill the vacuum he had created with positive democratic principles.

The Abyss of Aestheticism

Between 1897 and 1906, Mann turned his back on aestheticism as a life-style far more completely than he did in *Das Zwanzigste Jahrhundert*. This is clear from many of the novels and short stories dating from these years, some of which had a therapeutic value for Mann in that they permitted him to overcome through his characters certain limitations in his earlier outlook. In his *Die Göttinnen* trilogy, for example, he created an aesthetic protagonist (Violante, the

Duchess of Assy) who tries to live apart from society as a voluptuary and devotee of beauty. Portrayed as an epicurian pleasure-seeker who feels no responsibility for others, Violante lives only for the sensations of the moment. In this respect, her personal credo is close to that of Walter Pater's, who wrote that the goal of life is to "give the highest quality to [our] moments as they pass" and to get "as many pulsations as possible into [our] given [interval of] time."[18]

Despite all the resources at her command, Violante's attempt to live an amoral aesthetic life is a colossal failure. Her project leads at first to disappointment, then to boredom, and finally to a frenzied pursuit of pleasure for its own sake. She and her friends eventually fall into meaningless patterns of sensuality and, in the end, despair. Significantly, she is left without children, which was Mann's way of saying that her kind of life had literally come to an end. To Mann, aestheticism now seemed both unfeasible and unheroic, since something more socially responsible was needed to make life worthwhile. The aesthetic stance was judged unsatisfactory because it all too quickly degenerated into dilettantism. At one time, in the early 1890s, when he felt that the goal of life was to acquire style, this would have made little difference. But now, as Mann began to reconsider his own middle-class heritage and to reappraise the qualities of character and ethical behavior he found there, he came to view the life of the detached artist as something not only questionable but fundamentally dangerous if carried to an extreme. For these reasons the figure of Violante in *Die Göttinnen* in no sense represents an ideal, as Mann tried to make clear at the time to a readership that wanted to interpret things differently.[19] Through her, he both criticized and parodied the aesthetic excesses of the *fin-de-siècle* which he was leaving behind. Though many of his readers badly misunderstood him on this point, the thrust of his novel was that aestheticism is untenable and undesirable as a means of facing the realities of modern life.[20]

This message comes across even more forcefully in "Pippo Spano" (1903), the only noteworthy novella Mann wrote during his transitional period.[21] In this work Mann vicariously pushed the aesthetic posture as far as it could go, and then rejected it. Mario Malvolto, who lives only for his art, is incapable of human love, even when it is offered to him by the beautiful Gemma Cantoggi. As a dramatist and poet, he thinks only of how this relationship can advance his art.

Hence he is incapable of feeling tenderness or love since his emotions always become intellectualized. Malvolto's fault is that of the typical aesthete for whom "the whole world . . . is only raw material for a phrase." To the degree that he attempts to seek meaning by verbalizing rather than experiencing an impression, he finds that he is unable to give himself unreflectively to the moment; he even laments the fact that time spent in love-making has already cost him half a novel. In the end, the aesthetic pose costs Malvolto more than a novel: it costs him the genuine experience of life itself. By treating every sensation as merely an impression, he eventually loses the ability to distinguish qualities of impressions, as for example between the lovely Gemma and her facsimile in a painting. To him, both are only sensory data, and consequently he is unable to relate to the flesh-and-blood contessina in any special way, though it is obvious that she is in love with him. Malvolto is condemned for his failure to be human. His aestheticism has destroyed him.

In "Pippo Spano," Mann portrayed some of his own tendencies of the 1890s. Just as Goethe wrote *The Sorrows of the Young Werther* to crystallize a period of his life in order to transcend it, Mann wrote "Pippo Spano" to objectify and then cancel out his own aesthetic proclivities. With this novella he virtually abandoned his preoccupation with aestheticism and "turned to artistic endeavors . . . of political and sociological import."[22]

If in *Die Göttinnen* Mann rejected aestheticism because it led to the frenetic pursuit of pleasure, in "Pippo Spano" he rejected it because it was perversely self-centered and prevented any genuine love of others. This emphasis on love was still largely undeveloped (as it had been when it appeared in his early work of the 1890s); but in a few years it was to become the source of his confidence in democracy. By a simple equation Mann concluded that wherever love prospered, democracy and community were real possibilities, but wherever aestheticism was the rule there could only be egoism, hatred, and tyranny.[23] The triumph of love and democracy, he began to feel, had to coincide with the fall of aestheticism and social domination. This was an important insight which Mann went on to elaborate in various ways before the First World War. More will be said about the political implications of these ideas later. For the time being it is enough to point out that during his transitional years Mann came to regard aestheticism as a symptom of decadence. To him, it seemed to be the last gasp of basically "exhausted stock."[24]

Overcoming Nietzsche

Before Mann the moral democrat could emerge, not only aestheticism but also the influence of Nietzsche had to be overcome.

Mann first read Nietzsche in the early 1890s and, like many in his generation, misunderstood him. It was the misunderstood Nietzsche whom he criticized and turned away from during the years 1897–1906. It should be noted that when Mann initially encountered Nietzsche he was still a disciple of Bourget, and thus tended to see the German philosopher through the lenses of Bourget's neo-conservatism.[25] This meant that Mann's relationship to Nietzsche was indirect, since Mann's primary allegiance was to the philosphy of Bourget. On the one hand, Mann respected Nietzsche for his "aristocratic radicalism" since it was, after all, compatible with Bourget's elitism; but on the other, he sometimes looked upon Nietzsche as one of the "great decadents" of the era. While Mann occasionally found himself in agreement with Nietzsche about what was wrong with the age, he could not always agree with him about what should be done about it. At this stage Mann still hoped for social renewal through the family, which was something Nietzsche had no interest in promoting.

This ambiguous relationship to Nietzsche continued through the essays in *Das Zwanzigste Jahrhundert*. Here Mann increasingly drew Nietzsche into his own neo-conservative framework and made the philosopher both a "shifting and elusive" patriot and a symbol of German destiny.[26] When, in the years after 1897, Mann turned away from the politics of reaction, he also abandoned his reactionary interpretation of Nietzsche. Even so, continuing the ambivalence still longer, he held onto a few of Nietzsche's ideas for the leverage they gave him in criticizing existing society. Mann revealed Nietzsche's influence over him when he attacked Wilhelmian Germany for its tendency to produce not autonomous personalities but only *Untertanen* for whom he, like Nietzsche, had nothing but contempt. When Mann painted a scathing picture of the government bureaucrat Glumkow in "Das gestohlene Dokument" ("I have always waited for the nod from above," "I have never expressed an opinion I have not first heard in higher places"), he may have had in mind Nietzsche's own relentless critique of the German civil servant.[27]

As time passed, Mann began looking upon French republican ideas more favorably, and the few remaining Nietzschean concepts he had borrowed were quietly discarded. French thought offered Mann a more effective fulcrum for criticizing the Wilhelmian era than Nietzsche could provide. In place of the individual as a critical reference point, Mann gradually began using two other reference points which could not be found in Nietzsche's philosphy and which were, in the long run, more devastating instruments of criticism. One was the notion that the human ideal is not a well-rounded individual (the *Übermensch*), as Nietzsche believed, but a well-rounded, healthy, and vibrant *people*. The other was the notion that society ought to be based on moral laws and humanitarian principles, not on the will-to-power or the struggle of each against all. As Mann perceived it, Nietzsche's thought was compatible with, rather than antithetical to, the stress on power and domination which he found in pre-war Germany. For this reason, Nietzsche seemed unable to provide the cutting edge for attacking society at its weakest point. The ideals of ethical democracy appeared, by contrast, to strike at the very heart of society since they revealed the absences and weak foundations upon which the Wilhelmian order was built. In short, Nietzsche, as an anti-democrat and anti-moralist, was part and parcel of the contemporary problem and therefore could not be helpful in working out a long-term solution. Only those ideas which were at bottom antagonistic to the status quo could be fully effective in revealing its shortcomings. Hence democratic radicalism, not aristocratic radicalism, was what Mann was moving towards.

On the whole, between 1897 and 1906 Mann concluded that Nietzsche's thought was not only dangerous, but also inferior to the philosophy of liberal humanism. Furthermore, he inferred that when lesser men try to implement Nietzschean principles they always misinterpret them. In this way, the will-to-power over oneself degenerates into the will to exercise power over others, and the concept of "beyond good and evil" turns into licence or licentiousness. Mann's work during this decade is filled with characters who think they are *Herrenmenschen* but who are really cowards or criminals. Generally, he drew two conclusions about these "little supermen"; first, that their Nietzscheanism leads to tyranny or brutality, and second, that it is the product of physical or moral weakness.

In regard to the first conclusion, there are several instances in Mann's fiction where Nietzschean values are used to justify corrupt power. Immanuel Raat, the "tyrant of the school" in *Professor*

Unrat, thinks he is transvaluing values, but is actually driven by the same resentment that Nietzsche attributed to the masses; his whole life is spent attempting to catch and destroy others before they can destroy him. Similarly in *Im Schlaraffenland,* the financier James L. Türkheimer prides himself on being an amoral "Renaissance man"; in truth he is a petty tyrant and exploiter who hides his true features behind an image of dynamic individualism. This same message was conveyed in a number of Mann's shorter pieces as well.

The second conclusion—that Nietzscheanism is the recourse of weak or depraved types—was also a frequent thème in Mann's work. The artist Mario Malvolto in "Pippo Spano" is a decadent aesthete but he likens himself to the great Spano, a Renaissance *condottiere* and ruthless man of action. In reality there is no comparison. If Pippo Spano was a Nietzschean adventurer who lived dangerously, Malvolto is a pathetic weakling, afraid of involvement, repulsed by violent action, and enervated by artistic foppery. When, toward the end of the novella, he arranges to commit suicide with Gemma, he has her go first only to find that he is too cowardly to follow. By acting on pseudo-Nietzschean convictions Malvolto becomes responsible for the death of an innocent girl. This same connection between weakness and the Nietzschean "master morality" was made in some of Mann's novels. Claude Marehn in *Die Jagd nach Liebe (The Pursuit of Love,* 1903) is a disciple of Nietzsche, but he is shown to be a self-indulgent epigoni without any possibility of greatness. His friend, the actress Uta Ende, is not much different. She practices the Nietzschean principle of hardness towards oneself but only because she is an empty person, drained of emotion and incapable of loving others.[28] In *Die Göttinnen* and *Zwischen den Rassen (Between the Races,* 1907), a similar message is conveyed. Here, too, weakness masks itself as Nietzschean virtue.

Later on, in the 1940s, Mann developed this theme still further. He began to suggest that when Nietzscheanism exists side by side with weakness or aestheticism, the conditions are always ripe for fascism. Though he could not have labelled them such at the time, many of the figures he created during his transitional period were in fact proto-fascist types (e.g., Claude Marehn in *Die Jagd nach Liebe,* and Count Pardi in *Zwischen den Rassen).* Even Immanuel Raat and Mario Malvolto, because of their moral flacidity and fascination with raw power, would probably have been willing recruits for a right-wing, anti-democratic movement. In *Ein Zeitalter wird besichtigt (An*

Age is Surveyed, 1945) Mann went so far as to theorize that fascism
was *au fond* the result of unsublimated erotic instincts. Weaklings
and aesthetes became fascists mainly because the ideology of power
satisfied frustrations they could not overcome on a personal level.
Mann may have had D'Annunzio in mind when he wrote: "I discovered and portrayed [the fascist type] even before he became aware
of himself or sought political power. His fascism did not reside in
his view of the world. . . . It lay in the lust for power in the blood,
a part of the erotic legacy. The same tyrannical blood which great
artists can sublimate into beautiful objects is manifested brutally in
petty fascists" who are too weak to master their impulses.[29] In the
same way Mann felt that any reader who admired or wanted to
imitate Mario Malvolto was probably a fascist at heart.[30]

Mann was certain, by the turn of the century, that Nietzsche's ideas
were incompatible with his own convictions. His conclusion was that
Nietzsche, and all the excesses his name legitimized, had to be
disavowed. When, in his 1910 essay "Geist und Tat" ("Spirit and
Deed"), Mann raised the question of the ultimate consequences of
Nietzsche's thought, he gave an answer that was short and unequivocal.
Nietzscheanism, he wrote, encouraged everything "from tragic
ambition to miserable vanity, from foolish arrogance . . . to the nausea
of nihilism,"[31] Some years later, in his final evaluation of Nietzsche,
Mann had not changed his opinion. He still maintained that Nietzsche's
"work is fearful. . . . It contains chaos, along with the will to set it
loose."[32]

New Models, New Themes

At the same time that he began questioning the assumptions he had
taken for granted earlier, Mann entered a phase of intense literary
experimentation which took him well beyond the boundaries of his
previous work.

Later in life, Mann tried to pin-point the decision which led him to
break with Impressionism and move in new directions. "At age
twenty-five," he recalled, "I said to myself: it is necessary to write
novels of social commentary. German society does not recognize
itself; it is divided into classes which do not admit the existence of
each other, and the ruling class is securely hidden behind the clouds."[33]
Of course Mann exaggerated both the decisiveness of his break with

the past and the clear-sighted way he went about setting new tasks
for himself. Actually, he moved slowly toward a new conception of
authorship, and even then he continually intermixed old ideas with
new literary forms and methods.

One of the major interests Mann developed around 1900 had to do
with the *Zeitroman,* or the novel of contemporary social criticism. A
crucial factor propelling him in this direction was the influence of
French literature. In the years after 1897, Mann devoted himself to a
study of several French novelists, preëminent among them Balzac,
Hugo, Maupassant, Zola, and Anatole France.[34] From these he
learned how to broaden his powers of observation and to write novels
wherein large panoramas were coupled with trenchant class analysis.
In this respect, the difference between his first novel *In einer Familie*
and a work like *Im Schlaraffenland* is almost immeasurable. Where
the former is essentially a psychological novel dealing with the close
interaction of four people, the latter is a *roman à moeurs* in the
French tradition, dealing with what Bourget called the *vie extérieure*
rather than the *vie intérieure.*

It is true that as a result of these French models Mann simply
learned how to write better.[35] But there was also a more significant
development. As Mann gradually assimilated the techniques of the
French novel, he also began to take up the ideals of French *civilisation*
and to consider them superior to those of German *Kultur.* This
aspect of Mann's development cannot be underestimated. The more
he acclimated himself to French literature, the more he became
convinced that the ideas it embodied could not be dismissed as
"foreign" (as he did in *Das Zwanzigste Jahrhundert*). Instead, he
began to feel that French rationalistic values were morally, spiritually
and politically more advanced than anything the German tradition
could offer. In essence, Mann increasingly felt that France represented
an enlightened, humanistic, and republican legacy which was missing
in Germany. He began to argue that French ideals ought not to be
condemned but rather transported and implanted on German soil
(again, precisely what he had once argued should not be done). To
be sure, it was not until 1910 and after that these arguments acquired
any degree of sophistication. Nevertheless, as early as 1904 Mann
was making distinctions between the "chauvinism and reaction" he
found in Germany, and the potential for a "great democracy" he saw
in France.[36] In a letter to *Die Zukunft* (1904)—his first political statement since his reactionary journal articles eight years earlier—Mann

strongly protested against an anti-French piece by the essayist Karl Jentsch. "France," Mann wrote, "has not become a superficial civilization, but has inexorably pushed forward, strong in its innermost resolve, its intransigent sense of human rights, its critical literary perspective, and its intellectual scrupulousness. In a way that [Jentsch] cannot understand, France is a state entirely subject to the rule of *Geist*."[37]

The word *Geist* was important here. In Mann's view, France had more "spirit" than Germany because it displayed very little blind reverence or obedience. On the contrary, Mann thought he saw, both in French literature and in the French people, a lively sense of political responsibility bouyed up by strong currents of liberal humanism. For this reason he felt that a political writer with liberal convictions could play an influential role in France by calling attention to the democratic culture which already existed, at least in embryo. In Germany, by comparison, writers had no similar foundations to draw on, and consequently were more inclined to retreat into themselves instead of confronting the realities of power. This is why Mann, in his desire to be an effective rather than an ornamental author, sometimes regretted that he was not writing for a French audience. "My real tragedy," he lamented in 1910, "is that I must write in German. What results are being denied me which might have been attainable in France!"[38]

Given his shift toward French ideals, as well as the growing moral and humanitarian content of his social critique, it is not surprising that Mann was drawn into a prolonged period of artistic experimentation. The old impressionist language and the aloof, interior style no longer seemed adequate. Both were, after all, designed to convey the kind of private, aestheticized message Mann was in the process of leaving behind. This being so, how did he cope with the obvious split between his former impressionist forms and his new liberal material? Put differently, what new modes of expression did Mann devise to make his literary methods more compatible with his changing social and political ideas?

Three improvisations could be mentioned in this regard, all dating from the years 1897–1906. First, Mann began to experiment with the techniques of what Lukács called "critical realism," an approach to writing which few German authors took seriously before the turn of the century.[39] More will be said about this in a later chapter, but for the time being it is enough to point out that Mann's overriding interest began to be what he termed "the observed reality."[40] By this he meant the actual world around him: a world which, as he put it, did not recognize itself and where "the ruling class [was] securely hidden behind the clouds."[41] Increasingly, Mann's goal was to penetrate illusions and expose society for what it was. As a novelist he thought he could do this best by focusing on concrete social reality, not on private moods, impressions, or emotional states as he had done earlier. It should be added, however, that Mann did not want merely to describe the "observed reality" with the photographic exactness of the Naturalists. Instead, he wanted the freedom to stress one thing more than another, to use exaggeration and caricature when he saw fit, and in every instance to approach his material from his own particular point of view. The methods of critical realism allowed him to do this and still capture the totality of social relations. This is why Balzac, who was especially accomplished at portraying "typical people in typical circumstances," meant more to him at the time than Zola, and why even later it was Zola the radical democrat and not Zola the Naturalist, that attracted him most.

Second, Mann began to develop a crisp, abrupt and concise mode of writing far different from the elliptical style of the early 1890s. To be sure, there was still the occasional showy metaphor or flamboyant allusion (more in *Die Göttinnen* than elsewhere), but these tended to diminish with time. During his impressionist stage, his goal had been to achieve an almost tonal quality in his style—to force language to approximate music. After the transitional period his goal was nearly the opposite, i.e., absolute clarity and transparency, a language as close to mathematics as possible. "I always," Mann later wrote, "had to fight in myself the tendencies toward 'German' unclarity and extravagance; for this reason I submitted myself to a predominately logical language and literature, as others . . . [would submit to] mathematics."[42]

Finally, during these transitional years Mann began to explore the possibilities of satire as a method of social criticism. Traces of a satirical style can be found in Mann's earlier work, for instance in "Fantasien," but for the most part these remained dormant throughout the 1890s. However, in novels like *Im Schlaraffenland* and *Professor Unrat* Mann once again used satire as a mode of social commentary. This suited him perfectly since, as a rule, satire is the weapon of those who know what they are against, but are not entirely clear about what they are for. His manner of writing thus permitted him to ridicule his age without having to propose solutions (a difficult enough task for a novel). In time, Heinrich Mann mastered the satirical style to the same extent that his brother Thomas mastered the ironical, but more will be said about this in subsequent pages.

Given all the changes Mann underwent during the decade 1897–1906, it was extremely difficult for his audience to keep abreast of what was happening. To complete the discussion of these pivotal years in his development, it is necessary to look for a moment at the strained relationship that existed between Mann and his reading public.

Mann and His Readership

A writer's rapport with his audience is a crucial factor in his literary success, and yet little attention has been paid to this relationship.[43] In Mann's case, what happened between 1897–1906 was that he severed himself from one public (an aesthetic and neo-conservative one) and tried at the same time to establish contact with another (a liberal middle-class readership). Mann, like any other writer, was aware that authorship means reciprocity. Just as a reading public needs to be able to "place" a writer and have some notion of what his intentions are, so too a writer needs to have a feel for the audience to which he addresses himself. If this reciprocal understanding breaks down—and this sometimes happens when an author, by experimenting with new techniques or messages, loses touch with his established readership—then the problem of the writer's image begins to come to the fore. If, in spite of this rupture, a writer still wishes to continue his literary career, he must first try and grasp what it is he wants to do, and then either re-establish ties with his old audience or cast about for another one more compatible with his new intentions. When Mann found himself in this situation around 1900, his choice was to push ahead toward a new reading public.

The audience he wanted to reach was one concerned with social issues and interested in a critical approach to contemporary problems. For this reason, all Mann's novels during the transitional years were socially critical to one degree or another. Even *Die Göttinnen,* which was his most aesthetic, has been correctly described as "an almost complete document of all the addictions and fashions, all the hysterias and artistic excesses, all the illusions and intellectual and material wastefulnesses ending in nothing, all the political and human charlataneries of the period around 1900."[44] Nevertheless, many people

failed to read the work with these things in mind, and hence Mann
had a hard time establishing contact with the desired readership.

After the turn of the century Mann was sure that he wanted to be a
"consequential" writer. As he put it, he wanted his work to have
"results" and to help change society (as he believed the writings of
Hugo or Zola did in France, and those of Tolstoy did in Russia). The
obstacle to this goal, at least during the first decade after 1900, was
that his reputation as an aesthetic author obfuscated his social
criticism and prevented others from grasping his new message. This
is why he complained that his novel *Die Jagd nach Liebe* was misunderstood by many readers to be an "effusion of sensuality"
whereas, according to Mann, it was something very different.[45] The
fact that at this time Mann was viewed as "only a literary success"
was another source of disappointment to him and another sign that
he was being misinterpreted.[46] To be *merely* a literary success was to
be appreciated only for style and form, not for content. But it was
precisely a new critical content that Mann wanted to get across to
his German readers after 1900. This was one reason why he sometimes envied his French counterparts their ability to write critical
prose without being plagued by misunderstandings.

That Mann was in fact misinterpreted during his transitional period
seems undeniable, judging from the reception his works received.
Some of his most ardent supporters missed the critical and satirical
points, and instead read his work for its lingering afterglow of
Impressionism. Ironically, in doing so they attached themselves to the
very qualities he was transcending. The literary historian Hanns
Ludwig Geiger reported that in some circles Mann was spoken of as
"the apostle of beauty and sensuality," or an advocate of dilettantism
and the *Übermensch*.[47] In others, he was seen as a stylist, a purely
artistic writer, a skillful creator of images.[48] To the extent that a considerable portion of Mann's audience agreed with these opinions, it
failed to grasp what he was doing. Very few noticed, for example,
that in *Im Schlaraffenland* Mann parodied the Stefan George cult,
Huysmans, and the French Symbolists—all idols of the German
aesthetes. Likewise, it seems that most readers did not comprehend
what Mann was trying to say about contemporary Germany in
Professor Unrat. Indeed, when this novel first appeared in 1905 it received almost no attention at all and sold far worse than the other
books Mann wrote at the time. Apparently, his established aesthetic
audience viewed it as an aberration without redeeming "artistic"

merit, while at the same time the liberal middle-class readership had not yet taken note of its critical point of view.

Despite his overtures towards a new readership, it must be admitted that Mann did not do all he could have to dispel the notion that he was an aesthete. In 1904, in an autobiographical sketch for his publisher's catalogue, he pointed out that he was a product of two races, the Latin and the Germanic. This fact, he said, caused him to be a "reckless and very impressionable" writer; it led him to move in opposite directions at the same time, laying "the bestial side by side with the idyllic, enthusiasm beside satire, tenderness beside misanthropy."[49] In this passage Mann depicted himself exactly as his aesthetically-oriented readers liked to think of him, as an alienated, "impressionable," literary type—one interested in conveying, as Mann phrased it in the same sketch, "sensations" woven out of his own experience.

Perhaps this ambiguity indicates that he was somewhat afraid to cut himself off from the only reading public he had established so far, which would be understandable since it is literary suicide to break with one readership before making contact with another. It may be that Mann wrote what he did for his publisher because it was through this firm, the Albert Langen Verlag, that his more aesthetic works were printed, including his impressionist novellas of the 1890s.[50] Possibly Mann was simply playing the role expected of him by those who knew of his works only through the Langen editions, hence affecting an aesthetic pose to match his aesthetic image. It is significant that when Mann entered a more politically-engaged period after 1907 he switched publishers, going over to the new, more socially conscious, Kurt Wolff Verlag in Leipzig. With this gesture Mann symbolically divorced himself from the aesthetic audience he had built up during his years with Langen. Instead, he now attempted to make contact with a (still small) liberal reading audience which Kurt Wolff was also trying to reach.

After 1907, many began to see the direction in which Mann was moving. Then, and not before, it became possible both for the reactionary press to attack him,[51] and for a liberal writer like Otto Flake to talk about the "extraordinary impression" he was making "on the political youth."[52] No one had said this in the previous decade, not even Thomas Mann who, in 1905, criticized his brother for being, as he put it, "nothing more than an artist."[53] But if Heinrich Mann occasionally became exasperated with his readership for being obtuse and not catching his new intent, it was not entirely the public's fault. Not until *Zwischen den Rassen* (1907), *Die kleine Stadt (The Little Town,* 1909), and his activist essays around 1910 was it unmistakably clear that Mann was no aesthete but a "radical" democrat.[54] When this transition was complete, Mann found that he had an audience which read and respected him for entirely different reasons than the audience he had dealt with a few years earlier.

Throughout this period, Mann struggled to find an attitude adequate to the world around him, for the world was changing and he wanted his comprehension of it to keep pace. The old aesthetic, neo-conservative outlook which had served him well in the mid-1890s now seemed not only insufficient but also dangerous. As Mann re-thought his situation he tended to gravitate towards a liberal-democratic perspective, and in the wake of this came new models, new forms, a new style, and eventually a new reading public. Of course, this transition occurred slowly, over the course of nearly a decade and with many advances and retreats. But the net result by 1907 was that Mann had become virtually a different kind of writer and thinker than he was when he wrote for *Das Zwanzigste Jahrhundert.*

These changes quite naturally led to an entirely different notion of what literature was and what role it should play in modern society. They also raised the question of what tasks he, as a writer, had to fulfill as an advocate of liberal democracy. This question must now be dealt with since Mann was, in many ways, a path-breaker in his conception of the role and function of the literary intellectual in German society.

Footnotes
Chapter 5

1. Wilhelm Reich, *The Mass Psychology of Fascism*, pp. 3–33.

2. Both novellas were published in Mann's second collection of short stories, *Ein Verbrechen und andere Geschichten* (Leipzig, 1898).

3. See Heinrich Mann's letter to Maximilian Harden in *Die Zukunft* (1904), XLIX, no. 2:67; and his autobiographical sketch in the *Albert Langens Verlags-katalog 1894–1904* (Munich, 1904), p. 92.

4. Friedrich Nietzsche, cited in George Morgan, *What Nietzsche Means* (New York, 1965), p. 31.

5. When Ernst Kantorowicz, the first director of the Heinrich-Mann-Archiv in East Berlin, began sorting out Mann's *Nachlass* in the early 1950s, he was surprised to find the reactionary material dating from the 1890s. These early manuscripts were not generally known, even to someone like Kantorowicz, who had been fairly close to Mann in his later years.

6. Thomas Mann, cited in Richard and Clara Winston, "Introduction", *Letters of Thomas Mann 1889–1955*, p. xix.

7. See Heinrich Mann, "Das gestohlene Dokument," *Novellen I, Ausgewählte Werke* VIII:98–108. For differing views of the significance of this novella see Manfred Hahn, "Heinrich Manns Beiträge in der Zeitschrift 'Das Zwanzigste Jahrhundert'," *Weimarer Beiträge*, XIII, no. 6:1014; Klaus Schröter, *Heinrich Mann*, p. 39; and André Banuls, *Heinrich Mann*, p. 46.

8. The subtitle of the novel reads: "Ein Roman unter feinen Leuten."

9. Heinrich Mann, *Die Göttinnen, oder die drei Romane der Herzogin von Assy* (Berlin, 1957), p. 123.

10. This, of course, was nothing new in Germany. Since at least the end of the eighteenth century, it was a familiar ideal among German writers and philosophers. See W. H. Bruford, *The German Tradition of Self-Cultivation: 'Bildung' from Humboldt to Thomas Mann* (London, 1975).

11. Note particularly the characters Glumkow in "Das gestohlene Dokument" and Starke in "Ein Verbrechen." Both novellas are included in the collection cited in footnote 2 above.

12. André Banuls, *Heinrich Mann,* p. 56.

13. See Heinrich Mann, "Gustave Flaubert und George Sand," *Essays* I, *Ausgewählte Werke,* XI:107; and "Der Fall Murri," *Die Zukunft* (1906), LV, no. 31:161-68.

14. See the comments by Edgar Kirsch, cited in Klaus Schröter, *Anfänge Heinrich Manns,* p. 83.

15. Terms such as these—meaning respectively "coarse," "grotesque," "filthy," "without charm," and "coarse pursuits"—were common to Mann's vocabulary, particularly before 1910.

16. Harry Pross, "Heinrich Mann—der letzte Jacobiner," *Deutsche Rundschau* (1957), LXXXIII, no. 10:1052-53.

17. Heinrich Mann, letter to Maximilian Brantl, November 23, 1907, in "Heinrich Manns Briefe an Maximilian Brantl," *Weimarer Beiträge* (1968), XIV, no. 2: 398. Though Mann used the term "radical," in contemporary parlance his meaning was something closer to the word "liberal" or "left-liberal."

18. See Walter Pater, "Conclusion" to *Studies in the Renaissance* (1873) in *Selections From Walter Pater,* ed. Ada Snell (Boston, 1924), p. 40.

19. Heinrich Mann, letter to Ines Schmied, July 25, 1905; included in *Heinrich Mann 1871-1950: Werk und Leben,* pp. 106-07.

20. Some reviewers believed Mann was actually defending aestheticism and one even saw him as a new German "Erotiker" in the manner of D'Annunzio. See, for example, René Schickele, "Heinrich Mann: Skizze zu einem Portrait," *Werke in drei Bänden,* III:916; Heinrich Hart, review in *Velhagen und Klasings Monatshefte* (1903), XVII:473f.; and M. Jacobs, "Die Herzogin von Assy," *Die Nation* (1903), XX:506-08.

21. Heinrich Mann, "Pippo Spano," *Novellen* I, *Ausgewählte Werke,* VIII: 293-338.

22. Rolf Linn, "The Place of 'Pippo Spano' in the Work of Heinrich Mann," *Modern Language Forum* (1952), XXXVII:143.

23. These ideas were developed in novellas such as "Die Branzilla" (1906), "Der Tyrann" (1908), and "Auferstehung" (1910), as well as in novels like *Zwischen den Rassen* (1907) and *Die kleine Stadt* (1909).

24. As aesthetes, both the Duchess of Assy and Mario Malvolto are what Mann elsewhere called *Spätgeborene* ("late-born ones"). They are literally at the end of the line. While their ancestors performed great deeds, they simply play at living or

else sacrifice life for art. Mann made the same point in *Die Jagd nach Liebe,* where the dissipated Munich artists are portrayed as exhausted members of once great families. Rather than live for society they live only for themselves, but without any vitality or robustness. (Since the novel was, in part, a *roman à clef,* it became an embarrassment to the entire Mann family, most of whom were living in Munich at the time the book was published. See Julia Mann's letter to Heinrich, November 20, 1904, in *Thomas Mann—Heinrich Mann Briefwechsel, 1900–1949,* ed. Hans Wysling [Frankfurt, 1969]. pp. 256–58.)

25. Klaus Schröter, *Anfänge Heinrich Manns,* p. 72. Schröter's book provides the best discussion so far on Mann's relationship to Nietzsche (see especially pp. 69–115).

26. See Heinrich Mann, "Zum Verständnisse Nietzsches," *DZJ,* VI, Halbband 2, pp. 245–51; and "Friedrich Nietzsche und•das Deutschthum," *DZJ,* VI, Halbband 1, pp. 561–62.

27. Heinrich Mann, "Das gestohlene Dokument," *Novellen* I, *Ausgewählte Werke* VIII:98–108.

28. Rolf Linn, *Heinrich Mann* (New York, 1967), p. 37.

29. Heinrich Mann, *Ein Zeitalter wird besichtigt,* p. 462.

30. Heinrich Mann, letter to Karl Lemke, April 20, 1948, in *Briefe an Karl Lemke, 1917–1949,* p. 97.

31. Heinrich Mann, "Geist und Tat," *Essays* I, *Ausgewählte Werke,* XI:12–13.

32. Heinrich Mann, *Nietzsche* (London, 1939), pp. 1–2.

33. Heinrich Mann, *Sieben Jahre, Chronik der Gedanken und Vorgänge* (Berlin, 1929), p. 267.

34. See Klaus Schröter, *Anfänge Heinrich Manns,* pp. 115–58; Ulrich Weisstein, *Heinrich Mann,* pp. 25–28; André Banuls, *Heinrich Mann,* pp. 72–73, 110–16; and Heinrich Mann, "Anatole France," *Sieben Jahre,* pp. 176–85.

35. "At twenty I could hardly write at all," Mann later acknowledged, "but at thirty I learned the techniques of the novel." See Mann's "Kurze Selbstbiographie," dated March 27, 1947, in manuscript in the Schiller-Nationalmuseum, Marbach-am-Neckar.

36. See Mann's letter to Maximilian Harden in *Die Zukunft* (1904), XLIX:67f.; reprinted in *Heinrich Mann 1871–1950: Werk und Leben,* pp. 77–79.

37. *Ibid.,* p. 78.

38. Heinrich Mann, cited in Klaus Schröter, *Anfänge Heinrich Manns*, p. 114.

39. The term "critical realism" has specific connotations which will be discussed more fully in chapter 7.

40. Heinrich Mann, from a hand-written draft of a letter dated February 24. 1904, included in *Heinrich Mann 1871–1950: Werk und Leben*, p. 84.

41. See footnote 33 above.

42. Heinrich Mann, quoted in Klaus Schröter, *Heinrich Mann*, p. 38.

43. The best book on this subject, though often highly speculative, is Lorenz Winter, *Heinrich Mann and His Public*, trans. John Gorman (Coral Gables, 1970). See also, Jean-Paul Sartre, *What is Literature?*, trans. Bernard Frechtman (New York, 1966); Robert Escarpit, *The Sociology of Literature*, trans. Ernest Pick (Painesville, Ohio, 1965); Levin Schücking, *The Sociology of Literary Taste*, trans. Brian Battershaw (London, 1966); and the dated but still useful Q. D. Leavis, *Fiction and the Reading Public* (London, 1932).

44. Herbert Ihering, *Heinrich Mann*, p. 23; Rolf Linn, *Heinrich Mann*, p. 26.

45. Heinrich Mann, letter to Ines Schmied, July 25, 1905, *Heinrich Mann 1871–1950: Werk und Leben*, p. 106.

46. See Heinrich Mann, letter to Alfred Kantorowicz, March 3, 1943, reprinted in Herbert Ihering, *Heinrich Mann*, p. 142; also Lorenz Winter, *Heinrich Mann and His Public*, p. 46.

47. Hanns Ludwig Geiger, *Es war um die Jahrhundertwende* (Munich, 1953), p. 62.

48. See the comments by Heinrich Hart and Rainer Maria Rilke, included in *Heinrich Mann 1871–1950: Werk und Leben*, pp. 85, 109–10; and Gottfried Benn, "Heinrich Mann zum sechzigsten Geburtstag," *Gesammelte Werke in acht Bänden* (Wiesbaden, 1968), III:694–95.

49. Heinrich Mann, ["Autobiographische Skizze"], *Albert Langens Verlagskatalog*, p. 92.

50. Besides publishing novels like *Die Göttinnen* and *Die Jagd nach Liebe*, Albert Langen Verlag also published three volumes of Mann's short stories: *Das Wunderbare* (1897), *Flöten und Dolche* (1905), and *Stürmische Morgen* (1906).

51. See Heinrich Mann's letter to Maximilian Brantl, November 23, 1907, in "Heinrich Manns Briefe and Maximilian Brantl," *Weimarer Beiträge*, XIV, no. 2:398.

52. Otto Flake, "Von der jüngsten Literatur," *Die Neue Rundschau* (1915), II:1279.

53. Thomas Mann, letter to Heinrich Mann, February 18, 1905, in *Thomas Mann—Heinrich Mann Briefwechsel, 1900–1949,* p. 35.

54. See footnote 17 above.

Chapter 6

The Role of the Writer in Society

Der Literat ist . . . [ein] Moralist im doppelten Sinn: Er ist Seelenkundiger
und Sittenrichter, und er ist beides aus Künstlertum.

Thomas Mann

Mann's Changing Conception of the Writer's Task, 1890–1910

In 1910, Mann published an essay entitled "Geist und Tat." It was
his first overtly political article since the tendentious pieces of *Das
Zwanzigste Jahrhundert* fifteen years earlier.[1] To many at the time it
seemed to indicate that Mann's decision to discard his aesthetic
interests and become a "political writer" was sudden.[2] This view-
point was mistaken, as should be clear from the last chapter. The
argument in "Geist und Tat," that it was the duty of the writer to
become a politically engaged intellectual, had a long pre-history with
roots going back at least to the mid-1890s.

Except for the unusual (and usually suspect) "conversion experience,"
an intellectual *volte face* is, historically speaking, a rare occurrence.
What often appears to be a sudden change may only be a surface
phenomenon, the last stage of something that has been prepared long
before. When an allegedly new idea surfaces in a writer's work,
chances are that implicit traces of it can be found in his earlier
personal or social experiences. As these experiences change qualitatively, they generate new ways of looking at things. The apparently
new ideas in "Geist und Tat," for instance, were undoubtedly the
result of more than a decade of intense but unrecorded struggle to
convey Mann's evolving perceptions of his milieu and his own
relationship to it as a writer.

Four factors should be mentioned which had a bearing on Mann's
changing view of the writer's task. The first was the German socio-
political reality, which he participated in and which strongly affected
him, whether he liked it or not. The very fact that Mann lived at a
specific time, and therefore experienced the contemporaneity of

certain events, meant that he had to face up to and deal with unavoidable social tendencies. Among these were such developments as
the industrialization of Germany, the growth of the working class,
the rationalization and centralization of the state apparatus, and the
increasing fragmentation of life due, as the German sociologists put
it, to the transition from "community" to "society." Because all
these forces were concrete realities in Germany between 1890 and 1910,
Mann had no choice but to acknowledge their existence and try to
cope with them.

The second factor was the altered nature of Mann's perceptions of
reality. In its essential configurations, this reality did not change
drastically between 1890 and 1910. But like all writers, Mann was
shaped not directly by what was actually happening in the world, but
by the extent to which he was cognizant of these changes and interpreted them in relation to his own life. The changes in his surroundings merely set the conditions for his responses; they decided what he
would ultimately have to react against or affirm. Thus Mann never
saw these tendencies, these manifest "social facts," exactly as they
were, without filters or mediations. Instead, he formed *impressions* of
them and of the world in general, which is to say, he conferred
meaning and significance on the reality confronting him and then
reacted to these impressions more than to the reality itself. This is
not suprising, but in Mann's case it meant that the role he assigned
the modern writer was not only based upon, but was a logical extension of, the values he had forged in response to his social environment.

The third factor was an ideological one. As Mann's impressions of
social reality gradually coalesced into a unified outlook on life, they
began to take on what must be called a political dimension. This
meant that the role he allocated to the writer began to be affected
by subtle and not always recognizable political considerations; these,
too, must be kept in mind if one is to understand the kinds of commitments Mann eventually demanded of the *littérateur*.

Lastly, Mann's view of the writer's function was also shaped by the
audience for which he wrote. The more the composition of Mann's
established reading public shifted, the more he tended to assume a
different pose and visualize new tasks for the man-of-letters. This
was as much because he was changing himself (in response to a
changing world) as because his audience demanded new attitudes and
roles from him.

All of these elements came into play with regard to Mann's conception of what the writer *qua* writer was supposed to do. The same was true for other members of Mann's literary generation. Writers like Bernhard Kellermann, René Schickele, Georg Kaiser, and Lion Feuchtwanger also began to change both their self-concepts and their notions of what kind of literature should be written as they, too, responded to a changing world situation in accordance with the factors mentioned above. Though there will be no need to mention these points again in detail, it must be remembered that all four provided a collective *point de départ* for Mann and the others even though they often made only passing reference to them.

Having mentioned the factors which affected Mann's evolving notion of the writer's role, it is important to examine this notion itself and to trace its evolution.

Up until the time he became editor of *Das Zwanzigste Jahrhundert,* Mann talked about two roles for the writer. The first, which predominated around 1890, was that the writer should have no social function at all. The only responsibilities he had were to himself and to his art. If this led to an uncritical acceptance of existing power relationships, Mann was not disturbed by it. In fact, he seemed to feel that the writer could develop most fully only by attaching himself to the upper echelons of society, where the material for psychological observation was richer and more diversified.[3] To the extent that an artistic mission was involved here, it was simply to observe well, to combine these observations with one's own "qualities of soul," and then to write, preferably in a mannered and highly nuanced style.

By about 1894, however, Mann began to entertain another conception of the writer's role—one that was a step closer to social commitment. While he still maintained that there was a perilous cleft between art and life, the beautiful and the banal, he now suggested for the first time that it might be possible to bridge it. The writer's role was, as before, to enter the realm of the "marvellous," but not in order to stay there. Instead, Mann now inferred that the writer ought to return to earth and try to ennoble a base reality. In the novella "Das Wunderbare" (1894), for example, Mann expressed the idea that if art could be made to permeate life, a new unity might be achieved in which the "spirit" would no longer be alienated, and life would no longer be un-spiritual.[4] But of course this would work only if the reconciliation were effected exclusively on the terms laid down by art. It was, after all, the sensitive artist who was invested with the task of uplifting society. If a unity of the spiritual and the real were to be achieved according to the existing reality principle, then the world would not be aestheticized, but art merely degraded and trivialized.

Before the middle of the decade, then, Mann propounded two different roles for the artist: the one emphasizing withdrawal, and the other withdrawal-and-return. Only the second contained within it an incipient social function, since in this the writer bore some responsibility for his world and had a spiritual obligation to improve it. But despite these differences there was one consistent theme which ran through both, namely, the sacerdotal notion of the literary calling, where the writer was treated as the equivalent of a priest and literature was given the status of a holy rite. The crucial point that separated the two concepts of a writer's role was the same one which separates a cult from a religion, i.e., that the first "saves" by drawing people into the *mysterium,* and the second by administering the sacraments. By 1894, Mann had begun to take up the latter position as the more correct one.

This shift seems obvious in many of the essays he wrote at mid-decade for *Das Zwanzigste Jahrhundert.* But one can also detect other noticeable departures from his earlier work. By 1896, Mann had began to argue explicitly, no longer just implicitly, that the writer should place himself in "the service of ideas."[5] The man-of-letters, Mann now insisted, should not only stand up for high ideals and defend them when they are threatened, but he should also strive to "grasp" his times, and "feel the pulses of [his] age" by intimately involving himself in it.[6] This represented an enormous step away from the aesthetic views he had held just two years before. It was even an advance over his mystical concern for actualizing the "marvellous"—an idea which at least started him on the road to literary politics. But when it came to describing the exact content of the ideals the writer was suppose to serve, Mann faltered somewhat. Instead of invoking the ineffable or transformative power of art, he fell back upon the vague conservative slogans long familiar to *Das Zwanzigste Jahrhundert* readers: rootedness, national renewal, an integral German self-consciousness.[7] These were the principles which writers were asked to represent, since only through them could German society be spiritualized and redeemed.

At this point Mann was still in his neo-conservative phase, so it was natural that the tasks he prescribed for literary intellectuals should also be politically conservative. Nevertheless, despite this apparent regression, the position he arrived at in 1895–96 represented something of a minor breakthrough. This had nothing to do with Mann's ideals, since these were not innovative and would soon be discarded and forgotten altogether. Rather, it had to do with, first the way he began to concretize his views and talk in terms of real social needs instead of vague generalities like "the marvellous"; and secondly, with the way he began to argue for a more activist, agitational relationship on the part of writers toward reality. Ironically, the first traces of Mann's socially-involved literary activism are to be found not in 1910, but in 1895, hidden away in the pages of his reactionary journal.

During the nearly fifteen years which separated *Das Zwanzigste Jahrhundert* from "Geist und Tat," Mann's conception of the writer's role underwent several further changes. Here it is necessary to mention only the most important: namely, that while Mann continued to ask the writer to concern himself with social renewal, he began to define this term in a quite different way. By 1910 the intellectual posture Mann called for was much the same as previously (to be "engaged" and to "serve ideas"), but both the substance of his ideals and the kind of society he wanted for Germany were revised drastically.[8] Now his demand was that writers agitate for democracy and humanity, not national self-consciousness.

Signs of this change in accepted ideals began to appear in his Flaubert essay of 1905. Here one can find no mention of nationalistic values, but in the mouth of George Sand (a "socialist," a "child of the people"!) there is an assertion of new priorities: the love of humanity, universal reconciliation, and the principles of the French Revolution.[9] Two years later, in *Zwischen den Rassen*, these priorities were re-enforced; the novel ends by affirming the "goodness of democracy" because of its ability to "awaken dignity, deepen humanity, and spread tranquility."[10] In his next work, *Die kleine Stadt,* these same goals appear again. This time the setting is Italian, but there is no doubt that when Mann wrote the book he had Germany in mind, especially the relationship between German literary intellectuals and Wilhelmian society. In a letter to René Schickele he wrote: "The hatred of the intellectuals towards the infamous materialism of the German Reich is considerable. But what can [we] do to make [our] influence felt? . . . . We can do this: hold up our ideal, and hold it up so purely, brightly, and unshakably, that the best will become alarmed and develop a longing for it."[11]

The following year, Mann's famous "Geist und Tat" essay appeared in the journal *Pan*. Far from being a sudden reversal, as some have maintained, the essay represented the culmination of a long personal development. In it, Mann briefly and succinctly laid out his views on the writer's role in society. First of all he contended that it was not enough to "renew" society in the old conservative sense. In his view, Wilhelmian Germany was too much rooted in injustice, in the "rule of the fist" and in lies, to be redeemed by such easy solutions. Furthermore, he argued, there was nothing between the classes but "an iceberg of estrangement," and the monarchy itself was a "tyranny, an organization of misanthropy."[12] In light of this, Mann made his second point—that entirely new values were needed, precisely the ones Germany might once have had but turned away from after 1848. Throughout the essay he made mention of the ideals of freedom, justice, human dignity, reason, equality, and democracy. Each of these had to be injected into the body politic in order to transform Germany into a different kind of society. This led Mann to his conclusion that it was the duty of the literary intellectual to accomplish this task. Hitherto, German men-of-letters had "explained away stupidity and legitimized the injustice of their deadly enemy, power."[13] Now, Mann wrote, it was imperative that the activist writer, filled with *geistige* ideals, oppose untruth and oppression whenever he finds it. In order to accomplish this he must ally with the people against all the power cliques in the nation. For too long the representatives of the spirit (intellectuals) and the broad masses of the population have been separated from one another by mutual suspicion and distrust. The times demand, Mann continued, that this alienation be ended and that the literary intellectuals "finally fulfill their obligations by becoming agitators, by uniting with the people against power, and by dedicating themselves to fighting for the spirit with all the strength of language they possess."[14] From now on, Mann warned, any intellectual who associates with the "ruling clique" (*Herrenkaste*) should be considered a "traitor to the spirit."

In "Geist und Tat" Mann did indeed defend the notion that German writers should become *engagé*. And perhaps more than any other established literary figure of his time, he tied this activism to the goals of humanitarian and democratic values. Nevertheless, this fact should be noted: despite his substantial evolution from the ideal of the writer as a "beautiful soul" to the writer as a fighter for humanity, Mann's conceptions always remained within the parameters of German middle-class thought. Structurally, he was working with only two basic ideas. The first was that the spiritual individual should withdraw from the world altogether, and the second was that he should face the world and transform it in the name of some higher principle, whether it be the "marvellous," national regeneration, or ethical democracy. Despite great variations among the higher principles sought in the second type—from a mystical to a neoconservative to a democratic conception—the core idea was still the same, that the writer must be committed to the spiritual task of ennobling society.

This central idea is a common thread throughout nineteenth-century German thought. The crux of it is that there is a deep cleavage between spirit and matter, "culture" and material existence; the only way the gap can be bridged is from above, either by an individual being subsumed into culture and therefore escaping the world, or by culture "permeating and transfigur[ing] . . . the realm of necessity," thereby bringing spirit down to earth.[15] Even though these solutions are very different, the problem each is intended to solve is the same. Both take for granted that a dualism exists between high principles and low life. Furthermore, both assume that this antinomy can be overcome only by means of the spirit, that is to say, only when *Geist* becomes an active, shaping, reconciling force. This function of *Geist* can occur either when spirit lifts up a single individual to its own higher level *(Bildung)*, or when it takes hold in the soul of an entire people *(Kultur)*, thereby transforming and elevating them.

Even though Mann's ideas underwent great changes between 1890 and 1910, they always remained within the bounds of a dualistic, middle-class mode of thinking. Throughout these two decades, Mann continued to make the same assumptions about *Geist*, to see the world in sets of antipodes, and to write for an essentially middle-class reading public. To be sure, the composition of this audience changed (becoming presumably more progressive and democratic), but it remained a middle-class public nonetheless. The ideas Mann's readers embraced in his work were precisely the ones they found already implicit in their own traditions going back to the *Aufklärung*, viz., the emphasis on social responsibility, ethical duty, and moral ideals which, as Kant and Schiller said, had to be manifested here on earth.

What is particularly interesting about Mann is that while he did not overturn certain basic patterns of thought, he did make an effort to politicize them, especially after the turn of the century. This is why by 1910 he had become a radical democrat rather than merely a "spiritual personality."[16] But he never became a revolutionary thinker, either in 1910 or afterwards, because for that, entirely new modes of thought would have been required. Mann never developed these new modes of thought; on the contrary, even as a "fellow traveller" in the 1930s and 1940s, he still relied on most of the key ideas he had worked out earlier in "Geist und Tat" and other essays.

Mann managed to politicize his views of the writer's role (without at the same time discarding his dualistic intellectual framework) by simply changing the nature of the antinomies with which he dealt. At first it was the simple opposition of art against life; then it was the "marvellous" against reality; and finally, by 1910, it was *Geist* against *Macht*, or "spirit" against "power." In each stage along the way, the realm of the spiritual became increasingly less ethereal until, in the end, it was synonymous with morality, intellect, and reason. When this happened, the man of spirit became nothing other than the *geistige Mensch*, the engaged literary intellectual. At the same time, the realm of *Macht* was also transformed into a specific socio-historical concept. By 1910 it was not power in general that the writer was asked to oppose, but rather a particular kind of social power based on domination, repression, and lies—that of the Wilhelmian Empire. Now, the masses were no longer condemned as unspiritual; instead, it was only the ruling elite (which was accused of making the population inert and profiting from its submissiveness) that was singled out for criticism. It was implied that the "people," if inspired by spiritual intellectuals, could rise up against established power in the name of democratic principles. Then there would be a chance for Germany to return to the mainstream of liberal democracy from which it strayed in the nineteenth century.[17]

This politicization of categories was extremely important because it meant that Mann had to re-define the tasks of the writer in society. Since the enemy was now not abstract power but rather specific forms of power, including the monarchy and large-scale capitalism, the writer's role had to be made more concrete and socially meaningful. To merely "represent" ideas was no longer enough; the literary intellectual also had to do something about them. Actions had to follow awareness, since *Tat* was said to be an implicit imperative within *Geist*. Here Mann confronted another major theme of the nineteenth century—the hoped-for unity between thought and practice. Mann argued that such a unity could be achieved through the act of writing itself, where the engaged *littérateur* fused both elements into one through his active literary opposition to power in all its forms.

At this point it may seem that Mann came close to the Marxist concept of praxis, especially with his emphasis on the writer's need to vigorously oppose the status quo in thought and deed. But it would be a mistake to draw this inference. In "Geist und Tat," Mann's position was liberal rather than Marxist. Nowhere in the essay, or in any he had written before, was Marx's name mentioned. Instead, working entirely within the confines of middle-class Jacobinism, Mann's central reference point was the French Revolution of 1789 (which signaled for him a decisive victory of spirit over power).[18] In France, Mann's mode of thinking would have been recognized for what it was: an extension of nineteenth-century liberal theory. In Germany, because of the reactionary climate of the Wilhelmian era, it was taken to be radical or even revolutionary. Within the context of the German milieu, one can grant the radicalism of his views. But the inherent dualism of Mann's thought, his rejection of dialectics, and his persistent ethical idealism all kept him very far removed from the Marxist revolutionary tradition.

Literary Politics, 1910–1914

By this stage in his life, Mann had arrived at a notion of literary politics which was to remain with him *mutatis mutandis* for the next four decades.

In essence, literary politics meant that the writer, after having placed himself in the service of democratic and humanitarian principles, would then go on to use literature to combat a bad sociopolitical reality and inject into it a sense of the ideal. By means of literary politics a writer would consciously politicize his work and turn it into a force for the betterment of mankind.[19] Literature could then become a mode of political action. It could take on what Roland Barthes has called an "assertive value" and assume a position on "all that happens or does not happen in the world."[20] In this way, writing would become a thoroughly partisan activity since the writer's job would be to oppose illegitimate power on the one hand,

and promote the "party of humanity" on the other.

Once this conception of literary politics was established, Mann's views underwent several changes. For one, the *Künstler* as a model literary figure was replaced by the *Literat,* since social commentary rather than phantasy was to be the writer's main concern. For another, the literary work began to be viewed more as a tool than as a beautiful object in itself, because for Mann its deepest value resided in the moral or political message it conveyed rather than in the aesthetic impressions or moods it evoked.[21] Writing had become fully and completely a social act. The engaged writer was not only the bad conscience of his age—the moral and intellectual legislator of spiritual values—but his work was invested with the status of a "social power" in its own right.[22]

There were several ways in which the writer could go about exerting his social influence. He could, for example, play the role of witness, by simply taking upon himself the task of describing things as they actually were and thereby exposing to others a reality which the dominant elites would prefer to shroud in darkness. Mann had already hit upon this option by around 1900, when he decided that the task of the novel was to portray accurately contemporary society and by this means to reveal, as he put it, "the ruling class hidden behind the clouds." Later he refined this insight by pointing out that the writer had a special obligation to "see through" things, i.e., to penetrate, dissect, and analyze existing relations in order to lay bare the psychology of power as well as the reality of power. This he did himself in several novels, most notably *Professor Unrat* and *Der Untertan (The Good Subject,* 1918).

Besides this approach, Mann also believed that the writer could assume the more polemical role of forcefully satirizing and discrediting prevailing ideologies. Here he had in mind not only the ideologies of materialism, nationalism, and statism (all of which he cleverly attacked in much of his own work during this period), but also such apparently harmless notions as the "great man" theory. Mann strongly denied that the presence of a few great men was in any sense a compliment to a nation. The uniqueness of great individuals, he maintained, was usually built upon the humility, self-contempt, and degradation of the rest of the population, which was thereby sacrificed for a handful of real or imagined geniuses. Like so many other ideologies, this fascination for greatness seemed to be a German *idée fixe* which Mann wanted to subject to criticism and parody. "Has anyone ever measured," he wrote, "what it costs a people to have 'great men'? . . . No people today can afford [this luxury] while the issue of humanity is still on the agenda."[23]

Finally, the writer could assume an ethical role with regard to society. In addition to exposing reality and satirizing it, he could be an advocate of reason and the moral law. This would mean grasping concrete distinctions between good and evil and pronouncing on them.[24] It would also mean mediating between *Geist* and the flawed world of *Macht,* awakening people to the differences between the two, and arousing them to take one side against the other. Here the writer would become a kind of law-giver. Even though this role would be essentially that of intermediary, he could speak for higher ideals over against an obstinate reality principle.

As Mann outlined these tasks he quickly came up against a new problem which he had not had to deal with as an aesthete. What if a writer performs each of these roles superbly, and yet there is no concerned public to receive his message? What if even his best work is consistently misunderstood, not because he is unclear, but because the mass is obdurate, uninformed, or willfully misled by others? If this happened there could be no meaningful literary politics, and the writer's *Geist* would for all practical purposes be a chimera. The *littérateur* would be talking past his audience and his message would never congeal into a real social force to oppose the world of power.

In the years preceding World War I, Mann addressed himself to this disturbing notion. The result was yet another task for the writer, but one which now stood out as the most urgent, at least up to 1914. It was that the German *Literat* had the responsibility for virtually "creating a people," that is, for engendering a citizenry which could receive, internalize and act upon the ideals conveyed to them by intellectuals.

For literary politics to be effective, Mann argued, two factors would have to exist simultaneously: spirit, in the form of the engaged writer, and a people, the material base. If only the first were present, writing as an activity would be nothing but "meaningless play."[25] If only the second, there would exist nothing but an inert conglomeration of individuals, a dumb mass not yet worthy to be labelled a "people." It is important to note here, however, that though Mann acknowledged that both should co-exist and be interdependent, he did not say there should be equal reciprocity between them. On the contrary, all the action was one way, since spirit descends and takes hold of the people rather than the other way around. The trappings of a hieratic and clerical notion of the writer's role were still in evidence here. This view sharply demarcated him from Marx who believed that the intellectual's task was not to "give" the people anything but simply to help them articulate their own needs and to formulate theoretically what they already knew through experience. As Marx saw it, the *geistige Mensch* was to serve the people, not abstract ideals; his job was to draw out of the working class ideas and aspirations which they already had but were not fully cognizant of and did not know how to convert into practice.

Such dialectical premises were as foreign to Mann's way of thinking as they were to nineteenth-century middle-class thought in general. According to Mann's dualistic interpretation, a "people" must exist so that it can absorb the intellectual's message, become ennobled, and then ally with spirit against power. The people were needed only insofar as they had to be drawn into the eternal struggle between good and evil, and hence democratized so they would join the right side in the struggle. The writer's mission to actualize ideas in society required a receptive agent—a "people"—as fertile ground on which the word could become flesh. Thus Mann began to visualize the possibility of the German reading public being converted into a vast political public.

It was not until 1910 that he formulated this idea in a serious way. Earlier, he had been more pessimistic about people in general, believing that if the writer were to circulate among them it was likely he would be corrupted, as were Andreas Zumsee and other pseudo-artists in *Im Schlaraffenland.* This attitude made it easy for Mann occasionally to fall back upon the notion of a literary clerisy. After all, if the man-on-the-street could not be redeemed, then maybe it was necessary to draw rigid distinctions between the *cognoscenti* and the *ignoranti* so that writers could represent ideals only to one another. Even as late as 1908, in a letter to his friend Maximilian Brantl, Mann wondered if the German people were mature enough for a political awakening. He tended to think not, and he ridiculed those who took the momentary uproar over the Daily Telegraph Affair as a sign of "revolutionary courage."[26] A year later, in a letter to René Schickele, he seemed to doubt that the Germans had the capacity to be instruments of *Geist.* "The German Empire is without spirit," he wrote. "Possibly [the] people can politicize themselves apart from *Geist,* but what would we, who are alienated from them, know of that?"[27]

By the time "Geist und Tat" appeared the following year, Mann changed his mind, at least publicly. "What must be created," he announced, "is a people who will struggle for the spirit and be its *ratio militans*."[28] In France, it seemed, such a people already existed. It was ushered in by both the Enlightenment and the Revolution and had remained a political public ever since. This was why French literary intellectuals from Voltaire to Zola had been able to turn their works into autonomous forces for social change. Fortunately for them, there existed a genuine political community which could be activated to counter the threats of illegitimate authority. This, Mann argued, was not the case in Germany, where *Geist* had remained as impotent as ever. On the one hand, a people had not yet been forged out of the mass, and on the other, the intellectuals remained too aloof and contemptuous of the crowd. Such a situation was abominable and could only be ended by the advent of a democratic community instigated by spiritual intellectuals.[29] These same ideas were re-enforced in "Voltaire-Goethe" and other essays Mann wrote between 1910 and 1914. The point was to engender a people which would become both a tribune and a receptacle for humanitarian ideals. In this way words could "move things" and, through the medium of a political public, bring about a union of spirit and action in the world.[30]

This, in sum, was the concept of literary politics which Mann had developed in the period just before the First World War. Several things remained vague or unanswered, especially the exact nature of the writer's duties and the procedures by which he was supposed to create a people. But Mann never became more precise than this until the tumultuous German Revolution of 1918–1919, when events themselves forced him to become more specific.

Mann's Literary Generation: The Turn Toward Engagement

Mann was not alone in suggesting that the writer become *engagé*. Other German authors writing between 1900 and 1914 arrived at similar positions, and often in the same way, i.e., by struggling with, and then rejecting, a previously acquired aesthetic attitude towards life.

The reason for this is not hard to find. German reality changed, and along with it so did the outlook of many serious writers. The very conditions which once permitted idyllic withdrawal ("power-protected inwardness") had worsened and now seemed to call for involvement.

The whole tone of the Wilhelmian Era—with its arrogance and authoritarianism, its imperalism abroad and militarism at home— appeared increasingly odious and threatening. To the most perceptive writers of the period, a major war seemed imminent unless something decisive were done to prevent it. But what could be done? Among those who acknowledged that the situation was critical, there was general agreement that, at the very least, intellectuals had to arm themselves with the weapons of *Geist* in order to fight for a freer, more rational society. The insolence of power, it was agreed, would become still more insufferable unless someone spoke up for ideals and attempted to realize them by fusing "spirit" and "deed." The task of rectifying matters was given to the man-of-letters, often with the most extravagant claims made on his behalf.[31] The same writers who had earlier extolled the virtues of the aesthetic poet (*Dichter*) now began to speak of the merits of the committed author (*Literat*).

Signs of this change in mood and direction can be found everywhere in German literature around the year 1910. There appeared quite suddenly a spate of political-literary journals, each oriented toward the Left to one degree or another, and each advocating a socially-committed notion of art. The most important among these were *Das Blaubuch* (founded 1906), *Pan* (1910), *Der Sturm* (1910), *Die Aktion* (1911), *Revolution* (1913), *Die weissen Blätter* (1913), and *Das Forum* (1914).[32] Two new literary movements compatible with Mann's principles also made their appearance at this time, mainly in the pages of the above journals. The first of these was Expressionism, and the second Activism.

Expressionism called for the creation of a "new man," brotherhood, and the humanization of the world. Like Mann, whom many adherents of the movement adopted as their mentor, it took the position that existing society had to be transfigured since it was based on hate rather than love. Again like Mann, expressionist writers recognized that Germany was sorely in need of "ideals" which could redeem life on earth. But in every case, the Expressionists failed to mention how the world could be improved at the social level (though they thought they knew how to do it on a personal and private one). All of them yearned for transformation but lacked a method. Consequently, the movement became essentially a protest against bourgeois society by writers who merely "represented" spiritual ideals but were not clear about how to implement them.[33]

In contrast, the literary movement of Activism was more political

and radical. Led by young writers like Kurt Hiller and Ludwig
Rubiner, it called for immediate social reform based on the dictates
of reason and ethics. Child-rearing had to be rationalized, war
banned for good, the death penalty abolished, state power democratized, justice equalized, the churches weakened, and education
humanized—and in all this the writer was given a central role. Using
almost the same words Mann did in "Geist und Tat," the Activists
demanded that the *littérateur* dedicate himself to improving the
world. At one and the same time he was asked to become "the
voice of the public conscience, a warner, a bearer of truth, an accuser,
a defender, and a representative of the people in the best sense of the
word."[34]

Beside these new voices, several older ones also began to articulate
a kind of literary politics. A significant segment of Mann's literary
generation—a segment which, like him, had embraced an impressionist
Weltanschauung in the 1890s—now slowly came around to a more
engaged notion of what writing is and what the writer is supposed to
do. René Schickele, whose early work around 1900 was purely
aesthetic and lyrical, had become by 1914 a radical pacifist and
kindred spirit of the Activist movement.[35] In 1913 he became associated with *Die weissen Blätter* (soon to be the most important of the
anti-war journals), and in the following year wrote an anti-militarist
and vaguely socialist novel, *Benkal der Frauentröster*. Lion Feuchtwanger also turned away from what he called "the overemphasis on
the aesthetic and the formal" which characterized his youth. By the
time of the First World War, he began to focus his attention on
larger issues of man's responsibility for action in the face of power.[36]
Carl Sternheim abandoned his early experiments in Neo-Romanticism
and went on to write brilliant and biting satires of Wilhelmian
Germany. His attacks on the greed, pettiness, and hypocrisy were
already well-known before 1914. Georg Kaiser also developed a
more engaged notion of the social function of art, especially in *Von
morgens bis mitternachts* (written 1912) and *Die Bürger von Calais*
(1913). He now argued that art could present ideals and criticize
society at the same time. In this view his early Nietzscheanism,
with its emphasis on self-renewal, was played down; instead, stress
was placed on social renewal, since he now believed that a healthy
community automatically engendered healthy individuals.[37] Alfred
Döblin similarly put aside his impressionist approach to literature,
and began to insist that writers deal with modern life and its

problems. In a 1913 essay addressed "to novelists and their critics," Döblin called for a shift away from the purely psychological to a more imaginative portrayal of everyday phenomena (something he called "de-spiritualized reality").[38] It was essential, he said, that writers grasp the totality of their age—including contemporary forms of alienation, depersonalization, and degradation—and not merely confine themselves to the boundaries of their own psyches.

All of these developments were tokens of important changes in German literature after 1900. Some observers looked upon them with anxiety, others with enthusiasm. What could not be denied by either group, however, was that what Thomas Mann called a "democratic movement" in German letters had indeed established itself as a force to be reckoned with.[39]

In April, 1914, on the eve of World War I, Heinrich Mann surveyed the German scene with a mixture of hope and uneasiness. He felt hopeful because he believed (wrongly) that no significant literary figure stood on the side of the regime in power. On the other hand, he had to admit that literary intellectuals were still "without influence" and not likely to attain any in the near future.[40] Moreover, a "people" had not been created, which meant that for the time being the writer had to fight his battles alone. But this was no reason to lose confidence. The spirit, Mann pointed out, had previously survived and triumphed under conditions worse than in Wilhelmian Germany. And in any event the committed writer could find encouragement in the fact that "everything great in contemporary Germany lived against the regime" and was imbued with "hatred and contempt" for it.[41] What Mann could not have known at the time was that precisely these "great" tendencies which "lived against the regime" were the ones to be silenced four months later with the outbreak of war.

Footnotes
Chapter 6

1. The one exception to this was his untitled 1904 letter to Maximilian Harden, published in *Die Zukunft,* XLIX, no. 2:67f.

2. Typical of this view is the following statement: "From the proud and aloof Bohemianism of his youth Heinrich Mann turned in 1910 to social analysis and criticism." See Fred Genschmer, "Heinrich Mann (1871–1950)," *South Atlantic Quarterly* (1951), L, no. 2:209.

3. See Heinrich Mann, "Mein Plan," November 11, 1893; included in *Heinrich Mann 1871–1950: Werk und Leben,* p. 55.

4. Though the idea of such a fusion is suggested, it does not actually take place in the novella. The contradictory nature of the "marvellous" and what Mann earlier called "satisfied existence" (*gesättigte Existenz*) finally seemed too great to reconcile.

5. Heinrich Mann, "Religiöse Kunst," *DZJ,* VI, Halbband 2, p. 201.

6. Heinrich Mann, "Decentralisation," *DZJ,* V, Halbband 2, p. 513. This passage is cited and discussed further in Manfred Hahn, "Heinrich Manns Beiträge in der Zeitschrift 'Das Zwanzigste Jahrhundert'," *Weimarer Beiträge,* XIII, no. 6:1012–13.

7. See, for example, Heinrich Mann, "Bauerndichtung," *DZJ,* V, Halbband 2, pp. 79–81; and "Niederlage des Naturalismus, *DZJ,* VI, Halbband 2, pp. 467–68.

8. It should be said that there were times (particularly around 1900) when Mann was tempted to slip back into an elitist, custodial view of the literary calling. In the figure of Köpf, for instance, who is the only "hero" in the novel *Im Schlaraffenland,* Mann presented an image of the writer as aloof, cynical, and reserved. Köpf is aware of, and despises, everything that is wrong with German bourgeois society, but he does not commit himself to action. Instead, he rejects the masses and seems more interested in forming a clerisy above society than in involving himself in it. Involvement, it is inferred, usually ends in compromise or opportunism, and in any case the effort is not worth the reward. Significantly enough, this very notion of the writer as an elitist, self-appointed custodian of values (which Mann still occasionally flirted with around the turn of the century) was precisely the one he attacked most bitterly in his "Geist und Tat" essay.

9. Heinrich Mann, "Gustave Flaubert und George Sand," *Essays* I, *Ausgewählte Werke,* XI:102–03, 108. Mann was careful to let Sand herself speak for these

values (as a counterpoise to Flaubert's aestheticism). Although he was obviously sympathetic, Mann did not yet wish to directly identify himself with liberal-democratic concepts.

10. Heinrich Mann, *Zwischen den Rassen,* in *Ausgewählte Werke,* II:430.

11. Heinrich Mann, letter to René Schickele, October 27, 1909; in *Heinrich Mann 1871–1950: Werk und Leben,* p. 121.

12. Heinrich Mann, "Geist und Tat," in *Essays* I, *Ausgewählte Werke,* XI:10–11.

13. *Ibid.,* p. 12

14. *Ibid.,* p. 13.

15. See Herbert Marcuse, "The Affirmative Character of Culture," *Negations,* trans. Jeremy J. Shapiro (Boston, 1968), p. 91.

16. The term is Georg Simmel's. See Georg Simmel, *The Conflict in Modern Culture and Other Essays,* trans. K. Peter Etzkorn (New York, 1968), p. 14.

17. For more on this see Klaus Schröter, *Anfänge Heinrich Manns,* pp. 74–77, 135–46; Manfred Hahn, "Heinrich Manns Beiträge in der Zeitschrift 'Das Zwanzigste Jahrhundert'," *Weimarer Beiträge,* XIII, no. 6:1007–14; and Hanno König, *Heinrich Mann: Dichter und Moralist* (Tübingen, 1972), pp. 62ff.

18. Heinrich Mann, "Geist und Tat," in *Essays* I, *Ausgewählte Werke,* XI:7–8.

19. Mann believed that this had already happened by 1910 in France, but not in Germany. See Heinrich Mann, "Voltaire–Goethe," *Essays* I, *Ausgewählte Werke,* XI:16–17.

20. Roland Barthes, *Critical Essays,* trans. Richard Howard (Evanston, 1972), pp. xvii, 155.

21. This does not mean that Mann lost interest in considerations of form or beauty in the literary work, or that he went over to some crude type of Naturalism. Far from it. He remained highly sensitive to these matters, but turned away from the exclusive preoccupation with them that he had shown earlier. Lorenz Winter has made a somewhat similar distinction between literature as a *Produkt* and literature as a *Werkzeug.* See Lorenz Winter, *Heinrich Mann and His Public,* p. 19.

22. Heinrich Mann, *Ein Zeitalter wird besichtigt,* p. 252; and Hanno König, *Heinrich Mann: Dichter und Moralist,* p. 213.

23. Heinrich Mann, "Geist und Tat," *Essays* I, *Ausgewählte Werke,* XI:11–12;

and "Voltaire—Goethe," *Essays* I, *Ausgewählte Werke,* XI: 17.

24. See Hanno König, *Heinrich Mann: Dichter und Moralist,* p. 213.

25. Heinrich Mann, "Voltaire—Goethe," *Essays* I, *Ausgewählte Werke,* XI:17.

26. Heinrich Mann, letter to Maximilian Brantl, November 14, 1908, in "Heinrich Manns Briefe an Maximilian Brantl," *Weimarer Beiträge,* XIV, no. 2:400.

27. Heinrich Mann, letter to René Schickele, December 27, 1909, in *Heinrich Mann 1871-1950: Werk und Leben,* p. 121.

28. Heinrich Mann, "Geist und Tat," *Essays* I, *Ausgewählte Werke,* XI, p. 8.

29. Mann does not say precisely how this was to be done, except through the force of words. *Ibid.,* p. 13.

30. See, for example, Heinrich Mann, "Voltaire—Goethe," *Essays I, Ausgewählte Werke,* XI:16-17, 20.

31. See, for instance, Ludwig Rubiner, *Der Mensch in der Mitte* (Berlin, 1917).

32. For a description of the contents of these journals, see Fritz Schlawe, *Literarische Zeitschriften: 1885-1910* (Stuttgart, 1961), and *Literarische Zeitschriften: 1910-1925* (Stuttgart, 1962).

33. On the socio-political character of Expressionism see Adolf D. Klarmann, "Der expressionistische Dichter und die politische Sendung," *Der Dichter und seine Zeit.* ed. Wolfgang Paulsen (Heidelberg, 1970), pp. 158-80; Georg Lukács, " 'Grösse und Verfall' des Expressionismus," *Essays über Realismus* (Neuwied and Berlin, 1971), pp. 109-49; and Wilhelm Emrich, *Protest und Verheissung* (Bonn, 1963), pp. 135-54.

34. Paul Pörtner, "Einführung," *Literatur-Revolution 1910-1925,* 2 vols., (Neuwied and Berlin, 1961), II:26. For more on the ideology of Activism see the texts by Hiller, Rubiner and others in *ibid.,* pp. 387-472; also Wolfgang Paulsen, *Expressionismus und Aktivismus* (Bern, 1935), pp. 35-71.

35. See René Schickele, "Politik der Geistigen," *März* (1913), VII:405-07, 440-41.

36. See Lion Feuchtwanger, "Versuch einer Selbstbiographie," *Die Literatur* (1927), XXIX:569, also Horst Hartmann, "Die Antithetik 'Macht-Geist' im Werk Lion Feuchtwangers," *Weimarer Beiträge* (1961), VII, no. 4:667-93.

37. For a discussion of the limitations inherent in Kaiser's view of "engagement,"

see Wilhelm Steffens, *Georg Kaiser* (Hannover, 1969), pp. 45–48.

38. See Alfred Döblin, "An Romanautoren und ihre Kritiker," *Aufsätze zur Literatur,* ed. Walter Muschg (Olten and Freiburg, 1963), pp. 19–23.

39. Thomas Mann, letter to Kurt Martens, January 11, 1910, in *Letters of Thomas Mann,* p. 55.

40. Heinrich Mann, "Der Bauer in der Touraine," *Essays* II, *Ausgewählte Werke,* XII:251.

41. *Ibid.,* p. 252.

Chapter 7

Social Criticism and Literary Form

The more profoundly an epoch and its great problems are grasped by
the writer, the less can his portrayal be on a commonplace level.

Georg Lukács

Combative Writing

In the years prior to the First World War, Heinrich Mann worked
out a theory of literary politics which appeared to bring literature
into critical conjunction with the new realities of Wilhelmian
Germany. According to this theory, existing society, with its emphasis
on world power and national prestige, was fundamentally off course,
since it was based on force and authority and fueled by hate and
greed. To remedy the situation, higher ideals were needed. Germany
had to be spiritualized through values like humanity, democracy, and
rationality. But for this to happen a people had to be created who
could receive these values and, by acting on them, carry them into
daily life. Here is where the committed writer could be instrumental
in the cause of social change. If the German *Literat* could politicize
his reading public; if he could embody democratic and humanitarian
ideals in his work; and if he could fight against dangerous social
tendencies through the "force of words," then it might be possible to
change drastically the contours of existing reality. According to
Mann, it had been done before. He argued that in France, the
literature of the Enlightenment had helped prepare the way for the
Revolution, and that in Russia, the tradition of the social novel from
Gogol to Tolstoy had laid the groundwork for the events of 1905,
and later for the Russian Revolution itself.[1]

From Mann's point of view, there were essentially two mediums
through which a writer could make an impact upon society: the
novel and the political essay.[2] Mann believed that literature, when
properly executed, was not only a critique of life but an instrument
for social change. It now remains to be seen how well he accom-

123

plished the tasks of literary politics which he urged upon others. In the pages that follow no attempt is made to explicate Mann's works in detail or to give a precise description of their contents. The concern here is only with how well Mann was able to place these two forms, the novel and the essay, in the service of social criticism.[3]

The Novel

A writer who sets out to use the novel as an instrument for social change has several possible ways in which to accomplish this goal.

First, if his assumption is that reality is unjust or oppressive, he could simply portray the world exactly as it is, without commentary or embellishment. By describing things with photographic exactness, the writer would presumably force people to face the true nature of social existence, and perhaps eventually to change it for the better. This was the method of many Naturalists, who believed that a mirror-like reflection of the facts of life might raise consciousness and inspire the reading audience to action.

Second, a writer could take the approach of imaginatively recreating, rather than simply describing, what is. When a novelist describes, he tries to let facts speak for themselves, but when he re-creates he intentionally organizes and interprets reality through his own critical consciousness. In a re-created work, the surface characteristics of one's age are not simply transcribed; rather, the age itself is imaginatively reproduced in what Georg Lukács called its "distilled essence." A novelist chooses this approach to social criticism when he attempts to make transparent the totality of society, that is, the complex ensemble of social relations which might not be obvious if a multiplicity of external social facts were merely recorded. This type of writing, often referred to as critical realism, contains the implicit assumption that society can be fundamentally changed only when people grasp the essence of the whole and become aware of the basic processes which constitute it.

Third, a novelist could transmit his social criticism by writing in such a way as to induce his readers to identify with certain model characters in his work. If these heroic characters are made to take critical or even radical stances toward society, it is possible that, through identification or an empathetic transfer of emotion, the reader would also wish to act in the same way (or at least acknowledge that acting in such a way is an ideal to be emulated). In a similar vein, a good writer could use the theme of the novel to awaken or energize human values which would otherwise remain mired and lost in the routine of everyday life. A novelist who chose this path might be able to put his readership in touch with social goals which it had once set for itself, but had since been unable or unwilling to carry out in practice. By first recalling and then cata- lyzing these ideals (as Mann believed Tolstoy and Zola did), the novelist could lay the groundwork for mass movements of a demo- cratic or humanitarian nature which would eventually lead to basic changes in society.

As a fourth alternative, a writer could turn literature into a critical weapon by using it to attack society through satire and parody. Here the objective would be to represent the world as grotesque by illumi- nating its ugliest features in the worst possible light. Through this approach a novelist could pierce the façade of society and unmask selected truths. But it is doubtful whether such a method could inspire meaningful social action, since it is not specifically designed to convince the uninitiated and could easily generate more hostility and confusion than social involvement.

Finally, a committed writer could choose to agitate for social change by depicting a utopia. He could paint a picture of what society should be like and, by playing on the contrast between the "is" and the "ought," he could presumably arouse in people a desire for a new kind of social reality. Several writers, like William Morris in *News from Nowhere* or Bernhard Kellermann in *Der Tunnel*, have tried to use the utopian novel as a critical-literary device, but with only a modicum of success.

Of these five types of critical literature Mann opted for the second and the fourth. All of his social novels between *Im Schlaraffenland* and *Der Untertan* (i.e., between 1900-1918) fell into one or the other of these two categories; they were either attempts at capturing the essential totality of social relations or they were efforts at satirizing existing evils, and sometimes they were both simultaneously. Gener- ally, Mann felt uncomfortable with the other modes of writing mentioned above. He rejected the first type, typified most fully by Naturalism, because he considered it essentially uncreative; he felt that the writer who used this method tended to become, as Stendhal had already said, nothing but "a mirror walking down the road." Mann also had reservations about the third type, which would have encouraged readers to identify with positive ideals represented in novels, though there is evidence that at times he wanted to try this approach, but was unsuccessful at it. As for utopian criticism, Mann showed no interest in it since he recognized that his talent lay not in future projections but in a careful analysis of the physiognomy of existing society.[4]

The choices of critical realism and satire were not purely arbitrary ones for Mann. They were, in fact, the most likely modes of writing open to him, given his historical placement in pre-World War I Germany and his desire to develop an engaged form of literature. Despite Mann's alleged radicalism, he still worked and thought within an historically-conditioned literary milieu. The characteristics of this milieu—which at its broadest reach included the legacy of the nineteenth-century French novel, as well as the satirical achievements of Heine and Wedekind, both of whom Mann drew on to a considerable extent—made it probable that he would move in the direction he did. This historical influence does not negate the innovative side of Mann's work, although it does help to explain both his accomplishments and his shortcomings. When Mann wrote that the novel should be an instrument of "political humanism," that it should speak to men about the whole, that it should "not merely describe but improve," and that it should show how "human relations" are based on and perverted by "the power relations of society," it seemed self-evident to him (as it may not have to a similarly motivated author of another period) that the most effective way of achieving these ends was through social satire and critical realism.[5]

One can find these two methods as early as *Im Schlaraffenland,* even though Mann had not yet worked out a clear conception of what he meant by literary politics. The satirical elements in the novel are obvious and well-executed. Even the title, which translates as "In the Land of Cockaigne: a Novel about Fine People," is a parody of the *haute bourgeoisie* whose life Mann made the main focus of the book. The novel takes place in Germany during the 1890s, so Mann was able to use the setting in order to hold up to ridicule everything he disliked about contemporary German society. By this means he hoped to portray society at its most grotesque, and thereby force the reader to become shocked at things he might otherwise overlook. The central message of the novel is that Wilhelmian Germany not only rewarded hypocrisy, but was also founded on it. At bottom, social life is pictured as thoroughly immoral and corrupt.

In order to succeed one had to compromise oneself, which usually meant selling oneself for money. The whole of Imperial Germany is shown to have been undergoing a process of *embourgeoisement* whereby the most ruthless types were brought to the top and the hangers-on left to scramble for recognition as best they could.

Mann made these points through literary distortion and hyperbole. By satirizing moralists who commit infidelities, authors who become famous without writing a word, "radical" playwrights who write proletarian dramas to amuse the bourgeoisie, aristocrats who prostitute themselves for money, and workers who, despite their show of militancy, are eager to be admitted into "the Land of Cockaigne," Mann was able to expose what he felt to be the basic fraudulence of contemporary society. There was in this an ingenious use of types, each representing a different social stratum or different kind of corruption. By elaborating on what Friedrich Engels called "typical characters in typical circumstances," Mann captured the entire spectrum of society with all of its weaknesses and self-deceptions. And by confronting these with irony and satire, he drew the most negative conclusions about his age—conclusions which he hoped would also be picked up by his reading audience.

But Mann went still further in *Im Schlaraffenland*. He tried to portray not only the surface hypocrisy but also the motivating principles of society. To capture the very laws by which society was run, satire was not enough. For this, one had to grasp more than just the flat panorama of social types; the reader had to be shown the totality of interconnecting social relations, including the historical forces at work at any given moment. In order to accomplish this larger task, Mann adopted the methods of critical realism, which he acquired largely from the French novelists.

According to Georg Lukács, the model critical realist is one who attempts to do the following: first, capture the essential characteristics of an age holistically; second, focus on the central contradictions of an era rather than on its extraneous details; third, grasp the major historical trends at work, and show how social types emerge or develop in relation to these trends; fourth, render visible the qualitative depth of social life as much as possible, especially its richness, complexity, and dynamic potentiality; fifth, portray the world with a reasonable amount of objectivity and critical detachment; and finally, remain at least open-ended toward the idea of socialism, even if there is no effort to affirm or support it in the novel.[6] Probably no critical realist has ever embodied all of these qualities simultaneously, but each has possessed most of them most of the time. If Lukács' categories are accepted, it is fair to say that Mann did indeed move into the camp of critical realism with *Im Schlaraffenland*. In this novel, a far cry from his psychological and highly subjective *In einer Familie*, Mann utilized each of the above approaches except the last. The acceptance of socialism as a viable possibility did not appear in any of Mann's novels before 1917.

Mann captured and criticized the major features of his age in several ways. First of all, he typologized his characters, making each of them represent a particularly hateful tendency in society. Thus Andreas Zumsee personifies the petty bourgeois opportunist, the Baron von Hochstetten the effete aristocracy, James L. Türkheimer the bourgeois parvenu, and so on. By then setting each of these social types in motion and allowing them to interact with one another, Mann in effect recreated Wilhelmian society in microcosm. However, he did not do this mechanically, for by exaggerating and manipulating his characters he was able to determine the kind of effect he would evoke in his readers. The result is that in *Im Schlaraffenland* Mann offers more than a mirror-reflection of modern social life. He shaped and re-worked his image of society in such a way that a powerful critical message is inherent in his reproduction of the social whole.

Just as important is Mann's portrayal of what he called "bourgeois absolutism."[7] In this same novel, Mann tried to demonstrate that one class ruled while the others gravitated into its orbit. In the process of making this point he went on to attack monopoly capitalism, German imperialism, and the kind of society which subordinated all values, including cultural ones, to an exploitative money economy. Similarly, Mann attempted to show not only that acquisitiveness and commodity fetishism were the motive forces of Wilhelmian Germany, but also that these attitudes were encouraged by bourgeois plutocrats like Türkheimer, whose hegemony depended on the acceptance of these attitudes by the population at large. Real power, Mann indicated in numerous ways, is economic, and once this is acquired political power follows. Hence, when the multi-millionaire Türkheimer prepares to invest abroad, the German government paves the way for him by forcefully opening up overseas markets. This action is of course taken under the guise of "moral and economic progress," but when the rhetoric is dropped it means railroads and lottery

tickets from which Türkheimer profits. When the venture fails, the
German navy is ready to intervene "to show the world how far the
strong arm of Germany reaches."[8] The same sort of message is repeated in other ways throughout the novel. Money, for example, is
the sole gauge of worth in "Schlaraffenland," so that it is impossible
to measure the inherent value of a person in other than cash terms.
Thus at the beginning Bienaimee Matzke, the daughter of a common
laborer, possesses no worth at all. But when Türkheimer begins
showering her with gifts valued upwards of 500,000 marks, she
suddenly becomes worthy of respect.[9] Andreas Zumsee's human
value also rises in proportion to his income, and at the height of his
social esteem he is reckoned to be worth the equivalent of almost a
million marks.[10] Still, this places him far behind the so-called great
men of the age, e.g., the financeer Ratisbohr who is appraised at
eight million, and Türkheimer whose value is incalculable.

It is hard to think of another German novel of the time which
contains such a damning indictment of the status quo. Friedrich
Spielhagen wrote social novels about Berlin, but they were not
basically critical. Even Theodor Fontane, when he dealt with problems of modern society, did not make capitalism or bourgeois domination the central concern of his work. Thus, the East German critic
Hans Kaufmann may be right in calling Mann's *Im Schlaraffenland*
the first novel to picture Germany as a modern, thoroughly capitalistic society.[11] However, Mann did not do this from a Marxist perspective. His motivations for writing what is essentially an anti-
bourgeois and anticapitalist novel were still moral and even partly
aesthetic. Simply put, Mann was revolted by contemporary German
society because he believed it was completely bereft of principles. But
at this point he had no real theoretical grasp of society, nor any
special knowledge of political economy on which to base an even
stronger case against his age.

Im Schlaraffenland was Mann's first attempt to use the novel to
criticize society, and as such it represents a significant achievement.
Nonetheless, the work does have its faults. Most noticeable perhaps
are the lack of positive characters in the novel and the absence of
anyone representing ideals which could point the way toward the
future. Furthermore, there was no indication that people could
actually do anything about the oppressiveness of bourgeois domination. The ascendency of Türkheimer and his class was taken as an
irreducible fact of life, and no alternatives were suggested to tran-

scend it. As Mann hinted, neither the working class, the *Mittelstand,* nor the intelligentsia could offer viable solutions since no one knew the way back to a pre-capitalist *Gemeinschaft* or forward to a new age. Even the writer Köpf (the only figure in the book with whom Mann seemed to identify) was forced to remain a skeptical outsider, critical of the system yet too dependent on it for his livelihood to challenge forcefully the world as given.

To be sure, Mann offered one small ray of hope. At the end of the novel he indicated, symbolically, that a society as enervated by corruption as "Schlaraffenland" (i.e., Wilhelmian Germany) had to be on the verge of collapse. Türkheimer, for instance, has no children to carry on his empire, which for Mann was always a sign of decay.[12] Likewise, the moods of Renaissancism and flamboyant sexuality are signs of arrested development, and possibly hints of some future decline and fall. If society should collapse, Mann seems to have been saying, it would be under its own weight. Activist elements within the old order, even if they existed, could not topple Türkheimer's world. Hence Mann staked out no role for literary politics, since the ideals of democracy and humanity could not change the status quo.

Mann's next social novel set in Wilhelmian Germany was *Professor Unrat* (1905). In this work, Mann continued to criticize his age but now on a different plane. Instead of concentrating on an elite of "fine people" he turned his attention to the petty bourgeois world of a North German *Gymnasium* teacher. By showing what happens to Unrat, a man unflinchingly loyal to the dominant value system of his time, Mann tried to point out what it costs in human terms to live in an immoral society. Unrat is portrayed as having a thoroughly warped personality—a condition due precisely to his complete integration into the ethos of the Wilhelmian era. Like Türkheimer, Unrat is set up as a type and his importance rests on the way he embodies certain social tendencies. But, whereas Türkheimer appears to be the master of his situation, Unrat mentally collapses under the pressure of the prevailing value system. Mann's point seems to be that contemporary Germany was both socially and psychologically untenable. In certain respects this represents an intensification of his critique, but even this novel is unable to offer a positive solution. Unrat's personal breakdown does not symbolize an imminent social breakdown, since after he is removed to an asylum, everything goes on as before.

In *Professor Unrat,* Mann's indictment of Wilhelmian society was double-edged. First, he attacked the German school system for the way in which it propagated a false and dangerous set of values. Second, he struck out at the power relations of society, particularly those based on hatred as the chief nexus between individuals. So long as these kinds of attitudes prevailed, Mann inferred, tyranny and authoritarianism would be standard fare, and an ideal society based on love and cooperation would be further away than ever.

Mann's approach to the first part of his critique, that directed against the school system, was not entirely original. During the two decades prior to the publication of *Professor Unrat,* a unique genre of literature had taken hold in Germany—a genre which dealt with the schoolroom and school conflicts, with puberty and the painful rupture between the "creative young" and their authoritarian elders.[13] Mann simply continued this tradition in, for instance, his novella "Abdankung" ("Resignation," 1905), where he echoed nearly all the motifs of this so-called "literature of the school," even to the extent of having his youthful hero commit suicide.[14] But in *Professor Unrat,* Mann shifted his focus. He made the schoolmaster and all he typified, not the students, the main object of concern; and furthermore, he showed how the values of the classroom (regimentation, submission, blind obedience) were exactly those which Wilhelmian society rewarded in its day-to-day functioning. By this method, Mann added a socially critical tone to his work which most other school novels lacked due to their psychological emphasis. Where other writers were interested in penetrating the adolescent mind, Mann was chiefly interested in revealing how the ideology of the school related to the social structure of contemporary Germany. The difference here is immense and cannot be overlooked.

What becomes immediately clear about Mann's portrayal of the German classroom is that it is founded on reciprocal hatred, hatred not only of the pupils for the teacher but also of the teacher for the pupils. On the one hand, Unrat tries to catch his students in some minor infraction of the rules so he can "ruin their careers" (and there is clearly a class bitterness involved in this); on the other, the students, impelled by fear as well as hatred, strive to hurt and humiliate Unrat. The result appears to be a Hobbesian state of nature where classroom deportment is geared to permanent, internecine warfare. Mann's point is that this makes the school a perfect preparation for society as it actually is. The school is, in fact, a

paradigm of mistrust and *ressentiment*. It undercuts all possibilities
of cooperation, or, as in the case of Lohmann, Unrat's most
rebellious student, it turns one's natural sensitivities into hopeless
cynicism. According to Mann, the educational system by its very
nature is designed to produce an acquiescent and unthinking mass of
obedient subjects who follow orders no matter what.[15] Even the
students' derision of Unrat fits into the scheme of things, for antagonism is the motive force of social life and the lubricant which keeps
the wheels of society running.

The second part of Mann's attack was aimed at Unrat as a social
and psychological type. Here, Mann used him to personify certain
qualities he considered typical of the entire period rather than just of
the petty bourgeoisie to which Unrat belonged. To give one example,
the professor is portrayed as an archetype of the acquisitive character,
a man whose greed for possessions has escaped all reasonable bounds.
Self-realization, for him, is ownership: being is having. Only in accu-
mulating things, including his mistress Rosa Frölich, who he feels he
owns like any other object, does Unrat experience himself as a
person. Everything external to himself is converted into property,
since the only way he can relate to things is to exploit them for his
own use. Through the example of Unrat, the acquisitive character
type is carried to such an extreme that it becomes almost pure caricature. Similarly, Unrat's hunger for power is not simply a personal
idiosyncrasy; it is represented as typical of Wilhelmian Germany,
where Nietzsche's will-to-power, brutalized and misunderstood, has
become a social norm. In the course of the novel it becomes obvious
that Unrat believes he is an *Übermensch*. He distinguishes himself
from the "common philistine" and thinks of himself as a strong
individual in comparison to the mass of ordinary weaklings.[16] On
closer inspection, however, it is evident that for Unrat strength only
means the power to manipulate others. Behind his pseudo-Nietz-
scheanism there is nothing but a desire for revenge and a bad conscience. Mann's message is that at the core of Unrat's urge to dominate and destroy others there is a fundamental weakness of character.[17]
And the inference is that when the social norms of an entire age are
tyranny and the love of authority, it too is basically sick and lacking
in character.

In terms of effective social criticism, *Professor Unrat* was not an
improvement over *Im Schlaraffenland*. The satire in the later book
often lacked subtlety, and the overdrawn portrait of Unrat was

generally unconvincing. Once again, there were no forward-looking
characters nor any indication of how things might change for the
better in the near future. It is true that the work offers a thoroughly
critical view of society, including a careful dissection of some of the
most egregious features of the age. But this is an entirely negative
perspective; one can glimpse the way things should be only by
imagining the reverse of all that Mann described. Moreover, since
Unrat is shown to be in many respects the product of his times, he is
portrayed as not entirely responsible for what he has become. After
all, as an educator and a civil servant, he is only acting out the role
assigned to him, and if he is petty and tyrannical it is because everything in his age had conspired to make him so. He fully embraces
the values of society, which is what makes him both tragic and comic
at the same time. As an individual within a social totality, Unrat
continually reproduces the whole in his every thought and deed. To
Mann, it appeared that contemporary Germany, filled as it was with
Unrat-types, was a one-dimensional society which offered no possibilities for transcendence. His theory of literature at the time reflected
this depressing point of view. The novel, he felt, could only be a
forum for criticizing what is, not a means for suggesting what to do
about it.

Mann's next important novel, *Die kleine Stadt* (1909), appears to
be a complete turnabout. In it, one can find not only positive characters and values, but also a basically optimistic attitude toward
social change. For the first time, the ideals of democracy and brotherhood entered into Mann's work, and not as "wish dreams" but as
real possibilities that could be actualized in the present. Again for the
first time, Mann concluded a novel on a strong note of hope. The
world, he inferred, could be made better, and even a genuinely
democratic society was not altogether out of the question.

Die kleine Stadt is qualitatively different from the two earlier
novels, and consequently it represents a major breakthrough in
Mann's conception of the relationship between literature and society.
It demonstrates that the novel could do more than criticize. It could
also do at least three other things: present a model of functioning
democracy; portray in human terms the meaning of love, compassion,
and civic cooperation; and lastly, represent affirmative values worth
emulating, especially those of a truly democratic culture. This is not
to say that *Die kleine Stadt* was in any sense a utopian novel. Far
from it. The setting was Italy in the 1890s, and the treatment was

realistic rather than imaginary. But it is precisely this realism which Mann turned to good effect. By demonstrating how ordinary human beings, filled with good and bad qualities, were nonetheless able to rise above their situation and create a workable community, Mann implied that the same could be done by anyone. It was simply a matter of will and effort, not a superhuman feat which one reads about only in fairy tales.

It is no accident that *Die kleine Stadt* was completed at exactly the time Mann began to formulate his views on literary politics. The work represents his attempt to bring the novel format into line with his new social and intellectual outlook. Methodologically, it was his most innovative novel to date. Mann restrained himself, as the all-wise narrator, as much as possible in the (democratic) interest of letting his characters, all ordinary people, speak for themselves.[18] Furthermore, he abandoned the caustic, cryptic tone of his earlier work, and replaced his usually biting satire with a gentler irony.[19] Finally, he temporarily dispensed with the device of highlighting anti-heroes like Andreas Zumsee or Immanuel Raat and chose, instead, to create the most positive heroic type to be found in any of his early novels, i.e., the people themselves. The book is in fact a celebration of the "genius" of the community, a paean to democratic values.[20] In *Die kleine Stadt* he attempted to do what he had never done before: to build, as he put it, "a temple to the people, to mankind."[21] He wanted his novel to be a carry-over from, or perhaps the literary equivalent of, the commitments he had assumed in actual life. "I believe," Mann wrote at the time, "that in this democratic age only he whose work is related to the final victory of democracy can really create anything beautiful. My spiritual radicalism ... is inseparable from the political."[22]

What messages does the novel convey to the reader? First, there is the simple injunction to substitute the quality of love for that of hate as the propelling force behind modern society. When hatred predominates, regimental order and tyranny replace community and cooperation. Only when the energies of love prevail—and not privatized love, but love sublimated and politicized into compassion and the readiness to help others—can a free, democratic and wholesome civic life emerge.

This is a view which Mann had not made explicit before. In the early 1890s, he had depicted love as essentially personal; it could bind together two people, but often at the expense of separating them from the larger community. Later, under the influence of Bourget, Mann emphasized the integrative value of familial love, but it was not until *Die kleine Stadt* that love began to mean "social love," brotherhood, and the urge to bind oneself directly to the community. In short, as the word was de-eroticized it was raised to a principle of communality. The person who loved most was the one who lived constructively and in fellowship with others, not the one who loved privately and in isolation.[23] Mann used this framework to make two points simultaneously. On the one hand, he showed that democracy was possible in the "little town" of the novel because possessive love had been transformed into a generalized mutuality and good will. (After much confusion, the citizens in the novel experience what Mann called "a moment of love," which allowed them to take "an irreversible step towards greatness."[24]) On the other hand, Mann used the same framework to explain why Germany had not yet achieved community. The reason lay in the fact that the Germans still held onto an egotistic, acquisitive notion of love, and hence were prevented from reappropriating it as a social principle. Once these points are grasped, a character like Unrat becomes more understandable. In him, the natural energies that might have become love were turned into hate, and the will to unite with others was converted into the will to acquire power over them.

From the view that love must be socialized in order to become the binding force of a democratic society follows a second message, that the people as a whole are fundamentally good whenever they listen to their natural social instincts. If left alone, despite all their prejudices and shortcomings, they will find means for settling their differences and forging a decent society. Mann never exuded this sort of confidence in mankind before, and the sudden appearance of this attitude is striking. It seems that he had been reading Rousseau and Michelet at the time, and certainly their influence is obvious in *Die kleine Stadt*. "Have no fear for the people, their hearts are noble," says one character.[25] Another declares that "the will of all is more worthy of respect than the will of one."[26] Significantly, and in stark contrast to Wilhelmian Germany, the little town runs smoothy without any intrusion from a state apparatus.

A third and last message of the novel is that a people can be created through the influence of art. In *Die kleine Stadt* the catalyzing agent for democratization is a travelling troupe of players which inadvertently arouses the latent passions of the townfolk, and then

helps convert these passions into binding cooperative principles. If
the outside artists had not come and activated the masses, there
would presumably have been no happy reconciliation at the end—no
progress "towards greatness," as Mann put it. This is exactly the
point he repeated more forcefully the following year in "Geist und
Tat": the role of the intellectual (or artist) is to stimulate the masses
to achieve self-consciousness. However, there is at least one crucial
difference between *Die kleine Stadt* and "Geist und Tat" which
cannot be overlooked. In the novel, Mann simply assumed naturally
good intentions on the part of the Italians. It was taken for granted
that a healthy *volonté générale* was present just below the surface,
and that in order for the Italian people to get hold of themselves and
control their own destinies, it needed only to be aroused. In the
essay, which was addressed to a specifically German audience, the
matter was approached differently. Mann acknowledged that no such
democratic propensity existed among his countrymen, and that even
if one granted that the Germans were potentially as cooperative as
the Italians, they were in practice prevented from becoming so because of the nature of Wilhelmian society and its institutions. Thus,
in the first case the task of the intellectual or artist was merely to
activate what was already there, but in the second it was to forge a
people by means of ideals which were not indigenous and which
therefore had to be imposed from without. This is why the relationship between the German *Literat* and the *Volk* seemed so problematic
to Mann. Even though he hoped a novel like *Die kleine Stadt* would
have some effect in Germany (by portraying the "ideal" if nothing
else), he knew that it would be much harder to bring about democratization there than in Italy.

   When the reviews of his book began to appear, Mann of course
complained that he was misunderstood.[27] But in spite of his innovations, much of the criticism was deserved. The emphasis on love,
while well-intended, is somewhat naive. Likewise, the Italian setting
was unconvincing to a German readership that could not relate to the
quixotic events of an almost preindustrial town. Most of the liberal
political perspective which appears in the novel, takes the form of a
simple, and probably ineffectual, counter-image to Wilhelmian
Germany which, again, no doubt seemed meaningless to most of his
readers. As Lorenz Winter correctly summarized it: "The 'humanity'
of *Die kleine Stadt* was, to a great extent, economically independent
and politically unaffiliated. . . . Vast economic conflicts and political

intrigues . . . were unfamiliar to [a German audience], as were those social upheavals that, like the French Revolution, had spread out from the large cities. Nowhere did Mann's novel state clearly whether the small town was part of a monarchy or a republic."[28]

Thus, Mann's achievements in form were largely offset by weaknesses in content. The major strength of the novel was its positive model for social action, the major drawback its foreign locale. The apparent solution would have been to utilize the same format in a German setting, but then it would have been impossible to be optimistic. Hence, the dilemma Mann faced as a serious novelist was as much social as literary; he could not solve his fictional problems without the use of spurious techniques, but he could not resort to these and still be a good political novelist so long as reality remained what it was.

Mann's last, and best known, social novel before World War I was *Der Untertan* (written 1914, published 1918).[29] The most important thing to note here about this work is that methodologically, it did not break new ground. In it, Mann returned to the weapons of satire and critical realism which he had begun to develop in *Im Schlaraffenland*. However, his satire was now much more strident than before, and to many readers the work seemed so uncompromisingly hostile to everything that it could not be taken seriously. The conservative critic Werner Mahrholz, for instance, wrote in reference to the shrillness of the book's tone: "I maintain . . . that this German political satire . . . smacks of petty bourgeois narrowness. . . . [It] was not conceived and set down from freedom of soul . . . but from bitter hate and impotent rage."[30] Mahrholz goes too far, but it is true that Mann's use of parody and caricature was much more extreme than earlier. However brilliant his sardonic commentary may seem in retrospect, it undoubtedly appeared to many at the time as somewhat overdone.

The method of critical realism is raised to a higher level of sophistication in *Der Untertan* than had been achieved in either *Im Schlaraffenland* or *Professor Unrat*. On the one hand, its scope is broader since Mann's goal now was to portray not merely bourgeois domination, but, as he said, "the history of the public mood under Wilhelm II."[31] On the other hand, the novel has a more explicit political thrust, since Mann had widened his critique to include political types as well as socio-economic ones. In the work, the reader confronts old-fashioned liberals, National Liberals, Pan-Germans, Social Democrats, Prussian-agrarian conservatives, political anti-

Semites, and even the Kaiser himself. This side of Wilhelmian
Germany had previously been treated only tangentially, but now
Mann was willing to make it a center of attention. The result was an
attempt to represent the whole network of relationships which went
into the making of pre-war German society. With *Der Untertan,* in
fact, Mann began his project of writing a *Kaiserreich* trilogy modelled
on Zola's *Rougon-Macquart* series, which dealt with France under
Louis Napoleon. When completed in 1925, Mann's trilogy provided
a critical survey of modern Germany in its social, political, and
historical dimensions from 1871 to 1918. This was his major contribution to the genre of critical realism.

How effective was *Der Untertan* in raising the consciousness of the
reading public? This question can never be answered satisfactorily,
since the book was not allowed to appear until 1918, when an
entirely different climate of opinion prevailed. Then the novel sold
well, over 100,000 copies almost immediately, but it was often read
either retrospectively, as a period-piece, or for its prophetic anticipation
of the fall of the German Empire.[32] Nevertheless, if the purpose of
the book was to convey trenchant insights and a grasp of the social
terrain, it would have to receive the highest commendations. If, on
the other hand, Mann's goal had been to awaken social conscience
and goad people to do something about their conditions, then it
seems doubtful that *Der Untertan* would have been effective in this
sense even if it had been published before the war. Like former
works (though this is not absolutely necessary in a good realistic
novel), the book lacks positive figures which might have suggested a
better way into the future. More importantly, since most of the
characters seem to be helplessly entangled in the unfolding of larger
forces beyond their control, Mann failed to convey the notion that
human beings could do anything about their condition. It is easy to
feel depressed rather than encouraged by the novel, and ultimately to
resign oneself to the enormity of an apparently unchangeable social
reality.

The anti-hero of the novel is Diederich Hessling, a quintessential
"good subject," whose evolution from boyhood to a dubious maturity during the reign of Wilhelm II is one of the central themes of the
work. In what seems to have been intended almost as a mockery of
the traditional German *Bildungsroman,* Mann traced the development of Hessling from a "dreamy, delicate child" to a full-blown
capitalist and super-patriot. By the end of the novel, this authoritarian

figure appears to be in complete control of his situation, both economically (as owner of the only paper factory in town) and politically
(as founder of the locally powerful "Emperor's Party"). Mann subtly
attacked Hessling throughout the book, and the reader is never in
doubt about the character's basic lack of integrity, cowardice, and
fanatical hunger for power. Moreover, Mann ingeniously played on
the affinity between Hessling's weakness of character and the weak-
mindedness of his political thought, pointing out time and again the
intimate links between personal improbity and (right-wing) ideology.[33]
Nonetheless, Hessling wins out in the end, and hence he can be seen
as not only the ascendant man of the modern age, but by extension
of the future as well. No one is placed in the field to oppose him:
not the socialist Napoleon Fischer, who becomes his collaborator; not
the intellectual Wolfgang Buck, who becomes his lawyer; not even
Old Buck, the classical liberal and 1848 revolutionary, who dies fully
aware that Hessling stands unchecked and that daemonic forces are
still loose in the world.[34]

Thus, in spite of extraordinary insights into social reality, an
unshakable pessimism haunts the pages of Der Untertan. The most
talented character in the work, Wolfgang Buck, refuses to jeopardize
his career (or what he calls his "personality development") in order
to oppose certain tendencies which he knows are leading Germany in
in the wrong direction. The result is that he falls back upon irony
and skepticism, not only about politics but about everything.[35] On
the other hand, the one individual in Der Untertan who represents
Mann's political ideals—i.e., Old Buck, the bürgerlich liberal—is
depicted as an antiquated relic of the nineteenth century, and hope-
lessly out of step with the twentieth. He is shown to be wholly
incapable of dealing with the "new spirit," whose dangerous contours he just barely understands. Eventually his very obsolescence
makes him an object of contempt, and even small children begin to
fear him "just as the older generation, when it was young, felt un-
speakable pride on seeing him."[36] Symbolically enough, the elder
Buck is sentenced to death in 1848, though he is subsequently par-
doned and lives on until 1900. But it is obvious that he has outlived
his time and potential effectiveness. Even though he is pictured as a
genuine moral and spiritual antipode to the Wilhelmian era (at least
in terms of ideals), he is by no means represented as a real counter-
force to it. This point is made all the more poignant when Old Buck
dies, unappreciated and without followers, but not before Hessling,

again symbolically, expropriates what is left of his small estate. As the novel concludes with this laying of gray on gray, one is reminded of Walter Benjamin's incisive epigram which, it seems, could have been Mann's as well: "It is only for the sake of those without hope that hope is given to us."[37]

The Essay

"We must decide," says one character in *Der Untertan*, "whether people like Hessling will fill the prisons or join the country's ruling elite."[38] For Mann this was the central issue of the age, but in his novels virtually no one brings himself to make such a decision, let alone act on it.

This raises the question of whether or not the novel provides the best forum for treating, not to say resolving, highly charged political and social problems. Though more will be said about this shortly, it is worth suggesting here that many of the limitations of Mann's four critical novels, from *Im Schlaraffenland* to *Der Untertan*, were indirectly due to the constraints of the novel form itself. It may be that through the medium of fiction an author can criticize, and even portray an abstract ideal, but he cannot advocate solutions to specific problems or present a roadmap to a better society. To pursue these ends Mann seemed to feel that an entirely different format was required, and this he found in the form of the political essay.

The essay as a mode of expression was not well-developed in German literature. Lessing, Herder, Goethe, and Schiller, among others, utilized this genre in the eighteenth century, but not as successfully as had Montaigne in France, or Bacon in England, two centuries earlier. To most German classicists, the essay was viewed as an occasional piece, and therefore something on the periphery rather than at the center of their work. In the nineteenth century, however, the essay form became increasingly prominent and specialized, so that eventually it was possible to speak of three different kinds of essays in German literature. First, there was the political essay, which came to the fore during the 1830s and 1840s, but noticeably declined in the 1850s and thereafter. Second, there was the philosophical essay, which was used successfully by Schopenhauer and later by Nietzsche and Simmel. Third and last, there was the literary-cultural essay, which was the most conspicuous form during the

latter half of the nineteenth century. The practitioners of this type
of expression were generally elitist and culturally conservative. They
defended traditional values, viewed themselves as curators of an
important spiritual legacy, and wrote with urbanity and grace for a
refined *Bildungspublikum*. More often than not, their works were
lyrically conceived and playfully elegant. Argument by association
usually ruled over logic, and subjective impressions prevailed over
critical observation.

It is interesting to note, however, that by the beginning of the
twentieth century this kind of essay had begun to appear problematic
to many. Writing in 1910 on "The Nature and Form of the Essay,"
the young Georg Lukács argued that the prevailing essay form had
lost its *raison d'être*. It was no longer in touch with life itself but
only with the objectifications thrown up by life. For this reason, he
wrote, the modern essay was, at its core, a derivative and secondary
genre. The rich texture of life experiences, which would have to be
drawn upon to make it a vibrant medium, was missing, and so was
any direct contact with the immediate or the concrete. As a result,
nothing was left but for the traditional literary-cultural essay to be
recognized for what, in Lukács' opinion, it had already become: dilet-
tantish, precious, and even parasitic. The only way out of this
impasse was to transform the essay into something radically different.
This meant that in order to regain contact with the essential, it
would have to be converted into an instrument for both judging
society, and for getting back in touch with the ultimate questions of
life in a more satisfactory way than either poetry, philosophy, or the
previous essay forms had been able to do. In short, Lukács expressed
the notion that the essay, having become merely a playful work of
art, had been superseded by reality and hence was problematic. The
way to make it meaningful again would be to convert it into a
modality of the will-to-truth and personal integrity, that is, to make it
something entirely other than what it was.[39]

It was out of this critical situation described by Lukács that Heinrich
Mann revived the German political essay in 1910. He did so partly
by updating the pre-1848 political form inaugurated by the Young
Germans, and partly by borrowing from the French social essay as it
developed from Voltaire to Zola. In the process of producing a new
essayistic style and content, Mann fundamentally challenged the
predominant notion (shaped by essayists such as Hermann Grimm,
Rudolph Kassner, and Stefan George) of what the essay should be

like. He also revolted against his own previous conception of the essay, which was entirely compatible with the one held by the German cultured public. In fact, the sketches (they are not essays as such) which Mann wrote in the early 1890s are generally impressionistic, literary, and even *feuilletonist,* since the emphasis is almost solely on *Bildung* rather than politics.[40]

Between 1910 and 1918 Mann wrote eleven essays, all directly or indirectly political, incorporating his new conception of the essay form. Some are short, running roughly eight to ten pages; others, like the famous "Zola" essay, are several times longer and much more complex. In this chapter, which is concerned exclusively with the social and political implications of literary form, it is important to note exactly what was radical and innovative about the form of Mann's essays when viewed within the German context. The content will be discussed later.

The first characteristic of Mann's essays during this period is that they are all written in a tight, condensed style with no superfluous words or sentences. The language is sharp and to the point, lacking the emotionalism one finds in, say, the literature of Expressionism. Moreover, the essays usually contain only two or three major themes, rarely more; each of these is treated like a musical motif, presented at one point in the text and returned to later for elaboration. The result is that these carefully composed pieces are not only highly symmetrical but also easy to read, thereby showing the marks of the novelist and not merely of the journalist.[41]

In addition to this, all the essays are written in such a way as to make possible a direct attack on the evils which Mann had earlier assailed only obliquely through the illusion of fiction. Thus it became obvious to even the casual reader that Mann stood firmly against the existing power structure and advocated democratization as a means of transforming Wilhelmian Germany into a humane community. Furthermore, the essay form allowed him to be more concrete and prescriptive. He could now say specifically what he thought should be done, as he did in "Reichstag" (1911), or in "Sinn und Idee der Revolution" ("The Meaning and Idea of Revolution," 1918); he could also hold up for emulation models of committed individuals like Voltaire, Zola and La Révelliere.[42] Even so, Mann was not always able to be as straightforward as he would have liked. Over half of the essays he published between 1910 and 1918 were written during the war, and therefore had to be toned down to avoid censorship. Mann got around this limitation to some degree by resorting to *double entendre*. For example, when he discussed Zola and the Second Empire he was really talking about the intellectual in Wilhelmian society, and when he dealt with La Révelliere's opposition to Talleyrand he was actually stressing the superiority of the man of principle over the man of power. Nevertheless, to the extent that he was forced to be covert, his ability to get the point across was seriously eroded. Mann's political essays tended to be deciphered only by intellectuals, instead of by the general reading public whom he would have preferred to reach. Still, it must be said that no other prominent writer in Germany at the time expressed himself with as much political verve, and no one pushed as hard for the goals of justice, rationality, and democratization.

In order to assess the overall significance of Mann's political essays, two points need to be made. To begin with, Mann was one of the first writers in twentieth-century Germany to view the essay as a critical form *par excellence*. Neither Lukács nor the Expressionists, both writing between 1910 and 1918, arrived at this recognition quite as decisively as Mann did. Lukács was still mainly concerned with the essay as a personal and expressive medium, while most of the Expressionists treated it as a poetical or lyrical art form.[43] Mann, however, grasped the critical power of the essay, especially its ability to point out wrongs and suggest solutions without having to provide a detailed blueprint for action. Later in the century other German writers like Walter Benjamin, Theodor W. Adorno, and Hans Magnus Enzensberger would also come to see the critical potential of the essay, but Mann (along with perhaps Karl Kraus in Austria) was one of the earliest to perceive the essay as a social and political weapon.

Second, and related to this, Mann was one of the few German writers of his time to consider the essay as a basically ethical medium. For him, the motivating force behind the political essay was the need to take moral responsibility for what the world had become. Throughout essays like "Geist und Tat," "Der Europäer" ("The European," 1916), and "Die Bücher und die Taten" ("Books and Deeds," 1918), one finds both a vigorous moral tone and what Max Bense has called an "ethical style."[44] Criticism, ethics, and engagement were seen as intimately bound up with one another, since a *Kritik* implied a moral point of view, and morality implied intervention in the world. This notion did not, of course, originate with Mann. It

had existed as early as the eighteenth century, particularly among
those writers who defined themselves as opponents of their age. However, during the course of the nineteenth century, ethical motifs had
become less and less prominent in the German essay. The ideal of
Humanität was gradually replaced by *Bildung*, or the cultivation of
one's private, aesthetic sensibilities. Mann's significance lies in the
fact that he revolted against this tendency.[45] In his essays, he returned to the eighteenth-century goal of an ethical humanity, but
with one essential difference. Unlike the Enlightenment thinkers, he
was certain that humanity was synonymous with democracy and
could not be achieved without it. Thus, to Mann, ethics became
advocacy, and writing an expression of the categorical imperative.

On the whole, these characteristics, and the ways in which they
were used, are what made Mann's essays seem so novel and militant
at the time of their appearance. By rejecting the view that one should
write contemplatively, from an Archimedian point outside existence,
Mann in effect brought the essay back into the flow of history and
into an immediate confrontation with social and political reality. At
the same time he avoided the obvious danger of pure polemics since
his essays, however partisan, were nonetheless carefully composed
works of art which no one could mistake for crude propaganda.

Summary and Critique

"Politics and literature," Mann wrote in 1915, "have the same
object, the same goal, and each must penetrate the other so that
neither will degenerate."[46] This is a succinct statement of one of
Mann's primary goals: to effect social consequences by the use of
literary methods and to make literature relevant by politicizing it. In
his view, Imperial Germany was already degenerate, but he still had
hopes that it could be changed by means of combative writing or
what he termed the "power of words." To this end, Mann himself
tried to utilize both the novel and the essay in order to criticize
society as it then was, and to project as workable goals the ideals of
democracy, rationality, and humanity. By way of conclusion, a few
words ought to be said about how successfully he used these literary
forms in the service of his political principles.

In the first place, it should be acknowledged that Mann usually
over-emphasized the writer's capacity to affect society. No one,
Voltaire and Zola included, ever made as great an impact on the

world as Mann seemed to think. Writing, by its very nature, has profound limitations. Its boundaries generally go no further than an author's reading public, and even his readership is not likely to be changed by a literary work unless it is already predisposed in that direction. To be sure, if a writer were to address a broad, sympathetic audience—one already leavened with democratic and republican values—his words might be taken to heart and he could activate tendencies already latent in the population. But, as Mann lamented time and again, such as audience did not yet exist in Wilhelmian Germany. Most German readers expected literature to be an entertaining distraction from everyday life rather than a critique of it. For some, this meant that the writer should be a narrator of the inner life, a *raconteur* of the beautiful things of the soul.[47] For others it meant that he should be a spinner of epic tales or historical adventure stories, like those written by Karl May or Felix Dahn.[48] In either case, there was no strong demand that an author confront reality head-on in order to criticize and change it. Thus, except for Naturalism (which Mann disliked), Germany had been without a serious opposition literature for nearly sixty years. The result of this absence of any socially-oriented German literary tradition was a noticeable lack of sympathy or understanding for the writer who wanted to turn his craft into an instrument of radical social commentary. Under the circumstances, the effectiveness of an engaged literary genre seemed doubly difficult in Germany. Not only did few pay attention to what a committed author had to say,[49] but the critics and *feuilleton* writers who reviewed socially critical works usually misinterpreted or condemned them out of hand even before the public could read them without pre-formed judgments.

There were further obstacles to Mann's effectiveness as a political writer. His use of the essay as a mode of criticism was often brilliant, but it was not as efficacious as he might have hoped. This shortcoming was partly due to censorship and Mann's resultant need to disguise his meaning, at least during the war years. But equally important was his tendency to publish essays in small-circulation journals with a fairly selective readership and an orientation which was already left-liberal.[50] Needless to say, his impact on committed intellectuals like Kurt Hiller was great, but he had little influence on readers not already receptive to liberal views. Thus the diminutive audience Mann finally addressed prevented him from reaching the wider public he had set out to write for in the first place.

His novels enjoyed a much broader circulation, but even here the result was not all that Mann had expected. Too often the success of his books was, as he put it, merely "literary," while the underlying message remained unnoticed or forgotten. If this was so, the fault may not have been entirely Mann's. His novels, as works of critical realism, were as well-executed as those of any German author writing at the time. In fact, it seems fair to say that today they not only provide the best documents available for grasping the mood of Wilhelmian life, but they are also "the strongest cornerstone of the German realistic novel during the first quarter of the twentieth century."[51] Each of his social novels carefully depicts the dominant social antagonisms at the time. Moreover, all of them, especially *Der Untertan,* show a reliable socio-historical grasp of things which allows certain characters to speak for concrete historical tendencies rather than for universal principles *á la* Schiller. Also clearly evident is a grasp of the totality of social relations, though Mann frequently did not portray the whole from the point of view of "progressive forces," as a Marxist critic like Lukács would have preferred. And finally, Mann's critical novels between 1900 and 1918 consistently direct the reader's attention outward toward society, not inward toward the qualities of the "beautiful soul." Mann's break with the introspective legacy of German letters was perhaps more significant than that of any other writer of his age. As a genuine pathbreaker, Mann deserves credit for being probably the most radical critical realist in Germany at the time of the First World War.

Still, there were limitations to his method. Though Mann's characters were generally accurate reproductions of real types, they were usually portrayed as victims of circumstances beyond their control. None of them seemed to be able to overcome the given environment, but were instead shaped and dominated by forces they could do nothing to alter. Where this theme was most pronounced, as in *Professor Unrat* or *Der Untertan,* the conclusion of the novel was generally pessimistic; except for *Die kleine Stadt,* Mann offered few examples of what people might realistically aspire to. To be sure, Mann did occasionally uncover human potentialities in social life and even hinted at some political alternatives to the established order. But he failed to take full advantage of these opportunities and hence neglected to explore all the ways in which a novel could be used to turn random consciousness into coherent understanding and motivation.[52]

Of course, the novelist can only achieve so much. He cannot

directly change objective conditions, but he does have considerable latitude to affect the subjective will of the reader in a positive way, which means that he might at least indirectly lead others to change the world for the better. If this is the criterion for judging the success of Mann's work, he could probably be called a failure, since there is no evidence that his novels or essays influenced many people in a progressive direction. If, however, the criterion is the ability to portray the dangers and antagonisms of existing reality in such a way as to make them seem no longer tolerable, then Mann might be counted a success. Lukács would no doubt have argued the first line of thought while Theodor W. Adorno would have argued the second. A successful work, Adorno wrote, "is not one which resolves objective contradictions in a spurious harmony, but one which expresses the idea of harmony negatively by embodying the contradictions, pure and uncompromised, in its innermost structure."[53] This Mann did. His resulting pessimism may have been the direct reflection of a situation which seemed to require that the thoroughgoing realist be at the same time a thoroughgoing pessimist.

Footnotes
Chapter 7

1. Mann often (especially after 1917) made this point about a socially-conscious literature preceding great social changes. See his *Ein Zeitalter wird besichtigt,* pp. 250–51; and "Die Macht des Wortes," *Es kommt der Tag: Deutsches Lesebuch* (Zürich, 1936), pp. 224–32.

2. Surprisingly, Mann never placed any great importance on the drama as a medium of social commentary. Though he wrote of half-dozen plays between 1910 and 1914 (including probably his best, *Madame Legros,* 1913), he tended to dismiss the stage as a forum inappropriate for social criticism. This placed Mann outside a prevailing German tradition, running from Naturalism through Expressionism to Brecht, which saw the stage as a major platform from which to attack the shortcomings of the age.

3. It should be stressed that even when Mann used literature for social criticism, he never allowed questions of art to be set aside. To him every novel or essay had its own laws of composition, its own internal and formal demands, which had to be adhered to quite apart from the social or political implications the piece may have. But though Mann's literary art is certainly worth considering in its own right, it is not the main focus of this chapter.

4. The same must be said of the caricaturist George Grosz (1893–1959), who was in many ways Mann's artistic counterpart. Grosz tried briefly to portray in his art an image of the future socialist man, but failed miserably. His genius came to the fore only when he depicted *existing* forms of greed, hypocrisy, and brutality, especially in bourgeois society. See Beth Irwin Lewis, *George Grosz: Art and Politics in the Weimar Republic* (Madison, 1971).

5. Heinrich Mann, "Zola," *Essays* I, *Ausgewählte Werke,* XI:160 *passim;* and his letter to Paul Hatvani, April 3, 1922, in *Heinrich Mann,* ed. Heinz Ludwig Arnold (Stuttgart, 1971), p. 11. See also Hanno König, *Heinrich Mann: Dichter und Moralist,* p. 24; and Monika Plessner, "Identifikation and Utopie: Versuch über Heinrich und Thomas Mann als politische Schriftsteller," *Frankfurter Hefte* (1961) XVI:812–26.

6. Georg Lukács, *Realism in Our Time,* trans. John and Necke Mander (New York, 1971), chapters II and III.

7. Heinrich Mann, *Im Schlaraffenland,* in *Ausgewählte Werke,* I:49.

8. *Ibid.,* p. 89.

9. *Ibid.*, p. 288.

10. *Ibid.*, p. 394.

11. Hans Kaufmann, *Krisen und Wandlungen der deutschen Literatur von Wedekind bis Feuchtwanger* (Berlin and Weimar, 1969), p. 86.

12. See Manfred Hahn, "Zum frühen Schaffen Heinrich Manns," *Weimarer Beiträge*, XII, no. 3:387. Asta, his only child, is married to Baron von Hochstetten, who is impotent.

13. Examples of this genre written between 1885–1905 would include Frank Wedekind's *Frühlings Erwachen,* Arno Holz's *Der erste Schultag,* Emil Strauss's, *Freund Hein,* Rainer Maria Rilke's *Die Turnstunde,* Friedrich Huch's *Mao,* Leonhard Frank's *Die Ursache,* Otto Flake's *Das Freitagskind,* Ludwig Thoma's, *Lausbubengeschichten,* and Hermann Hesse's *Unterm Rad* and *Peter Camenzind.* The section of Thomas Mann's *Buddenbrooks* dealing with "Hanno's Day in School" (part XI, chapter 2, in the Lowe-Porter translation) can also be placed in this tradition, but the most brilliant of the school novels, Robert Musil's *Die Verwirrungen des Zöglings Törless,* was not published until 1906. For more on this subject see Robert Minder, *Kultur und Literatur in Deutschland und Frankreich* (Frankfurt, 1962), pp. 74ff.; and Martin Gregor-Dellin's "Nachwort" to *Vor dem Leben: Schulgeschichten von Thomas Mann bis Heinrich Böll* (Munich, 1965), pp. 292–302.

14. Heinrich Mann, "Abdankung," *Novellen* II, *Ausgewählte Werke,* IX:91–101.

15. Unrat's motto is: "Sie sollen nicht denken!" See Heinrich Mann, *Professor Unrat,* in *Ausgewählte Werke,* I:541.

16. *Ibid.,* p. 565.

17. *Ibid.,* p. 457.

18. David Roberts, *Artistic Consciousness and Political Consciousness. The Novels of Heinrich Mann 1900–1938* (Bern, 1971), p. 44.

19. Ulrich Weisstein, *Heinrich Mann,* pp. 105–06.

20. Heinrich Mann, "Prospekt für *Die kleine Stadt,*" manuscript in Schiller-Nationalmuseum, Marbach; and Mann's letter to René Schickele, December 27, 1909, in *Heinrich Mann 1871–1950: Werk und Leben,* p. 121.

21. Heinrich Mann, "Autobiographie," manuscript written *circa.* 1910, Heinrich-Mann-Archiv no. 471; see *Heinrich Mann 1871–1950: Werk und Leben,* p. 122.

22. Letter to J. N. van Hall, October 1, 1907; included in *ibid.,* p. 111.

23. These and related points are discussed in David Roberts, *Artistic Consciousness,* pp. 59–74; and Hanno König, *Heinrich Mann: Dichter und Moralist,* pp. 154–67.

24. Heinrich Mann, "*Die kleine Stadt.* Brief an Fräulein Lucia Dora Frost," *Die Zukunft* (1910), LXX:265–66; Hanno König, *op. cit.,* p. 76.

25. Heinrich Mann, *Die kleine Stadt,* in *Ausgewählte Werke,* III:147.

26. *Ibid.,* pp. 110, 211, 403.

27. Heinrich Mann, letter to René Schickele, February 19, 1910, in *Heinrich Mann 1871–1950: Werk und Leben,* 119.

28. Lorenz Winter, *Heinrich Mann and His Public,* pp. 54–55.

29. For a more wide-ranging discussion of this novel see Edgar Kirsch and Hildegard Schmidt, "Zur Entstehung des Romans *Der Untertan,*" *Weimarer Beiträge* (1960), VI, no. 1:112–31; Ulrich Weisstein, *Heinrich Mann,* pp. 111–41; David Roberts, *Artistic Consciousness,* pp. 84–124; and André Banuls, *Heinrich Mann,* pp. 96–106.

30. Werner Mahrholz, "Heinrich Manns 'Untertan'," *Das literarische Echo* (1919), XXI:518–19.

31. Originally the book was to be subtitled "Geschichte der öffentlichen Seele unter Wilhelm II." See Edgar Kirsch and Hildegard Schmidt, "Zur Entstehung des Romans *Der Untertan,*" *Weimarer Beiträge,* VI, no. 1:121.

32. See Lorenz Winter, *Heinrich Mann and His Public,* p. 70.

33. See, for example, Heinrich Mann, *Der Untertan,* in *Ausgewählte Werke,* IV: 220, 446–50.

34. *Ibid.,* chapter VI.

35. Wolfgang Buck's comprehension of his age is greater than that of any other figure in *Der Untertan.* He sees through the illusions of his epoch with great clarity. He is aware of a general and dangerous tendency toward self-deception ("What matters to each of us is not that we really change the world very much but that we have the feeling we are causing change."). And he perceives that the "representative type of the era" is not the Kaiser but the actor, i.e., the individual who can convince others by theatrics that the imaginary is in fact the real. Nevertheless, he cannot bring himself to do anything about what he knows. (See *Der Untertan,* pp. 195, 197, 436–37.)

36. *Ibid.,* p. 413.

37. Walter Benjamin, cited in Herbert Marcuse, *One-Dimensional Man* (Boston, 1964), p. 257.

38. Heinrich Mann, *Der Untertan,* p. 229.

39. Georg Lukács, "Über Wesen und Form des Essays: Ein Brief an Leo Popper," *Die Seele und die Formen* (Berlin, 1911).

40. See Dieter Bachmann, *Essay und Essayismus* (Stuttgart, 1969), pp. 73–78.

41. See Ludwig Rohner, *Der deutsche Essay. Materialien zur Geschichte und Ästhetik einer literarischen Gattung* (Neuwied and Berlin, 1966), pp. 240, 244, 248.

42. See "Reichstag," *Essays* II, *Ausgewählte Werke,* XII:7–11; "Sinn und Idee der Revolution," *ibid.,* pp. 22–25; "Voltaire–Goethe," *Essays* I, *Ausgewählte Werke,* XI:7–14; "Zola," *ibid.,* pp. 156–235; and "Gespräch mit Talleyrand," *ibid.,* pp. 142–49.

43. This was not true of the Activists, especially Hiller and Rubiner, who, like Mann, valued the essay for its critical possibilities.

44. Max Bense, "Über den Essay und seine Prosa," *Merkur* (1947), I, no. 3: 415. In using this term Bense does not refer specifically to Mann.

45. See Dieter Bachmann, *Essay und Essayismus,* pp. 69–73.

46. Heinrich Mann, "Zola," *Essays* I, *Ausgewählte Werke,* XI:209.

47. See Albert Klein, *Die Krise des Unterhaltungsromans im 19. Jahrhundert* (Bonn, 1969), pp. 82–94.

48. George L. Mosse, "Literature and Society in Germany," *Literature and Western Civilization,* 2 vols., ed. David Daiches and Anthony Thorlby (London, 1972), II:267–97.

49. According to Herbert Ihering, the attention of most people in Germany was focused on the latest drama, not the latest novel or essay. Hence "the appearance of the novel was not viewed as a noteworthy event; it was discussed by the *feuilleton* editor only when he had the time." This indifference was even more true with regard to the essay. See Herbert Ihering, *Heinrich Mann,* p. 20.

50. The essays "Geist und Tat" and "Reichstag" were printed in *Pan,* a radical bi-monthly; "Voltaire–Goethe" first appeared in Gustav Landauer's *Der Sozialist* (under the title "Französischer Geist") and was later reprinted in the expressionist weekly *Die Aktion;* "Der Bauer in der Touraine" was published in Wilhelm Herzog's left-leaning *Das Forum;* and "Zola" was published in the Swiss-based anti-war journal *Die weissen Blätter.*

151

51. Alexander Abusch, "Der Dichter des 'Untertan'," *Aufbau* (1950), VI:309.

52. On the provocative possibilities of the novel see Karl August Horst, *Das Spektrum des modernen Romans* (Munich, 1960); and Oskar Holl, *Der Roman als Funktion und Überwindung der Zeit* (Bonn, 1968).

53. Theodor W. Adorno, "Cultural Criticism and Society," *Prisms,* p. 32.

Chapter 8

The War Years: 1914–1918

My whole existence is based on the premise that moral efforts are possible.

Heinrich Mann

Mann's Political World-View in 1914

On the eve of World War I Mann began to be looked upon, with only partial justification, as a "radical" writer. Indeed, he even viewed himself that way and used this term with reference to his work. The irony in this is that by nature and inclination Mann in no sense possessed a radical personality. If it had been entirely up to him, it is possible that he would have remained a *Dichter* rather than a *Literat*. What drew Mann into social and political involvement was primarily his growing concern with "morality," derived, perhaps, from the latent legacy of his father. So long as the artist in him held the upper hand, he remained impervious to conditions around him; but when the ethical side became ascendant, especially after 1910, Mann could not resist judging his surroundings and criticizing a world which seemed to him morally untenable. In a way, it was Wilhelmian society itself which induced him to become political, for the more he became aware of its essential features, the more he realized that he had to oppose them. Thomas Mann, who also possessed the same rudimentary moralism, was much slower in coming to this recognition. In the years before World War I he chided his older brother for being a "passionate democrat" and getting involved in "a trivial and almost childish kind of radicalism."[1] For his part, Thomas confessed to Heinrich, there was "an inability to orient myself politically or spiritually as you have done. . . . My whole concern is with decadence and that of course hinders me from being interested in progress."[2] Later, however, especially in the 1930s and 1940s, Thomas became the same kind of ethical intellectual that

Heinrich had become before 1914.

It would be helpful at this point to take a brief inventory of Heinrich Mann's political opinions just prior to the outbreak of war. As will be seen shortly, many of his pre-1914 ideas had to be changed in light of the new realities of war-time Germany.

It has already been said that by 1914 Mann was committed to the goals of democracy, humanity, and rationality. However abstract these terms may seem, they were still what made him appear radical against the generally tepid background of the German Empire. Naturally, Mann wanted these goals to be embodied and realized in the German people. But for this to be accomplished, he argued, a mode of literary politics had to be devised which could mediate between the ideal and the real. Intellectuals had to bring higher values to the masses in order to rouse them out of their lethargy and inspire them with democratic principles. If this attempt were success-ful, an alliance could be forged between the intellectuals and the people against the ruling elites of the country. Once these two powerful forces united—the representatives of *Geist*, on the one hand, and the entire nation, its *ratio militans,* on the other—Germany would be on the verge of a major social transformation.

Having arrived at this point, Mann always backed away from the revolutionary implications of his argument. Before 1918, he refused to talk seriously about revolution as such. In all his writings up to this date there was no mention of the need for violent confrontation with the powers that be, because Mann wanted to rely exclusively on spiritual methods for bringing about needed social changes. He even refused to enter the political arena and fight for democratic ideals within the context of a party. The *littérateur,* Mann felt, was not suited for practical politics because his skills were incompatible with the give-and-take of parliamentary maneuvering.[3] Furthermore, he was convinced that what the ethical writer has to say could not be transmitted to just a single party; it had to be conveyed to society as a whole. As a result, Mann himself tried to assume a stance "above parties," fearing that his known allegiance to one party or another would damage his impact on the larger public.[4]

In addition to defending ideals, Mann attacked certain specific features of Wilhelmian society in the years before the First World War. Two features that were singled out for special criticism were German nationalism and militarism. Nationalism, according to Mann, was a threat to everything progressive and potentially democratic in

Germany. Not only did it lead men to treat one another like "blood-thirsty animals," thus making peaceful harmony in Europe impossible; it also furthered the notion that one's own state was the highest entity on earth and that all value flowed from service to it.[5] Still, Mann made a distinction between nationalism and nationhood. The first he rejected as harmful under all conditions, but the second he could accept as compatible with, and even necessary for, genuine democracy. "Up to now," Mann wrote perhaps too facilely, "the guarantee of nationhood has insured peace and [proved] that nationality and war do not go together; the durability of national unity is generally identical with democracy."[6] In contrast to this favorable view of nationhood, Mann expressed undisguised hostility toward nationalism, as in his cryptic comment that to be a "nationalist is the same as being a reactionary."[7]

German militarism was attacked with equal severity, and for many of the same reasons. Nowhere, Mann argued, had a military elite gained such hegemony over the life of a nation as in Germany. The very existence of a warrior clique living off of war and the threat of war made democracy virtually impossible. In scathing language Mann wrote that the German military had "disseminated the fear of enemies, ... stirred up hatred, ... ignited international crises, ... supported class conflict and chronic civil war," and tried to "reap its own advantages from the resulting anxiety and discord."[8] "What is the nation to them?," he asked rhetorically. "They know no nation, but only rulers and masses who are the raw material for their command." When it came to suggesting solutions to the problem of the military, however, Mann was again somewhat weak. He simply proposed that the entire country join together in a common effort against the militarization of life. If this happened, it would become clear that the army spoke for no one and that the collective will of the people openly opposed it. The generals would then be seen as a *Fremdherrschaft*, and presumably the rationale for their authority would dissolve. This answer was of course almost visionary, as many of Mann's answers were, but at least he identified militarism as an evil that had to be eliminated.

On the whole, Mann's political outlook just prior to World War I was liberal and idealistic. Nonetheless, it is important to note that it was an old-fashioned brand of liberalism (similar to Old Buck's in *Der Untertan*) which Mann embraced, not the new and much more fashionable "national liberalism" of the Wilhelmian era. The difference is essential for understanding Mann's alleged radicalism in comparison to the views of others who also considered themselves liberals.

Along with writers like René Schickele, Kurt Hiller, Wilhelm Herzog, Bernhard Kellermann, and Leonhard Frank, Mann repudiated the new directions that German liberalism was taking around 1900. Above all, he opposed the welding together of nationalism and liberalism—something which had become an accomplished fact after the liberal defaults of 1848, 1866, and 1871. Instead of considering these two ideologies to be integrally related, Mann proclaimed them deadly enemies. Wherever nationalism held sway, he felt an autocratic state would eventually emerge and prosper at the expense of liberty. Thus Mann tried to wrench the concept of liberalism away from the prevailing forces of nationalism and statism. Some of his bitterest attacks were directed not only against the far Right but also against those neo-liberals (personified by the young Wolfgang Buck) who insisted that the cause of liberty was furthered by chauvinism and the principle of authority. Under the guise of supporting freedom, liberal nationalists worked to destroy the possibilities of freedom "by putting a good face on things, by justifying with sophistry what is unjust—and this in the interest of the mortal enemy: authority."[9]

In effect, Mann disclaimed the national liberalism represented by men such as Friedrich Meinecke, Lujo Brentano, Friedrich Naumann, and Max Weber.[10] While these writers were infatuated with power, Mann struggled with a contrary notion already familiar to liberals in France and England—that concentrated power is intrinsically evil. It followed from this that the so-called "power state" was no ideal, and neither was Germany's "new course" of *Weltpolitik*. Here Mann stood directly opposed to the prevailing currents of Wilhelmian liberalism. In contrast to a liberal like Meinecke, who complained in his *Weltbürgertum und Nationalstaat* (1907) that pre-Bismarckian liberalism suffered from universalistic illusions and was too idealistic and humanitarian, Mann argued that precisely these qualities must be put back into modern liberalism. For him, the humanism and cosmopolitainism which inspired Kant's *Zum ewigen Frieden* (1795) was exactly what was needed. Such views made him seem somewhat out-of-date in comparison to a realist like Max Weber. But it was just this old-fashioned quality which gave Mann's thought an apparently radical cast—as if, by embodying what had been historically repressed, he was able to be the bad conscience of his age.

At the same time that Mann attempted to extricate liberalism from the snare of nationalism, he attempted to unite it with democracy. This, too, put him at odds with the dominant liberal ideology. Whereas men like Naumann, Meinecke, and Weber demanded first a power state, and then democratization, Mann demanded democratization, after which a power state would not be necessary. It was Germany's misfortune that after the Revolution of 1848 most liberals opted for nationalism over democracy. The result was that the socialist movement became the heir to democratic ideals, and it used these ideals to combat both a truncated liberalism and the principle of authority which the bourgeoisie came to cherish. Mann wished to reverse this process by fusing liberalism with what he called "the urge towards democracy."

These were the major features of Mann's political world-view immediately before the war. It remains to be seen what happened to these ideas during the next four years.

"An Outbreak of Madness"

From the moment war was declared in August, 1914, Mann took a critical attitude towards it. This was rare during the days following mobilization, when very few German writers doubted that the war was a great national blessing. The dramatist Gerhart Hauptmann, for instance, called it a "primordial experience." Karl Wolfskehl described it as a "divine struggle." Thomas Mann saw it as a "purification and liberation." And the Austrian novelist Robert Musil greeted it as a "primordial achievement," an "archetypal model" of the defense of one's "tribe."[11] Since these sentiments were echoed by numerous other writers as well, it was obvious that the war hysteria was not confined to beerhall patriots.

Heinrich Mann's negative reaction to the declaration of war was understandable, given his political philosophy and belief in the ethical imperative of democracy, because full-scale combat could only bring to the fore all the tendencies he opposed. Twenty years earlier, in the pages of *Das Zwanzigste Jahrhundert,* Mann approved of war as both a necessary purgative and a stimulus to the health of a nation. Now, he completely reversed himself and labelled it the ultimate evil. A war, he alleged, is always the product of a bad epoch and bad social conditions. It comes out of a milieu that lacks love or cooperation, an age that instead is permeated with hatred, resentment, and exploitation. War always leads to the intensification of immorality. No matter what its origin, according to Mann, the result is always the same: a triumph of destruction over construction, of death over life.[12] For this reason, he believed that war was not only intimately bound up with the Wilhelmian era, but was also perhaps the last pulse beat of a society which had become morally exhausted and spiritually bankrupt. Mann even hinted darkly that the First World War may have been a "preventive method" to put down the forces of change and perpetuate a decrepit system of government.[13] In short, the war could only be construed as contrary to the best interests of society since it was annihilating, rather than bettering, mankind.[14]

Mann's views on war were made clear in an exchange of letters with his brother, Thomas, in August and September, 1914. On August 7, Thomas wrote Heinrich that the war had thrown him into utter confusion and that he was forced to walk around "as if in a dream." "Personally," he continued, "I am prepared to completely change the material foundation of my life. . . . Shouldn't we be thankful for the totally unexpected chance to experience such great things? My overriding feeling is enormous curiosity . . . and deepest sympathy for this despised, fateful, and problematic Germany."[15] Heinrich replied by saying that the war could only bring unfortunate consequences both to him personally and to the German people as a whole.[16] In a return letter, Thomas expressed surprise and anger at this unpatriotic attitude. "I do not share your pessimism . . . but, rather, I think you do a disservice to German culture. Can you really believe that this great, basically decent, yes even solemn national war could cause the culture and morality of Germany to be set back so much?"[17]

At this point the record of correspondence temporarily breaks off and there is no indication of Heinrich's reply. Nevertheless, the differences between the two brothers had become evident. Heinrich continued to believe what he wrote to his wife on August 4, that the war represented to him an "outbreak of madness."[18] Thomas continued to defend the opposite position. In his essay "Gedanken im Krieg," published in November, 1914, he welcomed "the collapse of a peacetime world of which we had had enough, quite a bit more than enough."[19]

This is not the place to discuss the so-called "quarrel between brothers," since it has been dealt with at length elsewhere.[20] What is important at this point is to focus on Mann's political development between 1914 and 1918. Two aspects of Mann's social and political thought during this four-year period demand attention: his anti-war activities, and the changing nature of his world-view against the backdrop of total war.

The *Zivilisationsliterat*

Mann's opposition to both the war and the social structure that engendered it did not manifest itself in direct political action. Except for his peripheral involvement in at least one anti-war organization, Mann chose to convey his opposition mainly through writing.[21] Because of censorship, however, this was not as easy to do as it had once been. At first, he had to refrain from publishing his ideas at all, or else write for exile journals like *Die weissen Blätter*. Only after 1917 was it possible for him to address a large German audience through a liberal newspaper like the *Berliner Tageblatt* (which published three of his four most important wartime pieces). But even here, his articles had to be toned down so as not to offend the authorities. Just how much acrimony was sacrificed becomes clear when one compares the angry sentiments of his private wartime notebooks with the apparent moderation of his newspaper articles.[22]

Mann's essay on Zola, his masterpiece of *double entendre*, was published originally in *Die weissen Blätter* in 1915. It is deservedly remembered as his most important anti-war statement. This is so not simply because it condemns war, but because it points an accusing finger at those who cause it, notably the military and its supporters. Under the pretext of discussing Zola's relationship to the "militaristic and class-controlled state" of nineteenth-century France, it levels a critique against the same conditions in Wilhelmian Germany. And just as Zola is set up as the model of intellectual integrity, so, too, it is inferred that German intellectuals were duty-bound to oppose their own power state in the name of truth and democracy. This was exactly the response that the well-known French novelist Romain Rolland had asked for from all European men-of-letters in his book *Au-dessus de la mêlée.*[23] But throughout the first year of war Rolland was almost totally ignored in Germany, and his moral indignation was shared by only a few German writers and thinkers.

The contemporary relevance of the essay on Zola was unmistakable, and the points Mann scored against the French Empire were directly transferable to the German situation.[24] Essentially, Mann raised three issues which were relevant to wartime Germany. The first was that events like the Franco-Prussian War or scandals like the Dreyfus Affair do not happen accidentally. They come about because they are the fruits of a degenerate social order. To believe that wars are accidents is to mystify reality. In truth, they are always declared by particular groups of people ("ministers and millionaires") and waged for definite and recognizable ends. Until the "dark masses" realize this, they will never be able to institute fundamental changes because they will never see that the intentions of those in power are to continually form the world in accordance with their own interests. The nationalism produced by the excitement of war is a screen thrown up to cloud the issue. As a result, people fail to see that behind the apparent unity of patriotism there are still leaders and the led, cliques and masses.

Mann's second and third points follow logically from his first. He suggested that such elites had to be removed for the good of the nation, since as long as camarillas exist, oppressive hierarchical regimes would always be the primary reality of life. He then argued that the vacuum left by these old structures had to be immediately filled by democratic republics.

Mann supported his final point by quoting Zola. "[A] republic is not only a method of government, it is the essence of political truth, the unconditional affirmation of everything that has to do with real life."[25] Mann agreed with this statement and then expanded upon it. A republic, he insisted, brings equality. It returns the state to the people, and permits them to govern themselves. It even furthers the spiritual and artistic life of a nation and advances its general health and creativity. Hence Mann acknowledged that a republic is the best form of government. But at the same time, he knew that it was not enough merely to describe the ideal state. The real question was how to achieve it.

A democratic republic, Mann declared, could only be achieved through the breakup of the old power structure. The seeds of democracy and humanity always lie just below the surface of any repressive society; like young plants, they wait for the right moment to spring into the light and develop themselves in all their potentialities. Towards the end of the French Second Empire, for example, strong

republican sentiments existed, but before they could come to fruition
the old framework had to be shattered. This happened in the war of
1870–71, a catastrophe mitigated by the fact that it made way for a
democratic republic. The analogy with Germany was too obvious to
be missed. The "completely inhuman military regime," with its "lies
of false patriotism," had to be done away with. In its place, a "working democracy," a "true republic," needed to be given a chance to
grow.[26] As Mann put it, in words which could not be misconstrued:

> "No one really believes in the Empire, though people still [imagine]
> that they want to see it victorious. Rather, they believe above all in its
> almost insuperable power. But of what [value] is power if it is not
> commensurate with justice? . . . An Empire that is based solely on force
> rather than freedom, justice and truth, an Empire which relates to men
> only by commanding . . . and exploiting instead of respecting them, can
> never be victorious. . . . Power is useless and feeble if it only lives for itself
> and not for the *Geist* which stands above it.[27]

It was this kind of attitude which led Thomas Mann to ridicule his
brother in his romantic defense of German culture, *Betrachtungen
eines Unpolitischen* (1918). Though not mentioned directly by name,
Heinrich was accused of being a "belles-lettres activist," a "boule-
vard moralist," and a *Zivilisationsliterat*. These epithets no doubt
hurt Heinrich, especially since they came from someone whose
opinion he respected. But, as was often the case, he managed to turn
such terms of derision into positive values. Where *Zivilisationsliterat*
originally implied a superficial or second-rate literary journalist,
Heinrich Mann converted the word into a mark of esteem signifying
the highest type of writer: one who represented the aspirations of
humanity as a whole. Thus in the 1919 eulogy to his friend Kurt
Eisner, Mann honored the "belles-lettres activist" by specifically
referring to Eisner as a *Zivilisationsliterat*.[28] The man who speaks
and acts for democracy and freedom, Mann implied, is on a more
worthwhile course than the one who merely speaks for inwardness.

Search for the "Agent" of Social Change

As far as the tasks of the intellectual were concerned, Mann offered
nothing essentially new between 1914 and 1918, except a re-working
of ideas he had been elaborating on since 1910. When he assumed

the role of defending civilization and humanity in a time of crisis, as in the Zola essay, he was merely extending his earlier self-concept into a wartime situation.

This was not true, however, when one turns to his concept of the agent of social change. During the war, Mann did a great deal of thinking about which sector of society would be the receptacle for democratic values conveyed by intellectuals. He was still certain that intellectuals could not change the world by themselves. As "brain workers" they represented only one side of a proposition, but they needed a material base which could embody their ideas and carry them out politically and socially.

As early as 1895, Mann had flirted with the notion that the *Mittelstand* would be the source of social regeneration. If, he reasoned, the values of the traditional middle class (as opposed to the dominant bourgeoisie) could permeate the whole body politic, they might be able to turn a sick society into a healthy one. A decade later, however, Mann began to place his hopes in a "people" rather than a *Stand*. Most likely this was due to French influences, particularly Rousseau and Michelet. In any event, Mann began to visualize a kind of renewal based on the upsurge of a whole nation rather than only a part of it. But even here the core of the people was still the *Mittelstand*, as is obvious in a novel like *Die kleine Stadt*, where the honest burgher, drawing on a legacy of civic virtue and personal responsibility, becomes the mainstay of a new society.

By 1911–1912, Mann had shed some of this optimism regarding the potential effectiveness of the middle class. In a seemingly ambivalent essay entitled "Reichstag" (1911), he bitterly attacked the Reichstag delegates who were supposed to represent middle-class interests. A quick reading of this piece might lead one to conclude that Mann despised everything the burgher stood for. The middle-class delegates are ridiculed and mercilessly caricatured; they are portrayed as greedy, narrow-minded, and ambitious, and their "sly, plump faces" are said to show no concern for democracy but only for material gain, which they can pass on to their children and grandchildren.[29] Even their political positions are used for further social climbing rather than the improvement of mankind, and hence they play directly into the hands of the power structure. In a caustic, bitter passage Mann addressed the delegates with these words: "You smile, and this smile says: farce! While you chatter, the real business of the parliament goes unattended. It is a shameful comedy! Your

smile tells us that [we] are all the objects of legislation while you,
the subjects, sit here. . . . Your smile, it is the smile from Holofernes
to Genghis Khan. It is the swelling smile of all the pigs of world
history, the pigs who rule [*Herrenschweine*]."[30]

Despite the vitriolic tone of this essay, Mann did not intend it to be
an attack on the *Bürgertum* as such. Instead, it was an assault only
on the betrayers of this class. The delegates were specifically criticized
for cutting their ties with their own constituency, for attempting to
join a corrupt power elite, and for shunning the Reichstag's "radical
members" (who, it was inferred, stood closer to the popular will) in
order to make common cause with the far Right, the real "enemy of
the people." In short, Mann's hostility was vented on that part of
the middle class which had become untrue to its own principles. But
although the Reichstag was filled with a "despicable type of imperialistic subject," this did not mean that the situation was irremedi-
able. Two possible solutions existed. On the one hand, the old
middle class might yet come to its senses by renewing its concept of
civic responsibility within the existing political framework. On the
other hand, the entire populace might rise up outside the framework
of the Reichstag and, with the help of literary intellectuals, declare
itself against the ruling cliques and in favor of democracy. Of course
this latter option was unrealistic, but on the whole it was the one
Mann chose to emphasize between the appearance of his Reichstag
essay and the beginning of World War I.

The outbreak of war shattered what reasonable optimism Mann
still had that either the "middle strata" or the German people as a
whole could transform society in the near future. And yet, paradoxically, the less reason there was to think that the masses would
suddenly embrace democracy, the more hopeful Mann tended to
become on an abstract level, thus completely dissociating himself
from the immediate situation. For example, in his essay "Zola,"
Mann was inclined to deify the people and exaggerate their potential
for democracy, whereas in reality there was little to substantiate this
theoretical optimism. After all, the majority of Germans from all
classes rallied to the war and therefore to the side of the ruling class
rather than to that of Mann's "spiritual intellectuals."

As for the middle estate, Mann had to admit that it was not composed of the kind of people he had imagined. Earlier he thought that
it collectively embodied the virtues of political responsibility, ethical
duty, and grass-roots democracy. But by 1914 Mann arrived at the

notion that perhaps this was largely an illusion. The real *Mittelstand* was nationalistic, socially conservative, and status-oriented. Its world-view was based not on love of mankind, but on hostility toward the working class and fear that social change would lead to massification. It increasingly stressed its ties with the bourgeois world-order so as to distinguish itself from the manual laborer and the threat of proletarian socialism.[31] Hence, as the *Mittelstand* increasingly lost its sense of identity, its inner élan began to disappear. In order to fill this void, it chose the easy solution of embracing an outside source of power. This partly explained the middle class's veneration of the emperor, its acceptance of an authoritarian state, and its enthusiasm for war in 1914.

In short, Mann concluded that the *Mittelstand* was apparently no longer a progressive element in society. The liberal-democratic residues of the early nineteenth century had mostly faded, and the middle-class citizen had transformed himself into an obedient subject. Now the question was, who would carry on the once promising heritage which the *Bürgertum* had abandoned? In other words, what segment of society, if any, would now be most receptive to the "moral efforts" of spiritual intellectuals?

This was one of the most important issues Mann grappled with between 1914 and 1918. At the core of the problem was the question of who would be the agent of social change. The other elements of Mann's scheme were the same as before: the *geistige* intellectuals with their democratic principles and ethical ideals on one side, the "ruling cliques" with their instruments of power on the other. The only matter that needed to be solved concerned the third element, i.e., the group that would provide the material base to embody the intellectual's message and move Germany towards democracy. It should be said that Mann offered no definitive answers during the war years, but he did suggest two possible agents whose existence he hardly acknowledged before: the working class and the youth. At various times he inferred that one or the other could assume the progressive role that the old middle class had seemingly deserted.

Before the turn of the century, Mann had little regard for the working class, less for its socialist ideology, and still less for the party that represented it politically, the Social Democratic Party (SPD). In *Das Zwanzigste Jahrhundert,* Mann accused the socialists of being materialistic and un-German, and in *Im Schlaraffenland,* he portrayed the proletariat as opportunistic and easily compromised. Two

years later, in the *Münchener Neueste Nachrichten*, Mann spoke of
the "tyranny of socialism," and in his *Göttinnen* trilogy he made his
lone advocate of socialism look ludicrous.[32] The following year (1904)
he accused the German SPD of lacking principles and being "hypnotized
by the money question."[33] At this point, Mann never entertained the
notion that the working class might represent something positive.
And he viewed socialism not as an alternative to bourgeois society (as
did many of the Naturalists) but only as a parody of it. In the SPD,
Mann professed to see the same quest for power and domination
that pervaded bourgeois society at large.

Around 1906 or 1907, one can find the first hint of a change of
view. In a notebook kept during these years, Mann began to make a
distinction between the SPD and the working class itself. In contrast
to the party functionaries out to serve their own interests, there were
honest workers who justly rebelled against the brutalizing conditions of
their lives. Napoleon Fischer in *Der Untertan* represented the first
type, and preliminary notebook sketches show that as early as 1906
Mann had intended to portray him as an opportunistic Social
Democrat. However, another figure in the same notebook—a revolutionary name Mühsam—was never incorporated into Mann's novel,
and yet he was pictured as a strike leader who seems to have held the
people's wishes over his own.[34] Thus two kinds of working-class
personalities were drawn, one motivated by greed and the will-to-
power, the other by a humanistic concern for the oppressed. In his
"Reichstag" essay written a few years later, Mann again brought out
these differences. Social Democrats, he wrote, are often nothing but
"petty bourgeois types who want a life of narrow-minded content-
ment"; even talk of a general strike makes them "shudder with the
greatest fear."[35] But the same may not be so of the population they
supposedly represent. As was the case with the middle class and its
Reichstag delegates, Mann realized that careful distinctions had to be
drawn between working-class people and their official spokesmen.

It is important to note that Mann's re-evaluation of socialism and
the working class, which culminated in his "Zola" essay of 1915,
was not due to empathy with the physical suffering of the proletariat.
Rather, it was due to his tentative hypothesis that perhaps the working class was potentially more moral and democratic than the *Mittelstand,* which seemed to have forgotten its own past. After 1914
Mann was willing to accept the notion that despite the opportunism
of the SPD, socialism was nonetheless the legitimate heir of an

abandoned liberal democracy. For this reason Mann began to look more favorably on the socialist ideal, while at the same time not altering in the slightest his bad opinion of SPD leadership.[36] Unlike the Marxists, however, he was not inclined to invest the laboring masses with any special destiny or world-historical mission. Instead, the working class was seen only as an ally against the power elite which Mann, as a dissident intellectual, wanted to bring down. The proletariat had no unique status but was only a part, and hopefully a progressive part, of civil society. In this respect, Mann sometimes treated the working class like a surrogate *Mittelstand*. Nowhere was this made more clear than in the words he wrote a few months after the war's end: "The proletariat shall neither rule nor even exist. It struggles in order to disappear. Through social economy it will be uplifted, and made middle class (*verbürgerlicht*). . . . The new *Bürger*, now a worker, . . . will lay claim to the country and the epoch."[37] Here there was no mystique about the working class, only an assertion that it might be able to fill the role forfeited by the old middle class.

At the same time that Mann took a fresh look at the proletariat, he also tried to envision the new generation of young people as another possible agent of social change. In an article entitled "Das junge Geschlecht" ("The New Generation," 1917), Mann addressed himself to those Germans in their twenties who had not been corrupted by materialism and nationalism. He pointed out to them that they were in a unique position to change the world because they could see the horrors brought about by the old society and still muster the resolve to do something about them. It was wrong, Mann reasoned, that the "state and its greatness" were placed higher than "man and his happiness," and that the "power of things" was given precedence over the "power of the spirit."[38] A significant part of German youth, Mann was convinced, now realized this. It wanted to carry out the work of *Geist*, both by writing and by acting in the world. The best way to achieve this goal, this "great transformation" as he called it, would be by reaffirming the values of democracy and humanity which had been "pushed into the background since 1870."[39] Eventually the young could even start to re-build the state and shape it in their own image, but only after they had deepened their sense of responsibility and committed themselves to what Mann termed "the party of *Geist*."

Mann's essay was typically imprecise. This may be due in part to the fact that he wrote it for a newspaper audience during the war, and therefore had to simplify his argument. But his imprecision might also be the result of his insistence that the young use only spiritual methods for social change. All allusions to violence or mass upheaval were played down, and as a result the youth were left with this piece of harmless advice: "Your duty is to spirit; you must penetrate the world with spirit."[40] Perhaps it was no accident that just at this time Mann was personally close to another left-liberal writer, Leonhard Frank. In Frank's wartime writings there was not only a prominent accent on youth (his novel *Der Mensch ist gut* [1917] was dedicated to "the coming generations") but also a reliance on peaceful means to usher in the new society. Both Mann and Frank spoke about the need for a revolution, but they meant the revolution of love and reason.[41] They believed that the young people of Europe, shocked and repulsed by the World War, would be open to transforming the very societies that engendered the conflagration in the first place. Consequently they turned to the youth of all classes in order to suggest yet another path to the "new man" and the "new age."

At the end of the war in November, 1918, Mann was still searching for the most promising agent of social change. The political explosion which followed, however, soon made this quest academic. Rather than continue to speculate, Mann allowed himself to be drawn into the events themselves—the same events which also preoccupied millions of German youths and a good part of the working class. Before turning to Mann's involvement in the German Revolution of.1918–1919, it would be helpful to clarify the nature of his political thought just prior to the November upheaval.

Marx or Kant

At first sight it might appear that Mann's political outlook in 1918 was somewhat similar to that of the young Marx. Both defined themselves as opponents of their age in the strongest possible terms, and both rejected the militarism, authoritarianism, and injustice of the state (for Mann, the German; for Marx, the Prussian). Moreover, both seemed to feel that a new, more humanitarian, epoch was possible: one free from exploitation, wars, and ruling classes. Initially, both spoke in abstract terms about the intellectual's responsibility to the "party of humanity"; both even used this phrase. But in time each came to acknowledge that the ideal of humanity needed a material substratum in order to be actualized. *Geist,* in other words, had to be embodied in a real social group or it would not triumph over the powers that be. From this premise they both hit upon the working class as a possible instrument of social transformation. For Marx, it was the only possible agent for revolution, while in Mann's view it was simply the most likely one (more reliable, at least, than the *Mittelstand* and probably the younger generation as well).

Here, it seems, the affinities between Mann and Marx come to an end. In 1918, on the verge of a German Revolution and only one year after the Russian Revolution, more of Mann's opinions were incompatible with Marxism than were consonant with it. This fact goes a long way toward explaining why his behavior was radical, but not revolutionary, during the years 1918–1920. It also helps clarify why, as a fellow-traveller during the 1930s and 1940s, Mann supported the Soviet Union for what he considered exclusively ethical, not Marxist, reasons. What was it, then, about his mode of thinking or his manner of conceptualizing problems and formulating solutions that kept him out of the Marxist camp?

The answer is, of course, complex. Without going into great detail, let it suffice to say that Mann, unlike Marx, never developed a viable notion of praxis or even a rudimentary strategy for changing social institutions. Instead, he relied almost exclusively on intellectual methods—especially on writing or, as he said, on "words"—to make his effect. Similarly, Mann had no sound conception of the dialectic. He rarely talked about developing, unfolding, or bringing to fruition the latencies and tendencies within a given situation. On the contrary, he almost always spoke of injecting ideas from the outside, and of intellectuals bringing values to the masses. Though this way of thinking undoubtedly had something in common with Lenin,[42] it had very little in common with the young Marx or with the dialectical method. Moreover, Mann rejected the concept of class struggle, since it only increased the bitterness and hostility between people; he even looked with disfavor on day-to-day political activity. In his opinion, one should not dirty one's hands or become compromised by too much contact with a corrupt political system. Thus, by cutting himself off from institutional structures, Mann foreclosed many possibilities for change.

Herein lies perhaps the fundamental difference between Mann and Marx. Whereas Mann instinctively shunned anything that hinted of power relationships, Marx was bent upon seizing power in order to transform society. In the forefront of Marx's mind always stood the notion of not only a national, but a world, revolution. Not so with Heinrich Mann. Though he did use the word revolution, and though he did want fundamental change in Germany, his ultimate goal was still, perhaps paradoxically, a reconciliation between national units as they already existed. Marx talked of carrying revolution from one country to another via an international proletariat; Mann spoke only of democratizing Germany and then "adjusting" to the Western family of nations.[43] Marx argued for creatively undermining and destroying what exists in order to rebuild anew; Mann pleaded for "life, not destruction."[44]

At this point in his development, it was in fact not Marx but Kant to whom Mann stood closest. Though there is no direct mention of Kant in Mann's work until 1917 (when he is referred to as "the law-giver of reason"[45]), there can be no doubt that at least some aspects of Kant's thought had a considerable bearing on Mann's political philosphy. The most important influences seem to have been Kant's ethical idealism and his conception of the intellectual as a political moralist.[46]

Taking his cues from the Kantian categorical imperative, Mann assumed that ethical absolutes existed, and that these absolutes had to be used concretely to judge all aspects of social and historical reality. Wilhelmian Germany, for instance, had to be measured not so much against its immanent possibilities or suppressed futurity, as Marx might have said, but against universal categories of justice and freedom, humanity and rationality. If a given society compares favorably with the ideal, it may pass as a good society; if not, it needs to be replaced with something better. This, as a rule, was how Mann approached political questions—by criticizing "what is" with reference to "what ought to be." Whereas the realm of "ought" is always one of pure ideas and ethical principles, the realm of "what is" sometimes turns into an arena of crude power relations, coercion, and force without spirit. When this happens, the *Geist* of practical reason must be replaced by the *Geist* of pure reason, which is to say, absolute ethics must enter the world of *Macht* in the form of moral acts. This, in the view of both Mann and Kant, is what occurred in the French Revolution, which represented the breakthrough of reason into the world. In this instance, what was at first only an idea of change was converted into the imperative to change and then, ultimately, into the actuality of change (i.e., the Revolution itself). Ideas, then, were seen as weapons which carried an ethical force of their own. If an age was bereft of such ethical forces, it followed that it was also bereft of the *Geist* of pure reason and would eventually collapse, since power could not sustain itself without spirit.[47] It was this conviction, based not on evidence but on moral idealism, that allowed Mann a measure of optimism even when conditions did not seem to warrant it. In his view, literary politics was essentially a form of applied rationality. And reason would ultimately win out simply because it represented the universality of spirit against the narrow particularity of raw power.

Mann was also close to Kant in his notion of the intellectual as a political moralist.[48] The role of the engaged thinker was, for both the writer and the philosopher, not just to speak the truth but to educate others in the truth. Mere reflection on the nature of good and evil was not sufficient; the intellectual had also to "improve" the world, to change it for the better.[49] This could not be done through class struggle. Although, in Mann's opinion, such a conception of the writer's role at least had the merit of advocating concrete action, it was still too power-oriented and would therefore only alter reality without bettering it. The true role of the literary activist was to penetrate the world with spirit and make others aware of the moral law in their own hearts. As Mann put it in his Zola essay, "spiritualizantion" [*Vergeistigung*] can be achieved only where there is first "moralization" [*Versittlichung*]."[50] The urge to spiritualize existence by placing "reason and humanity on the throne of the world" was at bottom a moral urge, and the intellectual who committed himself to democracy was nothing less than a moralist in disguise.

Thus by and large Mann chose to work within a Kantian rather than a Marxist framework. This point seems borne out not only in his essays between 1914 and 1918 but also in the only novel he wrote during the war years, *Die Armen* (*The Poor*, 1917).[51] At first glance the title might suggest a Marxist orientation, and it is true that the novel does present the first and only thorough discussion of working-class life in Mann's entire corpus. But when one inspects the content of the novel it becomes obvious that the core message of the book is based on a Kantian rather than a Marxist perspective.

Die Armen was the second volume of the *Kaiserreich* trilogy, and contained many of the same characters as *Der Untertan*. One new figure, however, was a young worker named Karl Balrich, an employee in Hessling's paper factory. Through his experiences as a laborer, Balrich becomes "class conscious" and tries to arouse his fellow workers to action. Moreover, he comes to see Hessling as an expropriator of property and therefore as a class enemy. At this point, one might expect to see some type of workers' insurrection, but Mann abruptly changed the direction of the novel. Balrich suddenly discovers an old family document which proves that he and his relatives are legally entitled to a large share of Hessling's industrial empire. He attempts to acquire what is his by inheritance, but in doing so he turns away from revolutionary means and relies exclusively on intellectual and juridical ones. Now Balrich spends his time after working hours studying Latin, with the hope of becoming a lawyer, winning his case against Hessling, and then legally operating the factory more humanely for the benefit of the whole community. Needless to say, this was hardly the type of socialist revolution Marx had in mind.

What happens, in effect, is that midway through the novel Balrich is metamorphosed from a radical worker into a Kantian intellectual like Mann himself. The "early" Balrich wanted to unite *Geist* and *Tat,* but only in order to serve one class, not humanity at large; the logical result of this position would be to increase class hatred rather than effect reconciliation and harmony between men. The "later" Balrich, although he eventually fails,[52] is at least on the right ethical track. He understands that through the study of law he can put knowledge to use for everyone's benefit. Barlrich's friends and even his sister think that he has compromised himself, but in Mann's view he has simply chosen a more acceptable method for transforming society.

In nearly every respect, *Die Armen* was one of Mann's worst novels. And yet, aside from its literary weaknesses, the work was characteristic of Mann's rejection of strict Marxist categories in favor of ethical-humanist, or Kantian, ones. Ironically, the Russian Revolution took place the same year the novel was published, and the striking contrast between the methods of Balrich and those of Lenin must have been obvious to Mann's readers. It is hard to imagine two approaches more divergent than the ones represented by the fictional as opposed to the real-life revolutionary.

Footnotes
Chapter 8

1. See Thomas Mann's letter to Kurt Martens, January 11, 1910, in *Letters of Thomas Mann 1889–1955*, p. 55; and Mann, cited by Hans Wysling in "Zur Einführung," *Thomas Mann—Heinrich Mann Briefwechsel, 1900–1949*, p. xlvii.

2. Thomas Mann, letter to Heinrich, November 8, 1913, in *Thomas Mann— Heinrich Mann Briefwechsel, 1900–1949*, p. 104.

3. See Heinrich Mann, "Politik," *Pan* (1911), II, no. 8: 238–39.

4. Mann never publicly supported a political party, not even in 1933 when he made it known to the *Berliner Tageblatt* that he was a republican, but that he belonged to no party and above all was "not a communist." (See Mann's response to a questionnaire concerning his political affiliations in the *Berliner Tageblatt*, February 16, 1933.)

5. Heinrich Mann, "Der Bauer in der Touraine," *Essays* II, *Ausgewählte Werke*, XII: 246–48.

6. *Ibid.*, p. 249.

7. Heinrich Mann, letter to Maximilian Brantl, October 23, 1907, included in "Heinrich Manns Briefe an Maximilian Brantl," *Weimarer Beiträge*, XIV, no. 2:398.

8. Heinrich Mann, "Der Bauer in der Touraine," *Essays* II, *Ausgewählte Werke*, XII: 250.

9. Heinrich Mann, cited in W. E. Yuill, "Heinrich Mann," *German Men of Letters*, ed. Alex Natan (London, 1963), II: 205.

10. See James Sheehan, *The Career of Lujo Brentano* (Chicago, 1966); Richard Sterling, *Ethics in a World of Power: The Political Ideas of Friedrich Meinecke* (Princeton, 1958); Wolfgang Mommsen, *Max Weber und die deutsche Politik 1890–1920* (Tübingen, 1959); and Theodor Heuss, *Friedrich Naumann: der Mann, das Werk, die Zeit* (Stuttgart, 1937).

11. See Klaus Schröter, "Chauvinism and its Tradition: German Writers and the Outbreak of the First World War," *Germanic Review* (1968), XLIII: 129.

12. For a further discussion of Mann's views on war see Hanno König, *Heinrich Mann: Dichter und Moralist*, pp. 167–75.

13. See Heinrich Mann's "Notizbuch" (unpublished notebook dating from circa. 1917–1918), Heinrich-Mann-Archiv, no. 473.

14. Heinrich Mann, letter to Thomas Mann, January 5, 1918, in *Thomas Mann— Heinrich Mann Briefwechsel, 1900–1949*, pp. 137–38.

15. Thomas Mann, letter to Heinrich, August 7, 1914, in *op. cit.*, p. 108.

16. Heinrich Mann, letter to Thomas, undated but circa. mid-September, 1914, in *op. cit.*, p. 109.

17. Thomas Mann, letter to Heinrich, September 18, 1914, in *op. cit.*, p. 110.

18. Heinrich Mann, letter to Mimi [Maria] Mann, August 4, 1914, hand-written manuscript in the Heinrich-Mann-Archiv.

19. Thomas Mann, "Gedanken im Krieg," *Die Neue Rundschau* (1914), XIV: 1475; cited in Klaus Schröter, "Chauvinism and its Tradition," *Germanic Review*, XLIII, no. 2:134.

20. See Alfred Kantorowicz, *Heinrich und Thomas Mann* (Berlin, 1956); and André Banuls, *Thomas Mann und sein Bruder Heinrich* (Stuttgart, 1968).

21. Though there is not enough material available to provide many details, Mann does appear to have been involved in a peace league called the *Bund Neues Vaterland*. This organization was founded in November, 1914, by a number of socialists, liberals, and pacifists who wanted to see the war brought to a quick conclusion. The *Bund*'s purposes were threefold: to demand political and diplomatic efforts in all the European countries to end the hostilities; to argue for the desirability of an international federation for encouraging "peaceful competition" instead of war; and lastly, to work together with like-minded groups in the belligerent nations to bring about a "civilized universe." Initially, its members included a mixed bag of individuals such as Kurt von Tepper-Laski (the founder), Lilli Jannasch, Ernst Reuter, Albert Einstein, and Hugo Simon. Later others like Wilhelm Herzog, René Schickele, and Käthe Kollwitz joined the organization.
Mann's exact relationship to the *Bund Neues Vaterland* is still unclear. Following its inception he probably maintained some contact with it, though his name does not appear in connection with the League until September, 1915, and then only in passing in Romain Rolland's *Journal des années de guerre*. The next clear reference to Mann's involvement does not come again until April, 1917. By this time the *Bund* had been declared illegal. Nonetheless, according to Wilhelm Herzog, Mann travelled to Berlin in order to attend one of the League's meetings. By November, 1918, Mann was officially listed as the Munich representative of the organization. It is probably safe to say that Mann maintained some contact with the *Bund* throughout the war years but became especially close to it in 1917–1918. For further details, see Pierre Grappin, *Le Bund Neues Vaterland 1914–1916: Ses rapports avec Romain Rolland* (Paris, 1952); and Wilhelm Herzog, *Menschen, denen ich begegnete* (Bern and Munich, 1959), pp. 235–38.

22. Most of Mann's notebook jottings dating from the years 1916–1918 are in the Heinrich-Mann-Archiv. A short but revealing excerpt from these is included in Wilhelm Girnus, "Geist und Macht im Werk Heinrich Manns," *Weimarer Beiträge*, (1917), XVII; no. 8:43–44.

23. Romain Rolland, *Au-dessus de la mêlée* (Paris, 1915). The essay asking German writers to protest against the invasion of Belgium and the levelling of Louvain was written in September, 1914.

24. See, for example, Heinrich Mann, "Zola," *Essays* I, *Ausgewählte Werke,* XI: 196–97.

25. *Ibid.,* p. 199.

26. *Ibid.,* pp. 177, 196, 217, 230.

27. *Ibid.,* p. 198.

28. Heinrich Mann, "Kurt Eisner," *Essays* II, *Ausgewählte Werke,* XII:29.

29. Heinrich Mann, "Reichstag," *Essays* II, *Ausgewählte Werke,* XII:8.

30. *Ibid.,* p. 8.

31. See Jürgen Kocka, "The First World War and the 'Mittelstand': German Artisans and White-Collar Workers," *Journal of Contemporary History* (1973), VIII:101–23.

32. See André Banuls, *Heinrich Mann,* p. 56; and Lorenz Winter, *Heinrich Mann and His Public,* p. 19.

33. Heinrich Mann, letter to Maximilian Harden in *Die Zukunft* (1904), XLIX, no. 2:67–68.

34. The "Notizbuch" is in the Heinrich-Mann-Archiv. For an excellent discussion of part of its contents, see Edgar Kirsch and Hildegard Schmidt, "Zur Entstehung des Romans *Der Untertan,*" *Weimarer Beiträge,* VI, no. 1:115–19.

35. Heinrich Mann, "Reichstag," *Essays* II, *Ausgewählte Werke* XII:8.

36. See Mann's notebook comments on the "SPD leaders" dated March 25, 1916, cited in Wilhelm Girnus, "Geist und Macht im Werk Heinrich Manns," *Weimarer Beiträge,* XVII, no. 8:43.

37. Heinrich Mann, *Macht und Mensch* (Munich, 1919), pp. 213f.; see also Wilhelm Girnus, *op. cit.,* p. 50.

38. Heinrich Mann, "Das junge Geschlecht," *Essays* II, *Ausgewählte Werke,*

XII:13. This article was originally printed in the *Berliner Tageblatt* on May 27, 1917.

39. *Ibid.*, p. 14.

40. *Ibid.*, p. 16.

41. See Martin Glaubrecht, *Studien zum Frühwerk Leonhard Franks* (Bonn, 1965), pp. 71–78.

42. Lenin's separation of the professional revolutionary from the masses (who, by themselves, can only achieve "trade union consciousness") had no solid grounding in Marx's original thought. Structurally, at least, it resembled Mann's split between the spiritual intellectuals on the one hand and the "people" on the other. Both formulations existed outside the dialectical reciprocity of "heart" and "head" which Marx had formulated in his *Critique of Hegel's Philosophy of Right.*

43. Heinrich Mann, "Der Europäer," *Essays* II, *Ausgewählte Werke,* XII: 255–61.

44. Heinrich Mann, "Leben—Nicht Zerstörung," *Essays* II, *Ausgewählte Werke,* XII:17–18.

45. Heinrich Mann, "Das junge Geschlecht," *Essays* II, *Ausgewählte Werke,* XII:15.

46. Mann's relationship to Kant is discussed with great insight in Hanno König, *Heinrich Mann: Dichter und Moralist,* pp. 216–64.

47. Heinrich Mann, "Zola," *Essays* I, *Ausgewählte Werke,* XI:198.

48. See Hanno König, *Heinrich Mann: Dichter und Moralist,* pp. 264–70.

49. *Ibid.*, p. 266.

50. Heinrich Mann, "Zola," *op. cit.,* p. 206.

51. The novel, originally published by Kurt Wolff Verlag in Leipzig, has not been included in the East German edition of Mann's *Ausgewählte Werke.*

52. See Heinrich Mann, *Die Armen* (Leipzig, 1917), chapter VII. An abortive strike does eventually occur and is duly crushed by the military. World War I breaks out immediately thereafter, and Balrich is one of the first to be drawn into the conflict. The final irony is that Hessling's factory is converted into a munitions plant and its workers begin producing for the German army. For a discussion of this novel against the wartime background see Klaus Geissler, "Die weltanschauliche und künstlerische Entwicklung Heinrich Manns während des Ersten Weltkriegs," Ph.D. dissertation, Jena, 1965.

Chapter 9

Reason and Revolution

Philosophers have explained the world, the point is to alter it. For myself, I believe that the only way to alter it is to explain it. If one explains it plausibly, then one alters it in a peaceful manner through the spreading effects of reason. Only those who are unable to explain it plausibly attempt to alter it by force.

Lion Feuchtwanger

Pacifist revolutionaries—what a contradiction!

Leon Trotsky

The German Revolution

By September, 1918, the German High Command realized that it was no longer possible to win the war. The so-called Macedonian front had all but folded, and the German armies in the West were threatened with collapse. Under the circumstances, Field Marshal von Hindenburg asked that a new government be formed which might have a better chance for negotiating a peace settlement. In early October, Prince Max of Baden created a new ministry responsible to the Reichstag rather than to the Kaiser, ushered in a number of political reforms, and sent a peace note to President Wilson. Without fanfare Germany became, in effect, a constitutional monarchy. The feeling that the war would soon be over was widespread, but by the beginning of November no armistice had been declared. On November 3, some sailors of the Baltic fleet revolted when they learned that they were to make a senseless, final stand against the British. This was mutiny, and they were fired upon. Several were killed or wounded, and as the news spread so did the mood of insurrection. At Kiel and other coastal ports, sailor's councils were set up. A few days later, in military garrisons within Germany, others followed suit by establishing soldier's and worker's councils to re-

place the officer corps. On November 8, in Munich, socialists under
Kurt Eisner proclaimed the Bavarian Socialist Republic. The next
day in Berlin, Prince Max turned the federal government over to
Friedrich Ebert of the German Social Democratic Party, who became
acting Reich chancellor. Two days later, Germany was declared a
democratic republic.

With the collapse of the Second Reich, the old sources of power
and authority appeared to disintegrate, at least temporarily. Throughout November, Germany was for all practical purposes ruled by
councils (*Räte*) set up in all of the larger cities and most of the
smaller towns and villages. For a short while Germany had at least
the appearance of a *Räterepublik,* since the councils provided virtually the only firm basis for executive decision-making. Even the
civil service, which still existed intact alongside the councils, operated
only at the councils' behest.

The major question facing the supporters of the German Revolution, Heinrich Mann included, was the following: Should the councils
become the core institutions of the new Germany, or should they be
regarded as merely transitional phenomena to be put aside once parliamentary democracy had been restored? Between November, 1918,
and May, 1919, the question seemed to be thrust into the middle of
nearly every controversy, and how one answered it depended on
where one stood within the political spectrum.

Within the revolutionary camp there were at least three influential
positions, each corresponding to a leading socialist faction in Germany. First, the Majority Socialists (SPD) were not enthusiastic
about the council system, despite the fact that most of the workers
and soldiers on the councils were SPD supporters. To the leaders
of the Majority Socialists, who were mainly concerned with the issues
of legitimacy and continuity, the *Räte* had too much of an aura of
insurrection. These leaders wanted an easy transition from Reich to
Republic, not an apparent upheaval from below (which they viewed
as a rupture in the constitutionally-delegated authority that would
insure their succession to power). Though the Majority Socialists
went along with the council movement in November—they had no
other option—they were nonetheless reluctant revolutionaries who
hoped for a restoration of law and order, a return to parliamentary
democracy (with their party at the helm), and the convening of a
presumably moderate National Assembly at the soonest possible
moment. To them, the term "revolution" meant liberal republicanism

and the eventual nationalization of certain key industries. From this point of view, the revolution was virtually over when Friedrich Ebert had succeeded Prince Max as chancellor and Germany had became a "socialist republic" at least in name. The whole council movement seemed superfluous; it was looked upon as something that had to be overcome so that political life could return to normal channels.

A second, and altogether different, attitude toward the councils could be found among the more radical Independent Socialists (USPD). They embraced the council system as a model of direct democracy. Rather than wanting to disband the *Räte* as did the SPD, the Independent Socialists wanted to turn them into instruments for the complete democratization and socialization of Germany. Furthermore, the USPD wanted to delay the calling of a National Assembly until the German people had been sufficiently educated for political responsibility. They believed that the sooner such an Assembly convened, the less radical it would be.

Finally, there was the perspective of the Spartacus League, which represented the most extreme view of the councils during the revolutionary period. Originally part of the left-wing of the USPD, the revolutionary Spartacists broke away and formed their own League. Later, on December 30, 1918, they officially proclaimed themselves the Communist Party of Germany (KPD). As a matter of principle, the Spartacists declared themselves against bourgeois democracy. At the same time, they also opposed the idea of a National Assembly, since it would destroy the revolutionary momentum and turn the country over to the SPD and the forces of reaction. What the Spartacists wanted was an "armed worker's revolution" which would do away with the remnants of bourgeois rule. As they saw it, the council system had to be kept at all cost, not only because it provided the institutional means by which class struggle could be waged, but also because it supposedly contained within itself the framework for a future dictatorship of the proletariat.

From November 9 until the beginning of December, these three factions attempted to work together to some extent, with the USPD struggling to mediate the grave differences between the SPD and the Spartacists. By mid-December the strains and tensions within these groups had become too great to be resolved. Increasingly, the SPD moved towards restoration and rapprochement with the army, while the Spartacists moved towards revolutionary street action. At the National Congress of Worker's and Soldier's Councils in Berlin

(December 16–21, 1918), the controlling SPD element managed to push through the following resolutions: that there would be an election of delegates to a National Assembly on January 19, 1919, that the National Assembly itself would convene on February 6; and that in the meantime, power should not rest with the individual councils but with the elected representatives of the Central Council, who would possess authority equal to ministers in a provisional government. Finding this intolerable, and sensing that the SPD had become a party of reaction, the Independent Socialists withdrew from the Congress and moved closer to the Spartacists, who had chosen not to participate in the first place. On January 6, 1919, a mass demonstration was called in Berlin to protest the worsening situation, particularly the erosion of council rule and the firing of an USPD police commissioner. The most radical workers, perhaps two thousand altogether, occupied several buildings including the offices of *Vörwarts,* the SPD daily newspaper. The SPD leader Gustav Noske called on the right-wing *Freikorps* to evict the demonstrators and suppress the uprising, which they did with much bloodshed. By January 12, the Spartacist rebellion was crushed. A week later the National Assembly elections were held and the results showed a decided turn to the Right, with effective power being vested in the Majority Socialists, the Catholic Center Party, and the Democratic Party. On February 6, the National Assembly met as scheduled and set about drafting a new constitution which would provide the legal structure of the Weimar Republic.

At this point, it appeared to many that the revolution had been defeated. The coalition in power (SPD, Centrists, and Democrats) was precisely the one which had taken over the reigns of government in October, when Germany had become a constitutional monarchy with Prince Max as chancellor. And yet, the intervening four months were not without effect. The USPD and KPD continued to call for strikes and demonstrations, and as growing numbers of workers became unhappy with the new government, the ranks of the revolutionaries began to swell once again. From February until the beginning of May, 1919, muffled uprisings took place all over Germany, most notably in Berlin, Leipzig, Hamburg, Bremen, the Ruhr area, and Munich. In each case, there was much talk about class struggle, the socialization of production, and "all power to the soviets," but the solid base of working-class support that had existed in November of 1918 was clearly missing by April. All the uprisings were put

down more or less brutally. By the summer of 1919 the revolutionary élan was much diminished, and in some places it was wholly
eradicated (as in Munich, with the help of the *Freikorps*). The new
source of concern and anxiety for most Germans was the "dictated"
peace treaty that Germany was forced to sign and ratify in July. By
August the new constitution was approved and put into operation,
which meant that the Weimar Republic had been officially established.
For the time being, the period of revolutionary ferment appeared to
have come to an end.[1]

Heinrich Mann and the "Political Council of Intellectual Workers"

The fall of the German Empire in November, 1918, and the rapid
succession of events thereafter, made many of Mann's wartime specu-
lations obsolete. By now it no longer seemed important to ask who
the agent of social change would be or to talk about "creating a
people." After all, change was already a *fait accompli,* and even the
German people appeared not to have been created by intellectuals
but to have suddenly created themselves out of nothing. As for the
engaged writer, the new situation made it possible for him to go
beyond his merely literary activities. Now opportunities seemed to
abound for actually putting one's principles into action—that is, for
fusing "spirit" and "deed" in conjunction *with* others rather than by
simply writing *for* others.

Once again, a change in events induced a change in Mann's thought.
As Germany took a turn to the Left in November and December of
1918, so did Heinrich Mann. Not only his conception of himself as a
writer, but also his notion of what Germany needed socially and
politically, moved at least a few degrees leftward. In order to measure Mann's altered world-view against the background of his time,
a few words should be said about the Bavarian Revolution, since it
had a considerable impact on his thinking. Mann was in Munich
when the revolution broke out, and he remained there for some time
as an active participant. The militant and more socialistic tone of his
work during 1918–1919 is partly traceable to his reaction to, and
involvement in, the events he witnessed first-hand in Munich.

Munich was second only to Berlin as a center of revolutionary
activity.[2] In fact, the revolution in the Bavarian capital was underway
before the one in Berlin, and it lasted longer and was more bloody.

On November 7, a mass demonstration for peace was held in Munich's Theresienwiese. It was called by the SPD, USPD and the labor unions, and drew a crowd of perhaps eighty to a hundred thousand. After the crowd dispersed, the USPD leader Kurt Eisner, along with local workers and with the express approval of a nearby military garrison, seized government and newspaper buildings throughout the city. On the following day, a surprised populace learned that the Wittelsbach dynasty had been replaced by a Bavarian Democratic and Social Republic with Eisner as provisional prime minister. Councils were immediately set up as decision-making bodies, and both the police and the civil service subordinated themselves to the council system. At the same time, Eisner promised to hold elections for a National Assembly in January, 1919, so that the composition of the new government could be decided by popular vote. Thus in the interim Bavaria became, in effect, a council republic. All important decisions were made through participatory democracy, and real political power was invested in the Worker's, Soldier's and Peasant's Councils.

Several of the leading literary intellectuals in Munich endorsed Eisner's new Republic and were eager to cooperate with it. These included, besides Heinrich Mann, religious humanists like Martin Buber and socialists or left-bohemians like Wilhelm Herzog, Ernst Toller, Erich Mühsam, and Gustav Landauer (the latter two with some misgivings). What initially attracted these *littérateurs* to the Bavarian Republic was Eisner's intense idealism and his commitment to humanism, pacifism, and ethical socialism. Like them, Eisner was a novelist, journalist, and editor. Also like them, he believed in bringing ideals to the masses and transforming society in accordance with higher principles. Moreover, he was a Marxist, though in ideological matters far closer in spirit to the socialist humanism of Jean Jaures than to the Bolshevism of Lenin. Finally, he was a neo-Kantian (having studied with Hermann Cohen at Marburg), and therefore tied to a deeply moral perception of the world which was missing in the more extreme revolutionaries. All of these qualities made a strong impression on Mann as well as on other left-liberal writers in Munich. As Mann put it succinctly: "The hundred-day Eisner government provided more ideas, more intellectual inspiration, more mental stimulation, than the previous fifty years."[3]

Eisner's revolution pleased many intellectuals, but it did not satisfy the general population. The January election not only brought the

SPD to power (Eisner's USPD received only 3% of the vote), but it indicated that the electorate wanted parliamentary rule rather than council democracy. Acknowledging the people's will, but still determined to let the councils exist alongside parliament, Eisner was on his way to officially resign his ministry to the new Landtag on February 21, 1919, when he was shot by the young right-wing officer, Count Arco-Valley. Munich was immediately plunged into chaos, and the Bavarian government withdrew to Nürnberg. On April 7, some of Eisner's followers, none of whom had any political skill, announced the creation of a new Bavarian Soviet Republic. Virtually no one supported the new order except a few anarchists, Marxists, and numerous café intellectuals. When a rightist *coup* was attempted a week later, the only troops protecting the regime were KPD loyalists. However, the KPD itself did not approve of the fragile Soviet Republic. On April 13 it set up a government of its own, this time a Communist Soviet Republic which was to become the basis for a dictatorship of the proletariat. The socialist-humanist revolution was therefore succeeded by a Leninist one under the direction of Communist Party professionals (Eugen Leviné, Karl Levien, Rudolf Egelhofer, and others). By May 1, 1919, the scene was set for massive retaliation. As in Berlin a few months earlier, the exiled SPD government in Nürnberg called on the military to crush the Communist Republic and its Red Army. On May 8 Munich was subdued, but not before a "White Terror," which led to the deaths of several hundred and the arrest of thousands, had been unleashed.

Heinrich Mann was in Munich in November, 1918, and like most left-leaning intellectuals, was immediately swept up by the enthusiasm of the moment. Both the figure of Eisner and the idea of a Bavarian Republic strongly appealed to him, and he sought a way to work for the new government. In the early stages of the revolution, when power rested with the Soldier's and Worker's Councils, there seemed to be no place for people like Mann who made their living primarily by writing. His alternative, then, was to found a council for intellectuals which would represent what he called the *geistige Arbeiter,* the "mental" as opposed to the "manual" workers of Munich.

Mann was not the first to hit upon this idea. Shortly after the revolution had stabilized itself, the Munich aristocrat Alexander von Bernus established what he called his "Council of Intellectual Workers" (*Rat geistiger Arbeiter*). In reality, this was hardly more than a formal discussion group and its members, such as Paul Ernst, were not known for their republican or democratic sympathies. The impotence of the Council soon became apparent, and consequently another *Rat* was formed under the leadership of Heinrich Mann—this one called the "Political Council of Intellectual Workers" (*Politischer Rat geistiger Arbeiter*) to distinguish it from its predecessor.[4] The Political Council was both more left-wing and more closely in touch with the developments in the rest of Germany. For example, when other *geistige Räte* sprung up in cities like Dresden or Berlin, there was some attempt at communication with them in the hope of eventually forming a national council.

On the whole, none of these councils of intellectuals were very effective and hence most disappeared by the early months of 1919. The Dresden Council developed anarchist tendencies and quickly dissolved, though some of its members later joined the KPD. The more moderate Berlin Council came out, as one might expect, for pacificism and the "inviolability of human life"; in time it helped establish an amorphous "Congress of Radicals of the Spirit," but nothing much came of it.[5] The Munich Council organized by Mann seems to have been more closely aligned with the pacifist spirit of the Berlin group than with the greater militancy of the Dresden Council. For this reason, the more extreme Munich radicals turned away from it as a "useless nuisance."[6] Ernst Toller, for instance, was too busy being an activist to get involved in intellectual discussions. Gustav Landauer, who arrived in Munich at the end of November, also shunned the literary intelligentsia and immediately began working with another group called the Revolutionary Worker's Council to "drive the revolution forward towards a socialism constructed on the foundation of the *Räte* idea."[7] Erich Mühsam, too, chose direct action tactics instead of conversation; he founded a Union of Revolutionary Internationalists which tried to uproot counter-revolutionary elements by force of arms. Mann's Council stood far removed from such extremes. For the most part it was liberal-socialist in tone, and though wedded to the Eisner government, it was not noticeably upset when the *Räte* were usurped by the National Assembly. In fact, one of the few accomplishments of the Political Council of Intellectual Workers was to dispatch two or three delegates to the National Assembly to ratify the new constitution. This meant negating the most important achievements of the German Revolution, since the constitutional republic as outlined by Hugo Preuss signaled the end of the revolutionary impetus of the councils. Mann seemed either not to have realized this or, more likely, to have preferred parliamentary to council democracy. With this much understood, it goes without saying that he vigorously opposed the ill-fated Communist Soviet Republic in Bavaria during the three hectic weeks of its existence in April, 1919.

The journalist Franz Schoenberner was in Munich during this period, and attended some of the sessions of Mann's Political Council. His eye-witness accounts give a rather unfavorable picture of the proceedings. At one meeting he visited, Mann rose to give an opening address "of high literary perfection." Other speakers who followed him extolled the ideals of liberty, equality, and fraternity; still others called for a democratic republic and a democratic Europe. To Schoenberner, it seemed like 1848 all over again. All of the speeches were polished and ready for future publication, but somehow they seemed inappropriate and unrelated to events. This led Schoenberner to conclude that "the real test of political speeches is not so much that they make good reading, but that they make history, good history if possible. The speeches in the Political Council of Intellectual Workers made no history at all, either good or bad. . . . [T]he real struggle for power . . . was fought without the active participation of the organized intellectual workers."[8]

Schoenberner was undoubtedly right. Mann's Political Council of Intellectual Workers was not rooted in any work locale and did not speak for an identifiable constituency. For this reason it played no significant role in the Bavarian Revolution, nor was it even called upon in an advisory capacity. Naturally the proclamations of the Political Council were filled with humanitarian convictions, but that alone was not enough. A program which had only noble sentiments to recommend it would not last long against the bullets of the *Freikorps*. In fact, by the time the real trouble began in April, 1919, it appears that most of the members of the Political Council had already left the city.

Literary Politics Revisited

The development of Mann's political opinions in the weeks after the armistice can be traced fairly closely. In a programmatic draft written on November 13, 1918 for his Political Council of Intellectual Workers, Mann outlined some of his goals for post-war Germany. One of the first was that real democracy be established so that the idea of freedom could penetrate all of society. A second was that an international organization of intellectuals be created to facilitate communication and bring about a détente between the nation states. A third was that Germany be purged of all Pan-German tendencies so that the "will to goodness," which he now inferred might exist in latent form, could begin to assert itself.[9] Except for the last point (about which Mann was to remain ambiguous during the succeeding months), none of this was markedly different from the tone of his wartime essays. Apparently Mann had not yet come to grips with the full import of the revolutionary events around him. However, in his first published piece after the armistice—a piece entitled "Sinn und Idee der Revolution" ("The Meaning and Idea of Revolution") which appeared in the *Berliner Tageblatt* on December 1, 1918—Mann attempted to be more specific.

Germany, he wrote, must accept the defeat as justified, since of all the countries involved, it was perhaps most to blame for the "lies, the swaggering, and the rapacity" which polluted the atmosphere of pre-war society.[10] (This was also Eisner's position; in fact, Eisner actually made public incriminating documents from the Bavarian state archives which seemed to prove Germany's war guilt.) But Mann went on to argue that this "falsification of the national character," which was integral to the Wilhelmian period, was "now happily behind us."[11] The military collapse had given Germany a chance to start over again, and this time on the right foot. If the war had ended in a German victory, there would have been no revolution but only a continuation of arrogance and saber-rattling. The disaster, then, had its good side. By uncovering the ugliness of society which otherwise would not have been acknowledged, and by drawing Germans together again in a sense of mutual concern, the defeat had inadvertently become a catalyst for a greater spiritual triumph. The conditions were ripe for a new "moral earnestness" to rise from the ashes and prepare the way for a better tomorrow. The message, therefore, was to accept the defeat and turn it into a victory for democracy.

To accomplish this, Mann insisted that there had to be unconditional support for republican principles. Even matters of class interest had to be subordinated to political ideals. "What we want is that our Republic . . . be populated with republicans. We look on republicans as neither middle class nor socialist. These are super-fluous distinctions where higher matters are concerned. Republicans are simply those who place idea[s] above personal advantage, and the individual above naked power.''[12] According to Mann, Germany was poised on the verge of a new epoch, a dawning era of justice and rectitude. In order to arrive there, however, it was not essential to change the structure of German society; all that was necessary was that the "spiritual condition" of the Germans be improved—in other words, that *Geist* begin to achieve mental ascendency. This theme appeared with increasing regularity during the following weeks and months. Spiritual and moral change, not social and economic trans-formation, was the key to a healthy Republic. It was with this thought that Mann concluded his essay on the meaning of revolution:

> In this land, come what may, the spirit must still rule in the end. It is conquering Germany and the world; it alone is the real victor of the World War. Whoever resists it will be lost; whoever accepts it achieves equality and brotherhood. Our reconciliation with the world will finally come in the name of unifying eternal ideas. We intellectual workers want to be worthy of these in order to be among the first to reconcile Germany with the world.[13]

Two weeks later, in a few remarks entitled "Erneuerung" ("Re-newal"), Mann continued this line of thought.[14] The index to a good society, he insisted, is its mental and moral character, not its economic arrangements. This being so, the first step in getting the Republic on its feet was to clear the air of all the dangerous tendencies which had predominated in German life for two generations. After this, a thoroughgoing spiritual renewal would be essential, which for Mann meant reactivating the German heritage that pre-dated 1871—a heritage which he characterized, with customary vagueness, as one of reason, goodness, and humanity.

By the middle of January, 1919, Mann became somewhat less abstract in his formulations. In an article entitled "Wir wollen arbetien" ("We Want to Work,") he began for the first time to face up to some of the practical problems of the new state.[15]

By now it was clear to him that not everything was running smoothly for the Republic. Earlier, before November 1918, Mann had simply assumed that once a republic replaced the Empire, an age of democracy would immediately begin.[16] This faith was now being tested by events as deep divisions, even within the revolutionary

ranks, began to appear. Under the circumstances, Mann felt it
necessary to call for a re-dedication to the new government. All
citizens, he wrote, must work for the state so it will not go to ruin.
Since this had been the slogan of the German Right up to 1918,
Mann was quick to point out that working for the state no longer
meant what it had under the monarchy. Then, a tyrannical state
(*Herrenstaat*) had been forced upon the nation, but now there existed
a democratic state (*Volksstaat*) which actually belonged to the people
and which they had the responsibility to preserve. Everyone was
therefore duty-bound to see to it that the Republic became a success.

In concrete terms, this meant that there should be no excessive
wage demands by the workers since, according to Mann, this would
only cause a devaluation of the mark which would, in turn, weaken
the Republic. Furthermore, strikes should not be undertaken indis-
criminately, but only when what was demanded was in the interest of
the whole, and only when all of society benefited by them. Workers
should realize that the existing state was *their* state, and that by
working for it they served only themselves. In a democracy, Mann
maintained, the government is always disinterested; it is not a tool of
private capital, for its goal is only absolute justice, equality, and
happiness for its citizens.[17]

This being so, Mann was not able to understand why the proletariat would continue to work for its own interests as a class rather than
for a democratic state. To him it seemed that the Republic was the
embodiment of reason, and therefore to weaken it by strikes and
street demonstrations appeared wholly unreasonable. At this point,
Mann apparently saw only the danger from the Left, in the form of a
revolutionary working class, but closed his eyes to the far greater
(though temporarily quiescent) danger from the Right. Perhaps this
was because of the Spartacist uprising, which took place during the
same month he wrote his article.

The Spartacists naturally denied all the premises of Mann's argument. To them, the Republic was anything but objective and im-
partial, since it was the political expression of bourgeois and SPD
interests. Furthermore, they felt that the proletariat had to work for
its own interests rather than those of the Republic because, compared
to the direct democracy of the councils, the Republic was counter-
revolutionary and anti-socialist. To the Spartacists, then, the existing
state was only a façade behind which the same forces of the old
order would continue to develop. Mann later acknowledged the truth

of this interpretation,[18] but in 1919 he adamantly denied it. In his view the Republic was a fundamentally moral and rational creation, and to work for its advancement led to the highest kind of joy, the "joy of reason."[19]

In May, 1919, Mann summarized most of the opinions he had held since the previous November in his essay "Kaiserreich und Republik" ("Empire and Republic"). In this essay his earlier optimism was counterbalanced by a few deeply discordant notes, the first to appear in his post-war writings. Mann now admitted that grave, perhaps even mortal, problems confronted the Republic. Still, after examining these one by one, he concluded the essay with a sense of cautious optimism. The new Weimar Republic could yet become everything it should be, provided that the intellectuals and the German people at large performed certain necessary and clearly defined tasks.

Before describing these tasks Mann first explained what had gone wrong after November, 1918. For one, the Allies should not have imposed such harsh peace terms on Germany, since this only stimulated feelings of bitterness and revenge.[20] The triumph of *Geist* in Germany, Mann admitted, would be difficult under normal conditions, but because of the dictated peace it would be even harder to achieve. Now, thanks to the Allies, a mood of festering resentment was likely to spread, and the hoped-for victory of the spirit seemed further away than at any time since the beginning of the Revolution.

Equally serious were other problems generated within German society rather than inflicted from without. Mann was not slow to point these out. There was, he found, no real enthusiasm for political reform in either word or deed. The old lies of the monarchy were taken up again along with its personnel. The SPD had allowed itself to become the prisoner of the army. Liberal reformers were being stigmatized as "Bolshevists." Militaristic values were re-emerging and gaining ground everywhere. The universities were becoming centers of an "unabashed nationalism." Social injustice was rampant. And the climate of 1913, with its stress on power, authority, and force, seemed to be reasserting itself on a broad front.[21] Thus, by the late spring of 1919, Mann was complaining about most of the same things that had disturbed him during the years 1900–1918. The only difference was that earlier these problems had appeared within the framework of a tyrannical state and had not seemed alterable except through a new form of government. By 1918, however, a new governmental structure did exist and yet these problems still persisted. The simple change from Empire to Republic was apparently not enough; something else was needed to turn a nominal Republic into a functioning democracy.

Here Mann confronted the crux of the issue. According to him, the Germans were not ready for democracy because they still thought along pre-war, authoritarian lines and continued to conceptualize the world in a manner "hostile to the spirit." Even the Republic had not really been "earned" but simply fell into their hands. But now that it had come into existence it had to be consolidated; after all, it was better to have a republic than a monarchy since a republic at least moved Germany a step closer to democratization. Before 1918, Germany had been virtually in a dark age, when all efforts at change had to be negative, i.e., directed toward simply bringing down the Empire. Now that this had been achieved, under however dubious circumstances, the situation seemed brighter. For the first time it was possible to begin building rather than tearing down.

But how could this formal victory for democracy be turned into a real one? Not, according to Mann, by further political changes promoting council democracy, nor by any attempts at fundamental social or economic readjustment. Genuine democratization would only come by means of moral and intellectual changes, that is, by basically transforming the German mode of thinking and perceiving. According to Mann, it is only when ordinary citizens start placing a high valuation on freedom and democracy, and begin participating in governmental processes and taking responsibility for what the state is, that a republic can have either depth or substance. But Mann acknowledged that in the case of Germany the average citizen was not likely to do these things by himself. He recognized that this required a change of mind, and that such a mental re-orientation probably had to be induced from without, or at least shaped and cultivated by outside forces. Thus, in a circuitous way, Mann came back once again to his old starting point: literary politics. Even after the Revolution, the spiritual intellectual was given a crucial role to play in educating people for the responsibilities of participatory democracy.

Although Mann returned to his concept of literary politics, he placed it in an entirely different context. Now the engaged writer was to be constructive, not destructive. Moreover, he was not invested with the task of creating a people *ex nihilo* but only with that of steeping the existing population in democratic principles. And this was to be accomplished by drawing out its potential rather than by imposing demands upon it. As Mann summarized them in "Kaiserreich und Republik," the post-war German intellectual had the following major tasks to perform. First, he had to accept the Weimar Republic as the legitimate state authority, which meant abandoning all utopian aspirations and working instead for the slow improvement of the Republic from within. Second, he had to concentrate on altering the "mental disposition" (Denkart) of society in order to prepare the way for a thoroughgoing democratization.[22] Mann now assumed that by changing a society's pattern of thinking one could also change the moral and intellectual character of the population. He took it for granted that good ideas make good men, and that good men create good societies. The chief duty of the intellectual was to focus on the mental superstructure, not the socio-economic substratum. Germany had taken a wrong turn between 1871 and 1918 because the wrong ideas had come to the fore.[23] If democratic and humanitarian ideas could be made to prevail under the Republic, Germany could still be rescued from its past. As Mann put it in 1918, "spiritual well-being is more important [than material happiness] since it does more to determine the destiny of men than the laws of the economy."[24] And again: "[our goal] is to spiritually renew and purify Germany. First the air must be cleared so that men can breathe reason and truth; after that, a new life will follow naturally."[25] Finally, there was a third and last role prescribed for the German literary intellectual. This was to return to what Mann again called the "power of words" in order to agitate for spiritual matters.[26] Only after a revolution in spirit had occurred could a revolution in fact take place. Likewise, only when Germany became a land filled with genuine democrats could the Republic be called truly democratic.

In sum, by 1920 Mann was still hopeful and moderately optimistic. The Weimar Republic could become a success, but only if the spiritual intellectuals assumed the role of moral guides, constructive critics, and educators in popular democracy. Mann himself tried to perform each of these functions during the years 1920–1933. This, as he admitted, required long hours of patience and considerable self-discipline with no apparent rewards. Still, such efforts were necessary if one wanted a better society, for "democracy can be realized only through hard work." When the Second Reich was created in 1871, it was everything it could be from the very beginning (which for Mann was a measure of its worthlessness). But a republic always starts as a seed and hence has unlimited possibilities for growth, so long as people dedicate themselves to it with their hearts and minds. If the first generation to embrace a republican form of government Lenin makes this commitment, the second "will become better republicans through experience, and the third will be republicans by birth."[27]

Ethical Socialism

The German Revolution forced Mann to take stands he had not taken before, and this was especially true with regard to socialism. In "Sinn und Idee der Revolution," for example, Mann wrote: "Justice has long demanded an extensive implementation of socialism. This should now be realized. We support it not only with our reason but also with our heart."[28] Except for two or three ambiguous passages in the Zola essay, this was the first time he had publicly declared himself in favor of socialism. Before 1918 Mann had usually been identified with the call for democratization, not socialization. How did it happen, then, that within three weeks of the armistice he was openly advocating the "extensive implementation of socialism?"

The answer can be found by looking first at what Mann meant by socialism. His concept of socialism was not related to that of any political party such as the SPD or KPD. Mann refused to commit himself to either of these, and as late as 1933 still declared himself above parties. Similarly, his definition of socialism was almost entirely divorced from economics, and he seems to have had no notion of what it would mean in practical terms to "socialize" a country. Furthermore, Mann strongly rejected the idea of class struggle and was repulsed by concepts like the dictatorship of the proletariat. As he repeatedly insisted, the goal was not the triumph of the proletariat but its dissolution. The term "working class" had to be broadened to encompass all laboring elements in the population, including the old middle class;[29] in his view, the entire community had to triumph together or not at all. And finally, with regard to the Russian Revolution, which one might reasonably expect a socialist to have welcomed, Mann bitterly opposed it as a "fanatical" event. Lenin was described as "the most thoughtless of Russian dictators" and an "agent of the German General Staff against Russian democracy."[30] The Soviet regime itself was dismissed as "a deadly enemy of all democracy."[31]

Mann's understanding of socialism, then, was obviously not a Marxist one. He always intended the word to carry ethical and emotional connotations, since for him socialism was essentially a matter of the heart and will. Behind it lay not so much economic necessity as the moral impulse toward human dignity, equality, and freedom. Occasionally Mann did link socialism with the call to eliminate poverty, but at most this meant a more equitable sharing of goods, not outright expropriation.[32] In any case, even material betterment was seen as simply a pre-condition for something more important, namely spiritual development. At the core of Mann's socialism there was no historical materialism, but only "love" and the "idea of humanity." Consequently, there were few references to socio-economic matters except insofar as they prepared the way for moral and spiritual progress.

All in all, Mann regarded socialism as basically an extension of what he called the "will to goodness." Its motive force was not the dialectic, but conscience and the ethical imperative (which is why he later suggested that Tolstoy was closer to his ideal than Lenin).[33] The root of these ideas originated *before* 1918, that is to say, before Mann identified himself with the cause of socialism. Hence there does not appear to have been a decisive leap from liberalism to socialism, but rather a gradual transition, with most of the intellectual groundwork laid prior to the end of the war. If Mann, between 1914 and 1918, could be labelled a Kantian liberal (to distinguish him from neo-liberal statists and nationalists like Naumann or Weber), then after 1918 he could be labelled a Kantian socialist (to distinguish him from the Marxian socialists and communists). It should be added that Mann never used this term to describe himself. He may have wished to separate himself from both the academic neo-Kantian school of philosophy (Hermann Cohen, Ernst Cassirer, Paul Natorp) and from the burgeoning Kantian movement among some intellectuals within the ranks of the Social Democratic party. Despite this, Mann's affinity with the latter group is unmistakable, since many of the political opinions he articulated between 1918 and 1920 were similar in spirit to those expressed by the Kantian socialists. Both Mann and the Kantians (e.g., Kurt Eisner, Otto Bauer, Max Adler, Karl Vorländer) affirmed the existence of absolute moral laws above the flux of history, and both agreed that a socialist society would be one which conformed to these unchanging precepts. Mann and the Kantian socialists similarly believed that social relations should become moral relations, and consequently they denied the inevitability of class war. To them it seemed that unrestricted class struggle was unethical, and that, in any case, the ideal of humanity should take precedence over internal social factionalism.[34] Furthermore, both believed that "real ethical forces" were inherent in all men; once these were released, mankind would be propelled towards a good society on the basis of the moral imperative. Finally, both Mann and the left-wing Kantians placed a strong emphasis on reason (*Vernunft*) as a guide to action, since the ideal society would have to be rational as well as moral. When Mann wrote that "we support socialism not only with our reason but also with our heart," he was summarizing both his own political creed and that of the Kantian socialists as well.

To clarify Mann's political world-view, it is helpful to compare him with Kurt Eisner, perhaps the most prominent of the German Kantian socialists. Mann respected Eisner not only for his moral and pacifist view of the world, but also because he fused *Geist* with *Tat* and was a man of reason and moderation. True, Eisner was more theoretically oriented than Mann, and his conception of socialism was more closely tied to Marxism and the USPD. Nevertheless, Mann saw in Eisner the true representative of humanitarian democracy and ethical socialism. To him, Eisner's real virtue was that he stood for idealism and democratization in contrast to the authoritarianism of the old society.[35] "More idealism," Eisner once wrote, "that is the call today, more idealism and that means . . . more ethics."[36] Mann concurred wholeheartedly, and in fact had often expressed the same sentiments in different language.

Eisner's assassination in February, 1919, was a blow to Mann. In a commemorative address, he lamented this unnecessary death but also used the occasion to point out that Eisner's greatness lay in his humanity, and in the fact that he chose peaceful means rather than civil war to solve political problems. Eisner's goal was cooperation and social harmony, and to achieve this he relied on reason instead of brute force. To Mann, this distinguished him from all previous figures in public life; and it was precisely this quality which Mann thought made him an exemplary model for future statesmen.[37]

Mann's Literary Generation, 1918–1920

By 1920, Mann had completed his intellectual journey from neo-conservatism to liberalism to ethical socialism. He was not alone in this. A good part of his literary generation made the same transition from aestheticism to social democracy between the years 1900 and 1918. Then, during the tumultuous period of the German Revolution, most moved still further leftward. The number of artists and writers who, in 1918 and 1919, began advocating socialism, signing socialist manifestoes, and joining radical Councils of Intellectual Workers is striking. But there was no determinism involved in this turn to the Left, nor anything like a mysterious entelechy working itself out below the surface. Most moved in roughly the same direction at the same time because intellectually it seemed natural to do so, and because a commitment to humanitarian socialism appeared to be the logical unfolding of certain premises they all held in common. Consequently, by the end of 1918 or early 1919, nearly all of Mann's literary colleagues had begun to take public positions which would have been unthinkable ten years earlier.

It would be impossible to give a complete list of examples here, but a glance at even a few of the dozens of literary-political declarations of 1918–1919 would reveal the names of almost all those writers mentioned earlier as constituting, more or less loosely, Mann's literary generation.[38] In one way or another each embraced what might be called a socialist world-view. The paths which had led them to such a position were personal and idiosyncratic, though the overall pattern was nearly the same; likewise, the tone and accent they gave to their political writings (e.g., satirical, rational, apocalyptic, etc.), were entirely private and unique. Nevertheless, these writers shared certain common assumptions about who they were and what they wanted. Thus they were brought together not only because they knew what they were against, but also because they knew what they were for.

In retrospect it may seem that there were some noticeable differences between them, but it certainly did not appear so in 1918. As far as they could see, they were all moving together as a common front, and whatever conflicts existed could be worked out by rational discourse. A few comments from some of the writers involved may be instructive.

René Schickele, whose development had run parallel to Mann's since the turn of the century, had been a pacifist and a democrat during the war. But in December, 1918, in the lead article of his journal *Die weissen Blätter*, he made an emotional plea for socialism:

Now, now! Finally. Now! The new world has begun. It is the world of liberated mankind . . . . Now the new age has arrived, the socialist age. It declares: the world belongs to men. All men are the same, all belong together . . . . I believe that socialism must come with a great, deep flood of light which penetrates all men. I believe that it must expand inwardly and outwardly in an atmosphere which transfigures all men . . . . Therefore it seems to me that the socialist society—which is nothing more than the free, unconstrained, powerful solidarity of organized mankind—[is] the final center of gravity, the mature coming of age of all creation.[39]

The same note was struck by Bernhard Kellermann, who had long since abandoned his early Impressionism, as well as his cautious prewar liberalism, and now enthusiastically embraced the November Revolution.

The vanquished capitalistic and imperialistic Germany, with its officialism and police administration, will not in the least be missed by [German] writers. . . . Full of confidence and hope after being muzzled for centuries, the writer, inspired with the desire to cooperate, steps over the threshold of the German Republic. From it he expects the fulfillment of his demands for freedom, respect, and the protection of interests. . . . He will happily serve the new Republic and its leaders if they have the strength and the determination to fill the German people with new hopes, to inflame them with new ideals and lead them towards new goals. . . . Revolutionary in the deepest core of his being, the German writer now demands a permanent revolution in a spiritual sense.[40]

Wilhelm Herzog made a similar appeal in the pages of his journal *Das Forum*. Convinced that the German Revolution needed to identify itself with the goals of international brotherhood and solidarity, he printed the following (and generally typical) statement in his August, 1919, issue:

We want to build. For this we need good, fine, and proper material. . . . [Hence these demands]. First: thou shalt not kill! . . . Second: oppose every nationalistic ideology no matter how it disguises itself, as conservative, national-democratic, or social-patriotic. . . . Third: the true fighters for the spirit must transcend their subjective differences . . . and come together for the first time. The belief in the victory of idea[s] can surmount any doubts about the possibility of being together and working together. Solidarity of all torchbearers of the spirit against the despisers of spirit and the slanderers of revolution. Solidarity for a new world order which knows no capital punishment or enslavement. Solidarity for a classless society of all men. Solidarity for justice and goodness without boundaries, without murder, and without weapons. This is our goal."[41]

Examples such as these could be repeated for most of Mann's

literary generation. In the period immediately after the November Revolution, nearly all agreed that the fall of the Empire was a salutary event, that the German Republic should be affirmed and supported as a great step forward, and that some form of socialism ought to be implemented in Germany. Furthermore, all spoke abstractly (though with considerable enthusiasm) of the "new man" and the "new age," of humanity and brotherhood, of reason and spiritual revolution. This being the case, it was hardly accidental that, in the numerous articles which flowed from their pens at the time, each employed an almost identical vocabulary and set of metaphors, even if they used them in different ways. Momentarily, at least, they seemed to constitute the kind of organized "army of the spirit" which Herzog had called for in his *Das Forum* manifesto.

But this was so only in the first flush of revolutionary excitement. By the middle of 1919, the initial sense of unity began to dissolve. The group continued to agree on the long-range goals to be achieved, but disagreed over two other issues which became increasingly prominent after the beginning of 1919. One had to do with the nature of the Weimar Republic, and centered on the question of just how progressive it actually was; the other concerned the short-term means which were, or were not, permissible to attain the long-term ends of socialist humanism. Both issues raised important practical and theoretical problems. For example, should the spiritual intellectual support an ostensibly socialist government if that government calls out the army to shoot other socialists? Is it acceptable to use violence against such a state in order to usher in a non-violent, genuinely socialist society? And what about the working class? Is it the material embodiment of revolutionary theory, and therefore the cutting edge of social transformation, or is it merely one social group among many with no claim to a special destiny? These and similar questions tended to divide Mann and his literary colleagues.

Some became depressed and temporarily dropped out of the picture (only to reappear around 1930 as opponents of the Nazi movement). After a period of great euphoria in 1918–1919, this element of Mann's generation entered a stage of withdrawal and disillusionment. Precisely because its expectations were so high, its disappointment was all the deeper when it became clear that the Republic was a flawed and compromised institution. Rather than work either to streamline or overthrow it, this group of writers felt inclined to move to the sidelines and lament everything that went wrong. Many, though refusing to forswear their socialism or republicanism on principle, became bitter and cynical. Others, while remaining more optimistic, chose to heap scorn on the existing state of affairs, to question the efficacy of engaged political action, and to reject the status quo as hardly better than the Empire. Within this group one could mention Georg Kaiser, Carl Sternheim, Alfred Döblin, René Schickele, and most of the writers connected with the journal *Die Weltbühne*.[42] Georg Kaiser, for example, was initially enthusiastic about the German Revolution. As a friend of radicals like Mühsam and Landauer, he supported the Bavarian Soviet Republic of April, 1919 (which Mann, for one, rejected as far too extremist). By the 1920s, however, Kaiser turned away from political engagement. Though he continued to hold socialist sympathies and to write pacifist, anti-militarist, and anti-nationalist plays, he began to doubt whether the major problems of the age were susceptible to political solutions. "There are no political solutions," he wrote, "there are only human solutions. And these are prevented by the state."[43] Despite his growing pessimism, Kaiser spoke out against National Socialism in the early 1930s. In 1933 his books were burned and his plays banned from the theater. By 1938 he fled from the Gestapo into exile in Switzerland, where he died in 1945.

Carl Sternheim also maintained an "anti-authoritarian socialism" in the years after 1920, but like Kaiser he became increasingly disgruntled. His major fear was that the Republic would become "bourgeoisfied." To him, it seemed that both the SPD politicians and an acquisitive-minded working class were indistinguishable from the functionaries and *Untertanen* of the Wilhelmian Era. Thus, since no real spiritual revolution had occurred in 1918–1919, it was only a matter of time before the old moneyed interests would return to dominate Germany. Given this attitude, it is understandable why Sternheim's work took on a sarcastic and derisive tone almost from the beginning. Until he emigrated in 1933, his pose was that of a republican *manqué*. The following statement was typical: "The German Revolution, like everything the Germans lay their hands on, has become German business. . . . In the face of this gigantic historical comedy, which the other European peoples look upon with amusement, the Germans once again are blind to how silly they look . . . . What we have is a National Assembly of four hundred men, most of them famous political thinkers, who chatter with the same idiocy, feel at home in the same Reichstag, play the same card games, and drink no less Pilsner beer than their famous predecessors."[44]

René Schickele was not as cynical as Sternheim, but was just as upset by the course the Revolution took. At the start he greeted the November events as the beginning of a new age for mankind, an age of freedom, equality, and social renewal. After a short time, however, Schickele became disillusioned. The Republic, he felt, had turned out to be the same old power structure in disguise. To work within it was to become entangled in a tissue of lies. That left two possibilities: either to withdraw to the "ideal" of humanitarian socialism above factions, or to enter the political arena in order to overturn the Republic and establish a dictatorship of the proletariat. Schickele chose the first alternative. For him the goal was to hold on to the vision, to become a custodian of socialist and democratic values, and to prevent *Geist* from being tarnished by *Macht*. As for the second option—revolutionary agitation—Schickele gave little support to it during the 1920s. From his point of view the communists, especially the KPD intellectuals, represented "hate" rather than "love." Where they wanted class struggle, he wanted pacifism; where they were bent on a dictatorship of one class, he was interested in *Gemeinschaft,* the opposite of class rule. Thus the German Bolshevists seemed to Schickele no better than the German officer corps, since both clamored for power over spirit, force over reason. "I am a socialist," he wrote, "but if someone convinced me that socialism could only be realized through Bolshevik methods, I . . . would not want to see it realized."[45] From a position of abstract humanism, Schickele rejected both participation in the new Republic and revolutionary praxis against it. Instead, he fell back upon his own alternative, something he called "the dictatorship of ideals." "We have only one task," he argued, "and we must perform it under all conditions. It is to concern ourselves with the ideal . . . so that it does not fall into oblivion."[46] Throughout the 1920s, Schickele remained devoted to socialist principles but did not fight for their realization in the political arena.

Finally, Alfred Döblin could be mentioned as still another writer whose initial excitement cooled with the passing months. In Döblin's view, the German Revolution was betrayed almost as soon as it began by the politicians of the SPD, business interests, and the military. The turning point was the abandonment of the councils, which, to him, represented the only real possibility for "republicanism, democracy, and civility." From Döblin's perspective, the council approach meant true socialism because it established the autonomy of the masses, self-help without dictatorial leaders, and freedom from officialdom.[47] Through the councils, the wants and needs of the population could have been dealt with directly since, according to Döblin, the spirit of the councils was identical with that of the people. Though he seems to have only vaguely understood the revolutionary social implications of the *Räte,* Döblin was convinced that a return to a manipulated parliamentarianism would only lead to the slow death of the Republic.[48] Despite this apprehension, he felt that there was very little a writer could do to improve the situation. Joining a party, he was sure, would not help, and so he rejected all leftist groups and abhorred their violence and authoritarianism. Throughout the Weimar period Döblin could find no place to anchor himself, except beside other alienated intellectuals.[49] He remained a socialist, and continued to argue for the abolition of capitalism, but was afraid of the kind of society which might follow, particularly if it were modelled on the Soviet Union. In 1933 he was forced to flee Germany. After various activities in anti-fascist organizations, and eventually escape to America in 1940, Döblin found a sense of belonging in the Catholic Church. He converted in 1941, and transferred his socialist longings to the figure of Christ, who became "the exemplification of justice and freedom."[50]

Besides the directions chosen by these writers (skepticism and the retreat to ideals), there was another option available to Mann's literary generation: that of communism. Instead of complaining about the failure of democracy in Germany after 1919, Mann's contemporaries could have joined the KPD and worked for the overthrow of the Republic, which many thought was untenable anyway. But very few writers made this choice during the 1920s. Of those who did, most were either much younger than Mann, or they did not go through a long transitional period from aestheticism to socialism during the critical years of their development. For most middle-class writers, the leap from Kantian socialism to communism was both too difficult and too frightening. It meant giving up one's freedom in order to submit to party discipline, authority, and a questionable emphasis on power. Among those whose development resembled Mann's even slightly, only Ludwig Rubiner (who died in 1920) and Friedrich Wolf—both of whom were several years younger than Mann—were willing to make this sacrifice. To them, the loss of bourgeois privileges seemed a small price to pay if the result were the triumph of justice and equality in the classless society.[51]

After Hitler seized power in 1933, the idea of communism seemed much less objectionable to many of Mann's friends and colleagues. Indeed, by then communism appeared to many to be the only logical choice, since no power in Europe seemed willing to oppose Nazism except the Third International. Hence a writer like Lion Feucht-wanger, who, in the 1920s, was suspicious of communism and looked upon the Soviet Union as a repressive state, swung around to the opposite point of view ten years later. By the late–1930s, he had become a paradigmatic fellow-traveller, latching onto everything he considered good (Stalinist Russia) in order to oppose everything he considered bad (Germany under Hitler).

Finally, there was a third way open to Mann's literary generation, a way which avoided the two extremes of psychological withdrawal or political conversion. This was to defend actively the Weimar Republic, despite its flaws and shortcomings, and do all one could to improve it from within. There was nothing appealing about this alternative. In a sense it was the most difficult of the three, since it meant a general lowering of expectations and the abandonment of hope for great changes in the near future. It also hinted of compromise, reformism, and "selling out" to the status quo. Nevertheless, this was the direction chosen by several writers including Heinrich Mann, Georg Hermann, Bernhard Kellermann, and later in the 1920s, by Thomas Mann as well. In some respects, supporting the Republic in this manner seemed like a step backwards because it implied, once again, merely a rudimentary defense of democracy, civil rights, and the constitution just to secure the ground for later, more important changes. Because there was nothing grandiose about this option, there were not many who chose it. But the lack of prestige accorded this position did not bother Heinrich Mann. He had already rejected the heroic image of the writer as a relic of the nineteenth century. In his view, the modern man-of-letters needed to become more modest; he needed to struggle not in order to discover his personal genius, but to awaken the genius within his own people. And yet, once this spark was kindled, his task was still not over. He then had to deepen continually the spirit of democracy so that men could become better in a moral, as well as in a social, sense.[52]

Footnotes
Chapter 9

1. The literature on the German Revolution is extensive. For the best discussion in English see A. J. Ryder, *The German Revolution of 1918* (Cambridge, 1967); Arthur Rosenberg, *A History of the German Republic,* trans. Ian Murrow and L. M. Sieverking (London, 1936), pp. 1–124; and Reinhard Rürup, "Problems of the German Revolution," *Journal of Contemporary History* (1968), III, no. 4: 109–35.

2. The best book on the Munich events is Alan Mitchell, *Revolution in Bavaria: Kurt Eisner and the Bavarian Socialist Republic* (Princeton, 1965).

3. Heinrich Mann, "Kurt Eisner," *Essays* II, *Ausgewählte Werke,* XII:26; see also Paul Pörtner, "The Writer's Revolution: Munich 1918–1919," *Journal of Contemporary History* (1968), III, no. 4:147.

4. Franz Schoenberner, *Confessions of a European Intellectual* (New York, 1965), pp. 108–10.

5. Klaus Geissler, "Entwicklung Heinrich Manns," pp. 192, 195.

6. This phrase was used by Gustav Landauer in November, 1918. See Eugene Lunn, *Prophet of Community. The Romantic Socialism of Gustav Landauer* (Berkeley, 1973), p. 303.

7. Erich Mühsam, *Von Eisner bis Leviné* (Berlin, 1929), p. 14; cited in Eugene Lunn, *Prophet of Community,* p. 297.

8. Franz Schoenberner, *Confessions of a European Intellectual,* p. 115.

9. Heinrich Mann, "Entwurf einer programmatischen Erklärung," hand-written manuscript dated November 13, 1918, in Heinrich-Mann-Archiv, no. 252.

10. Heinrich Mann, "Sinn und Idee der Revolution," *Essays* II, *Ausgewählte Werke,* XII:22–23.

11. *Ibid.,* p. 23.

12. *Ibid.,* p. 24.

13. *Ibid.,* p. 25.

14. Heinrich Mann, "Erneuerung," hand-written manuscript dated December 16/17, 1918, in Heinrich-Mann-Archiv, no. 337. These notes were later revised and published in the *Berliner Tageblatt,* January 1, 1919.

15. Heinrich Mann, "Wir wollen arbeiten," *Macht und Mensch* (Munich, 1919), pp. 192–97.

16. See Friedrich Boek, "Heinrich Manns politisches Glaubensbekenntis," *Preussische Jahrbücher* (1920), CLXXXII, no. 2:254.

17. Heinrich Mann, "Wir wollen arbeiten," *Macht und Mensch,* pp. 192–93.

18. Heinrich Mann, *Ein Zeitalter wird besichtigt,* pp. 339–67.

19. Heinrich Mann, "Wir wollen arbeiten," *op. cit.,* p. 194.

20. The conditions of the Versailles Treaty were announced to the German delegation on May 7, 1919. They caused a furor in Germany when they were made public a few days later. For Mann's comments see "Kaiserreich und Republik," *Essays* II, *Ausgewählte Werke,* XII:54–55.

21. *Ibid.,* pp. 55–58.

22. In a letter to Maximilian Harden, August 14, 1919, Mann wrote that the essence of "Kaiserreich und Republik" was the call for "the renewal of the German mental disposition." This letter is reprinted in *Heinrich Mann 1871–1950: Werk und Leben,* pp. 191–92.

23. This point is developed at length in Heinrich Mann, "Kaiserreich und Republik," *op. cit.,* pp. 31–52.

24. Heinrich Mann, "Sinn und Idee der Revolution," *Essays* II, *Ausgewählte Werke,* XII:23.

25. Heinrich Mann, "Kurt Eisner," *Essays* II, *Ausgewählte Werke,* XII:27.

26. Heinrich Mann, "Kaiserreich und Republik," *op. cit.,* p. 58.

27. *Ibid.,* pp. 60–61.

28. Heinrich Mann, "Sinn und Idee der Revolution," *op. cit.,* p. 23.

29. Heinrich Mann, "Kaiserreich und Republik," *op. cit.,* pp. 62–63. Mann envisioned a grand reconciliation of classes based upon common recognition that the class system was obsolete. He even had kind words to say for the *Kleinbürgertum.* According to him, this "down-to-earth" segment of the middle class had natural propensities towards justice, truth, and morality but was misled and

then side-tracked by the "liars and adventurers of imperialism" (i.e. the bourgeoisie). The Munich activist Gustav Landauer made virtually the same point. "The concept of the worker," he wrote, "must be widened; all technical, commercial, and other organized activities must be included. Not the dictatorship but the *abolition of the proletariat* must be the slogan." (See Eugene Lunn, *Prophet of Community*, p. 301)

30. See the original hand-written manuscript of "Sinn und Idee der Revolution," Heinrich-Mann-Archiv, no. 296. The part on Lenin and the Russian Revolution was not included in the East German edition of the *Ausgewählte Werke*.

31. Heinrich Mann, cited in Klaus Geissler, "Entwicklung Heinrich Manns," p. 201.

32. In a letter to Carl Sternheim in January, 1919, Mann confessed his doubts that the destruction of a private economy would change anything. The same sentiment was expressed in the original copy of "Sinn und Idee der Revolution" (see above, footnote 30) where Mann declared himself for a "radicalism of the spirit" but against a radicalism bent on "economic upheavals."

33. Heinrich Mann, "Die Macht des Wortes," typewritten manuscript dating from the year 1936, in Heinrich-Mann-Archiv, no. 323.

34. See Karl Vorländer, *Kant und Marx* (Tübingen, 1926), pp. 158ff.; and Carl Landauer, *European Socialism* (Berkeley, 1959), I:306–07.

35. Friedrich Boek, "Heinrich Manns politisches Glaubensbekenntnis," *Preussische Jahrbücher,* CLXXXII, no. 2:252. Alan Mitchell has pointed out (in *Revolution in Bavaria*, p. 121, and *passim*) that for Eisner "the democratization of the whole people" took precedence over socialization.

36. Kurt Eisner, cited in Karl Vorländer, *Kant und Marx*, p. 212.

37. Heinrich Mann, "Kurt Eisner," *Essays* II, *Ausgewählte Werke*, XII:29–30.

38. To mention only one instance: among those names endorsing Kurt Hiller's *Bund zum Ziel* program (for a "radical social republic") were the familiar ones of Wilhelm Herzog, Rudolf Leonhard, Paul Zech, René Schickele, Otto Flake, Ludwig Meidner, and Heinrich Mann. Such examples could be multiplied many times over.

39. René Schickele, "Revolution, Bolschewismus und das Ideal," *Die weissen Blätter* (1918), V, no. 6:102–10 *passim*.

40. Bernhard Kellermann, "Der Schriftsteller und die deutsche Republik," in *Deutscher Revolutions-Almanach für das Jahr 1919 über die Ereignisse des Jahres 1918,* ed. Ernst Drahn and Ernst Friedegg (Hamburg, 1919); included as a document in Friedrich Albrecht, *Deutsche Schriftsteller in der Entscheidung* (Berlin and Weimar, 1970), pp. 494–97.

41. Wilhelm Herzog, "Unabhängigkeits-Erklärung des Geistes," *Das Forum* (August, 1919), III, no. 11:830–31.

42. On the *Weltbühne* circle, a topic which is beyond the scope of this work, see István Deák, *Weimar Germany's Left-Wing Intellectuals* (Berkeley, 1968).

43. Georg Kaiser, cited in Ernst Schürer, *Georg Kaiser*, p. 171.

44. See Carl Sternheim, "Die deutsche Revolution," *Zeitkritik, Gesamtwerk*, ed. Wilhelm Emrich (Neuwied am Rhein, 1966), VI:85–86.

45. René Schickele, "Revolution, Bolschewismus und das Ideal," *Die weissen Blätter*, V, no. 6:125.

46. *Ibid.*, p. 128.

47. Alfred Döblin, "Republik," *Die Neue Rundschau* (1920), XXXI, no. 1:76–77.

48. On this see Leo Kreutzer, *Alfred Döblin, Sein Werk bis 1933* (Stuttgart, 1970), p. 76.

49. He tried to bring himself into contact with the poor and the working class, but more for cultural than political reasons. (To him it seemed that the poor contained most of what was still good in German life.) One of Döblin's problems was that he could never achieve any real identity with the working class even though there was some poverty in his own background; hence he always talked about the writer's duty to work "with" the poor or "along side" of them. Like Heinrich Mann, he viewed the intellectual barriers between classes as perhaps too great to overcome very easily, though he agreed one was duty-bound to try. See Alfred Döblin, "Die Vertreibung der Gespenster," *Der neue Merkur*, January 1919, pp. 11ff.; reprinted in Döblin's *Schriften zur Politik und Gesellschaft* (Olten, 1972), pp. 71–82; and Gordon Craig, "Engagement and Neutrality in Weimar Germany," *Journal of Contemporary History* (1967), II, no. 2: 57.

50. George L. Mosse, "The Heritage of Socialist Humanism," *Salmagundi* (Fall, 1969—Winter 1970), X–XI: 132. Döblin later explained his intellectual odyssey in *Schicksalsreise* (Frankfurt, 1949).

51. On Rubiner's transition to communism, see Friedrich Albrecht, *Deutsche Schriftsteller*, pp. 101–07; on Wolf, see Walter Pollatschek, "Friedrich Wolf, Dichter und Kämpfer," *Wolf: Ein Lesebuch für unsere Zeit*, ed. Else Wolf and Walther Pollatschek (Berlin, 1969), pp. xxiii–xxxvii.

52. See, for example, Heinrich Mann, "Unser Einfluss und diese Zeit" (1927), in *Sieben Jahre*, pp. 350–55; and "Dichtkunst und Politik" (1928), in *ibid.*, pp. 498–516.

Part III

WRITING AND POLITICAL POWER

Chapter 10

The Weimar Era

I write and write—and what effect does it have on the conduct of the country?

Kurt Tucholsky

I never thought that I would call for a dictatorship, [but now] I do—a ditatorship of reason.

Heinrich Mann

Literary Politics and Republican Politics

As has already been pointed out, Mann greeted the new German Republic with great enthusiasm at its inception in November, 1918. A republic was precisely the form of government he had hoped for throughout the war, even though he had been unable to decide who should usher it in: intellectuals, the *Mittelstand,* youth, or the proletariat. Now such questions were beside the point, since a republic already existed as a by-product of military defeat. This method of creation was, in Mann's opinion, unfortunate since it lent a questionable legitimacy to a state already beset with numerous internal problems. Nonetheless, Mann immediately embraced the new Republic and, as an engaged literary intellectual, began working for its success.

During the first few months of the Republic's existence, however, several problems arose which called into question its integrity. Mann tried not to notice these problems, and when he did acknowledge them he played down their seriousness. Above all, it seemed to him essential that people not abandon the state *in toto* just because it contained internal contradictions. For instance, when the SPD defense minister Noske called on counter-revolutionary troops to quell the Spartacists in January and again in March, 1919, Mann did not protest. However, these episodes permanently alienated other leftist intellectuals like Kurt Tucholsky, who never forgave the

207

Republic for allying with reactionary forces to crush the radicals.
"We don't have revolution in Germany," he wrote in May, 1919,
"we have counter-revolution."[1] From this point on Tucholsky virtually gave up on the Republic. But from Mann's perspective, the
Spartacists (and later the communists in the Munich Soviet of April,
1919) had in some ways asked for the punishment they received.
Their error was that they believed in class warfare, were fundamentally anti-republican, and possessed the same craving for power and
domination that one found among the *Machtmenschen* of the old
Empire. Hence, to Heinrich Mann, as to many others at the time,
the far Left appeared to represent the greatest threat to the new state.
For this reason Mann wanted the radical Left held in check so the
Republic could be preserved (just as he wished that the Kerensky government in Russia had been able to maintain itself against Lenin).[2]
Later, Mann admitted that perhaps he had been too short-
sighted. The end of the Republic, he concluded after 1933, may have
been implicit in its beginnings, since the attitudes of men like
Scheidemann and Noske seemed to foredoom the republican experiment from the start.[3] But this opinion came only with hindsight. At
the time of the left-wing disturbances Mann was convinced that
almost anything done in defense of the Republic was correct.

During the early summer and fall of 1919, however, Mann was
forced to modify his views somewhat. By now the terms of the
dictated peace of Versailles were known, and the mass reaction
against both the treaty and the government which accepted it had
grown enormously. During the uproar that followed, Mann began to
detect some conspicuous flaws not only in the German people but
also in their new government. Most notable, perhaps, was his dis-
comfort with the continued prevalence of militaristic values. He was
equally distrubed by what he sensed to be a dangerous reliance by
the state on an army which refused to call itself republican. Yet
despite these problems, Mann still retained a basic faith in the
Republic's abilities to overcome these difficulties and move towards
genuine democracy.

There were several things which appear to have inspired Mann's
confidence. For one, a people now existed which he felt was both
teachable and potentially democratic. (At this stage, Mann tended to
define the "people" as a fusion of working-class and middle-class
elements, i.e., as laborers who had become good citizens [*Arbeiter-
bürger*] and middle-class individuals [*Kleinbürgertum*] who had

become laborers "of head and hands."[4] He assumed that this fused group would provide the basis for a broad and educable reading public.) For another, a spiritual intelligentsia had emerged which was willing to guide the masses toward democracy and encourage them to take responsibility for the Republic. Finally, an effective literary politics now seemed possible in Germany, perhaps for the first time in history. If great efforts were made, Mann was certain that the influence of "spirit" could be spread and cultivated; it was even possible for it to flow over the borders into France, which, after the Versailles Treaty, also seemed in need of it.[5] Mann felt that *Geist* could still be triumphant because it was potentially more powerful than either money or armies. In light of these factors, which spoke well for the future, Mann continued to support the Republic, even with all of its shortcomings. "The spirit of our democracy," he wrote at the time, "can save us and, who knows, perhaps also the world."[6] Significantly, the dedication in his collection of essays entitled *Macht und Mensch*—the only book he published in 1919—was "to the Weimar Republic."

Optimism of the Will: 1920–1923

The first three years of the twenties saw a steady erosion in Mann's optimism regarding immediate improvements in the Republic. Nevertheless, his long-range hope for the new state did survive—mainly, it seems, because of a strenuous effort of will.

From the beginning, Mann did what he said the activist writer should do: he rejected aloofness, confronted the concrete issues of his age, and addressed himself to the "problems of the living." But this created a dilemma, for the more Mann familiarized himself with the reality of the Weimar Republic, the more difficulties he saw which had to be overcome. In order to maintain hope it was necessary, at least on occasion, to shut his eyes to certain facts, since presumably too much knowledge of the actual situation would lead to a pessimistic point of view. A curious dichotomy thus emerged between what Mann saw and what he hoped for. On the one hand, events themselves suggested that the problems of Weimar were deep-seated rather than merely superficial, as he had at first thought. On the other hand, there were certain "moral facts" such as the rightness of the German Republic which had to be believed in at all costs. Mann's tendency during the early 1920s was to let the second cast of mind obscure the first. That is, he let his will to believe dominate his will to observe and assess the reality of the situation. The result, at least until the beginning of 1922, was a facile optimism in Mann's published writings which failed to take account of the more disturbing aspects of German society and politics.

Typical in this respect was his essay "Berlin," written in October, 1921. In this piece Mann claimed to have found the beginnings of a healthy German democracy in the give-and-take of urban life. Berlin, he thought, encouraged the qualities of patience and skepticism, irony and rationality, class-mixing and class collaboration, all of which proved that the republican experiment was succeeding. The metropolis, it seemed, had become a "school for democrats" and "the strongest bulwark of our reason."[7] More importantly, Mann felt that what was happening in Berlin could spread to other parts of Germany if the *Länder* would follow the lead of the capital. On the whole, the future looked bright, but only so long as one assumed (wrongly as it turned out) that Berlin was simply setting a pattern which would soon take hold elsewhere.

In the following year another essay entitled "Tragische Jugend" ("Tragic Youth") appeared. Though not nearly as exuberant as the essay on Berlin, it nevertheless ended on a strong note of optimism. "I would still hope," Mann wrote, "that the entire world and above all [our] most suffering country can be saved by the power of *Geist* and continue to live on into the future. If the first consequences of the catastrophe [World War I] are overcome, it may be shown that our spirit has become clearer and more animated in all areas of human endeavor. . . . The trials which the world lays before us will simply make us stronger."[8]

These sentiments represented the face Mann revealed to the world. Privately, he seemed much less sure of himself and less confident about the progress of democracy. In personal letters to friends (where it was not necessary to put up appearances or worry about discouraging an already shaky reading public) Mann was more frank in his opinions. In effect, he felt free to speak more about what he saw than about what he merely wanted to believe. Here an ambiguity began to manifest itself, making it hard to determine exactly what Mann's deepest attitudes toward the Republic were. In a letter to his lawyer, Maximilan Brantl, written in January of 1920 in the midst of the counter-revolutionary atmosphere in Munich, Mann was depressed though not yet in complete despair.[9] He seemed to think that the climate in Munich (the city at this point was trying the leaders of the overthrown Soviet Republic of 1919) had taken a turn for the worse, but fortunately was still not typical of Germany as a whole. The following year, in a letter to Félix Bertaux, Mann had become more pessimistic. He indicated that Germany was a long way from true democracy and would have to endure an extended period of "purely capitalistic democracy" before things would get better.[10] Two months later, in a letter to a young writer, Mann appeared slightly more hopeful,[11] but then at the beginning of 1923 he again seemed uncertain about Germany's future.[12] This shifting back and forth was due not only to Mann's spontaneous reaction to events, but also to his slow and often reluctant confrontation with certain underlying realities of the Weimar Republic.

In this respect, the year 1923 was an important turning-point. It was at this time that Mann directly and publicly acknowledged some of the major shortcomings of the Republic and demanded that these be remedied so that democracy could get back on course. As never before, Mann was able to fuse his capacity for realistic analysis with a fundamental impulse to hope, thereby preventing the one from excluding the other. The result was that in 1923 he probably embodied his conception of the man-of-letters as a practitioner of literary politics more satisfactorily than at any other time during the Weimar era. Not only did Mann carefully observe and interact with his concrete situation, but he also brought into play all his powers of interpretation and criticism. Even his literary style seemed to become more condensed and lucid as he shed much of his earlier naive, superficial confidence in the possibilities of German democracy.

To understand what Mann wrote in 1923, it is important to look briefly at the events of that year.

Since the signing of the dictated peace at Versailles, Germany had moved steadily to the Right. In the national elections of 1924, the Weimar Coalition (composed of the SPD, the Center Party, and the newly-formed German Democratic Party [DDP]) failed to be endorsed by a majority of the electorate. Nevertheless, the government attempted to carry out a "policy of fulfillment" toward the Allies, but always in the face of violent protests and assassinations by right-wing extremists. In Munich, where Mann lived throughout this period, both the *Freikorps* and various racist groupings had established themselves as forces to be reckoned with. There was even frequent talk in Bavaria of marching on Berlin and bringing about a *coup d'état,* as Mussolini had done in Italy. To exacerbate this rightward drift in Germany, there was also the issue of reparations, which the government had so far proven incapable of dealing with. At Versailles, the total amount of money which Germany had to pay was left unsettled, but an Allied Reparations Commission was later created which set the figure at 132 billion gold marks. At the same time the Commission warned that if this amount was not forthcoming, an Allied blockade would follow and parts of the Ruhr Industrial region would be occupied. When, in January 1923, there was a temporary default in payments, the French premier Poincaré sent troops into the Ruhr district to seize German mines and factories. By way of response, the German government called for passive resistance, but in order to subsidize this policy vast quantities of paper money had to be printed and distributed to the unemployed, thus adding to an inflationary spiral which was already excessive. For nine months, until the autumn of 1923, the situation became increasingly critical. By the time the new chancellor, Gustav Stresemann, put an end to the resistance, Germany's morale was as depressed as its currency.

By the end of 1923, the episode in the Ruhr was over but its effects lingered on. Two facts stood out in the minds of many observers and victims: first, that a broad stratum of the middle class (*Mittelstand*) was economically wiped out by the inflation; and secondly, that many wealthy industrialists and landowners profited from this same inflation. With regard to the first point, it became clear during the course of 1923 that large sections of the middle class (particularly those dependent of fixed salaries, pensions, or savings) had been proletarianized. This experience caused a good part of the rentier class to become disillusioned with the Republic, and to look more favorably upon the extremist ideologies of the Right. The second point—that some profiteers made large fortunes off of Germany's misery—was also not overlooked, least of all by Heinrich Mann. It was found that several of Germany's leading entrepreneurs and industrial magnates had been able to borrow at low rates of interest, then invest in real property and "vertical trusts" which returned their investments many times over. Others had simply taken advantage of the economic situation to expand their plants or buy new equipment while paying off old loans or wages with inflated money. Thus, while the state continued to exhaust its reserves, many industrialists and financiers remained unhindered in their attempts at building economic empires.[13]

It was against this background of inflation, profiteering, and political crisis that Mann began to re-formulate his view of the central problems of the Weimar Republic. In six essays written between April and October of 1923, specifically addressing the events just recounted,[14] Mann tried to explain the nature of Germany's difficulties and to suggest what might be done about them. For the first time in public since 1919 (but now much more forcefully), Mann argued that Germany's problems may not be due merely to a lack of *Geist* or to a failure of nerve in actualizing democracy. He pointed out that they might instead be structural and therefore extremely deep-rooted, just as they had been during the Wilhelmian era.

Three important ideas were central to each of Mann's 1923 essays. First, he asserted that the rich, or "industrial bourgeoisie," had acquired control of the state and were using it to advance their own interests; consequently they, not the French, were the true enemies of the German people. Second, Mann insisted that *Geist* could still save Germany but now, it seemed, only if it were accompanied by some changes in the material base of society. By itself, the power of spirit appeared insufficient so long as there was no mass receptivity to it, no popular willingness to have it become an active political force. Earlier, Mann had placed so much hope in *Geist* that he had assumed it could virtually create its own material conditions and then transform them; but this had been during a period of Kantian idealism, when he had felt that thought alone might be enough to spiritualize and democratize Germany. Now it was clear that something else—namely, more regulation of wealth and power, perhaps even more socialization—was needed in order to lay the groundwork for a free, genuinely republican society. Third and finally, Mann began to argue that all his previous talk about democracy had not gone far enough. By this time democracy seemed to be merely a catchword, a façade behind which all the old private interests could operate unchecked. Seeing this, Mann urged the institutionalization of "social democracy" as a counterpoise to what he called "capitalist democracy"; put differently, he wanted Weimar to become a social republic rather than merely the "advanced capitalist republic" it had been so far.[15] This stance appeared to lead him into a radical or revolutionary position, but as will be pointed out shortly, Mann believed that all the socialization Germany needed was already provided for in the Weimar Constitution.

The core of these new formulations appeared in Mann's first two essays of the year 1923: "Das Sterben der geistigen Schicht" ("The Death of the Intelligentsia") and "Wirtschaft 1923" ("Economy 1923"). Both pieces, written in the early and anxious months of the Ruhr occupation, defined German problems in the worst possible light. Four essays written later in the year, during a period of deepening inflation and social unrest, attempted to point the way out of the crisis. Taken together, the last four pieces represented a strong element of hope superimposed on what seemed to be a hopeless situation.

In "Das Sterben der geistigen Schicht," written in April, Mann argued against passive resistance on the grounds that it encouraged an extremist form of nationalism which demanded "victory" over the French.[16] The only kind of victory that Mann thought made sense was a victory of "reason" and "good will," two qualities which he believed could emerge if a different moral and spiritual climate prevailed in Germany. In this respect, the most valuable resource Germany possessed was its spiritual intellectuals, since they alone could prepare the groundwork for the emergence of a society where material interest would be subordinated to *Geist*. But this was not happening in 1923, mainly because the Republic had fallen into the hands of the rich, who had turned the state into an instrument of economic policy. The result was a pervasive "poverty of ideas" and even a "hostility to ideas" in Germany. Now, for the first time, Mann singled out the existence of a plutocracy as one of the greatest problems of the Weimar Republic. He argued that because the wealthy controlled politics, economic matters were given primacy while spiritual values were discarded, along with the intelligentsia which fostered them.

The fact that Mann now had a specific enemy for his *j'accuse* allowed him to focus his analysis much more sharply than before; this also opened the way for a clear-cut solution, namely, the unseating of the rich from the centers of power so that Germany could become truly democratic. "What victory means," he wrote, "can never be discovered by economic thought but only by a determined breakthrough to spiritual goals. Who prevents this and forces us all into a position of dependence? The excessively rich [*Der übermässige Reichtum*]. Who brings about ever new entanglements . . . in both the domestic and foreign sphere? The wealthiest people. The state is, suddenly and in an illegal way, in their hands. . . . Even without a putsch they have achieved dictatorship."[17]

From this premise Mann concluded that the very rich, who had already acquired control of the state, were now systematically destroying their rival, the old middle class. As he had thirty years earlier, Mann proceeded to identify culture as such with the continued existence of the small but "firmly established and independent *Mittelstand*."[18] In an interesting way he linked the fate of the spiritual intelligentsia to the endangered middle class, indicating that both had to reassert themselves together against the rich and powerful or else perish together. The *Mittelstand*, even though it had greatly disappointed him by succumbing to the mystique of economics, was still portrayed as the repository of value and therefore as the core audience which intellectuals had to reach and spiritualize. Mann even envisioned the emergence of a new politics based on an alliance between the intelligentsia and a middle class redefined as encompassing all those oppressed by monopoly capitalism, including workers. This alignment of forces would oppose the existing "politics of power" and usher in an age of social reconciliation in place of the prevailing social exploitation.[19]

The following month, in "Wirtschaft 1923," Mann expanded his argument by giving it an historical dimension. Now he contended that ideas or ideologies gain ascendency mainly because there are social or material interests behind them, a point he had not made before. Nationalism, for example, was pervasive because big business funded it; the ideals of freedom and equality, on the other hand, did not have wide currency in Germany because business was not interested in supporting them. Historically speaking, Mann felt that the existing "ruling class"—a term he now used freely to describe the bourgeoisie—began to have a stake in nationalism in the 1870s, when it discovered that the economy was the mainstay of the state and that loyalty to the state (i.e., nationalism) necessarily meant loyalty to an industrial-capitalist economy. In World War I nationalism became even more equated with capitalism when, with the encouragement of the state, a powerful *Kriegsindustrie* emerged. By the Weimar period, Mann believed that the state had become so subservient to economic interests that appeals to nationalistic emotions were actually intended to maximize profits, for instance by means of a larger armaments industry.

Throughout 1923, Mann was convinced that what Marxists at the time were calling "the reification of the economy" had gone beyond all reasonable bounds. Greed and self-aggrandisement were now stressed as the motive forces of social activity, while any sense of responsibility for the exploited and dispossessed was entirely lacking. Only power and wealth counted, and the two terms were interchangeable to the bourgeoisie. Mann continued to emphasize that the *Mittelstand,* still apparently the reservoir of value and moderation, was being swallowed up in the whole process of the "survival of the greediest."[20] As a result, the "mental workers" were losing their function because the social base which their ideas were to penetrate was disappearing. But as bad as all this seemed, Mann still saw a way out. The ruling class could be dislodged, since it was not as untouchable as it imagined itself to be. A great nausea against avarice could emerge, sweeping away the existing value system and with it, the economic leaders who profited from a "dictatorship of the economy." If this happened, spiritual values could return, implemented by spiritual intellectuals. Apparently, it would be only after a thorough social and structural house-cleaning that the Weimar Republic would have a chance to become a genuinely democratic state. This hope was formulated with characteristic vagueness, but nevertheless it remained one which Mann professed to believe in.[21]

In the remaining essays Mann wrote in 1923, he continued to emphasize the theme of hope rather than despair. In "Anfänge Europas" ("European Beginnings"), he spoke optimistically about the possibilities of a united Europe based on Franco-German cooperation. If the spiritual intellectuals could make this unity a reality, the foundations would exist for the gradual elimination of two major European evils: nationalism and vulgar materialism.[22] In "Noch ein Krieg mit Frankreich" ("A Further War with France"), Mann expressed confidence that the influence of monopoly capitalism on the state and economy could be overturned in both France and Germany. Then decision-making would be returned to the people of each country, who would find their way to reconciliation and understanding. Mann strongly argued that democracy was alive in Germany, but that it needed to be tended and cultivated in order to achieve its fullest potential.[23] In still another essay entitled "Wir feiern die Verfassung" ("We Celebrate the Constitution"), he again sounded a hopeful note. Germany, Mann contended, could renew and advance itself if only it would live up to the principles already embodied in the Weimar Constitution of 1919. The highest ideals of democracy and freedom were embedded and codified in this central document of state, and it only remained to enforce the Constitution so that its spirit could permeate the whole climate of the Republic. If this happened, the industrial magnates and their allies, the nationalists, would not be allowed to wield so much influence. In Mann's opinion, these people had usurped power because the terms of the Constitution had not been carefully implemented. Now this problem could be remedied by straight-jacketing monopoly capital, encouraging the growth of an independent middle class, enforcing at least a minimum of socialization, and seeing to it that "the spirit of the Weimar Constitution" took hold in the population at large.[24] On the whole, Mann felt that there was reason to be confident about the future of the Republic, provided it carried out the obligations it had already imposed upon itself in the Constitution.

In October of 1923 Mann published the last of the six essays he wrote that year. It was entitled "Diktatur der Vernunft" ("Dictatorship of Reason") and took the form of an open letter to Chancellor Gustav Stresemann. Significantly, October was perhaps the low point of that difficult and tragic year. Though passive resistance had ended in September, inflation was still rampant (one dollar bought 2,520,000,000,000 marks in November), the Black Reichswehr was in rebellion, counter-revolutionary agitation was rampant in Bavaria (later leading to Hitler's putsch on November 9), and general alarm existed concerning an alleged communist takeover in Saxony and Thuringia, where KPD representatives joined the SPD in a cabinet coalition.

In the midst of this, Mann called upon Stresemann to restore the rule of law before the forces of the Right established a dictatorship. Ironically, Mann overlooked the fact that Stresemann, as a member of the German People's Party (DVP), was himself a man of the moderate Right and would therefore be reluctant to enforce policies which ran counter to the interests of his class or party. Nevertheless, the situation in Germany seemed so urgent that literary politics, as Mann understood it, required intellectuals to make certain demands upon politicians in order to save the Republic. This was the express purpose for writing "Diktatur der Vernunft." In specific terms Mann insisted, first of all, that the chancellor institute some form of press censorship to prevent the proliferation of well-financed right-wing ideas which made it difficult for reason to achieve hegemony in

Germany. Second, he urged Stresemann to forbid "irrational gangs" of fanatics and racists from organizing and moving freely throughout the country. (It was in this connection that the National Socialists were mentioned for the first time in Mann's writings). Third, he demanded elimination of the power of the German plutocrats by strictly enforcing the Constitution, guaranteeing basic human rights and establishing "social democracy." Fourth, Mann called for state control of monopoly capitalism by means of the socialization of heavy industry, while at the same time asking for the protection of the "small proprietor" (*Kleinbürger*) as provided for in the Constitution. Fifth and last, he insisted that Stresemann secure total rapprochement and reconciliation with France, since this was the only "rational" foreign policy that could be followed.[25]

If all this happened, Mann inferred, Germany would be on the road to political and spiritual recovery. He claimed that each of the points mentioned above was entirely reasonable, and that if Stresemann acted upon them he would be acting in a thoroughly rational manner—which is to say, he would be establishing the "dictatorship of reason" that Mann believed would command the support of a majority of the German people. Just as importantly, he would be acting under the advisement of a spiritual intellectual, namely Heinrich Mann himself. Here was an opportunity for the chancellor to set a momentous example for other leaders to follow. The intellectual could begin to have an influence on politics by becoming a kind of spiritual advisor to decision-makers, very much in the Enlightenment tradition of the resident *philosophe* at court. The role of the intellectual, Mann now wrote, was to warn people against corruption and exploitation, while the role of the politician was to do something practical to eliminate these evils.[26] The two human types—the thinkers and the doers—could work together for the common good. If this process of cooperation resulted in a healthy interaction on both sides, where politicians became more spiritual and intellectuals more political, then one could be hopeful about the future of Germany.

Pessimism of the Intellect: 1924–1929

Mann's social and political world-view of 1923 has been described in some detail because it was this outlook which he maintained, with only slight variations, for the duration of the Weimar Republic. But although there was little change in the content of Mann's thought, i.e., in his definition of what was wrong with society and what had to be done to remedy the situation, there were noticeable changes in his forced sense of confidence about the future. Between 1924 and 1929, it seems that what Antonio Gramsci called the "optimism of the will" gave way in Mann's case to a more pervasive and realistic "pessimism of the intellect." The more he interacted with his age in a direct and immediate way, the more Mann became discouraged by what he saw. Eventually it appeared that not the peripheral structures, but perhaps the central pillars, of Weimar society were undemocratic or anti-republican. This insight, which many other radical democrats had arrived at some years earlier, had a sobering effect on his thought. It led him toward a less hopeful, though not exactly despairing, assessment of the Republic's chances for survival; it also forced him to re-evaluate his own relationship to the political reality of Weimar and to alter somewhat, in method if not in goal, his conception of the tasks of literary politics.

Paradoxically, Mann's growing pessimism after 1923 coincided with a period of at least superficial prosperity and stabilization in Germany. By the beginning of 1924 a new *Rentenmark*, which helped put an end to the inflation of the previous year, had been introduced. At the same time the Dawes Plan, which also facilitated Germany's economic recovery, went into effect. A year later, Stresemann signed the Locarno Pact, thus ushering in a spirit of détente with the West which led to Germany's admittance into the League of Nations the following year. Domestically, Germany experienced more tranquility in the mid-1920s than at any time since the war. The *Freikorps* units, which throve on the crisis of 1923, were now much diminished except for the nationalist Stahlhelm organization. Likewise, support for racist parties fell precipitously after the December elections of 1924 and did not revive again until 1930; the Nazi Party (NSDAP), for example, lost one-half of its voters and eighteen seats in the Reichstag by the end of 1924 and virtually disappeared from national politics for the remainder of the 1920s. Political power was held by a coalition of middle-class parties which, despite much anti-democratic sentiment, had the effect of preserving rather than dissolving the Republic. Even Field Marshal von Hindenburg, when he became president in 1925, surprised many by upholding the Weimar Constitution regardless of his own monarchical tendencies.

Rarely, in his writings after 1924, did Mann seem encouraged by these events.[27] Much more prevalent was his conviction that Germany's recovery was only a façade behind which neglected problems continued to fester and grow. Most of the evils he had in mind had been mentioned in 1923, but others were added. For example, Mann now believed that despite the apparent return to normalcy there had as yet been no serious attempt to reform the civil service or republicanize the army. Consequently, anti-democratic forces were consolidating themselves at a time when the masses were caught up in the euphoria of an illusory stabilization. The judicial system similarly appeared to be in the hands of reactionaries, which meant that there was little real justice in Weimar, particularly for republicans or leftist sympathizers.[28] Most unsettling of all, however, was the continuing influence of big business on German economic, cultural, and political life. In Mann's opinion, monopoly capital had more power to shape and determine the nature of social reality in the 1920s than any other single factor. For these reasons he concluded that, despite appearances, the Weimar years represented a "period of reaction."[29] At the deepest structural level nothing seemed to have changed much since the Wilhelmian era, except that the bourgeoisie had replaced the aristocracy as Germany's ruling class.[30]

The consequences of this situation did not appear promising to Mann. Because Weimar society had not only grown indifferent to injustice and criminality but also had begun to let industrial magnates decide questions of political policy and cultural value, the mass of average citizens, which under ideal conditions would have been the bulwark of the Republic, was slipping into moral and spiritual lethargy. The result was a new level of greed and acquisitiveness in the German people, and a concomitant decline of interest in spiritual matters. In Mann's view, intellectual and ethical concerns were becoming burdensome to many to the same degree that sports, dancing, and other diversions became the norm. In short, Weimar Germany appeared to be transforming itself into a standardized mass society which perfectly suited the needs of the prevailing system of "advanced capitalism" (Hochkapitalismus). As selfishness gradually replaced conscience, and the image of the consumer undermined the model of the citoyen, Weimar increasingly operated "without spiritual laws." Not surprisingly, Mann thought he saw a new type of "good subject" emerging out of all this and labelled him a "monarcho-republican" (meaning the spiritually empty, anti-democratic, and money-oriented individual who thinks only of himself and not of the social whole). The concept of a spiritual and moral "people," which Mann had earlier invested such confidence in, now appeared increasingly unrealistic because of the control which predominant economic forces exerted upon the masses.[31]

This conclusion had a great effect both on Mann's conception of himself as a writer and on his view of literary politics in the Weimar period. If it was true that not *Geist* but a "dictatorship of the economy" ruled Germany, then the population at large was materialistic and "hostile to the spirit" almost by definition. And to the extent that this was so, society was also necessarily resistent to the forces of reason and intelligence. (According to Mann, wherever materialism gains the upper hand, spiritual and ethical ideals lose their impact). But the hostility to the spirit which was spreading everywhere was not due to some inherent flaw in the German people; it existed because certain manipulative economic interests, which were by nature antagonistic to all things spiritual, had planted it there and wanted it to thrive. The question then was: what could be done to remove such harmful influences so that Germany could recover its spiritual potential? Ostensibly, the answer would be to free the masses from materialism so that they could join with spiritual intellectuals in opposing the worst aspects of monopoly capitalism. In Mann's view, however, this was no easy matter, since the economically and socially conditioned *Geistfeindlichkeit* had become so pervasive in the Weimar era that it made an effective penetration by "spirit" virtually impossible. On the surface, at least, this would imply that the role of the engaged *littérateur* had become meaningless, because no receptive audience existed to carry out the message of literary intellectuals.

Mann was thus trying to deal with the disturbing notion that an intelligent and influential reading public (which was always crucial to the concept of literary politics) might no longer carry real weight in Germany. In 1918, Mann had believed that there existed precisely the right kind of readership for literary politics: one composed of the most progressive middle and working class elements (those who labor with "head and hands"). By 1923, however, he thought he saw this audience destroyed by the inflation. It seemed to him that large sections of the German population had become indifferent to literature and thought.[32] He claimed not to know why people read at all any more, but presumably it was only to remain *au courant,* not to satisfy any driving inner need. As an author approaching his mid-fifties, it also occurred to Mann that maybe he was read, if at all, mainly for nostalgic or sentimental reasons and not for instruction or elevation, which for him was the whole point of writing. In a letter to Tucholsky, he complained that no one understood his recent work; perhaps, he concluded, it might be better to write fairy tales instead.[33]

Mann's growing uncertainty about his audience was possibly best reflected in his concern with the youth of Germany. If the Weimar Republic was to endure, Mann felt that the younger generation had to embrace democracy.[34] This, for him, was another way of saying that it would have to embody and implement the ideas dispensed by spiritual intellectuals. For this reason, the youth question became pivotal throughout the 1920s, just as it had been in 1918, when Mann had thought the young might become a major agent for social transformation.

In general, it could be said that the more Mann observed and wrote about the younger generation, the more he slowly abandoned his once hopeful attitude toward it. In 1922, he complained that the young seemed more filled with hate than love, which explained why they tended to reject the status quo and opt for "absolutist" solutions of the Left or Right.[35] However, from 1924 onward Mann shifted the focus of his argument. Now it appeared that the main problem was not that young people were being politically radicalized, but that they were becoming completely indifferent to social and political issues. The young, he pointed out (meaning particularly middle class youth), seemed unconcerned about injustice or exploitation and had only a minimum of social conscience. Furthermore, they lacked any real historical sense or feeling for tradition, and lived only in order to enjoy themselves. Sports, dancing, jazz, cars, and sexual freedom represented the "totality of their wishes."[36] Most disturbing of all was their lack of responsibility. For the most part they failed to acknowledge social duties and obligations, above all the duty to turn a flawed "conservative Republic" into a genuinely "radical" Republic.[37] All these shortcomings led to an enervating political passivity which seemed to bode ill for the future of democracy in Germany. Perhaps, Mann speculated, the generation of 1940 would be more socially and spiritually aware, since it usually took fifteen to twenty years after a war for the best qualities of youth to come to the surface. In any event, he was certain that the present generation was not ideal, nor was it easily reachable as a supportive reading public.[38]

This being the case, it was necessary for the practitioners of literary politics to change their tactics to better attain their goals. Since youth and the middle class had moved beyond the reach of *geistige* intellectuals, it was essential for writers to try and spiritualize life in Weimar by different means. Mann had two alternative methods in mind. First, literary intellectuals could address themselves to the leading political figures of the Republic in order to help them democratize society from the top down. To be sure, Mann believed that many of these leaders were for the moment in bondage to capitalist interests, but that a tremendous "spiritual capital" existed which could be used by writers to convince men of state to implement more humane policies.[39] Intellectuals might even form a kind of shadow cabinet to help guide those in power. This was partly the intent behind Mann's letter to Stresemann in 1923, i.e. that writers would provide sound advice and politicans would act upon it; it was also the reason for his enthusiasm over President Thomas Masaryk of Czechoslovakia who, he said, always learned from the thought of others and was "not afraid of ideas."[40] Perhaps a group of "spiritually trained and spiritually motivated politicans" could be created to actualize spirit and reason in Germany in a way that the masses failed to do.[41] If this happened, it would be because the intellectuals served as objective advisors whose sole interest was in preserving and strengthening the Republic *as a state,* not because they involved themselves in partisan politics. In fact, the politicians would have to understand that the *Geist,* which is communicated by intellectuals, not only stands higher than the state but is actually the goal the state must strive for. Mann's model here seems to have been Kant who, as a philosopher, could make demands on political reality because he always spoke from the elevated position of moral-rational absolutes. This notion seemed highly attractive to Mann, especially since he was making few inroads into the population at large. Nonetheless, he insisted that although intellectuals could attach themselves to the state as advisors to those in power, they should not allow themselves to become government functionaries. Their higher mission was to *Geist* and *Geist* alone. The state, by contrast, could never become spiritual enough for Mann's taste because of its inherent practical, *realpolitisch* nature. Hence its importance lay in being an instrument for spiritual purposes, not an end in itself.[42]

Besides advising leaders of state, Mann suggested a second way in which German writers could help transform a recalcitrant reality. This was by joining other European men-of-letters in an organization of intellectuals dedicated to advancing the spirit of democracy, republicanism, and mutual cooperation between nations. The result, hopefully, would be the eventual emergence of a rational and moral supra-national state—presumably supervised by intellectuals—which would spread the influence of *Geist* throughout Europe.[43] Possibly this larger framework could help the individual nations to root out those tendencies which Mann considered incompatible with the highest levels of spiritual development. It might even lead to the creation of truly democratic societies which had so far not been attained within the context of the nation state. With this in mind, Mann frequently called for a pan-European union of intellectuals (and nations) throughout the 1920s. However, he apparently failed to notice that much of Europe was moving to the Right at the time and that a future supra-national state could take on a reactionary, if not a fascist, character.[44]

There was an undeniable air of elitism in both of the above roles which Mann suggested for intellectuals, but they seemed to represent the only way to get around the three major obstacles of the time, namely, the power of the rich, the pervasive cultural *Geistfeindlichkeit,* and the apparent rejection by the young of democratic values. Noting this new aloofness in Mann, the critic Lorenz Winter has argued that it represented an urge to withdraw from society into the cloister. In Winter's opinion, Mann developed an almost religious conception of the writer's task in the sense that he hoped to preserve *Geist* by founding a pure "church of literature" uncorrupted by the materialistic demands of the masses.[45] There is some truth to this. The idea of a church did become a model for Mann because the church was, as he put it, "the only form in which the West has seen the spirit triumphant over non-spiritual powers. . . . The church has become a power in itself. 'That was the stroke of genius'."[46] Mann certainly wanted the same thing to happen with German intellectuals, which is to say, he wanted them to become organized as an independent spiritual force. What he rejected, however, was the notion that they should separate themselves from life by addressing their message to posterity. For Mann, the objective was not that writers become secular monks, as Winter has inferred, but that they become the modern equivalent of Jesuits (and equally tight-knit and effective as advisors to the powerful). Thus, the literary clerisy was still explicitly urged to engage itself, to speak directly about the problems of the age, and to be activists for the spirit by rejecting the temptation to write for posterity.[47] But the methods used had to be changed, since the spiritual poverty of the age demanded that writers try new tactical approaches.

It is in this light that one can understand Mann's desire to address the political leaders of the German Democratic Party (DDP) at its convention in 1927, hoping to inspire them to move further leftward and develop more of a social conscience.[48] It also explains his acceptance of membership in the prestigious Prussian Academy of Arts in 1926, and his assumption of the presidency of the literary section of the Academy in 1931. Becoming a member of this organization was clearly a sign that Mann had joined the establishment, but he saw this high position as an opportunity to spiritualize Germany from above. His duties as an academician required, among other things, that he be a consultant to the Prussian Minister of Culture on literary matters, that he improve the quality and accuracy of school texts in the *Gymnasia* and universities, and that he establish connections with literary figures from other countries. In each of these capacities Mann believed he could further the cause of spirit in a way that would have been impossible in his function as merely a political *littérateur*. He anticipated, for example, that he could use his office to fight against censorship laws, root out anti-French prejudices from school texts, oppose *völkisch* currents in the curriculum, and speak for reason and freedom in all public places and at official gatherings.[49] In these ways Mann felt that the spiritual intellectual might be more effective working cautiously within the state apparatus than he would be by remaining simply a disgruntled outsider.

Throughout the 1920s, then, Mann tended to maintain an aristocratic conception of the writer's role. Literary intellectuals were seen as a special class of individuals whose interests were primarily spiritual and ethical. Nonetheless, these intellectuals were obliged to intervene in society in the name of eternal human values, though never as simply one interest group among others. Their responsibility as a caste was to spiritualize society from the top down so as to transform the whole and not merely a part of it.[50] These ideas had probably always been present just below the surface of Mann's thought. In the 1890s, for instance, the image of the writer as an aesthetic aristocrat was paramount, and around 1910 the notion that men-of-letters constituted a special mandarin class was central to Mann's thought. Even in 1918, with his Political Council of Intellectual Workers, the idea that the literati could become an independent spiritual and moral force in society persisted. Mann had always insisted that this intelligentsia be independent and free-floating, so that even when he later advised that writers attach themselves to the state for strategic purposes, he continued to insist that their primary loyalty must always be to reason and intelligence in the abstract. In contrast to his friend Kurt Hiller (who believed in "Logocracy," or direct rule by "the morally and intellectually superior"), Mann preferred that writers be only advisors so as not to get caught up in the practical side of power.[51] For him the highest goal, to put it in Kantian language, was to become the custodian and active defender of the categorical imperative.

As Mann interpreted the categorical imperative between 1924 and 1929, his duty was to preserve the Weimar Republic, however incomplete and unspiritual it was, and however subject to the control of monopoly capital. One could not simply give up on a state because it had numerous limitations. Rather, the task should be to cultivate all the democratic possibilities within it, even if it was hard to be optimistic about the success of such an undertaking. By 1929, Mann's enthusiasm and hope were no longer as naive as they had been in 1919, but the commitment to save the Republic remained.

Lengthening Shadows: 1930–1933

The last years of Weimar were difficult for Germany's republican writers. Heinrich Mann—along with others of his generation like Wilhelm Herzog, Bernhard Kellermann, Bruno Frank, and by now Thomas Mann[52]—found himself increasingly hard-pressed to defend a state which was only nominally republican after 1930. It was in this year that Heinrich Brüning, the new chancellor, abolished ministerial responsibility and created a presidential dictatorship under Hindenburg. This meant, in effect, the abdication of formal democracy in Germany, even though Brüning hoped this state of affairs would only be temporary. To make matters worse, the Great Depression soon enveloped Germany, strangling the middle class and impoverishing the proletariat for the second time in seven years. The deep fissures which were indigenous to the Republic from the beginning began to widen. In the elections of September, 1930, there was an unexpected surge of support for the Nazi Party. From 12 seats in the Reichstag, the NSDAP jumped to 107, and from a total voting strength of 600,000 (in 1928) it grew to 6,400,000, thereby becoming the second largest party in the country. Unlike most communist and a few liberal intellectuals, Mann took Hitler seriously from this point on. In fact, the so-called "threat from the far Right" became one of his major preoccupations throughout the early 1930s.

As the economic depression worsened, a good part of the middle class defected from the Republic and sought extremist solutions to its problems. At the same time the fortunes of the NSDAP steadily improved, both in terms of finances and the number of supporters. In the 1932 presidential election Hitler surprised many by collecting 13,400,000 votes, as compared to 19,300,000 for Hindenburg and only 3,700,000 for the Communist Party candidate Thälmann. Since Hitler's support amounted to only 37% of the vote, Hindenburg remained in office for another term, though he became increasingly anti-democratic and contemptuous of the procedures of the Republic as time went on. Gradually a reactionary clique formed around the aging president and convinced him first to replace Brüning with Franz von Papen, and then later to replace von Papen with General Kurt von Schleicher. By December, 1932, the Weimar Republic existed in name only, since von Schleicher represented virtually no one but himself and the Reichstag was not able to recoup its lost power. In the meantime Nazi support continued to grow. In July, 1932, the National Socialists became the largest party in Germany with 230 seats, nearly 100 more than their nearest rivals the Social Democrats. Despite some minor losses in the November elections, the NSDAP was still a force to be reckoned with. Though Hindenburg disliked Hitler intensely, he was finally convinced by his friends to appoint him as chancellor, provided that von Papen (who it was thought could control Hitler) remain as vice-chancellor. This appointment took place on January 30, 1933. During the next few months Hitler, instead of being held in check, rapidly strengthened his hold over most of the important social and political institutions of Germany.

In light of these events, Mann felt compelled to become *engagé* in a more direct sense than between 1924 and 1929. Once again it seemed that the situation demanded a change in tactics. The same shift toward commitment also occurred among others in Mann's literary generation. Apparently the economic and political crisis drew out of many writers a new sense of urgency and involvement, even among those who had been indifferent to the Republic in the 1920s.

In Heinrich Mann's case this meant a renewed defense of the German state, in spite of the fact that it was only a distorted image of what it should be. This put Mann in the awkward position of supporting a society that was unspiritual and a government that was undemocratic. Nevertheless, there seemed to be no alternative since, in his opinion, the Republic was the only thing that stood between a Nazi dictatorship and anarchy.[53] From 1930 to 1933 Mann continued to support the Weimar state, but his was a negative support *faute de mieux.* The old enthusiasm was gone and he rallied behind Hindenburg, as did other ethical socialists, only because the extremes of Left or Right seemed much worse. "So long as the Republic endures," Mann wrote in 1932, "there is hope. . . . [But] a National Socialist Reichspresident would mean: never again rest, never again a respectable atmosphere, never again a secure existence or human happiness but more and more hate, degradation, and catastrophe. If Hindenburg can erect a dam against this, then let us strengthen that dam with our votes!"[54]

In statements such as these Mann continued to defend the Weimar government, but still insisted on remaining above parties. According to him, democracy, like *Geist,* could not be embodied in any single party and hence it was important to remain unaffiliated; he believed he could do more good for Germany as a whole in this way than if he became a party intellectual.[55] But while Mann's desire to be free-floating persisted, his language became far more militant and direct than before. The sentiments he expressed were not new in the early 1930s, but the tone was. He repeatedly talked about the need to "go on the attack" and usher in a new "aggressive spirit." He called not for a long-suffering patience but for a "fighting democracy." Writers, he said, were engaged in a deadly war, a "war of the spirit against [unjust] power." They had, therefore, not only to organize but to actually go on the offensive.[56] Mann consciously became less an Olympian and more an embattled writer struggling against the forces of irrationality. By now the tactic of reaching enlightened politicians had failed, since Stresemann was dead and all the Liberals and Social Democrats were removed from cabinet positions. Hence there was nothing left to do but return to the people, and try to arouse in them a commitment to the Republic.

This position naturally earned Mann the wrath of both the Communists and the National Socialists. In *Linkskurve,* the leading communist literary journal of the early 1930s, the poet Johannes

R. Becher attacked Mann for supporting a corrupt bourgeois state and therefore delaying the advent of a dictatorship of the proletariat. He further criticized Mann for backing Hindenburg (the hero of Tannenberg and an exemplar of the old regime!) rather than Thälmann for president of the Republic.[57] Similarly, in the right-wing press Mann had long been singled out as one of the "worst men of the Left" (meaning a defender of the Republic). The Nazi *Völkischer Beobachter* was particularly virulent in this respect, because Mann had been hostile to their "Movement" since at least 1923 and had once labelled the Führer a threat to civilization itself.[58] Ironically, Mann was as unhappy with the Republic as some of his critics were, but often for very different reasons. He lamented the fact that a democratic culture had not been encouraged, that social reforms had not been instituted, that the government was indecisive toward Hitler and his S.A., and that no serious attempt had been made to republicanize the Reichswehr, the judiciary, or the universities.[59] Nonetheless, Mann continued to hope, however vainly, that the German people might shake off their lethargy and demand that the Weimar Republic become a genuine democracy.

The crucial question for Mann was this: did the authoritarian governments of Brüning, von Papen, and von Schleicher truly reflect the mood of the population? If they did, Germany was unsalvageable and literary politics was meaningless, since the country would surely embrace a fascist dictatorship. If they did not, as Mann hoped, there was still a chance that the Germans could be reached and spiritualized by literary intellectuals. The wayward state might then be reappropriated and humanized; as Fichte had said over one hundred years earlier, the "political nation" could be reclaimed by an awakened "cultural nation."

It is true that in the early 1940s, long after Germany had fallen to the National Socialists, Mann was reluctantly forced to accept the first interpretation. The German people, it appeared to him on reflection, had perhaps been ripe for Hitler's fascism from the start. In fact, by this time Mann thought that nearly all the characteristics of Nazi Germany had been implicit in the Weimar period, and therefore "every struggle for a true democratic republic was lost from the beginning."[60] But this assessment came only after the event. At the time Germany succumbed to the National Socialists, Mann had felt it might yet be possible to redeem the situation, though he had to admit that it was "evening if not already midnight."[61] Without supplying evidence, he had claimed, presumably on the basis of an intuitive moral judgment, that the German people still possessed a latent fund of rationality and good sense which, in the last analysis, might lead them to rally behind the Republic once the evils of the anti-republican forces became obvious to them. "The majority of the people," Mann wrote in 1932, "can be nothing else but republicans in spite of all the movements against the system. At bottom, open reaction is confronting a unanimous *Volk* which could eventually bring into existence a new age of reason."[62]

Mann's conception of his task between 1930 and 1933 was that of a contest (which may partly explain the appearance of his combative style and vocabulary). Put in simplest terms, the contest was between those who wanted to preserve the Republic and those who wanted to destroy it. Curiously enough, the Communists, who were as much opposed to the Republic as the Nazis, were virtually non-existent in Mann's discussions at this time. Apparently they were not perceived as a serious threat, even though their voting strength began to rise again after 1930. This meant that there were only two major contestants locked in struggle: spiritual intellectuals versus the National Socialists. To the victor would fall the most important prize of all: access to the German people in order to "win them over" to democracy or fascism. The role of the democratic *littérateur,* as Mann now conceived it, was not so much to celebrate the existing state (something which was impossible anyway given the nature of the government) but rather to effectively discredit the other side in whatever way one could. If the Germans had any rational or democratic instincts left, and if the Nazis could be exposed as "false nationalists" and "false socialists," then the population might be brought around to the side of the Republic before it was too late. The very future of Germany was at stake.

Mann tried to set an example for the other writers by pointing out in several sharply-worded essays that the Nazis were "common criminals," that their racial ideology was "utter nonsense," that their movement was based on lies and hatred, that they were not an *Arbeiterpartei* but despised everything the working class stood for, that they were "pawns of monopoly capital," that their overriding goal was not the welfare of the nation but power and "booty," and that, if a Third Reich were established, it would lead directly to external wars, an internal "bloodbath," and the "gassing of the masses."[63] If all this were made crystal clear, and "clarity" was what

Mann called for above all else during these years, then the Nazis might finally be seen for what they were, and rejected.[64] This, at least, was Mann's hope during the early 1930s.

In a strange, circuitous way Mann returned, in the last years of the Weimar Republic, to the same conception of literary politics he had held at its inception. Once again the German condition was described as "above all a spiritual fact."[65] This being the case, literary intellectuals had a major role to play, since they were most effective in dealing with spiritual matters. Their urgent task was to replace an unhealthy system of ideas (nationalism, militarism, immoralism) with an entirely new one based on ethics, rationality, and internationalism, thereby laying the groundwork for a future democratic society. Nonetheless, Mann insisted that the German situation was inherently unpredictable. Events could go in either of two directions, toward spiritual renewal or toward disaster, depending on the success or failure of the literati. "It depends on men and on their preparedness and will," Mann wrote in 1932, "whether or not an age of reason dawns. Irrationality has so far succeeded without effort, but reason never triumphs by itself; it ... must be fought for."[66] And elsewhere: "[The Germans] are listening once again to the call of the abyss. They have listened to it all too often. The question now is whether they will really follow it this time."[67] Intellectuals, then, could be catalysts for spiritual goals, but in the last analysis the fate of Germany lay in the hands of the people themselves.

The Novel and Political Commitment

Without doubt, Mann's forte during the Weimar period was the political essay. Altogether he wrote close to seventy, and nearly all of them dealt with different aspects of Germany's social and political reality. Many of these essays were as trenchant and aggressive as his pre-World War I pieces, while others were more avuncular and patronizing. All, however, contained some problems of style and form, stemming in part from Mann's uncertainty about exactly who he was writing for. These literary problems were also due to the great uneasiness he felt in defending a status quo which had never fully met with his approval, particularly after 1930. Mann had not felt compelled to argue for an existing state of affairs in Germany since the mid-1890s, and even then he had done it only theoretically. His arguments now were more specific, and precisely for this reason they were more difficult to formulate. No wonder Mann suggested that democracy had seemed more beautiful before 1914, when it was nothing more than a "slogan of opposition."[68] At that time his literary politics had been directed toward actualizing a pure ideal, not defending a compromised reality like the German Republic. This was an irony which the literary defenders of Weimar had to face throughout the period 1918–1933. All of them wanted to remain faithful to a republican vision, but they felt bound by circumstances to support a broken image of it. To have opted for one side or the other of this double bind would have meant giving up the project of literary politics altogether. Only the firm conviction that they, as writers, could still somehow preserve the creative relationship between the ideal and the real kept these individuals active and involved as *littérateurs*.

Mann's main concern during this period was the essay, but this did not mean that he abandoned the novel as a mode of literary expression. On the contrary, Mann wrote no less than five novels and more than a dozen short stories during the Weimar era, making this perhaps the most productive period of his life. Nonetheless, with the exception of two or three novellas and one novel, most of Mann's literary work during these years seems almost unreadable today. *Der Kopf* (*The Head*, 1925), the final volume of the *Kaiserreich* trilogy, was undoubtedly his best effort in the 1920s. In some ways it complimented his political essays since this novel is, in part, the story of an intellectual who attempts to reform society from above by reaching the men of power and spiritualizing them. (There is even a scene in which Terra, the idealist intellectual, tries to reach the chancellor after the people turn a deaf ear to his spiritual demands.) Furthermore, in *Der Kopf* Mann was highly critical of Germany's power elite of industrialists and diplomats, and he tried to portray the many hidden connections between economics and politics at the highest levels.[69]

With this exception, however, nothing Mann wrote during the Weimar era could equal *Der Untertan* or even *Im Schlaraffenland*. His novel *Mutter Marie* (*Mother Maria,* 1929), though subtly critical of the way money shapes values in the modern world, lacks a convincing form and is in places incoherent and confusing. *Eugenie oder Die Bürgerzeit* (*Eugenie or the Middle Class Epoch,* 1928) is certainly much better, but it represents a turning away from Weimar, back to the simpler, less frenetic, decade of the 1870s. Mann seems to have been searching for roots, and for a sense of moral order and responsibility that had vanished for many, especially the young, by the 1920s. In his next novel *Die grosse Sache* (*The Big Deal*, 1930) Mann returned to a contemporary setting to portray a materialistic society based on greed and "big deals." His concern here was to suggest that a life based on honor and moderation is the best way to cope with the world as it is. Finally, in *Ein ernstes Leben* (*A Serious Life*, 1932), Mann continued his description of what a decadent society (in this case the German demi-monde) does to morality and personal responsibility. Unfortunately, the points he tried to make are weakened by a disorganized plot and inadequate development of themes. In many of these novels Mann experimented with several styles and modes of expression (*Neue Sachlichkeit*, the detective story, etc.), possibly with the hope of broadening his appeal and enlarging his audience. But none of these works sold as well as earlier novels, undoubtedly because they lacked depth and integration.

It should be pointed out that writing novels is one thing and theorizing about them quite another. If, during the Weimar years, Mann had numerous shortcomings in the first area, he was at least much clearer and more compelling when it came to the second.

Throughout the 1920s and early 1930s he expressed himself often on the question of what the novel should do and what its moral tasks are *vis-à-vis* modern society. On the whole, one could summarize Mann's message in the following way. The purpose of a work of fiction is to be an instrument of *Geist* and a means of awakening social and political awareness. "The goal of the novel," he wrote in 1927, "is not simply to portray life but to improve it."[70] This meant that literature had first to criticize the reality of life unthinkingly accepted by the bulk of the population, and then make apparent the dangerous but largely unrecognized tendencies which lay half concealed within it. In some ways this was an updating of his earlier critical realism, but now Mann went further. The novel, he argued, should not merely instill conscience but should *be* conscience; that is, it should embody the deepest moral awareness of the age concretized in writing. Moreover, the novel should encourage progressive ideals and a sense of community and mutuality. It should, furthermore, spread the "European spirit" and arouse in people a commitment to democracy by trying to change bad habits and modes of thought and preparing the way for new ones. Finally, the novel should strive for "social effectiveness" by immersing itself in the life of the age, but only in order to cut through to the palpable truths below the surface and not, like the film (which Mann was often critical of), to become fascinated by the surface itself.[71]

Needless to say, Mann himself did not always live up to these imperatives during the Weimar period. Too often the superficial or trivial held his attention, usually resulting in an obsession with detail at the expense of the social whole. This discrepancy between his ideal of the novel and the kinds of novels he actually wrote did not disturb Mann as much as one might expect, for as time went on he gradually shifted away from a concern with novelists-as-authors and instead became more intrigued with novelists-as-men-of-action. Though the theory of the novel remained important to Mann, the politically-committed side of writers—that is, what they did as individuals rather than as novelists—began to seem more significant. Zola was a case in point. In the 1920s Mann admired him more as a prototype of what he called *"der aktive Mensch"* than for his skills as a writer.[72] The same was true with regard to German writers like Lessing and Heine;[73] they received Mann's respect less for their plays or poetry than for their personal courage and the way in which they viewed themselves as writing against the grain.

It must be remembered that at this late date Mann did not need instruction from anyone on how to write novels. He did, however, feel a need for inspiring examples of how to conduct himself as a political activist. The endemic crisis of the Weimar Republic forced him to assume a number of responsibilities outside the realm of the traditional novelistic genre, and Mann accepted this as part of his situation. For him and other like-minded contemporaries, it became more important to be an engaged intellectual than simply an engaging author.

Footnotes
Chapter 10

1. Kurt Tucholsky, "Preussische Studenten," *Gesammelte Werke,* ed. Mary Tucholsky and Fritz Radditz (Hamburg, 1960), I:407.

2. See Mann's comments cited in Klaus Schröter, *Heinrich Mann,* p. 94.

3. Heinrich Mann, *Ein Zeitalter wird besichtigt,* pp. 352ff.

4. Heinrich Mann, "Kaiserreich und Republik," *Essays* II, *Ausgewählte Werke,* XII:62.

5. *Ibid.,* pp. 55, 58.

6. *Ibid.,* p. 67.

7. Heinrich Mann, "Berlin," *Essays* II, *Ausgewählte Werke,* XII:96, 99.

8. Heinrich Mann, "Tragische Jugend," *Essays* II, *Ausgewählte Werke,* XII:88.

9. Heinrich Mann, letter to Maximilian Brantl, January 24, 1920; in "Heinrich Manns Briefe an Maximilian Brantl," *Weimarer Beiträge,* XIV, no. 2:407–08.

10. Heinrich Mann, letter to Félix Bertaux, October 19, 1922; in *Heinrich Mann 1871–1950: Werk und Leben,* pp. 192–93.

11. Heinrich Mann, letter to Karl Lemke, December 15, 1921; in *Briefe an Karl Lemke, 1917–1949,* p. 16.

12. Heinrich Mann, letters to Maximilian Brantl on February 3, and February 9, 1923; in "Heinrich Manns Briefe an Maximilian Brantl," *op. cit.,* pp. 408–10.

13. On the political and economic dimensions of the German inflation of 1923 see especially Erich Eyck, *A History of the Weimar Republic,* 2 vols., trans. Harlan P. Hanson and Robert G. L. Waite (Cambridge, Mass., 1962), I:227–301; Fritz Ringer, ed., *The German Inflation of 1923* (New York, 1969), pp. 34–96; and Arthur Rosenberg, *A History of the German Republic,* pp. 178–221.

14. These essays were collected at the end of 1923 and published under the title *Diktatur der Vernunft* (Berlin, 1923). They were later reprinted in Mann's *Sieben Jahre* under a new title ("Die Tragödie von 1923"), and reprinted again in his *Ausgewählte Werke,* vol. XII.

15. Some of these sentiments were already foreshadowed in Mann's letter to Félix Bertaux, October 19, 1922; included in *Heinrich Mann 1871–1950: Werk und Leben*, p. 193.

16. Heinrich Mann, "Das Sterben der geistigen Schicht," *Essays* II, *Ausgewählte Werke*, XII:98.

17. *Ibid.*, p. 101.

18. *Ibid.*, pp. 101–02.

19. *Ibid.*, p. 102.

20. Heinrich Mann, "Wirtschaft 1923," *Essays* II, *Ausgewählte Werke*, XII: 111–12, 115.

21. *Ibid.*, p. 102.

22. Heinrich Mann, "Anfänge Europas," *Essays* II, *Ausgewählte Werke*, XII: 119–26.

23. Heinrich Mann, "Noch ein Krieg mit Frankreich," *Essays* II, *Ausgewählte Werke*, XII:264–74.

24. Heinrich Mann, "Wlr feiern die Verfassung," *Essays* II, *Ausgewählte Werke*, XII:141–50.

25. Heinrich Mann, "Diktatur der Vernunft," *Essays* II, *Ausgewählte Werke*, XII:126–35.

26. *Ibid.*, p. 128.

27. Mann's most optimistic essay of the mid-1920s was probably his "Briefe ins ferne Ausland," written in 1926 and published in *Sieben Jahre*, pp. 219–50.

28. For Mann's view of Weimar's judiciary system see his two articles entitled "Justiz" (one written in 1927, the other in 1928) in *Essays* II, *Ausgewählte Werke*, XII:421–52; see also his "Richterliche Verantwortung" (1929), in *Das öffentliche Leben* (Berlin, 1932), pp. 139–40.

29. Heinrich Mann, letter to Kurt Tucholsky, May 12, 1924; in *Heinrich Mann 1871–1950: Werk und Leben*, p. 212.

30. Heinrich Mann, "Die jungen Leute," *Essays* II, *Ausgewählte Werke*, XII:158. Mann's critique of big business can be found in essays like "Geistiges Gesellschafts-kapital" (1924), in *Essays* II, *Ausgewählte Werke*, XII:154–56; and "Unser gemeinsames Problem" (1925), in *Sieben Jahre*, pp. 251–57.

31. On this aspect of Mann's thought see his "Deutsche Republik" (1929), *Essays* II, *Ausgewählte Werke*, XII:239–42; "Gräber des Geistes öffnen sich" (1928), *ibid.*, pp. 458–62; "Geistiges Gesellschaftskapital" (1924), *ibid.*, pp. 154–56; and "Unser Einfluss und diese Zeit" (1927), *Essays* I, *Ausgewählte Werke*, XI: 263–68. A discussion of some of these points can also be found in Klaus Thoenelt, "Heinrich Manns Psychologie des Faschismus," *Monatshefte* (1971), LXIII, no. 3: 220–34.

32. See Heinrich Mann, "Briefe ins ferne Ausland," *Sieben Jahre*, pp. 228–29, 242–44.

33. Heinrich Mann, letter to Kurt Tucholsky, May 12, 1924; in *Heinrich Mann 1871–1950: Werk und Leben*, p. 212.

34. Heinrich Mann, "Geistige Neigungen in Deutschland" (1925), *Essays* I, *Ausgewählte Werke*, XI:244.

35. Heinrich Mann, "Tragische Jugend," *Essays* II, *Ausgewählte Werke*, XII:75.

36. Heinrich Mann, "Bibi und andere Gestalten" (1929), *Sieben Jahre*, p. 532; "Der Bubikopf" (1926), *Essays* II, *Ausgewählte Werke*, XII:162–65.

37. Heinrich Mann, "Die jungen Leute," *Essays* II, *Ausgewählte Werke*, XII: 160–61.

38. Mann's discussion of the youth problem after 1924 (of which this paragraph is only the briefest summary) can be found in "Die jungen Leute" (1925), "Der Bubikopf" (1926), "Jugend früher und jetzt" (1926), and "Sie reichen sich die Hände" (1926), all in *Essays* II, *Ausgewählte Werke*, XII:157–76. Of these the last is by far the most hopeful. But Mann's pessimism returned in his final essay on youth during the Weimar period: "Morgen" (1931), *Essays* I, *Ausgewählte Werke*, XI:376–84.

39. Heinrich Mann, "Geistiges Gesellschaftskapital," *Essays* II, *Ausgewählte Werke*, XII:155–56.

40. Heinrich Mann, "Gespräch mit Masaryk" (1924), *Sieben Jahre*, p. 173.

41. Heinrich Mann, "Unser gemeinsames Problem," *Sieben Jahre*, p. 256.

42. On the relationship between the intellectual and the state see Heinrich Mann, "Dichtkunst und Politik" (1928), *Essays* I, *Ausgewählte Werke*, XI: 310–25.

43. Heinrich Mann, "VSE" (1924), *Essays* II, *Ausgewählte Werke*, XII:275–86. The letters VSE stand for *"Vereinigte Staaten Europas"* ("The United States of Europe").

44. In 1925 and again in 1927, Mann did acknowledge that a pan-European state, even if well-intentioned, would have its dangers. It might, for example, be taken over by financial and industrial interests (i.e., international capitalism) and used to maximize profits, enslave and exploit large masses of people, and probably prepare for a war with Russia. See Heinrich Mann, "Paneuropa, Traum und Wirklichkeit," *Sieben Jahre,* pp. 281–82; "Unser gemeinsames Problem," *ibid.,* pp. 351–57; "Gräber des Geistes öffnen sich," *Essays* II, *Ausgewählte Werke,* XII:458–62; and the comments by Alfred Kantorowicz, "Nachwort," *ibid.,* pp. 567–69.

45. Lorenz Winter, *Heinrich Mann and His Public,* pp. 87–89, 107–08.

46. Heinrich Mann, *Der Kopf* (1925), cited in *ibid.,* p. 87.

47. Heinrich Mann, "Geistiges Gesellschaftskapital," *Essays* II, *Ausgewählte Werke,* XII:154–56; and "Theater der Zeit," *Essays* I, *Ausgewählte Werke,* XI:273–74.

48. Heinrich Mann, "Der tiefere Sinn der Republik" (1927), *Essays* II, *Ausgewählte Werke,* XII:232–38; and Mann's letter to Félix Bertaux, May 14, 1927, in *Heinrich Mann 1871–1950: Werk und Leben,* p. 201.

49. See Heinrich Mann, "Dichtkunst und Politik" (his report to the Prussian Academy in 1928), *Essays* I, *Ausgewählte Werke,* XI:310–25; "Die Akademie," *ibid.,* pp. 330–38; and Mann's letter to René Schickele, September 7, 1927, in *Heinrich Mann 1871–1950: Werk und Leben,* pp. 235–36.

50. Heinrich Mann, "Dichtkunst und Politik," *op. cit.,* pp. 318, 324–25.

51. Kurt Hiller, cited in István Deák, *Weimar Germany's Left-Wing Intellectuals,* p. 5.

52. Thomas Mann began to support the Republic after 1922. His first public defense of Weimar came in his address "The German Republic" (1923), reprinted in *Order of the Day,* trans. H. T. Lowe-Porter (New York, 1942), pp. 3–45.

53. Heinrich Mann, "Morgen," *Essays* I, *Ausgewählte Werke,* XI:376–77.

54. Heinrich Mann, from a hand-written manuscript (1932?), in *Heinrich Mann 1871–1950: Werk und Leben,* p. 247.

55. Heinrich Mann, "Morgen," *op. cit.,* pp. 383–84.

56. See, for example, Heinrich Mann, "Der Schriftsteller und der Krieg" (1932), *Essays* II, *Ausgewählte Werke,* XII:485–87; and the comment by Alfred Kantorowicz in "Nachwort," *ibid.,* p. 596.

57. Johannes R. Becher, "Vom 'Untertan' zum Untertan," *Linkskurve* (1932),

IV, no. 4:1–5. The former Activist Kurt Hiller proposed in the *Weltbühne* that Mann himself run for president in 1932. Nevertheless, Hiller voted for Thälmann. See Kurt Hiller, "Der Präsident," *Die Weltbühne*, February 9, 1932, included in *Köpfe und Tröpfe* (Hamburg, 1950).

58. See Heinrich Mann, "Lebensfeinde," *Essays* II, *Ausgewählte Werke*, XII: 453–57; and "Wir wählen," *Das öffentliche Leben*, pp. 257–62.

59. On this see especially Heinrich Mann, "Das Bekenntnis zum Übernationalen' (1932), *Essays* II, *Ausgewählte Werke*, XII:503–11; "Die deutsche Entscheidung" (1931), *ibid.*, pp. 488–92; and "Situation de l'Allemagne" (1930), *ibid.*, pp. 387–404.

60. Heinrich Mann, "Skizze meines Lebens," *Eine Liebesgeschichte* (Munich, 1953), p. 42; Klaus Thoenelt, "Heinrich Manns Psychologie des Faschismus," *Monatshefte*, LVIII, no. 3; 221.

61. Heinrich Mann, "Die deutsche Entscheidung," *Essays* II, *Ausgewählte Werke*, XII:488.

62. Heinrich Mann, "Das Bekenntnis zum Übernationalen," *Essays* II, *Ausgewählte Werke*, XII:510–11.

63. See especially Heinrich Mann, "Die deutsche Entscheidung," *op. cit.*, pp. 488–92; and "Wir wählen," *Das öffentliche Leben*, pp. 257–62.

64. Heinrich Mann, "Morgen," *Essays* I, *Ausgewählte Werke*, XI:377–78; and "Der Schriftsteller und der Staat," *Essays* I, *Ausgewählte Werke*, XI:326.

65. Heinrich Mann, "Die deutsche Entscheidung," *op. cit.*, p. 489.

66. Heinrich Mann, "Das Bekenntnis zum Übernationalen," *op. cit.*, p. 511.

67. Heinrich Mann, "Die deutsche Entscheidung," *op. cit.*, p. 489.

68. Heinrich Mann, *Macht und Mensch*, p. 220.

69. The best brief discussion of this novel is N. Serebrow, "Heinrich Manns Antikriegsroman *Der Kopf*," *Weimarer Beiträge* (1962), VII, no. 1:1–33.

70. Heinrich Mann, "Entdeckung Zolas," *Essays* I, *Ausgewählte Werke*, XI:238.

71. For Mann's view of the function of the novel in society see the following essays: "Unser Einfluss und diese Zeit," *Essays* I, *Ausgewählte Werke*, XI: 263–68; "Was ist eigentlich ein Schriftsteller?," *ibid.*, pp. 306–09; "Der Schriftsteller und der Staat," *ibid.*, pp. 326–29; "Die neuen Gebote," *ibid.*, pp. 249–53; and "Mein Roman," *Das öffentliche Leben*, pp. 329–36.

72. Heinrich Mann, "Entdeckung Zolas," *Essays* I, *Ausgewählte Werke,* XI: 236–39.

73. Heinrich Mann, "Lessing," *Das öffentliche Leben,* pp. 13–23; and "Heinrich Heine," *ibid.,* pp. 27–30.

Chapter 11

Exile

In my day all roads led into a morass.
Words gave us away to the executioner.
There was little I could do.
Yet without me the rulers would have been more secure,
Or at least that was my hope.
And so passed the time
Allotted to me on earth.

Bertolt Brecht

Writers Without Readers

Despite his intellectual allegiance to socialist humanism during the Weimar period, Mann remained steadfastly above parties. His goal was to represent the whole of society and reconcile factions within the Republic, not to take sides with one group against another. However, the ascendency of Hitler in January, 1933, seemed to make this stance irrelevant. Realizing this, Mann signed (along with others like Käthe Kollwitz and Albert Einstein) an urgent appeal calling on the two major working-class parties, the KPD and the SPD, to join together in combatting the threat from the Right. This did not commit Mann to any particular party, but to the union of left-wing parties against fascism. The fact that he signed the so-called *Dringender Appell* caused an uproar among the Nazis and their supporters, who claimed that this politicized the Prussian Academy of Arts, of which both Mann and Kollwitz were members. After a formal deliberation in February, the Academy expelled the two signators due to their "political partisanship."[1] A short while later other members of the Academy either left voluntarily or were forced to leave under pressure. Significantly, those expelled included some of the most prominent members of Mann's literary generation, among them Bernhard Kellermann, René Schickele, Alfred Döblin, Jakob Wassermann, Georg Kaiser and Thomas Mann. Most not only left the

241

Academy but Germany as well. After the Reichstag fire of February 27, 1933, and more particularly after the book burning of May 10, thousands more fled the country. Those who were not fortunate enough to get out in time were imprisoned; some, like Kurt Hiller and Ludwig Renn, were later released and went into exile, but others like Erich Mühsam and Carl von Ossietzky died in the Nazi camps.[2] By the end of 1933 over fifty thousand Germans had emigrated, most of them writers, journalists, academics, lawyers, and labor leaders. The majority, but by no means all, were left-liberals, socialists, or communists, and nearly seventy-percent were Jewish. The greatest number of writers and intellectuals crossed into France, but others went to Czechoslovakia, Switzerland, Austria, Russia, Norway and England. Nearly all expected to be in exile for no more than a few weeks or months, since they were sure the Nazi regime could not last for long. In fact, it lasted for twelve years. Many of the emigrés never returned at all, or if they did it was after the war, and to East Germany.

Heinrich Mann's expulsion from the Prussian Academy took place on February 15, 1933. A few days later, on the advice of the French ambassador François-Poncet, he left for France just before the secret police ransacked his apartment. In the *Völkische Beobachter*, the attack upon Mann as a "Jewish" writer and enemy of Germany was accelerated, and false rumors were spread that he had been imprisoned. By May his name appeared on the first list of books to be burned and by August he was one of the first to have his German citizenship revoked. In the meantime Mann settled in Nice, living in the same house as the novelists Hermann Kesten and Joseph Roth.[3] Nearby, in Sanary sur Mer, were still other exiled writers: Lion Feuchtwanger, Ludwig Marcuse, René Schickele, Theodor Wolff, and Rudolph Leonhard. For most of the next seven years Mann stayed in southern France, with only occasional journeys to Paris; and yet, despite his relative isolation, he became the undisputed leader of the German exiles during the 1930s. In 1933 Mann was elected honorary president of the *Schutzverband deutscher Schriftsteller* (Association of German Writers), which had been disbanded by Goebbels and reconstituted in exile. The following year he became president of the anti-fascist *Deutsche Freiheitsbibliothek* (German Freedom Library), a research and informational institute. which attempted to embody the spirit of the "other Germany." Later, in 1935, he became the intellectual leader of the *Volksfront,* politically the most important of the German exile organizations. In 1940, after the Nazi invasion of France, Mann was forced to flee once again. With a forged passport and accompanied by his wife, Feuchtwanger, Franz Werfel, and his nephew Golo Mann, the sixty-nine year old writer escaped on foot over the Pyrenees to Spain. From there he travelled to Portugal and booked passage on a ship to New York. Once in the United States, he settled in California and lived there until his death in 1950.

Broadly speaking, Mann's experience in the 1930s was shared by many of his contemporaries. Virtually all the members of his literary generation, who have been discussed in earlier chapters, responded in similar or parallel ways to the same events after 1933. All, of course, were violently opposed to the "Nazi revolution" but they also rejected the notion of inner emigration. Instead, most of them made an immediate decision to go into exile, the majority leaving before May, 1933. Of all the major writers who shared Mann's point of view, only Georg Kaiser chose to wait until as late as 1938 before leaving. Moreover, all remained essentially left-oriented, identifying themselves by this time either as socialists or radical liberals. Nearly all eventually became fellow-travellers sympathetic to the Soviet Union, but only a few called themselves Marxists or communists. And finally, all continued to pursue the project which they had taken up years earlier, namely, to outline the contours of a "new man" and a "new society"—a quest that seemed all the more urgent now that their homeland had fallen under Hitler's sway.

Some writers, like Bruno Frank or Georg Hermann, thought their ideals had been realized in the U.S.S.R. But while they spoke out for the principles of socialism as embodied in this country, it was generally from the safe havens of Paris or Zürich. Bernhard Kellermann also believed he saw both a new culture and a new man emerging in the Soviet Union; he therefore attached his hope for a future age of truth, goodness, and justice to the fate of the Soviet Union. Like the others, however, he chose to emigrate to the West instead of to Russia.[4]

Other literary intellectuals, while remaining generally socialist in orientation, went through more complex developments in exile. Georg Kaiser initially decided to stay in Berlin after 1933, even though his plays were banned from the German stage because of their pacifist and humanist sentiments. The social values he had always wanted to see realized in Germany were simply transferred, in his unperformed plays, to "a utopian realm of ideas and ideals in order to protect them from the coldness of the real world."[5] After emigrating to Switzerland in 1938, Kaiser entered a period of anti-fascist activity, during which he tried to describe through literature the totalitarian nature of the everyday life he had experienced in Germany. In the mid-1940s, when it appeared to him that the major problems of the world were inherent in Western civilization as a whole and not indigenous to Germany, he succumbed to a mood of pessimism and resignation.

Alfred Döblin also had uncertainties about his tasks as a writer. Upon leaving Germany in 1933 he wrote: "I am no longer a German writer. I am simply and solely a Jew. Nothing interests me but Jewish problems."[6] Despite this disclaimer, Döblin remained active as a non-party socialist throughout the 1930s. In his novel *Pardon wird nicht gegeben* (1935) he forcefully repeated the militant ideals of literary politics. The writer, he asserted, should identify himself with the goals of brotherhood and justice and work for a broad democratic front that would oppose all existing threats to freedom. After being forced to leave France for America in 1940, Döblin underwent something like a religious experience which led to his conversion to Catholicism. Nonetheless, he never abandoned his humanitarian socialism, since one of his overriding concerns as a Catholic was to reconcile Christianity with the European revolutionary tradition.[7]

Lion Feuchtwanger was of course another member of the older generation whose development ran roughly parallel to Mann's after 1933. Like many others, Feuchtwanger fled to southern France after Hitler's seizure of power and there wrote numerous historical novels defending the Enlightenment values of reason and progress. He also became an outspoken supporter of the Soviet Union, which he viewed as perhaps the only viable bulwark against National Socialism. In America, where he lived from 1940 until his death in 1958, Feuchtwanger continued to defend socialism in the abstract and to argue for the implementation of reason and morality in the modern state.[8]

Regardless of the differences mentioned here among members of Mann's literary generation, all were informally unified. This unity was based, first of all, on personal friendships (formed for the most part in the 1920s), which tended to reinforce a sense of common identity; secondly, it stemmed from the similarities of their literary development and class background (all were inescapably middle class even as socialists, something the young communist critics were not hesitant to point out); and thirdly, it was related to the homogeneity of their world-views which, collectively, strongly emphasized reason, ethics, and social democratic values. Their sense of belonging together also came from sharing a condition of exile, which forced them to become much clearer about who they were as a group, what they wanted, and what they opposed. Nonetheless, exile had great disadvantages, the most important being the loss of a significant reading public. For writers to be effective, particularly in the area of literary politics, they must of course have a reachable audience; in fact, the presence of a large potential readership is the *sine qua non* of a political writer's existence. After 1933, however, no exiled German writer could count on reaching the audience that had supported him in the 1920s. Hitler forbade the publication or dissemination of books by "un-German" authors, i.e., those who had fled the country or whose works had been officially declared "worth being burned" (*verbrennungswürdig*). In a single stroke, the abolition of a reading public was also the abolition of a literary relationship for the German writer in exile; this immediately called into question the whole *raison d'être* of committed authorship.

The lack of an audience has often been overlooked, but it was a crucial problem for the émigré writer. Most German exiles never learned to write well in a foreign language and only a few found translators for their principle works. As a result, the majority fell into obscurity almost as soon as they left Germany. The loss of contact with a community which shared German culture and speech was tantamount to a sentence of death. This partially explains the sense of depression many writers developed as their months in exile stretched into years, and they found themselves deprived of both a language and an audience.[9] It was an impossible situation that ended in suicide for many (Stefan Zweig, Ernst Toller, Walter Hasenclever) and ineffectiveness, if not irrelevance, for many others.

The failure to reach a German reading public was also due in part to the tendency of some émigré writers to look toward the U.S.S.R. for a kind of surrogate audience since Russia frequently provided a major readership for leftist authors. Lion Feuchtwanger, for example, whose *Moscow 1937* was one of the strongest defenses of Stalinism in the 1930s, saw nine of his novels translated into Russian with a total printing of 260,000 copies. Heinrich Mann sold nearly two million copies of his books in Russia, which may partly explain his statement of 1943: "At present I love the Soviet Union completely. It is near to me and I to it. Russia reads me in a massive way, gives me life, and I can see there indications of how posterity will know me."[10] It was perhaps difficult to oppose a country which was willing to underwrite one's publications to such a degree.

France proved much less receptive to the German authors in exile, who therefore had no real effect on French public opinion. A few exiled writers were translated into French in the 1930s, most notably Thomas and Heinrich Mann, Joseph Roth, and Stefan Zweig, but the vast majority remained completely unknown. Döblin, who in the 1920s had been considered one of Germany's best novelists, made almost no impact in France. René Schickele, despite an Alsatian background and the capacity to write excellent French, was not able to find a publisher even though his novels dealt with Franco-German themes. In the 1930s, Franz Werfel's *Das Lied von Bernadette* and Siegfried Kracauer's *Offenbach* enjoyed brief successes because of their French subject matter, but the only best-seller by a German author was Hermann Rauschning's *Gespräche mit Hitler*.[11] Heinrich Mann who, unlike most of the other émigrés, could express himself well in French, found only a relatively small audience in France. Even his *Henri Quatre* novel, which dealt with French history and generally received good reviews, was not widely read. However, between 1933 and 1939 Mann was invited to write dozens of articles and editorials for a liberal French newspaper, the *La Dépêche de Toulouse*. This was an opportunity every German exile would have envied, but even here Mann's ability to influence French public opinion was only minimal, since the *Depêche* was a provincial paper which lacked the circulation and impact of a Paris daily.[12] On the whole, France was too xenophobic, particularly after the Stavisky Affair, to open itself up to the exiled authors who had fled there for protection. Much of the French press was reactionary and had no interest or sympathy for what was called "this quarrel among Germans." Except for a brief period under Léon Blum and the Popular Front (1936–37), the German émigrés were just barely tolerated; under the circumstances, the question of exerting real influence through writing was hardly worth raising at the time.[13]

After 1940, when so many German writers were once again forced into exile—this time to the United States, Mexico, or South America—the problem of an audience became more painfully acute. In this country and in the Spanish speaking lands there was even less public interest in the German exiles than there was in France. Paul Zech, who settled in Santiago, Chile, found himself in a state of continuous despair which often verged on suicide. Not only was he without a reading public, but, as a result, he had no clear sense of why he should go on writing. He felt unable either to change professions (by now he was nearly sixty) or to begin any significant literary work: "Today," he wrote a friend, "I am unable to write even a few columns of figures underneath one another."[14] The same experience was repeated by many who emigrated to America. Most émigré authors were completely unknown to American readers and therefore could not carry on their work as professional writers. Some continued writing anyway, hoping to publish their books later on, but many gave up temporarily and sought other forms of employment (e.g., as script readers for the Hollywood film studios). Except for the better-known authors like Thomas Mann, Feuchtwanger, or Stefan Zweig, the majority of German writers were condemned to languish in obscurity.

In the end, the main audience available to most exiled German writers in the 1930s was other exiled German writers. This was hardly the ideal condition for effective literary politics, but there was no alternative. This explains the proliferation of small-circulation journals throughout the decade, many of them with only a few hundred subscribers. The most prominent exile figures wrote for all or most of these journals, since they were often the only forums of expression available. Besides these periodicals—the most notable among them, *Das Neue Tagebuch* (Paris), *Die Neue Weltbühne* (Vienna and Prague), *Das Wort* (Moscow), and *Die Sammlung* (Amsterdam)—German publishing houses were established to print works which would otherwise not have seen the light of day. Like the journals, these books usually appeared in German and were read mostly by other Germans. These outlets allowed writers to continue the project of literary politics, but for a much circumscribed audience and under conditions which were far from ideal. Now it was no longer a literary politics *in* Germany but a literary politics *against* Germany; now one did not reach "the people" but only other émigrés and, with luck, a few people of influence in the host countries.

This new situation, brought on by the lack of a significant reading public, not only affected the nature of writing and the writer's evaluation of his role, but also directly affected the course of exile politics. This is particularly evident with respect to Heinrich Mann during his period of exile in France.

Fellow-Travelling: 1933-1940

Exile imposed severe restrictions on Mann but, paradoxically, it also afforded him greater freedom. Observing Germany from a distance not only allowed Mann to get "outside the whale," as George Orwell once put it, but also to see events in Germany as an integrated whole and attack them in their totality. In the last years of Weimar this had not been possible, since Mann had committed himself to defending a state of affairs which he did not like. He had never felt comfortable doing this; as he himself admitted, his strength lay not in defending the status quo but in attacking it. Thus when an aggressive posture became feasible again after 1933, Mann took full advantage of the situation. During the next few years he wrote over 350 essays and articles, all from the position of a critical outsider. Most were published either in the *Dépêche de Toulouse* or in various exile journals of every political shade, from liberal to communist. Some of the better pieces were collected and published by German exile presses like Querido Verlag in Amsterdam or the Europa Verlag in Zürich. It is in this way that Mann's three major essay volumes of the 1930s appeared in print. They were *Der Hass (Hate,* 1933), *Es kommt der Tag (A Day is Coming,* 1936), and *Mut (Courage,* 1939).

The essays in these books show great variety in form and technique. The majority are polemical but not didactic or rhetorical; others are rich in satire and metaphor, since Mann often drew upon his abilities as a novelist to make a point or describe a situation (as in the section of *Der Hass* entitled "Scenes from Nazi Life").[15] All the essays are direct and to the point, but none show signs of resignation or futility, preserving instead a hopeful, combative mood throughout.[16] For this reason the commentator Ludwig Marcuse has described Mann as perhaps the finest and most incisive political essayist of the exile period.[17]

Within the extraordinarily large corpus of his writings from the 1930s, there were notable shifts in Mann's political thought which reflected his continuous reassessment of the situation in Europe. During the first year or two of exile Mann refused to believe that the

German people really wanted National Socialism. His tendency was to think that the Germans had been misled by Hitler. As a "confidence man of power," Hitler played on their deepest fears and needs, and the Germans believed him because unfortunately they had been nourished by centuries of falsehoods.[18] Mann was hopeful that most of the German population still loved freedom and reason, and therefore would not long tolerate the Nazi regime. For this reason, the National Socialists were described as only "temporary victors." The "true Germany" still remained in the "hearts of all the people suppressed in that country," and would make itself heard sooner or later.[19] The tragedy, in Mann's view was that he and other exiled writers could not find an audience among these people, and hence were cut off from affecting events inside Germany. Nonetheless, Mann still treated the German people as a potential ally. He took it for granted that they would soon carry out an internal revolution against Hitler, presumably without the aid of literary intellectuals, most of whom were now in exile.

The best example of Mann's political position at the beginning of exile was his book *Der Hass* (dedicated affectionately to "my Fatherland"). Here he expressed confidence that the German people would not endure the "brown plague" imposed upon them. At bottom, Mann believed that most Germans recognized the inhumane and intolerant character of National Socialism. Hence in a crisis they would not defend the regime, since "a people defends itself only when it defends a revolution," and Germany had not experienced a revolution under Hitler. Mann's attack upon Nazism was based almost entirely on moral criteria. The Nazi movement was pronounced evil because it was fueled by hate rather than love, and because it was fundamentally anti-humanist. Virtually no attention was given to the socio-economic conditions which produced Nazism; instead, the movement was simply viewed as the obverse of reason and ethics, which seemed to Mann cause enough to oppose it.[20]

In the period from roughly 1935 to 1940, Mann altered his perspective somewhat, as is evident in the essays which appeared at the time in *Es kommt der Tag* and *Mut*. Though he continued to profess hope for an internal revolution based on an overly positive assessment of the German people, he increasingly began to rely on outside events to change the situation in Germany. The two outside events which came to the forefront of his attention were, first, the U.S.S.R. as a power state that could challenge Hitler in a way that the Western democracies failed to do (the policy of appeasement disgusted Mann); and secondly, the emergence of a "popular front" of exiled intellectuals who could help undermine the regime through literary-political work.

In a sense, the Soviet Union gradually became a substitute "people" and the *Volksfront* a substitute intelligentsia—both, unfortunately, existing beyond the borders of Germany. This revised understanding of the relationship between a people, its intellectuals, and political power completely imploded the theoretical framework Mann had used earlier to explain literary politics. Now the real people, the *Volk,* were inside Germany but unable to act because they were without *Geist.* On the other hand, the intellectuals who could dispense spirit were unable to do so because they were in exile; consequently, they were cut off from the reciprocal interaction with the German people which they needed in order to be effective. This meant that if literary politics were to remain viable, a different kind of alliance would have to take place, i.e., one between the intellectuals and a surrogate "people," the U.S.S.R. This would permit the Germans to be saved by outside efforts even if they could not save themselves. It would also give the exiled intelligentsia a real material force, a political state, to ally with. The new goal, therefore, was to form a coalition between the idealism of the *Volksfront* and the power interests of Soviet Russia. For the first time in his life, Mann became convinced that spirit without power simply added up to powerlessness. The Germans in exile, he now believed, could not wage their war against Hitler alone; they needed the support of *Macht,* particularly a rational and ethical form of *Macht* such as Mann believed Russia to possess. He could never have constructed such an argument ten or fifteen years earlier. In the 1920s, he had felt that power and spirit had to be kept separate so that spirit would not be contaminated by power politics. Now his argument was reversed: *Geist* should not oppose (rational) *Macht* but embrace it. In this way a spirit-power fusion would finally be achieved which would not only make the Russian state more spiritual, but the German *Volksfront* more powerful. Together they could presumably rescue the German people from the grip of National Socialism, though Mann never explained exactly how this was to be achieved.

Mann's new view of the Soviet Union represented perhaps his most important political change of the 1930s. At the time of the Russian Revolution he had been suspicious of the Bolsheviks because they emphasized class struggle rather than class conciliation. In the years that followed, Mann gradually began to look more favorably on Lenin and his accomplishments, but when he praised him he did so for pragmatic and not ideological reasons (as he put it, Lenin made people "happier").[21] Still, Mann insisted that communism was a Russian phenomenon; it was in tune with the Russian character but was in no way appropriate for importation to Europe. It was this position which led to Mann's hostility toward the German KPD and its hostility toward him (e.g., in the *Linkskurve* attack). It was also this conviction which forced Mann to develop an alternative to communism in Europe: to wit, a social-democratic pan-European union which explicitly excluded Russia from membership.[22]

By the middle 1930s, Mann saw the Russian Revolution as primarily a "spiritual event" prepared for by a century of Russian literature from Gogol to Tolstoy.[23] This was his way of indicating that the origins of the 1917 event were basically intellectual, not historical materialist. "The U.S.S.R.," he wrote at the time, "is the greatest realization of an idea since [the French Revolution]."[24] Moreover, Lenin, the catalyst of this extraordinary occurence, was celebrated not merely as a Bolshevik revolutionary but as one of the world's foremost moral leaders and educators.[25] The legacy he left behind was, in Mann's opinion, still embedded in the Soviet Union of the 1930s. This is why Russia was viewed as a far more progressive state than the Western democracies. Not only had it abolished greed and exploitation, but it had managed to integrate itself perfectly with the needs and even the human nature of the Russian masses in order to work more successfully for their "higher and better" development. Equally important for Mann was the fact that the Soviet state seemed to encourage the cultural betterment of its citizens. Mann saw this as a sure sign of its inherently spiritual nature, particularly when compared to the indifference toward cultural matters he found in the West, or the outright destruction of culture in Nazi Germany. Russia, then, was treated as a unique phenomenon. It was a place where people were respected rather than oppressed, where culture flourished, and where even the lowest worker could become an intellectual.[26] "To know that such a state exists," Mann wrote, "makes one very happy."[27]

Sentiments such as these made Mann a paradigmatic fellow-traveller. Along with such other writers in exile as Kellermann and Feuchtwanger, Mann defended nearly everything that happened in the

Soviet Union, including the Moscow Trials. By his reasoning, the Russian state was basically ethical and therefore what followed from it was also good. When thorny issues arose, as in the case of the purges, one had to make a decision: either one was for the Revolution and therefore progressive, or against it and therefore reactionary. There was no middle ground. The Revolution, as Mann put it, was "indivisible" and had to be supported or rejected *in toto*.[28] This was an argument that fellow-travellers often fell back upon. Just as, in the early years of Weimar, Mann refused to be as critical of the Republic as he might have been because it seemed essential to preserve the *moral fact* of its existence, so now he refused to attack the U.S.S.R. To nitpick about this point or that would only help discredit it in Western (and German) eyes, which was the last thing Mann wanted to do. Likewise, he supported Soviet foreign policy in the 1930s not only because it appeared to be the embodiment of rationality, but because the Western democracies continually failed him at every turn, in Spain as well as Germany.[29] And of course he spoke glowingly of Stalin as the dynamic leader of the Russian state. Not only was the Soviet premier praised as a great realist and intellectual, but he was hailed as one of the few figures of the twentieth century who had succeeded in combining *Geist* and *Macht* into one.

Related to Mann's new perspective on Russia was his work for the German *Volksfront* in exile. Mann's primary concern, it must be reiterated, was still Germany, not the Soviet Union. He wanted first of all to expel Hitler from power, and secondly to help create a new German state—alternately described as a "socialist republic" and a "democratic republic"[30]—which would succeed where Weimar had failed.

To achieve these ends he had to have all the leverage possible, including the aid of Russia, which now seemed to possess all of the qualities he had once hoped to find in Germany. But German *Geist* was also needed. It was imperative, then, that the émigrés organize themselves into a broad-based association which could provide the intellectual and practical basis for the new Germany after Hitler was driven out. This would work, however, only if such a front operated in conjunction with the Soviet Union, "without whose existence there [could] be no peace and no German *Volksfront*."[31]

Mann advanced the idea of a popular front in exile as early as 1934, but without eliciting much response. The reason was that the same divisions which separated the German Left during the Weimar period continued to separate it after 1933. Left-liberals were inherently mistrustful of socialists and communists; the socialists, in turn, formed their own exile organization in Prague and avoided making common cause with the communists; and the communists adamantly refused to look on the other two groups as anything but "bourgeois idealists" or "social fascists."[32]

Beginning in 1935, however, this situation started to change. To many, it began to appear that Hitler had entrenched himself in power and would not soon be removed unless an effective, unified opposition developed on the Left. More importantly, the Comintern changed its tactics for revolution, now ordering communist parties and organizations like the KPD to join with socialists and progressive liberals in popular front organizations bent on impeding the threat from the Right. Thus, in 1935, an exile anti-fascist front became possible for the first time. Its goals were to: first, develop an organized structure of opposition to Hitler; second, disseminate information to the West about events in Nazi Germany; third, try to effect, through writing and political agitation, the policies of other countries toward Germany; fourth, attempt to make contact with a German underground in order to smuggle literature into the Third Reich; and lastly, serve as a kind of steering committee for a new state after National Socialism had been defeated.

Heinrich Mann was elected president of the *Volksfront* at its founding convention in 1936, apparently because he stood above factions and best represented the "other Germany." It was an important facet of popular-front politics to convey the sense that intellectuals in exile were the true heirs of all that was great in German culture. If the Nazis could be intellectually discredited, the hope was that the West would then see them as nothing but usurpers or cultural barbarians. But there was another factor involved. Since the leadership of the *Volksfront* had turned out to be socialist and communist, it was necessary to win over the liberals by frequent reference to German culture and tradition, the legacy of the past, and the continuity of humanistic values. Mann hoped that through a vigorous defense of German culture, the *Volksfront* could bring together all the disparate elements in exile. In the 1930s the idea of "the defense of culture" (*die Verteidigung der Kultur*) became one of the cornerstones of his literary politics.[33]

For the purpose of strengthening the *Volksfront,* Mann wrote numerous essays calling for a firmer and deeper relationship between progressive middle class intellectuals like himself and the communist intellectuals in exile.[34] For a while this urging was effective, and differences were put aside. This happened in 1936–1937, a time corresponding with the success of the *front populaire* in France under Léon Blum. Even the orthodox communist Johannes R. Becher began working closely with Mann and praising his work; in fact he opened up the pages of his Moscow journal *Internationale Literatur* to virtually anything Mann wanted to write, despite the fact that just four years earlier, in the pages of *Linkskurve,* he had excoriated Mann as a petty-bourgeois opportunist.[35] By the end of the 1930s, however, the mood of cooperation began to break down. The Communist Party stalwarts, under Walter Ulbricht, tried to take over the *Volksfront* from within and make it a KPD organization tied to Comintern policy. This tactic alienated many liberals and socialists, who withdrew from active involvement in the organization. In spite of personal doubts about Ulbricht and anger at his subversion of the Front, Mann stayed on as president in an attempt to at least prevent the *Volksfront's* dissolution. He was aware that the real politics of the *Volksfront* took place behind his back; all he could do was acquiesce to events and, as he said, "let things take what course they may."[36] With the increasing internal disintegration of the organization, Mann had to admit that the German émigrés had failed in their task. They had not been able to unify, and therefore were in no position to change the situation in Germany by spiritual means. The power of the Soviet Union still remained, but the hoped for "second front" of exiled intellectuals was not able to sustain itself much beyond 1937.

There remained only two possible ways of changing Germany in the late 1930s, both of which required force: one was a war of Russia against Germany, the other was internal revolution. Mann felt certain that one or the other would soon occur, but he could not predict which one or when. He hoped it would be revolution, since an internal revolt would most likely cost fewer lives. But he knew that events would have to take their own course. As he wrote later on in 1943, "if the war had not come, the revolution would have; this was the only choice Hitler had."[37]

By 1938–1939, then, Mann began to return to the theme of a coming German revolution. Now, however (unlike during the years 1933–1934, when he had also felt that an uprising against Hitler was in the offing), Mann believed that the revolution would have to be

socialist and led by the working class. He did not arrive at this conclusion with enthusiasm, but rather backed into it because there was
not much else to hope for. By now Mann had virtually written off
the *Mittelstand,* which had disappointed him too many times in the
past. This class, it seemed, had been bought off by Hitler. In effect,
Mann transferred to the proletariat the qualities he had once believed
were inherent in the old middle class, particularly the qualities of
rectitude, integrity, and political responsibility. He even paid the
working class the highest compliment he could confer by labelling it
a "state-creating class" (*staatsbildende Klasse*) and a true "pillar of
culture" (*Träger der Kultur*).[38] This did not mean, however, that
Mann called for class rule or a dictatorship of the proletariat (an
idea still deeply repugnant to him). It only meant that he saw the
working class as the instigator of revolution, after which a rational,
humanist *Volksstaat,* composed of all social-democratic elements in
the new Germany, would eventually be set up in place of rule by one
class. He did not envision that Germany after the revolution would
be a communist state, since he felt that the term "communism" was
appropriate only to the Russian situation; rather, he believed that
Germany would be a state based on what he called "revolutionary
democracy."[39]

The Nazi-Soviet Pact of August 22, 1939, unfortunately put an
end to what few threads of hope still remained that Germany would
soon be transformed. Now there could be no successful worker's
insurrection, since Russia had come to terms with the Nazi state and
would not interfere in German domestic affairs. The Pact was a
serious blow to Mann's already shattered conception of literary
politics. It took two days and nights, as he later recalled, to recover
from the shock. But when he did he assumed, like many other
fellow-travellers, that Stalin must have had good reasons for signing
the non-agression treaty—reasons which he could not immediately
fathom. For the first time it appeared that all the options and all the
combinations of forces Mann had explored as means of changing
Germany were exhausted. Three months before the Pact, Mann had
written his brother Thomas that "Hitler will have to be struck down
before the new year or the future will be completely unpredictable, at
least for me."[40] Now, after August 1939, Hitler was perhaps more
secure than he had ever been, and the future which Mann had called
"unpredictable" would soon usher in World War II.

Politically speaking, Mann moved quite far to the Left between the years 1933 and 1939. But essentially this change involved an emphasis on new tactics and strategies, not new assumptions about politics or society. It is true that by the end of the decade Mann was calling himself a socialist intellectual and openly agitating for socialist revolution in Germany. Nevertheless, he did not abandon the old presuppositions which had informed his work for at least the two previous decades. The revolution, if it were to come, would have to be fundamentally moral, and its leaders would have to be inspired by inward "moral forces." Moreover, post-revolutionary society would be spiritual rather than materialistic, and literature would be strongly encouraged so that the masses could develop "literary instincts."[41] No class or party would be allowed to rule since this would mean tyranny, but instead all parties and interests would be encouraged to prosper together in an atmosphere of freedom. And finally, the intellectuals would have a major role to play in keeping state and society on the right track. As "officers of the revolution" they would be responsible for educating the people and leading them towards greatness; without them, the qualities of humanity, dignity, and "cultivation" would not take root in the population.[42] Even as a socialist, then, Mann still placed great stress on the role of *gesitige* intellectuals in transforming and spiritualizing society. At the very time that he began to rely, for strategic reasons, on the working class to carry out the revolution, he continued to insist that only intellectuals could truly guide and perfect it. "This is the reason," he wrote in 1939, "that intellectuals must lead the revolution. Everything would be dark and difficult without them."[43] Thus, although Mann became more radical in the 1930s, nearly all of his old premises remained. But now, they were often re-phrased in a more militant language and style.

The Novel in Exile: *Henri Quatre*

After 1933, the defeat of National Socialism became Mann's primary concern. Nearly everything he wrote as a publicist was subordinated to this end, so that his work increasingly took on the character of radical political journalism. But this did not mean that Mann abandoned the novel as a literary form. On the contrary, it was during his exile period that he wrote *Die Jugend und Vollendung des Königs Henri Quatre* (*The Youth and Maturing of Henri IV of*

France, 1935–1938), his longest and perhaps best work. No doubt it will be on the basis of this book and the *Kaiserreich* trilogy that Mann's purely literary reputation will ultimately rest.

Other émigré authors of Mann's generation also continued to express themselves as novelists in the 1930s. Now, however, the content of their novels was shaped decisively by the exile experience. The main reason, of course, was the loss of direct contact with daily life inside Germany. It would now be impossible for an author like Döblin, for example, to write another *Berlin Alexanderplatz* (1928), or for a Heinrich Mann to produce anything approaching *Ein ernstes Leben* (1932). Both works required an intimate and subtle knowledge of the German mood and atmosphere, to which all émigrés lacked accessibility after 1933. What emerged in place of the realistic novel or the *roman à moeurs* was a relatively new mode of expression for German writers: the historical novel. While in exile, Lion Feuchtwanger began writing about the Jewish War against Rome (*Der jüdische Krieg*, 1935) and the age of Nero (*Der falsche Nero*, 1936); Bruno Frank wrote about sixteenth-century Spain (*Cervantes*, 1934); Ferdinand Bruckner dealt with the Napoleonic Empire (*Napoleon I*, 1936); and Wihelm Herzog wrote about France during the Dreyfus affair (*Der Kampf einer Republik*, 1934). Still other émigré writers chose for their milieux such divergent historical settings as Reformation Germany, eighteenth-century Prussia, the Greece of Alcibiades, or the French Second Empire.[44] So many novels of this type were written that they began to be the rule rather than the exception. By the middle of the decade literary critics were already talking, though not quite correctly,[45] about the historical novel as a new genre of literature which was slowly taking shape under the difficult conditions of exile.

Despite appearances, the historical novel did not represent a flight into the past or an escape from political responsibility, as Kurt Hiller inferred at the time.[46] Instead, it represented a conscientious attempt on the part of many authors to make the best of a bad situation and find reasons for continuing to write even without access to "living material" from contemporary Germany. There were also political reasons for the emergence of the genre. Most of those who resorted to historical subject matters were, like Mann, active anti-fascists and strong advocates of socialist humanism. They hoped to participate in the struggles of their age, however indirectly, by making their historical works an extension of their politics. As Georg Lukács has pointed out, they could do this in at least three ways: first, by trying to recapture the truths of history which they felt were being distorted and falsified by the Nazis; second, by recalling in their novels the great humanist tradition which Hitler was attempting to obliterate; and third, by discussing earlier historical situations and ideals which could then inspire their contemporaries to fight for progress and reason.[47] In this way the past, by being recaptured through the novel, could "show the way mankind had gone and the direction in which it is [or should be] moving."[48] As far as the émigré writers were concerned, the historical novel, far from being a retreat into obscurantism, was one of the few avenues of literary-political engagement which was still open to them.

This is the way in which Mann perceived the tasks of the historical novel when he wrote *Henri Quatre*. The purpose of the work, as he put it, was to be neither "glorified history nor a genial fable but a true symbol" linking the age of Henri IV with the equally eventful 1930s.[49] This implied the fusion of two qualities which were difficult to reconcile: on the one hand, a realistic portrayal of situation and character (historical accuracy), and on the other, a firm sense of similarity and parallel development (historical symbolism). Both together, Mann felt, would deepen the impact of the past and enlarge its relevance for the present. Readers would then never be able to escape into history, but rather always find there something that draws them back into involvement with contemporary events. The particular would be raised to universal significance by means of symbolically attributing to specific historical detail a general, trans-historical meaning. In *Henri Quatre,* Mann frequently applied this method in order to indicate that history itself is only symbol. Hence the character of Henri Guise can be read as a representation of Hitler, the preacher Boucher as Goebbels, and the Duke of Mayenne as Goering. Similarly, an event like the Saint Bartholomew's Day Massacre hints at Hitler's "Night of the Long Knives," and the Edict of Nantes at Stalin's Constitution of 1936. Mann did not intend that his depictions of historical persons and events be directly identified with contemporary ones; he simply wanted the reader to become cognizant of, and perhaps more intelligently engaged in, the present at the same time that he reads about the past.

The two volumes of *Henri Quatre* which, taken together, amount to more than fifteen hundred pages, do not require a detailed summary here. All that need be said is that the book recounts the development of Henri of Navarre from childhood to kingship, against the rich texture of French life in the sixteenth century. The book resembles the traditional German *Bildungsroman*, except that the central figure is not dealt with in a private or exclusively spiritual way but is portrayed in and through his reciprocal relationships with his age. Mann represented Henri IV as one of the most progressive forces of his time. As Henri grows and matures he not only sees the need for tolerance, peace, the spread of reason and the end of factionalism, but he actively works to promote each of these ends. And yet Henri also exhibits human characteristics. He doubts himself, lies, deceives, abandons his own ideals, feels remorse and self-contempt, loves and hates with equal passion—in a word, he possesses the same strengths and weaknesses as any other mortal being. This realistic portrayal of character makes the novel both more concrete and more historically believable. The work is also firmly rooted in the epoch, and for this reason is of a different order than some *romans à clef* of exile (where Hitler and his friends are simply transposed to a different setting and milieu, as in the case of Feuchtwanger's *Der falsche Nero*). As the reader follows Henri from one encounter to another, from one political and social crisis to another, he sees him develop into a *Mensch* in the fullest sense of the word. Even if, by the end of the novel, Henri is defeated and dies without having achieved all he had hoped for, he is still the most positive figure Mann ever created in a novel. He completes himself by leaving the world a better place in which to live, an accomplishment which had become Mann's new criterion of success, in contrast to the Goethean ideal of well-roundedness and personal self-cultivation, which had so intrigued him in the 1890s.

The story of Henri IV's youth and maturation was also an attempt to communicate "symbolically" the following messages to the Europe of the 1930s.

First, Mann wanted to point out the essential correctness of Henri's ideas given the context of the year 1600. The ultimate goal of Henri IV, though never actually realized, is to unify Europe by applying reason to political life. With this in mind, the king attempts to put an end to the forces of hatred and bigotry as represented by the Catholic League under the Duke of Guise (cf. the Nazi Party under Hitler). Mann felt that Henri's ends were ethically and rationally justified; and since they were precisely the same ones that he and other exiles were fighting for at the time the novel was written, Mann sought to make a past age illuminate his own by implication. Henri, as Mann summarized it, was therefore intended to represent "the first good European": a king who attempted to establish "a free, happy, and united Europe" such as Mann himself hoped to see realized.[50]

Second, Mann tried to portray Henri IV as the model of a leader who could combine spirit and action, *Geist* and *Tat*. He showed the king to be a humanist but, as he tellingly expressed it, a humanist who could "ride and fight."[51] Intelligence had to be put into practice or it was of no use at all. Mann inferred that the reason Henri could so ingeniously be both a thinker and activist at the same time is that he had a good understanding of how reality could be utilized for spiritual purposes. In a sense, this made the king a personification of Mann's version of the intellectual in power, who was not only intelligent but was also not afraid of grasping and exercising power in order to implement his ideas. It seems possible that Mann may have had Stalin or perhaps Lenin in mind when he created the character of Henri, since he often praised the two Russian leaders for being pragmatic intellectuals. Indeed, Mann later wrote that "Henri IV handled himself like a revolutionary and today would be called a Bolshevik."[52] Nevertheless, even though the character Henri unites thought and deed in his own person he could not dispense with the advice of spiritual intellectuals, and neither, Mann inferred, could any contemporary leader like Stalin. To emphasize this, Mann gave the philosopher Montaigne an important role to play in the novel. As an informal advisor to the king, Montaigne makes a great impact on Henri, particularly by convincing him of the need for reason, moderation, and tolerance in human affairs. Even rulers, Mann implied, need guidelines; they need intellectuals to make them wiser and better men of action. "He who thinks, and he alone, must act," Mann wrote with respect to Henri IV. But Mann also made it clear that it is Montaigne, by supplying the king with knowledge of higher values, who converts Henri into a kind of "embattled humanist" to advance the cause of *Geist* in his own time.[53] In Mann's view, this symbiotic relationship between humanistic intellectuals and receptive leaders had to exist since, without it, rulers like Hitler would find it easy to resort to violence and brutality for immoral ends.

The third message of *Henri Quatre* is that true greatness comes only from intimate contact with the people. Henri is depicted as a monarch who never loses touch with ordinary men and women; his genuine empathy for his subjects, based on a sense of their common humanity, leads to an intuitive grasp of what they want and need. This quality is what Mann called "the power of goodness," and Henri is described as literally founding his reign upon it. This, too, the king learns from Montaigne, who often reminds him of Cicero's words: *nihil est tam populare quam bonitas* ("nothing is so popular as goodness"). In return for the king's benevolence the people give him their loyal support, causing a genuine mutuality to develop between Henri and the French population. This bond is the source of the king's strength and is the reason Mann labelled him "the prince of the poor and the oppressed."[54] Probably Mann intended this point to be a disguised approval of the Soviet situation in the 1930s, since he believed that Stalin's strength and popularity was founded on a similar rapport with the Russian masses.

A final message of the novel is that the exercise of power and even military force could be justified, but only so long as these actions are subordinated to *Geist*. Thus Henri's fight against the "fanaticism" of the Catholic League is legitimate, because power is placed in the service of reason and because it is designed to benefit an entire people rather than a particular class or interest group. Moreover, Mann indicated that *Macht* should be resorted to only by humanitarian rulers advised by intellectuals. If force were initiated from below, without the guidance of an intellectual elite, it could get out of control and become irrational. Had Mann dispensed with this notion of spiritual leadership from above, and instead viewed history as shaped by the masses' determination of what is right and reasonable, he would have agreed with the communist position and have won the approval of his Marxist critics. As it was, his outlook was still that of a middle class writer and humanitarian socialist who refused to abandon hope in the possibility of rational, benevolent leadership from the top. Lukács' critique of *Henri Quatre*, written in the 1930s, elaborates on this difference between Mann's socialism and his own Marxist perspective. The novel, Lukács felt, is too biographically oriented; hence it over-emphasizes the role that kings, as elite individuals, play in history and minimizes the active role of the masses. Furthermore, the work seemed to him to be based too much on idealism and not enough on historical materialism, and he therefore labelled it merely a "progressive" novel but not a socialist one.[55]

From the view-point of orthodox Marxist criticism, Lukács' comments are valid. Nonetheless, his remarks are not entirely relevent, because Mann did not intend to write a novel of socialist realism, nor did he try directly to affect events in the 1930s by means of his novel.

His chief goal in *Henri Quatre* was simply to convey the embodiment of ideals (rationality, humanism, the "power of goodness") to a world which needed direction. As a symbolic historical figure, Henri IV was used to represent enlightened values and to indicate that there was reason to hope even in bad times. Thus in *Henri Quatre*, Mann attempted a considerably more modest task than in the novels he had written before World War I. Now he felt that literature could clarify and explicate life by presenting ideals, but in and of itself it could not change the world.

In America 1940–1950: The End of Literary Politics

After the Nazi occupation of Paris in June, 1940, the German exiles in France were in danger of being arrested and imprisoned. Though Heinrich Mann lived in the south, and therefore fell under Vichy control, he hardly had grounds for feeling secure. In September, 1940, he decided to leave France for good, but since this was illegal for an émigré in Mann's position, it was necessary to acquire a forged passport, which he did under the pseudonym Heinrich Ludwig. Ten days after leaving Marseilles Mann arrived in Lisbon, and from there sailed for New York. He was never to see Europe again. The next ten years were spent in southern California where he was forced to observe European affairs from a distance. Now the sense of participating in important social and political issues all but vanished. For the first time in his life Mann realized that, as a writer, he was totally unable to make an impact on the events occurring around him.

At this point the active pursuit of literary politics, which had occupied Mann for fifty years, came to an abrupt end. Now no one, particularly in America, cared what he thought about any given issue. He was regarded as simply another German exile living in Santa Monica (Döblin, Feuchtwanger, Frank and others lived nearby). Time and again in his letters Mann complained that he was treated like an "insignificant author," known perhaps for *Der Untertan* but little else.[56] To one friend he wrote in 1942: "Here life drags on without any great necessity. No one takes notice of [my] presence except the tax-collector. Here one is forced to work in a void when under different circumstances . . . one could have touched the living."[57] Because of this feeling of purposelessness Mann published almost nothing during the early 1940s, certainly nothing geared to influence political decision-making.[58] More and more he withdrew into himself, a tendency which only increased after the suicide of his second wife in 1944.

Mann never felt comfortable in America since, like most German émigrés, he was revolted by American commercialism and "cultural philistinism." To make matters worse, he now had no steady source of income, except a one-year job as script reader for MGM Studio with a pay of $6000. Apart from this he was forced to rely on monthly checks from his brother Thomas (who was securely situated at Princeton University) and on an occasional royalty check from the sale of his books in Russia.[59] As far as Americans were concerned, the mantle of intellectual leader of the German opposition to Hitler belonged not to Heinrich Mann, but to Thomas. This fact, which Heinrich accepted with some bitterness (not toward Thomas but toward the American public), caused him to re-evaluate himself and his work. Now, for the first time since the 1890s, he began to regard himself more as an "author" (for whom writing is an end in itself) than a literary activist. This also meant that Mann became centrally concerned about his place in posterity, despite the fact that in the 1920s he had insisted that one should never write "for posterity" but only for the immediate situation.

Mann's turn away from literary activism was reflected in the novels he wrote in the 1940s, all of which revealed a diminished contact with the real world. The frequent reliance on surreal settings and the use of a reflective inner monologue indicated that Mann was no longer attempting to write within the genre of critical realism on which he had built his later reputation. In *Lidice* (1943), for example, he focused on the theme of reality versus unreality, just as he had done in his impressionist work of the 1890s. Though the novel is set in Nazi-occupied Czechoslovakia, the action and characterization are not very believable, mainly because Mann was not interested in historical accuracy but in the altogether different issue of how appearances can turn into "truths." In *Der Atmen* (*Breath*, 1949) he dealt with the last hours of an eccentric and enigmatic woman who had been, at different times in her life, both a countess and a communist. Set in the chaotic world of early September, 1939, when Hitler invaded Poland, the novel essentially portrays an individual trying to come to terms with her past in order to find some degree of inner peace. Even though the work contains a certain amount of social commentary (particularly regarding something Mann termed "synarchism"), it is for the most part abstract and ineffective. The last novel Mann wrote, *Empfang bei der Welt* (*Reception in the World*, published posthumously in 1956), is chiefly concerned with the corruption of art in modern society. The novel has almost no plot and the characters are identified only by their first names. Even the locale is never specified, though it appears to be southern California.

Aside from his novels, Mann completed one other work in the 1940s: an intellectual memoir entitled *Ein Zeitalter wird besichtigt* (*An Age is Surveyed*, 1945). Written in the closing years of the war, this unusual book represents a moralist's attempt to comprehend a world which seems to resist comprehension. In format, the work combines autobiographical sections with commentary on some of the major events and personalities of the twentieth century. Since Mann had by now given up the attempt to influence public opinion through literature, his only interest in writing the book was to catalogue, presumably for future generations, his personal opinions about the age in which he lived. Despite many astute observations, the book is strangely unemotional and detached. It reads like the memoir of an out-dated survivor, that is, of a man who has outlived his age and cannot really grasp the new one that has replaced it.

When the war ended in 1945, Mann did not feel inclined to return to West Germany. In personal letters he complained about how neglected he had become there: "My name," he wrote Karl Lemke, "is hardly mentioned in the West anymore."[60] Significantly, the same fate befell such others of Mann's generation as Schickele, Kellermann, Frank, and Feuchtwanger, none of whom recovered their prewar literary reputations in the German Federal Republic. The attitude of the East German regime, however, was markedly different. Officials there were eager to have Mann return so that he could give the newly formed German Democratic Republic an aura of intellectual respectability. Writers a generation younger than Mann had already taken up residence there, among them Johannes R. Becher, Bertolt Brecht, and Anna Seghers. What East Germany still needed for real literary prominence, however, was an older writer of Heinrich Mann's stature. Efforts to attract him began in the late 1940s, when the Humboldt University awarded Mann an honorary doctorate and the DDR granted him its National Prize for Art and Literature. Later he was offered the presidency of the newly constituted German Academy of Arts, with the promise that this office would entail real power to affect the cultural policies of East Germany. There was also the implication that he could expect a sizeable and appreciative readership, since his works would be reprinted in large numbers by the state. Despite considerable reservations about the Ulbricht regime, these inducements proved too irresistible for an author who had been without a public for so long. Mann made arrangements to return to the DDR but died unexpectedly in Los Angeles on March 12, 1950, two weeks before his eightieth birthday.

The year 1950 marked the end of Mann's life, but the end of his effectiveness as a practitioner of literary politics had occurred ten years earlier. With the outbreak of total war in 1939–1940, the European world Mann had known disintegrated, and with it the very possibility of literary politics as a meaningful undertaking. To try and improve society through writing implies, at the very least, the existence of a stable and comprehensible world open to rational discourse. Mann could no longer take this for granted after 1940, and consequently the project which had occupied him for most of his career suddenly seemed an exercise in futility. He spent this last decade unable to live out a life-choice that had become untenable once the conditions which supported it had disappeared.

Footnotes
Chapter 11

1. For a broader discussion of this incident see the documents included in *Literatur und Dichtung im Dritten Reich: Eine Dokumentation,* ed. Josef Wulf (Gütersloh, 1963), pp. 16–21; and Eberhard Dreher, "Keine Untertanen: Heinrich Mann, Käthe Kollwitz, Martin Wagner," *Études Germaniques* (1971), XXVI, no. 3: 344–48.

2. On the fate of the various émigrés see Hans-Albert Walter, *Bedrohung und Verfolgung bis 1933,* in *Deutsche Exilliteratur 1933–1950,* 2 vols. (Darmstadt and Neuwied, 1972), I: 197–250; and Matthias Wegner, *Exil und Literatur: Deutsche Schriftsteller im Ausland 1933–1945* (Frankfurt, 1967), pp. 32–54.

3. Mann's first wife, Maria Kanova, whom he married in 1914 and divorced in 1930, fled to Prague in March of 1933 along with their daughter Leonie. Maria died in 1947 as a result of illness stemming from her war-time internment in Theresienstadt. Heinrich Mann went to Nice with the actress Nelly Kroeger, whom he married in 1939. She committed suicide in California in 1944.

4. On the whole, it was only members of the younger radical intelligentsia who selected Russia as a place of exile, e.g. writers like Erich Weinert (b. 1890), Johannes R. Becher (b. 1891), Alfred Kurella (b. 1895), and Willi Bredel (b. 1901). What separated these individuals from Mann's generation was the fact that (1) they never went through a period of aesthetic development, (2) they came to literary maturity in the very different atmosphere of the 1920s, and (3) they had all opted for communism before 1933. By contrast, those whom contemporary Marxist critics call "bourgeois-humanist writers" (Mann, Schickele, Hermann, Werfel, etc.) chose to emigrate westward, mainly to France and later to America.

5. Ernst Schürer, "Verinnerlichung, Protest und Resignation: Georg Kaisers Exil," *Die deutsche Exilliteratur 1933–1945,* ed. Manfred Durzak (Stuttgart, 1973), p. 278.

6. Alfred Döblin, cited in Erika and Klaus Mann, *Escape to Life* (Boston, 1939), p. 199.

7. See Alfred Döblin, *Schicksalsreise: Bericht und Bekenntnis* (Frankfurt, 1949); and Heinz Graber, "Politisches Postulat und autobiographischer Bericht: Zu einigen im Exil entstandenen Werken Alfred Döblins," in Manfred Durzak, ed., *Die deutsche Exilliteratur 1933–1945,* pp. 418–27.

8. Marcel Reich-Ranicki, "Lion Feuchtwanger oder Der Weltruhm des Emigranten," in Manfred Durzak, *op. cit.,* pp. 443–54; Hans Mayer, "Lion Feuchtwanger oder die Folgen des Exils," *Neue Rundschau,* (1965), LXXVI: 120–29.

9. On this problem see Ernst Bloch's interesting essay "Zerstörte Sprache–zerstörte Kultur," in *Verbannung: Aufzeichnungen deutscher Schriftsteller im Exil*, ed. Egon Schwarz and Matthias Wegner (Hamburg, 1964), pp. 178–88.

10. Heinrich Mann, "Kurze Selbstbiographie," dated March 3, 1943: included as an appendix in Herbert Ihering, *Heinrich Mann*, p. 146.

11. See Ernst Erich Noth, "Die Exilsituation in Frankreich," in Manfred Durzak, *Die deutsche Exilliteratur 1933–1945*, pp. 73–88.

12. *Ibid.*, p. 84. This did not prevent the German representative in Paris from trying to suppress Mann's articles in the *Dépêche*. But he had no success; the owner of the paper was the French Minister of the Interior, Albert Sarraut. See Heinrich Mann, *Ein Zeitalter wird besichtigt*, p. 407.

13. Hans-Albert Walter, "Die Asylpolitik Frankreichs von 1933 bis zur Annexion Österreichs," *Exil und innere Emigration*, ed. Peter Uwe Hohendahl and Egon Schwarz (Frankfurt, 1973), II:47–63.

14. Paul Zech, letter to Max Hermann-Neisse, March 10, 1938, cited in Matthias Wegner, *Exil und Literatur*, p. 101.

15. Heinrich Mann, *Der Hass. Deutsche Zeitgeschichte* (Amsterdam, 1933), pp. 197–235.

16. See Werner Herden, "Aufruf und Bekenntnis: Zu den essayistischen Bemühungen Heinrich Manns im französischen Exil," *Weimarer Beiträge* (1965), XI, no. 3: 324–25, 329.

17. Ludwig Marcuse, "Farewell to Heinrich Mann," *Books Abroad* (1950), XXIV, no. 3:249.

18. Heinrich Mann, *Es kommt der Tag* (Zürich, 1936), pp. 81ff.

19. Heinrich Mann, *Der Sinn dieser Emigration* (Paris, 1934), p. 26.

20. Heinrich Mann, *Der Hass*, pp. 63–78, 104–14.

21. See Heinrich Mann, "Antworten nach Russland" (1924), *Essays* II, *Ausgewählte Werke*, XII: 136–37; "Geistige Neigungen in Deutschland" (1925), *Sieben Jahre*, p. 235; and "Fünf Jahre nach dem Tode Lenins" (1928), *ibid.*, p. 556.

22. Mann abandoned this scheme after 1927, when he saw that the anti-Russian bias built into pan-Europeanism was being used by international capitalism to weaken the Soviet state.

23. Heinrich Mann, "Die Macht des Wortes," *Es kommt der Tag*, p. 228.

24. Heinrich Mann, cited in Alfred Kantorowicz, *Der Einfluss der Oktober-revolution auf Heinrich Mann* (Berlin, 1952), p. 15.

25. Heinrich Mann, "Lenin, fünfzehn Jahre nach seinem Tode," *Mut* (Paris, 1939), pp. 145–46.

26. Heinrich Mann, "Eine grosse, historische Sache," *Verteidigung der Kultur: Antifaschistische Streitschriften und Essays* (Hamburg, 1960), pp. 514–15.

27. Heinrich Mann, cited in Alfred Kantorowicz, *Der Einfluss der Oktober-revolution*, p. 17.

28. Heinrich Mann, cited in Hans-Albert Walter, "Heinrich Mann im französischen Exil," *Heinrich Mann*, ed. Heinz Ludwig Arnold (Stuttgart, 1971), pp. 133–34.

29. Heinrich Mann, *Mut*, pp. 70–85.

30. Compare Mann's comments in his letter to Arnold Zweig, August 2, 1935, with those expressed in his speech to the German *Volksfront* on April 11, 1937. Both documents are included in *Heinrich Mann 1871–1950: Werk und Leben*, pp. 262, 284.

31. Heinrich Mann, *Mut*, p. 292.

32. The best brief discussion of the background of the *Volksfront* is Hans-Albert Walter, "Heinrich Mann im französischen Exil," *Heinrich Mann*, pp. 129–32; but see also Gisela Berglund, *Deutsche Opposition gegen Hitler in Presse und Roman des Exils* (Stockholm, 1972), pp. 11–43.

33. See Heinrich Mann, "Die Verteidigung der Kultur," in *Verteidigung der Kultur: Antifaschistische Streitschriften und Essays*, pp. 132–37; "Verfall einer geistigen Welt," *ibid.*, pp. 104–08; "Aufbau einer geistigen Welt," *ibid.*, pp. 109–13; and also Werner Herden, *Geist und Macht: Heinrich Manns Weg an die Seite der Arbeiterklasse* (Berlin, 1971), pp. 75–100.

34. For example, Heinrich Mann, "Ein denkwürdiger Sommer," *Verteidigung der Kultur*, pp. 149–51.

35. See Werner Herden, "Heinrich Mann und Johannes R. Becher," *Weimarer Beiträge* (1971), XVII, no. 4:114–20.

36. See the critical comments on Mann by Babette Gross, cited in David Roberts, *Artistic Consciousness*, p. 183.

37. Heinrich Mann, letter to Alfred Kantorowicz, March 3, 1943: included in Herbert Ihering, *Heinrich Mann*, p. 146.

38. Heinrich Mann, cited by Wilhelm Girnus, "Geist und Macht im Werk Heinrich Manns," *Weimarer Beiträge*, XVII, no. 8:51.

39. Heinrich Mann, *Es kommt der Tag*, p. 16.

40. Heinrich Mann, letter to Thomas Mann, May 25, 1939, in *Thomas Mann—Heinrich Mann Briefwechsel, 1900–1949*, p. 185.

41. Heinrich Mann, "Die Macht des Wortes," *Es kommt der Tag*, p. 230.

42. *Ibid.*, pp. 224–232; see also "Geheime Schulen," *ibid.*, pp. 212–18; and "Die Führung," *ibid.*, pp. 218–24.

43. *Ibid.*, p. 221.

44. For a partial bibliography of historical novels written by German exile authors see Walter A. Berendsohn, *Die humanistische Front: Einführung in die deutsche Emigranten-Literatur* (Zürich, 1946), pp. 115–17.

45. Among some of the writers who remained inside the Third Reich there was a similar turn to the historical novel in the 1930s.

46. Kurt Hiller, *Profile* (Paris, 1937), p. 160.

47. Georg Lukács, *The Historical Novel*, trans. Hannah and Stanley Mitchell (Boston, 1963), pp. 270–72. On the historical novel in exile see also Klaus Jarmatz, "Aktivität und Perspektive im historischen Roman des kritischen Realismus 1933 bis 1945," *Weimarer Beiträge* (1965), XI, no. 3:350–76; and Alfred Döblin, "Der historische Roman und wir," *Aufsätze zur Literatur* (Freiburg, 1963), pp. 163–86.

48. Georg Lukács, *The Historical Novel*, p. 271.

49. Heinrich Mann, *Die Vollendung des Königs Henri Quatre*, in *Ausgewählte Werke*, VII:915, italics added.

50. Heinrich Mann, "Die Tage werden kürzer," Heinrich-Mann-Archiv, no. 230; in *Heinrich Mann 1871–1950: Werk und Leben*, p. 265.

51. Heinrich Mann, *Die Jugend des Königs Henri Quatre*, in *Ausgewählte Werke*, VI:565.

52. Heinrich Mann, *Ein Zeitalter wird besichtigt*, pp. 164–65.

53. Heinrich Mann, *Die Jugend des Königs Henri Quatre*, p. 565.

54. Heinrich Mann, "Ein denkwürdiger Sommer," *Verteidigung der Kultur,* p. 151.

55. Georg Lukács, *The Historical Novel,* pp. 279–322 *passim.*

56. Viktor Mann, *Wir waren fünf,* p. 573.

57. Heinrich Mann, letter to Klaus Pinkus, April 5, 1940: in Heinrich Mann, *Briefe an Karl Lemke und Klaus Pinkus* (Hamburg, 1963), pp. 148–49.

58. Between 1943 and 1945 Mann wrote four "political" articles for *Das Freie Deutschland,* an émigré journal in Mexico, but they were really addressed to a future post-war audience rather than an existing one. Each article was only one or two pages in length and none contained ideas which had not already been expressed in the 1930s.

59. See Heinrich Mann's two letters to Katia and Thomas Mann, dated April 4 and April 5, 1942, in *Thomas Mann—Heinrich Mann Briefwechsel, 1900–1949,* pp. 214–16.

60. Heinrich Mann, letter to Karl Lemke, May 27, 1949, in *Briefe an Karl Lemke, 1917–1949,* p. 138.

Chapter 12
Conclusion

The Categories of Literary Politics

One of the factors which originally attracted Mann to writing was the unique aura attached to the literary profession. "Being a writer" meant something special in Germany in the late nineteenth century. Not only did the term "author" carry with it connotations of high culture and sacerdotal mission, but it also suggested a privileged status far removed from, and unrelated to, the commonplace world of everyday life. Authorship was thus regarded as a means to rise above middle-class existence by escaping into a realm of beauty. Literature, it seemed, possessed almost religious qualities which could redeem those who felt too sensitive for the banal reality around them. When Mann appropriated these views, which were widely held in Germany during the 1880s and 1890s, especially among large segments of the middle-class reading public, he was simply accepting the basic literary assumption of his age. His earliest conceptions of what an author was like (aesthetic, introspective, priest-like in his "calling") were wholly compatible with those of the German *fin-de-siècle* audience for whom he initially wrote.

By 1910, some twenty years after he published his first piece, Mann had become a quite different kind of writer. Previously authorship had meant the creation of beautiful things, but now it meant agitation to promote democracy and humanity; formerly, the writer had been asked to withdraw from the world for his personal good, but now Mann called upon writers to become *engagé* for the good of all. This change occurred not only because the reality Mann confronted was different from the one he had confronted in 1890, but also because he began to perceive and assimilate reality differently. This implied both a rejection of the images he had originally associated with being a writer, and the forging of new ones more in keeping with his increasingly liberal world-view. This shift from aestheticism to moralism, from *l'art pour l'art* to literary politics, was the major transition of Mann's life. It goes without saying that

271

in the years after 1910 the world continued to evolve and so did Mann's relationship to it. However, from 1910 until 1940, when he was forced to emigrate to America and abandon the pursuit of literary politics, Mann's outlook on life, though continuing to develop, tended to change only in particulars and not in basic orientation. Compared to the real "epistemological break" which took place during the years 1895–1910, all subsequent alterations until the last decade of his life were matters of degree.[1] Only once, in other words, was there a genuine transformation of the modalities and categories of Mann's thought. By contrast, between 1910 and 1940 one finds fluctuations more than shifts, and variations on themes rather than qualitative rifts in his patterns of thought.

Here it is necessary to single out and briefly comment upon three of the relatively fixed elements of Mann's *Weltanschauung*, since they became the mainstays of his literary and political thought during the years when he was at the height of his career. They are, first, that ethics is the yardstick of valuation; second, that reason is the guide to social betterment; and third, that writing is "active humanism."

From these premises, several different conclusions were possible, as Mann's later evolution made amply clear. Starting from essentially the same three points, Mann embraced at least three different political positions: in 1910 he was a liberal democrat, in 1918 a Kantian socialist, and in 1938 a fellow-traveller and defender of Stalin and the Soviet state. Thus, regardless of divergences, each ideological stage was an extension of an identical set of presuppositions about ethics, rationality, and literary politics. The variations appeared when Mann drew different conclusions from the same core ideas, but even here his thought was still part of the same logical continuum. For example, had Mann not started from these three major principles, he could *not* have arrived at a sympathetic view of communism no matter how much he stretched his thought, horizontally or vertically. The reason is that before the epistemological break of his transitional years, the framework in which Mann operated was basically aesthetic and neo-conservative. In order for a new politics to emerge, a new world-view had to precede it.

The best way to understand the fluctuations of Mann's ideas, especially between the years 1910 and 1940, is by applying Goethe's concept of "permanence in change." The three poles of Mann's thought already referred to were constant, but at the periphery there was a great deal of movement. For instance, the notion that ethics is a universal reference point that can never be abandoned was an *ideé fixe* for Mann; but from this pivotal center he both condemned communism as immoral (in 1920), and later hailed it as the embodiment of the categorical imperative (in 1940). In concluding this treatment of Heinrich Mann it is important to look more closely and critically at these three elements of Mann's thought; taken together, they reveal not only some of the strengths but also many of the shortcomings of his conception of literary politics.

Ethics as the Yardstick of Valuation

The word "ethics," as Mann used it, was much too abstract. In time it seemed to become almost a reference point without substance, then a sacred word, and finally, a religious incantation. Until the mid-1930s Mann never stopped to consider that an absolute ethic, under certain conditions, might only tend to advance the forces which he opposed. To be "ethical" in the face of the Nazi movement (for example, to abjure the use of force under any circumstances) would in effect mean willing oneself out of the struggle, for what good was moral idealism if one's adversary refused to abide by the rules of the game?

More importantly, the reliance on ethics as a mode of valuation, often without a solid grounding in history or political economy, led Mann to view things far too simplistically. Almost invariably he saw the world in terms of the opposites, good and evil, with very few distinctions in between. This worked satisfactorily in a few cases. For instance, although Mann's opposition to Hitler was couched in ethical language few in the West minded this approach, since the whole struggle against Nazism took on the character of a moral crusade. In other cases, however, his working definition of ethics led him into problems from which he could extract himself only with the greatest effort. By the 1930s, for example, Mann had decided that National Socialism was the most morally unacceptable doctrine on earth; therefore he concluded that its direct opposite, communism, had to be fundamentally moral. Once this conclusion was reached, Mann was full of excessive praise not only for the humanistic principles underlying communism, but also for Stalin and the U.S.S.R. "Communism is synonymous with morality," he wrote in *Ein Zeitalter wird besichtigt*, ". . . . It *is* its moral background."[2] Furthermore, Mann assumed that wherever morality was present, progress and rationality necessarily had to exist along with it. These qualities, he was sure, could never be artificially separated, since it was the nature of things that they flourish interdependently. Hence, because Nazi Germany was clearly immoral, it had by definition to be unprogressive and irrational, too; and because Soviet Russia seemed to have "ethical integrity," Mann took it for granted that it must be fundamentally progressive and rational. Earlier, particularly in the 1920s, he could not have made this assessment because he had not yet acknowledged that the essential core of communism was its "moral impluse," its concern with goodness.[3] Instead, he had castigated the Bolsheviks for their fanaticism and power-madness, and dismissed Leninist Russia as simply another form of dictatorship. Only in the 1930s, when he decided that communism was the embodiment of ethical principles, did Mann change his mind. In this case, as in so many others, his political judgments were an extension of his moral perceptions.

One would think that an emphasis on ethical criteria would lead one to become intransigent, resolute, unchanging. This was far from the case. Ethics led Mann, as it did others of his generation, from one extreme to another. The difficulty came not in supporting morality in the abstract, but in deciding which states, institutions, or organizations embodied ethical virtue. Once this was determined, political commitment followed. Often, it was enough to elicit commitment that the "underlying motives" or the "basic intentions" of an institution like the Soviet state be considered moral. It was this kind of loophole that allowed Mann and others to tolerate "surface contradictions" like the purges and the Nazi-Soviet Pact so long as their faith in the essential goodness of communism remained unshaken. Even strict ethical prohibitions against the use of force were lifted slightly in the 1930s when it became clear that perhaps Hitler could be defeated only by a real (not a spiritual) revolution, or by armed invasion from outside. As has already been pointed out in the above discussion of Mann's novel *Henri Quatre,* he believed that a moderate use of force could be acceptable if it were wielded for ethical ends and in the name of a whole people rather than a single class.

Almost all of the follow-travellers of the 1930s were ethical idealists like Mann, embracing the Soviet Union for moral reasons. It was precisely their ethical valuations which allowed them to make so many practical misjudgments and to frequently appear naive or "used." The twentieth-century world does not lend itself to being dealt with in terms of black and white, good and evil. The major shortcoming of Mann and the other ethical socialists was that too often their moral instincts replaced concrete political analysis and understanding. It was precisely because they frequently lacked a firm grasp of the socio-historical situation that they were thrown to and fro by the categorical imperative.

Reason as the Guide to Social Transformation

For Mann, the good society was by definition a rational one. Rational did not necessarily imply sound economic or technological planning, since Mann rarely thought in these terms. Instead, it meant a society which was permeated with *Geist* and which did everything possible to draw out of its citizenry a sense of reason and justice. At first Mann thought such a society could be achieved merely by the introduction of democracy. This accounts for the optimism of his 1910 essays and his early support for the Weimar Republic. Later, he began to think that democratic reforms were not enough. Perhaps the truly rational society would have to be socialist, since the existence of capitalism and the profit-motive (which are always encouraged in middle class democracies) was incompatible with rationality and justice. It was this sort of logic that led Mann to celebrate the Soviet Union in the 1930s. Like Feuchtwanger, he saw Stalin as a thoroughgoing rationalist trying to construct a "gigantic state [based] on reason alone."[4] Mann wholeheartedly supported this effort. As he put it in 1937: "At last a state is trying to make out of men what we have always wanted: a rational existence, the collective working for the benefit of the individual . . . and each individual becoming a better person in a community moving toward greater perfection."[5]

As may be clear from this example, Mann tended to idealize reason (*Vernunft*) in the same way that he mystified ethics. So important was the concept to him that he was willing to call for a "dictatorship of reason," despite the dangers this notion suggested. For this solution to be valid, Mann was obliged to see a degree of "reasonableness" in everything, even where it did not, in fact, exist. Thus, in order to give a rational explanation for any difficulty, Mann simply pretended that all existence is fundamentally reasonable, and therefore subject to rational solutions. At best this avoided the issue, at

worst it led to a simplistic treatment of the most problematic questions of the day. National Socialism, for instance, was seen as essentially a revolt against "reason and its defenders."[6] Presumably, if the
irrationality could be pointed out and argued away, everything would
return to normal. Similarly, Mann never fathomed the depths of anti-
Semitism in Germany, and consequently lost all effectiveness in
arguing against it. As far as he was concerned, it was nothing but a
pseudo-issue designed to mask the German sense of inferiority.
Furthermore, he believed it originated not in the German heartland
but in border areas like East Prussia, where Germans were a minority
who experienced their existence as "problematic." For these people
the Jew became a scapegoat, but unfortunately they "overcom-
pensated" and produced the phenomenon of anti-Semitism.[7] This
attempt on Mann's part to look for rational, psychological expla-
nations completely missed the point; so did his repeated efforts to
expose the weaknesses of racial theories by means of rational argumentation.[8] In every sense Mann failed to grasp the dynamics of German anti-Semitism. In fact he may have made matters worse, if that
were possible, by trying to prove that in their deepest essence the
Jews were even more German than the Germans. Hence, in Mann's
opinion anti-Semitism was hardly more than a clever ploy, and even
as late as 1935 he was still arguing that the Jew was merely a
"bogeyman" (Popanz) which Hitler used as an excuse to take power.[9]
The notion that Hitler came to power by virtue of a popular movement and not through trickery and deceit, or that anti-Semitism
might have had indigenous social origins and far-reaching ideological
implications, does not seem to have been convincing to Mann at the
time. To entertain such notions would be to acknowledge man's
basic irrationality, and this he was not prepared to do.

By the overwhelming importance he placed on Vernunft, Mann
consciously linked himself to the tradition of the French Enlightenment. Like his eighteenth-century predecessors, he assumed that if
reason could become an "objective historical force" it would automatically make the world a happier place in which to live. Moreover, he believed that in most instances reason alone, not the resort
to weapons, would "triumph over social irrationality and overthrow
the oppressors of mankind."[10] However admirable the sentiments,
this naive faith in the power of reason seemed to be out of place in
the twentieth century. In the course of Mann's lifetime, major break-
throughs were made by Freud and others in exploring the dark

underside of the human personality. Important findings about the instinctual dimension of men and the proclivities toward mass behavior under the veneer of civilization became widely known. Nevertheless, Mann does not appear to have re-evaluated the meaning of reason in the light of these new discoveries about the unconscious and irrational in human nature. To put it simply, he tried to cope, anachronistically, in eighteenth-century terms, with tendencies that sprung up not only outside of, but also against, the legacy of the Enlightenment. That he would fail to deal adequately with the problems of his age was virtually a foregone conclusion. For the most part, he chose the wrong weapons to fight adversaries he could neither properly identify nor really understand.

Writing as "Active Humanism"

The notion that writing is a political gesture, that it is in fact humanism applied and made concrete, remained constant for Mann after the beginning of the century. What changed, however, were his feelings about its effectiveness. Though there was never any thought of giving up writing altogether (this would be a betrayal of the spirit), there were times when Mann wondered if something more was needed. He was not slow to observe, for example, that a book like *Der Untertan* "was devoured but did not change a thing."[11] What, then, was the act of writing really accomplishing? These doubts about his occupation seemed to grow in direct proportion to his loss of a reading public; naturally, the fewer readers he had, the less meaningful, for his own purposes, the written word appeared to be. This was especially true when, as Mann put it in 1934, he no longer had a feeling for who his readers were because they were "scattered over the whole earth" and consequently he was forced to address them, through translations, in "strange languages."[12] The experience of exile, at least up to 1940, did not change the fact that his sense of personal integrity demanded that he write, but it did raise legitimate questions about how effective writing was as a mode of political expression.

Until the early Weimar period, Mann never doubted what he called the power of words. He was sure that the *littérateur* could affect reality through the medium of language by spreading *Geist* throughout society and thereby creating a people receptive to democratic ideals. Later, misgivings crept in when it occurred to him that most of the important decisions of the time were being made well beyond the boundaries of literary influence. This did not throw him into despair, since he still believed that writers could be instrumental in reaching the leaders who were making these outside decisions. In the 1920s, partly by trying to influence political leaders, Mann tried harder than perhaps any of his contemporaries to make the written word an autonomous force to be reckoned with, even to the extent of writing an "Open Letter to Gustav Stresemann" and expecting results. Although at times he talked about a "clerisy" of writers, or about the need for literary intellectuals to "found their own church," it was not because he wanted them to withdraw from the world but because he wanted them to solidify their forces and unite for more effective action. This was the crux of Mann's literary politics during the Weimar era.

In the early years of exile, Mann continued to have confidence in the potency of words. But since his works were not reaching Germany, he had to use language for a different purpose than when he wrote for a German audience, that is, to encourage the *Volksfront* efforts and inform the West about the dangers of National Socialism. By the late 1930s, Mann was forced by circumstances (e.g., the continued lack of accessibility to a German readership, the collapse of the *Volksfront,* and the obvious impotence of literary politics in a condition of exile) to do some re-thinking about the efficacy of the written word. Before, he had argued that "the voice of the writer [must] be strengthened through the entire authority of the people or he will carry no weight whatever;"[13] now, the "people," his audience, had shrunk to a fraction of what it had been and literature no longer seemed as useful as before. Even the goal of "spiritualizing" the heads of states, and through them the millions they commanded, did not seem to be working. This fact eventually led Mann to a conclusion which his friend Kurt Hiller had reached some years earlier: that it may not be enough for intellectuals to advise leaders, as Montaigne did Henri IV, but they would have to become leaders themselves. Hence by 1942 Mann could write: "We must have learned one thing: we cannot control events that are not of our own making. When the intellectuals do not wield power there is the danger that someday they may be thrown out. . . . It [is] imperative that in all countries in the future only creative spirits come to power and determine the trend of events. Only so would life be worthwhile for men to live."[14]

The above observations raise two related questions which need to be asked: Why did Mann place such an extraordinary emphasis on the power of words, and where did he derive the conviction that writing could change life? It goes without saying that writing can be influential, but prior to the 1930s, Mann and his contemporaries claimed more. They argued that writing, because it is a spiritual activity, takes primacy over, and is superior to, any material approach to change. The spirit rules life, and therefore revolutions must occur in the spiritual realm before they can percolate down to the material base. To be sure, from the 1920s on Mann argued that profound socio-economic changes were needed, but mainly in order to soften up society and make it more amenable to the penetration of *Geist*. Even socialism was merely a means, the end being the triumph of spirit. "The spiritual seems to me to be primary," Mann wrote in direct contrast to Marx. "It comes first in history." The same attitude was conveyed elsewhere when he expressed the conviction that "the ideas of today [become] the realities of tomorrow."[15]

Statements like these represent something more than a writer's conceit. It may be that every author tends to magnify the significance of what he does, but with Mann and others of his literary generation this sense of importance turned into a sense of mission. Writing became an essential part of a total *Weltanschauung*, nor merely a private vocation. The philosophical ground of this was neo-Kantianism, though often misunderstood or re-interpreted. Mann and his contemporaries simply assumed that the mind shapes reality. Consequently, they believed that if people could be made to become more rational and moral, they would proceed to fashion a world which reflected these qualities.[16] The key to this kind of social change was writing, though they sometimes doubted that their audience was as aware of this fact as they should have been. Just as the spirit organizes existence and determines its course, so the written word organizes the spirit and determines its character. Everything was seen as moving from *Geist* to matter, and those who could make an impact at the highest, most spiritual level could be certain of reaching the lowest as well. Implicit in this outlook was an anti-materialism which kept Mann outside the ambience of Marxism even after he had become a fellow-traveller. As was the case with the other writers mentioned earlier, Mann never scrutinized the idealistic assumptions at the center of his literary politics as thouroughly as he might have. The result was that these assumptions contained too many unwarranted notions about the ability of words to affect reality. Furthermore, Mann never seriously considered that writing itself might be a form of social production which, as Walter Benjamin argued, legitimizes the existing order even when this is not intended.[17]

Thus Mann's shortcomings were not entirely personal. In large measure they were bound up with his class and literary generation, for the tendency to place hope in ethics or the "spreading effects of reason" was not unusual among those who underwent a development similar to Mann's. To many engaged middle-class writers, the idea of a "free-floating intelligentsia" seemed to be a sane compromise between social despair and an exclusive commitment to the proletariat. In this *via media,* the practice of writing was fetishized. It became not what it should be, a preparation for action, but action itself.

This led to an exaggerated notion of what the written word could accomplish, as Mann belatedly realized when his essays neither saved the Weimar Republic nor brought down the Hitler regime.[18] Still, both he and the others needed to believe, at least into the 1930s, that the act of writing could make a difference. Without this as a working hypothesis they would have had less of a conception of who they were as individuals, for only by writing about the world did they feel a sense of personal involvement and meaningful participation in it.

Footnotes

Chapter 12

1. The concept of the "epistemological break" is utilized in different contexts by Louis Althusser and Gaston Bachelard. See Louis Althusser, *For Marx*, trans. Ben Brewster (New York, 1969).

2. Heinrich Mann, *Ein Zeitalter wird besichtigt*, p. 87.

3. Heinrich Mann, "Revolutionäre Demokratie," hand-written manuscript without place or date (written *circa*. 1934), Heinrich-Mann-Archiv, no. 287.

4. Lion Feuchtwanger, cited in David Caute, *The Fellow-Travellers* (New York, 1973), p. 255.

5. Heinrich Mann, cited in Alfred Kantorowicz, *Der Einfluss der Oktober-revolution*, pp. 16–17.

6. Heinrich Mann, *Der Hass*, p. 75.

7. Heinrich Mann, "Ihr ordinärer Antisemitismus," *Der Hass*, pp. 125ff.

8. See Heinrich Mann, "Der Antisemitismus und seine Heilung," *Essays* II, *Ausgewählte Werke*, XII:469–70; "Gut geartete Menschen," *ibid.*, pp. 471–77; and "Die Deutschen und ihre Juden," *Es kommt der Tag*, pp. 51–52.

9. Heinrich Mann, "Die Juden," hand-written manuscript dated August 19, 1935, in Heinrich-Mann-Archiv, no. 321.

10. On the Enlightenment nature of these views see Herbert Marcuse, *Reason and Revolution: Hegel and the Rise of Social Theory* (Boston, 1964), p. 7.

11. Heinrich Mann, "The German European," *Decision* (1941), II, no. 4: 39.

12. Henrich Mann, "Sammlung der Kräfte," *Die Sammlung* (1934), II, no. 1:p. 7.

13. Heinrich Mann, "L'Avinir de la culture," *Essays* II, *Ausgewählte Werke*, XII:376.

14. See Heinrich Mann's contribution to "Transplanted Writers: A Symposium," *Books Abroad* (1942), XVI, no. 3:268–69.

15. Heinrich Mann, *Sieben Jahre,* pp. 350–51, 360; and Lorenz Winter, *Heinrich Mann and His Public,* p. 101.

16. On the intellectual premises of neo-Kantianism see Timothy Raymond Keck, "Kant and Socialism: The Marburg School in Wilhelmian Germany," Ph.D. dissertation, University of Wisconsin, 1975, pp. 209–300; and George L. Mosse, *Germans and Jews* (New York, 1970), pp. 171–88.

17. See Walter Benjamin, "The Author as Producer," *New Left Review,* July-August, 1970, LXII: 83–96.

18. Heinrich Mann, *Ein Zeitalter wird besichtigt,* p. 202.

BIBLIOGRAPHY

The following bibliography includes only works footnoted in the text. In addition, I have made use of several unpublished sources which are not listed below. The most important of these can be found in the Schiller-Nationalmuseum, Marbach-am-Neckar, and the Heinrich-Mann-Archiv, in the Deutsche Akademie der Künste, East Berlin. The latter collection is particularly significant. It contains the bulk of Mann's *Nachlass,* including over 22,000 pages of letters, essays, newspaper articles, fragmentary notes, and drafts of novels, novellas, and poems. Some of the more pertinent of these documents have been reprinted in Sigrid Anger, ed., *Heinrich Mann 1871–1950: Werk und Leben in Dokumenten und Bildern* (Berlin, 1971).

I. Books by Heinrich Mann

Mann, Heinrich. *Die Armen.* Leipzig, 1917.
    Ausgewählte Werke in Einzelausgaben, ed. Alfred Kantorowicz. 12 volumes. Berlin, 1951–1962.
        I. *Im Schlaraffenland* and *Professor Unrat.*
        II. *Zwischen den Rassen.*
        III. *Die kleine Stadt.*
        IV. *Der Untertan.*
        V. *Eugenie oder Die Bürgerzeit.*
        VI. *Die Jugend des Königs Henri Quatre.*
        VII. *Die Vollendung des Königs Henri Quatre.*
        VIII. *Novellen* I.
        IX. *Novellen* II.
        X. *Schauspiele.*
        XI. *Essays* I.
        XII. *Essays* II.
    Briefe an Karl Lemke, 1917–1949. Berlin, 1963.
    Briefe an Karl Lemke und Klaus Pinkus. Hamburg, 1963.
    Es kommt der Tag. Deutsches Lesebuch. Zürich, 1936.
    Die Göttinnen oder die drei Romane der Herzogin von Assy. Berlin, 1903.
    Der Hass. Deutsche Zeitgeschichte. Amsterdam, 1933.
    Heinrich Mann 1871–1950: Werk und Leben in Dokumenten und Bildern, ed. Sigrid Anger. Berlin, 1971.
    In einer Familie. Munich, 1894.
    Die Jagd nach Liebe. Munich, 1903.

Eine Liebesgeschichte. Munich, 1953.

Macht und Mensch. Munich, 1919.

Mut. Paris, 1939.

Novellen. Hamburg, 1963.

Das öffentliche Leben. Berlin, 1932.

Sieben Jahre. Chronik der Gedanken und Vorgänge. Berlin, 1929.

Der Sinn dieser Emigration. Paris, 1934.

Thomas Mann—Heinrich Mann Briefwechsel, 1900–1949, ed. Hans Wysling. Frankfurt, 1969.

Ein Verbrechen und andere Geschichten. Leipzig, 1898.

Verteidigung der Kultur: Antifaschistische Streitschriften und Essays. Hamburg, 1960.

Das Wunderbare und andere Novellen. Munich, 1897.

Ein Zeitalter wird besichtigt. Stockholm, 1945.

II. Articles by Heinrich Mann

Mann, Heinrich. "Barbey d'Aurevilly," *Die Gegenwart* (1895), XLVIII, no. 47–48: 325–28, 342–46.

"Bauerndichtung," *Das Zwanzigste Jahrhundert* (1895), V, Halbband 2, 347–54.

"Bei den Deutschen," *Das Zwanzigste Jahrhundert* (1895), V, Halbband 2, 575–83.

"Bourget als Kosmopolit," *Die Gegenwart* (1894), XLV: 53–58.

"Brief an Paul Hatvani," in *Heinrich Mann,* ed. Heinz Ludwig Arnold. Stuttgart, 1971.

"Briefwechsel Johannes R. Becher—Heinrich Mann," *Sinn und Form,* (1966), XVIII: 325–33.

Contribution to a symposium on the intellectual and politics, *Decision* (1941), I, no. 1: 44–45.

Contribution to "Transplanted Writers: A Symposium," *Books Abroad* (1942), XVI, no. 3: 268–69.

"Decentralization," *Das Zwanzigste Jahrhundert* (1895), V, Halbband 2, 513–17.

"Degeneration—Regeneration," *Das Zwanzigste Jahrhundert* (1895), V, Halbband 2, 185–91.

"Der Fall Murri," *Die Zukunft* (1906), LV, no. 31: 161–68.

"Friedrich Nietzsche und das Deutschthum," *Das Zwanzigste Jahrhundert* (1896), VI, Halbband 1: 561–62.

"The German European," *Decision* (1941), II, no. 4: 36–39.

"Hauptmanns *Weber* und die Sozialdemokratie," *Das Zwanzigste Jahrhundert* (1895), V, Halbband 2, 396–98.

"Heinrich Manns Briefe an Maximilian Brantl," *Weimarer Beiträge* (1968), XIV, no. 2: 393–422.

"Jüdischen Glaubens," *Das Zwanzigste Jahrhundert* (1895), V, Halbband 2, 455–62.

"*Die kleine Stadt.* Brief an Fräulein Lucia Dora Frost," *Die Zukunft,* February 19, 1910, LXX: 265–66.

"Kriegs-und Friedensmoral I," *Das Zwanzigste Jahrhundert* (1895), V, Halbband 2, 590–98.

"Kriegs-und Friedensmoral II," *Das Zwanzigste Jahrhundert* (1896), VI, Halbband 1, 17–26.

"Moderne Literatur," *Das Zwanzigste Jahrhundert* (1895), V, Halbband 2, 402–04.

"Neue Romantik," *Die Gegenwart* (1892), XLII, 40–42.

"Niederlage des Naturalismus," *Das Zwanzigste Jahrhundert* (1896), VI, Halbband 1, 467–68.

"Nietzsche," *The Living Thoughts of Nietzsche.* London, 1939.

"Politik," *Pan* (1911), II, no. 8: 235–39.

"Reaction," *Das Zwanzigste Jahrhundert* (1895), V, Halbband 2, 1–8.

"Das Reichstags-Wahlrecht," *Das Zwanzigste Jahrhundert* (1895), V, Halbband 2, 469–79.

"Verehrter Herr Harden . . . ," *Die Zukunft* (1904), XLIX, no. 2: 67–68.

"Reichstag," *Pan* (1911), II, no. 5: 133–36.

"Zum Verständnisse Nietzsches," *Das Zwanzigste Jahrhundert* (1896), VI, Halbband 2, 245–51.

"Weltstadt und Grossstädte," *Das Zwanzigste Jahrhundert* (1896), VI, Halbband 1, 201–13.

III. Secondary Sources

Abusch, Alexander. "Der Dichter des 'Untertan'," *Aufbau* (1950), VI, no. 4: 309–13.

Adorno, Theodor W. *Prisms,* trans. Samuel and Shierry Weber. London, 1967.

"Zum Verhältnis von Soziologie und Psychologie," *Sociologica: Aufsätze für Max Horkheimer.* Frankfurt, 1955.

Alberti, Konrad. "Die Bourgeoisie und die Kunst," *Die Gesellschaft* (1888), IV: 839–41.

Albrecht, Friedrich. *Deutsche Schriftsteller in der Entscheidung.* Berlin and Weimar, 1970.

Albrecht, Günter, *et. al. Deutsches Schriftstellerlexikon.* Weimar, 1963.

Albrecht, Milton C., Barnett, James H., and Griff, Mason, eds. *The Sociology of Art and Literature.* New York, 1970.

Althusser, Louis. *For Marx,* trans. Ben Brewster. New York, 1969.

Anshen, Ruth, ed. *The Family: Its Function and Destiny.* New York, 1955.

Antonovsky, Helen Faigin. "A Contribution to Research in the Area of the Mother-Child Relationship," *Child Development* (1959), XXX: 37–51.

Bachmann, Dieter. *Essay und Essayismus.* Stuttgart, 1970.

Banuls, André. *Heinrich Mann.* Stuttgart, 1970.

——. *Thomas Mann und sein Bruder.* Stuttgart, 1968.

Baron, Hans. *The Crisis of the Early Italian Renaissance.* 2 vols. Princeton, 1955.

Bartels, Adolf. *Die deutsche Dichtung der Gegenwart.* Leipzig, 1907.

——. *Heimatkunst.* Munich, 1904.

Barthes, Roland. *Critical Essays,* trans. Richard Howard. Evanston, 1972.

Becher, Johannes R. "Vom 'Untertan' zum Untertan," *Linkskurve* (1932), IV, no. 4: 1–5.

Bechtel, Heinrich. *Wirtschaftsgeschichte Deutschlands.* 3 vols. Munich, 1951–1956.

Benn, Gottfried. *Gesammelte Werke in acht Bänden,* ed. Dieter Wellershoff. Wiesbaden, 1968.

Bense, Max. "Über den Essay und seine Prosa," *Merkur* (1947), I, no. 3: 414–24.

Berendsohn, Walter. *Die humanistische Front: Einführung in die deutsche Emigranten-Literatur.* Zürich, 1946.

Berglund, Gisela. *Deutsche Opposition gegen Hitler in Presse und Roman des Exils.* Stockholm, 1972.

Bloch, Ernst. "Zerstörte Sprache—zerstörte Kultur," *Verbannung: Aufzeichungen deutscher Schriftsteller im Exil,* ed. Egon Schwarz and Matthias Wegner. Hamburg, 1964.

Bithell, Jethro. *Modern German Literature 1880–1938.* London, 1939.

Bleibtreu, Karl. *Revolution der Literatur.* Leipzig, 1886.

Boek, Friedrich. "Heinrich Manns politisches Glaubensbekenntnis," *Preussische Jahrbücher* (1920), CLXXXII, no. 2: 251–56.

Böhme, Helmut. *Deutschlands Weg zur Grossmacht.* Cologne, 1966.

Bradley, Francis. *René Schickele: der Kampf um einen persönlichen Stil.* New York, 1942.

Brofenbrenner, Urie. "The Study of Identification through Interpersonal Perception," *Person Perception and Interpersonal Behavior,* ed. Renato Tagiuri and Luigi Petrullo. Palo Alto, 1958.

Bruford, Walter Horace. *The German Tradition of Self-Cultivation: 'Bildung' from Humboldt to Thomas Mann.* London, 1975.

Caute, David. *The Fellow-Travellers.* New York, 1973.

Cooper, David. *Psychiatry and Anti-Psychiatry.* New York, 1971.

Craig, Gordon. "Engagement and Neutrality in Weimar Germany," *Journal of Contemporary History* (1967), II, no. 2: 49–63.

David, Claude. "Stefan George: Aesthetes or Terrorists?" *The Third Reich,* ed. Maurice Baumont, *et. al.* New York, 1955.

Deák, István. *Weimar Germany's Left-Wing Intellectuals.* Berkeley, 1968.

Dietzel, Ulrich, ed. *Aus den Familienpapieren der Manns.* Berlin, 1965.

Dittberner, Hugo. *Heinrich Mann: Eine kritische Einführung in die Forschung.* Frankfurt, 1974.

Döblin, Alfred. *Aufsätze zur Literatur,* ed. Walter Muschg. Olten and Freiburg, 1963.

"Republik," *Die Neue Rundschau* (1920), XXXI, no. 1: 73–79.

Schicksalsreise: Bericht und Bekenntnis. Frankfurt, 1949.

Schriften zur Politik und Gesellschaft. Olten, 1972.

Dreher, Eberhard. "Keine Untertanen: Heinrich Mann, Käthe Kollwitz, Martin Wagner," *Études Germaniques* (1971), XXVI, no. 3: 344–48.

Dreitzel, Hans, and Wilhelm, Jürgen. "Das Problem der 'Kreativität' in der Wissenschaft: Ein Beitrag zur Wissenschaftssoziologie," *Kölner Zeitschrift für Soziologie und Sozialpsychologie* (1966), XVIII, no. 1: 62–83.

Durzak, Manfred, ed. *Die deutsche Exilliteratur 1933–1945.* Stuttgart, 1973.

Eisenstadt, S. N. *From Generation to Generation.* Glencoe, 1956.

Emmerich, Walter. "Young Children's Discrimination of Parent and Child Roles," *Child Development* (1959), XXX: 402–19.

"Parental Identification in Young Children," *Genetic Psychological Monographs* (1959), LX: 32–51.

Emrich, Wilhelm. *Protest und Verheissung.* Bonn, 1963.

Escarpit, Robert. *The Sociology of Literature,* trans. Ernest Pick. Painesville, Ohio, 1965.

Eyck, Erich. *A History of Weimar Germany.* 2 vols., trans. Harlan P. Hanson and Robert G. L. Waite. Cambridge, Mass., 1962.

Feuchtwanger, Lion. "Versuch einer Selbstbiographie," *Die Literatur,* June 5, 1927, XXIX: 569–70.

Flake, Otto. "Von der jüngsten Literatur," *Die Neue Rundschau* (1915), XXVI, no. 9.

Forrest, Tess. "Paternal Roots of Male Character Development," *The Psychoanalytic Review* (1967), LIV, no. 1: 51–68.

Freud, Sigmund. *On Creativity and the Unconscious,* ed. Benjamin Nelson. New York, 1958.

Fromm, Erich. "Über Methode und Aufgabe einer analytischen Sozialpsychologie," *Zeitschrift für Sozialforschung* (1932), I: 28–54.

"Sozialpsychologischer Teil," *Studien über Autorität und Familie,* ed. Max Horkheimer. Paris, 1936.

Geiger, Hanns Ludwig. *Es war um die Jahrhundertwende.* Munich, 1963.

Geissler, Klaus. "Die weltanschauliche und künstlerische Entwicklung Heinrich Manns während des Ersten Weltkrieges," Ph.D. dissertation, Jena, 1965.

Genschmer, Fred. "Heinrich Mann (1871–1950)," *South Atlantic Quarterly* (1951), L, no. 2: 208–13.

Girnus, Wilhelm. "Geist und Macht im Werk Heinrich Manns," *Weimarer Beiträge* (1971), XVII, no. 8: 39–57.

Glaubrecht, Martin. *Studien zum Frühwerk Leonhard Franks.* Bonn, 1965.

Goldmann, Lucien. *The Hidden God,* trans. Philip Thody. New York, 1964.

Pour une sociologie du roman. Paris, 1964.

"The Sociology of Literature," *The Sociology of Art and Literature,* ed. Milton C. Albrecht, James H. Barnett, and Mason Griff. New York, 1970.

Structures mentales et création culturelle. Paris, 1970.

Graber, Heinz. "Politisches Postulat und autobiographischer Bericht: Zu einigen im Exil entstandenen Werken Alfred Döblins," *Die deutsche Exilliteratur 1933–1945,* ed. Manfred Durzak. Stuttgart, 1973.

Grappin, Pierre. *Le Bund Neues Vaterland 1914–1916. Ses rapports avec Romain Rolland.* Paris, 1952.

Gregor-Dallin, Martin. *Vor dem Leben: Schulgeschichten von Thomas Mann bis Heinrich Böll.* Munich, 1965.

Gross, David. "Heinrich Mann and the Politics of Reaction," *Journal of Contemporary History* (1973), VIII, no. 1: 125–45.

Grünberg, Emil. *Der Mittelstand in der kapitalistischen Gesellschaft: Eine ökonomische und soziologische Untersuchung.* Leipzig, 1932.

Guntrip, Henry. *Personality Structure and Human Interaction.* London, 1961.

Hahn, Manfred. "Heinrich Manns Beiträge in der Zeitschrift 'Das Zwanzigste Jahrhundert'," *Weimarer Beiträge* (1967), XIII, no. 6: 996–1019.

"Das Werk Heinrich Manns von den Anfängen bis zum 'Untertan'." Ph.D. dissertation, Leipzig, 1965.

"Zum frühen Schaffen Heinrich Manns," *Weimarer Beiträge* (1966), XII, no. 3: 363–406.

Hamann, Richard, and Hermand, Jost. *Gründerzeit.* Berlin, 1965.

Impressionismus. Berlin, 1966.

Naturalismus. Berlin, 1959.

Stilkunst um 1900. Berlin, 1967.

Hamerow, Theodore. *The Social Foundations of German Unification,* 2 vols. Princeton, 1969–1972.

Hart, Heinrich. ["Die Göttinnen"], *Velhagen und Klasings Monatshefte* (1903), XVII, no. 2.

Hartmann, Heinz, and Löwenstein, Rudolph. "Notes on the Super-ego," *The Psychoanalytic Study of the Child,* ed. Ruth Eissler, Anna Freud, and Heinz Hartmann. New York, 1962. Vol. XVII.

Hartmann, Horst. "Die Antithetik 'Macht-Geist' im Werk Lion Feuchtwangers," *Weimarer Beiträge* (1961), VII, no. 4, 667–93.

Hegel, Georg Wilhelm Friedrich. *Philosophy of Right,* trans. T. M. Knox. London, 1952.

Herden, Werner. "Aufruf. und Bekenntnis: Zu den essayistischen Bemühungen Heinrich Manns im französischen Exil," *Weimarer Beiträge* (1965), XI, no. 3: 323–49.

Geist und Macht. Heinrich Manns Weg an die Seite der Arbeiterklasse. Berlin, 1971.

"Heinrich Mann und Johannes R. Becher," *Weimarer Beiträge* (1971), XVII, no. 4: 102–26.

Herzog, Wilhelm. *Menschen, denen ich begegnete.* Bern and Munich, 1959.

"Unabhängigkeits-Erklärung des Geistes," *Das Forum* (August, 1919), III, no. 11: 830–31.

Heuss, Theodor. *Friedrich Naumann: der Mann, das Werk, die Zeit.* Stuttgart, 1937.

Hiller, Kurt. *Köpfe und Tröpfe*. Hamburg, 1950.

   Profile. Paris, 1937.

Hoffman, Max. *Geschichte der freien und hansestadt Lübeck*. Lübeck, 1889.

Holona, Marian. *Die Essayistik Heinrich Manns in den Jahren 1892–1933*. Warsaw, 1971.

Horkheimer, Max. *Kritische Theorie,* ed. Alfred Schmidt. 2 vols. Frankfurt, 1968.

Ihring, Herbert. *Heinrich Mann*. Berlin, 1951.

Ilberg, Werner. *Bernhard Kellermann in seinen Werken*. Berlin, 1959.

Jacobs, M. "Die Herzogin von Assy," *Die Nation,* May 9, 1903, XX.

Jarmatz, Klaus. "Aktivität und Perspektive im historischen Roman des kritischen Realismus 1933 bis 1945," *Weimarer Beiträge* (1965), XI, no. 3: 350–76.

Kantorowicz, Alfred. *Der Einfluss der Oktoberrevolution auf Heinrich Mann*. Berlin, 1952.

   Heinrich und Thomas Mann. Berlin, 1956.

Karst, Roman. *Thomas Mann oder Der deutsche Zwiespalt*. Vienna, 1970.

Kaufmann, Hans. *Krisen und Wandlungen der deutschen Literatur von Wedekind bis Feuchtwanger*. Berlin and Weimar, 1969.

Keck, Timothy Raymond. "Kant and Socialism: The Marburg School in Wilhelmian Germany." Ph.D. dissertation, Madison, 1975.

Kellermann, Bernhard. "Der Schriftsteller und die deutsche Republik," *Deutscher Revolutions-Almanach für das Jahr 1919 über die Ereignisse des Jahres 1918,* ed. Ernst Drahn and Ernst Friedegg. Hamburg, 1919.

Kesten, Hermann. "René Schickele," introduction to *René Schickele: Werk in drei Bänden*. Cologne and Berlin, 1959.

Kirsch, Edgar and Schmidt, Hildegard. "Zur Entstehung des Romans *Der Untertan,*" *Weimarer Beiträge* (1960), VI, no. 1: 112–31.

Klarmann, Adolf. "Der expressionistische Dichter und die politische Sendung," *Der Dichter und seine Zeit,* ed. Wolfgang Paulsen. Heidelberg, 1970.

Klein, Albert. *Die Krise des Unterhaltungsromans im 19. Jahrhundert*. Bonn, 1969.

Klemperer, Klemens von. *Germany's New Conservatism*. Princeton, 1957.

Kocka, Jürgen. "The First World War and the 'Mittelstand': German Artisans and White-Collar Workers," *Journal of Contemporary History* (1973), VIII, no. 1: 101–24.

König, Hanno. *Heinrich Mann: Dichter und Moralist*. Tübingen, 1972.

König, René. "Family and Authority," *The Sociological Review* (1957), V, no. 1: 107–27.

   Materialien zur Soziologie der Familie. Bern, 1946.

Kreutzer, Leo. *Alfred Döblin, Sein Werk bis 1933*. Stuttgart, 1970.

Laing, R. D. *Politics of the Family and Other Essays*. New York, 1972.

Lambi, Ivo Nikolai. *Free Trade and Protection in Germany, 1868–1879*. Wiesbaden, 1963.

Landauer, Carl. *European Socialism*. 2 vols. Berkeley, 1959.

Langenbucher, Helmuth. *Volkhafte Dichtung der Zeit.* Berlin, 1941.

Leavis, Q. D. *Fiction and the Reading Public.* London, 1932.

Lebovics, Herman. *Social Conservatism and the Middle Class in Germany, 1914-1933.* Princeton, 1969.

Lewis, Beth Irwin. *George Grosz: Art and Politics in the Weimar Republic.* Madison, 1971.

Lienhard, Fritz. *Neue Ideale.* Leipzig, 1901.

Lion, Ferdinand. *Thomas Mann in seiner Zeit.* Zürich, 1935.

Linden, Walther. *Geschichte der deutschen Literatur.* Leipzig, 1944.

Linn, Rolf. "The Place of 'Pippo Spano' in the Work of Heinrich Mann," *Modern Language Forum* (1952), XXXVII, no. 3: 130-43.
  Heinrich Mann. New York, 1967.

Lukács, Georg. *Essays on Thomas Mann,* trans. Stanley Mitchell. New York, 1965.
  Essays über Realismus. Neuwied and Berlin, 1971.
  The Historical Novel, trans. Hannah and Stanley Mitchell. Boston, 1963.
  Realism in Our Time, trans. John and Necke Mander. New York, 1971.
  Die Seele und die Formen. Berlin, 1911.

Lunn, Eugene. *Prophet of Community. The Romantic Socialism of Gustav Landauer.* Berkeley, 1973.

Lütge, Friedrich. *Deutsche Sozial- und Wirtschaftsgeschichte.* Berlin, 1966.

Mahrholz, Werner. "Heinrich Manns 'Untertan'," *Das literarische Echo* (1919), XXI, no. 9: 518-20.

Mann, Erika. *Das letze Jahr: Bericht über meinen Vater.* Oldenburg, 1968.

Mann, Erika, and Mann, Klaus. *Escape to Life.* Boston, 1939.

Mann, Thomas. *Autobiographisches,* ed. Erika Mann. Oldenburg, 1968.
  "Gedanken im Krieg," *Die Neue Rundschau* (1914), XXV, no. 2: 1474-84.
  Last Essays, trans. Richard and Clara Winston. London, 1959.
  Letters of Thomas Mann 1889-1955, ed. Richard and Clara Winston. New York, 1971.
  The Magic Mountain, trans. H. T. Lowe-Porter. New York, 1961.
  Order of the Day, trans. H. T. Lowe-Porter. New York, 1942.
  Schriften und Reden zur Literatur, Kunst und Philosophie. Frankfurt, 1960.

Mann, Viktor. *Wir waren fünf: Bildnis der Familie Mann.* Constance, 1949.

Mannheim, Karl. *Essays on the Sociology of Knowledge,* ed. Paul Kecskemeti. London, 1959.

Mayer, Hans. "Lion Feuchtwanger oder die Folgen des Exils," *Neue Rundschau* (1965), LXXVI, no. 1: 120-29.

Marcuse, Herbert. "Autorität und Familie in der deutschen Soziologie bis 1933," *Studien über Autorität und Familie,* ed. Max Horkheimer. Paris, 1936.
  Negations, trans. Jeremy J. Shapiro. Boston, 1968.

One-Dimensional Man. Boston, 1968.

Reason and Revolution. Hegel and the Rise of Social Theory. Boston, 1964.

Marcuse, Ludwig. "Farewell to Heinrich Mann," *Books Abroad* (1950), XXIV, no. 3: 248–49.

Matthais, Klaus, ed. *Heinrich Mann 1871/1971.* Munich, 1973.

Minder, Robert. *Kultur und Literatur in Deutschland und Frankreich.* Frankfurt, 1962.

Mitchell, Alan. *Revolution in Bavaria, 1918–1919: Kurt Eisner and the Bavarian Socialist Republic.* Princeton, 1965.

Mitscherlich, Alexander. *Society Without the Father,* trans. Eric Mosbacher. New York, 1969.

Mohler, Armin. *Die konservative Revolution in Deutschland 1918–1932.* Stuttgart, 1950.

Mommsen, Wolfgang. *Max Weber und die deutsche Politik 1890–1920.* Tübingen, 1959.

Morgan, George. *What Nietzsche Means.* New York, 1965.

Mosse, George L. *Germans and Jews.* New York, 1970.

"The Heritage of Socialist Humanism," *Salmagundi* (1969–70), X–XI: 123–39.

"Literature and Society in Germany," *Literature and Western Civilization,* ed. David Daiches and Anthony Thorlby. London, 1972.

Mühsam, Erich. *Von Eisner bis Leviné.* Berlin, 1929.

Müller-Salget, Klaus. *Alfred Döblin: Werk und Entwicklung.* Bonn, 1972.

Mussen, Paul, and Distler, Louis. "Masculinity, Identification, and Father-Son Relationships," *Journal of Abnormal and Social Psychology* (1959), LIX: 350–56.

Nietzsche, Friedrich. *Beyond Good and Evil,* trans. Walter Kaufmann. New York, 1966.

Noth, Ernst Erich. "Die Exilsituation in Frankreich," *Die deutsche Exilliteratur 1933–1945,* ed. Manfred Durzak. Stuttgart, 1973.

Parsons, Talcott, and Bales, Robert. *Family, Socialization, and Interaction Process.* New York, 1966.

Pater, Walter. *Selections from Walter Pater,* ed. Ada Snell. Boston, 1924.

Paulsen, Wolfgang. *Expressionismus und Aktivismus.* Bern, 1935.

Petersen, Julius. *Die literarischen Generationen.* Berlin, 1930.

Peyre, Henri. *Les générations littéraires.* Paris, 1948.

Plessner, Monika. "Identifikation und Utopie: Versuch über Heinrich und Thomas Mann als politische Schriftsteller," *Frankfurter Hefte* (1961), XVI, no. 12: 812–26.

Pohle, Ludwig, and Muss, Max. *Das deutsche Wirtschaftsleben seit Beginn des neunzehnten Jahrhunderts.* Leipzig and Berlin, 1930.

Pollatschek, Walther. "Friedrich Wolf, Dichter und Kämpfer," *Wolf: Ein Lesebuch für unsere Zeit,* ed. Else Wolf and Walther Pollatschek. Berlin, 1969.

Pörtner, Paul, ed. *Literatur-Revolution 1910–1925.* 2 vols. Neuwied and Berlin, 1961.

"The Writer's Revolution: Munich 1918–1919," *Journal of Contemporary History* (1968), III, no. 4: 137–152.

Pross, Harry. "Heinrich Mann—der letze Jacobiner," *Deutsche Rundschau*, (1957), LXXXIII, no. 10: 1050–55.

Rank, Otto. *Art and Artists*, trans. Charles Francis Atkinson. New York, 1968.

Rasch, Wolfdietrich. *Zur deutschen Literatur seit der Jahrhundertwende.* Stuttgart, 1967.

Rehm, Walther. "Der Renaissancekult um 1900 und seine Überwindung," *Zeitschrift für deutsche Philologie* (1929), LIV: 296–328.

Reich, Wilhelm. *The Mass Psychology of Fascism*, trans. Vincent Carfagno. New York, 1970.

Reich-Ranicki, Marcel. "Lion Feuchtwanger oder Der Weltruhm des Emigranten," *Die deutsche Exilliteratur 1933–1945*, ed. Manfred Durzak. Stuttgart, 1973.

Ribbat, Ernst. *Die Wahrheit des Lebens im frühen Werk Alfred Döblins.* Münster, 1970.

Ringer, Fritz, ed. *The German Inflation of 1923.* New York, 1969.

Roberts, David. *Artistic Consciousness and Political Consciousness. The Novels of Heinrich Mann 1900–1938.* Bern, 1971.

Rohner, Ludwig. *Der deutsche Essay. Materialien zur Geschichte und Aesthetik einer literarischen Gattung.* Neuwied and Berlin, 1966.

Rolland, Romain. *Au-dessus de la mêlée.* Paris, 1915.

Rosenberg, Arthur. *A History of the German Republic,* trans. Ian Murrow and L. M. Sieveking. London, 1936.

Rubiner, Ludwig. *Der Mensch in der Mitte.* Berlin, 1917.

Ruprecht, Erich, ed. *Literarische Manifeste des Naturalismus 1880–1892.* Stuttgart, 1962.

Rürup, Reinhard. "Problems of the German Revolution 1918–1919," *Journal of Contemporary History* (1968), III, no. 4: 109–36.

Ryder, A. J. *The German Revolution of 1918.* Cambridge, England, 1967.

Sandler, Joseph, and Rosenblatt, Bernard. "The Concept of the Representational World," *The Psychoanalytic Study of the Child,* ed. Ruth Eissler, Anna Freud, and Heinz Hartmann. New York, 1962. Vol. XVII.

Sartre, Jean Paul. *L'idiot de la famille: Gustave Flaubert de 1821–1857.* 3 vols. Paris, 1971–1973.

——. *What is Literature?*, trans. Bernard Frechtman. New York, 1966.

Schafer, Roy. *Aspects of Internalization.* New York, 1968.

Schickele, René. "Politik der Geistigen," *März* (1913), March 15, 1913, VII: 405–07; and March 22, 1913, VII: 440–41.

——. "Revolution, Bolschewismus und das Ideal," *Die weissen Blätter* (1918), V, no. 6: 97–130.

——. *Werk in drei Bänden*, ed. Hermann Kesten. Cologne and Berlin, 1959.

Schlawe, Fritz. *Literarische Zeitschriften 1885–1910.* Stuttgart, 1961.

——. *Literarische Zeitschriften 1910–1925.* Stuttgart, 1962.

Schoenberner, Franz. *Confessions of a European Intellectual.* New York, 1965.

Schramm, Percy. *Hamburg, Deutschland und die Welt.* Munich, 1943.

Schröter, Klaus. *Anfänge Heinrich Manns. Zu den Grundlagen seines Gesamtwerks.* Stuttgart, 1965.

"Chauvinism and Its Tradition: German Writers and the Outbreak of the First World War," *Germanic Review* (1968), XLIII: no. 2: 120–35.

Heinrich Mann. Hamburg, 1967.

Thomas Mann. Hamburg, 1964.

Schücking, Levin. *The Sociology of Literary Taste,* trans. Brian Battershaw. London, 1966.

Schürer, Ernst. *Georg Kaiser.* New York, 1971.

"Verinnerlichung, Protest und Resignation: Georg Kaisers Exil," *Die deutsche Exilliteratur 1933–1945,* ed. Manfred Durzak. Stuttgart, 1973.

Schwarz, Egon, and Wegner, Matthias, ed. *Verbannung: Aufzeichungen deutscher Schriftsteller im Exil.* Hamburg, 1964.

Sebald, Winifred Georg. *Carl Sternheim: Kritiker und Opfer der Wilhelminischen Ära.* Stuttgart, 1969.

Serebrow, Nikolai. "Heinrich Manns Antikriegsroman *Der Kopf,*" *Weimarer Beiträge* (1962), VIII, no. 1: 1–33.

Sheehan, James. *The Career of Lujo Brentano.* Chicago, 1966.

Simmel, Georg. *The Conflict of Modern Culture and Other Essays,* trans. K. Peter Etzkorn. New York, 1968.

Soergel, Albert. *Dichtung und Dichter der Zeit.* Leipzig, 1911.

Solomon, Alice, ed. *Forschungen über Bestand und Erschütterung der Familie.* Berlin, 1930.

Sombart, Werner. *Der Bourgeois: zur Geistesgeschichte des modernen Wirtschaftsmenschen.* Munich and Leipzig, 1923.

Die deutsche Volkswirtschaft im neunzehnten Jahrhundert. Berlin, 1903.

Spalek, John, ed. *Lion Feuchtwanger: the Man, His Ideas, His Work.* Los Angeles, 1972.

Steffens, Wilhelm. *Georg Kaiser.* Hannover, 1969.

Sterling, Richard. *Ethics in a World of Power: the Political Ideas of Friedrich Meinecke.* Princeton, 1958.

Stern, Fritz. *The Failure of Illiberalism.* New York, 1972.

The Politics of Cultural Despair. New York, 1965.

Sternheim, Carl. *Zeitkritik. Gesamtwerk,* ed. Wilhelm Emrich. Neuwied, 1966.

Thoenelt, Klaus. "Heinrich Manns Psychologie des Faschismus," *Monatshefte* (1971), LXIII, no. 3, 220–34.

Tucholsky, Kurt. *Gesammelte Werke,* ed. Mary Tucholsky and Fritz Radditz. Hamburg, 1960.

Vajda, Mihàly, and Heller, Agnes. "Family Structure," *Telos* (1971), VII, 99–111.

Vorländer, Karl. *Kant und Marx.* Tübingen, 1926.

Yuill, Y. E. "Lion Feuchtwanger," *German Men of Letters,* ed. Alex Natan. London, 1964. Vol. III.

"Heinrich Mann," *German Men of Letters,* ed. Alex Natan. London, 1963. Vol. II.

Walter, Hans-Albert. "Die Asylpolitik Frankreichs von 1933 bis zur Annexion Österreichs," *Exil und innere Emigration,* ed. Peter Uwe Hohendahl and Egon Schwarz. Frankfurt, 1973. Vol. II.

Bedrohung und Verfolgung bis 1933, in *Deutsche Exilliteratur 1933–1950.* Darmstadt and Neuwied, 1972. Vol. I.

"Heinrich Mann im französischen Exil," *Heinrich Mann,* ed. Heinz Ludwig Arnold. Stuttgart, 1971.

Wegner, Matthias. *Exil und Literatur: Deutsche Schriftsteller im Ausland 1933–1945.* Frankfurt, 1967.

Weinstein, Fred, and Platt, Gerald. *The Wish to be Free: Society, Psyche, and Value Change.* Berkeley, 1969.

Weisstein, Ulrich. *Heinrich Mann. Eine historisch-kritische Einführung in sein dichterisches Werk.* Tübingen, 1962.

Winkler, Heinrich A. "Der rückversicherte Mittelstand," *Zur Soziologischen Theorie und Analyse des 19. Jahrhunderts,* ed. W. Rüegg and O. Neuloh. Göttingen, 1971.

Winston, Richard, and Clara. "Introduction," *Letters of Thomas Mann 1889–1955.* New York, 1971.

Winter, Lorenz. *Heinrich Mann and His Public,* trans. John Gorman. Coral Gables, 1970.

Wulf, Josef, ed. *Literatur und Dichtung im Dritten Reich: Eine Dokumentation.* Gütersloh, 1963.

INDEX